Also by Joel Achenbach

It Looks Like a President, Only Smaller:
Trailing Campaign 2000

Captured by Aliens:
The Search for Life and Truth in a Very Large Universe

Why Things Are:
Answers to Every Essential Question in Life

Why Things Are, Volume II:
The Big Picture

Why Things Are & Why Things Aren't:
The Answers to Life's Greatest Mysteries

SIMON & SCHUSTER
New York   London   Toronto   Sydney

The
GRAND
IDEA

*George Washington's
Potomac and the Race
to the West*

JOEL ACHENBACH

SIMON & SCHUSTER
Rockefeller Center
1230 Avenue of the Americas
New York, NY 10020

SIMON & SCHUSTER and colophon are
registered trademarks of Simon & Schuster, Inc.

For information about special discounts for bulk purchases,
please contact Simon & Schuster Special Sales:
1-800-456-6798 or business@simonandschuster.com

Designed by Leslie Phillips

Manufactured in the United States of America

1   3   5   7   9   10   8   6   4   2

Library of Congress Cataloging-in-Publication Data
Achenbach, Joel.
The grand idea : George Washington's Potomac and the race to the West / Joel Achenbach.
p.   cm.
Includes bibliographical references and index.
1. Potomac River—History—18th century.   2. Potomac River—Navigation—
History—18th century.   3. Potomac River Valley—Description and travel.
4. Washington, George, 1732–1799—Travel—Potomac River Valley.   5. Washington,
George, 1732–1799—Political and social views.   6. Political culture—United States—
History—18th century.   7. United States—Politics and government—1783–1809.   I. Title.

F187.P8A23 2004
975.2'02—dc22   2004045307

ISBN 0-684-84857-0

To Mary, Paris, Isabella, and Shane,
for going along

CONTENTS

MAPS

THE GRAND IDEA

1

The Surveyor

Mount Vernon, 1784

*T*HE MAN WHO could have been king was just a farmer now, at peace with the world. He would live out his few remaining years amid fields of corn and wheat and rye. He would rotate his crops, experiment with seeds. He would design nets for catching shad in the river. He would breed jackasses, perhaps plant a vineyard. *Stick to the plantation, stay above the political fray*—that was the plan, that was the crucial plot device of the elaborate script he'd written for his retirement. Perhaps no man had ever quit his job with such a flourish of Enlightenment virtue. By giving up his sword, by tossing aside the power he had earned in battle, by choosing agriculture over monarchy, George Washington had authenticated the rhetoric of the American Revolution.

"I am become," he informed the Marquis de Lafayette, "a private citizen on the banks of the Potomac, & under the shadow of my own Vine & my own Fig tree, free from the bustle of a camp & the busy scenes of public life . . ."

That was his favorite image: a man on his river, under his vine and fig tree, unburdened, unhurried—serene. He trundled out the vine and fig-tree reference (from 1 Kings 4:25: "And Judah and Israel dwelt safely, every man under his vine and under his fig tree") many times as he sat at his desk that first winter at Mount Vernon. Washington lived an active life governed by ambitious desires and big ideas. The desires made him acquire western land aggressively and seek to become a powerful man, a Virginia planter supreme. The big ideas propelled him to the leadership of a revolution that would change the world, and now, at the close of the war, had spurred him to strike this retirement pose, this affectation of a genteel farmer superintending his peas and oats.

The image did not reflect the gritty, chaotic reality of his riverside plantation. Mount Vernon was a thriving village, with five distinct farms and nearly 8,000 acres of reddish soil washing steadily into the brown Potomac. His domain included a mill, a dairy, more than 100 cows, more than 600 sheep, and too many pigs to count, the swine left free to roam the woods and fatten up on chestnuts. Mount Vernon was home to a small number of hired white laborers and white indentured servants, but this was essentially a black community, with more than 200 slaves working as carpenters, blacksmiths, farriers, fishermen, cooks, maids, coopers, millers, weavers, and field hands. The slaves were considered by Virginia law a form of property, much like the dining room table or the chairs on the piazza. The air was filled with the sound of their voices and carried the odors of a vital agrarian enterprise, of smoke and roasting meat and salted fish, of mud, manure, lye, animal hide, privies, and human sweat. The place had precisely the bustle of a camp. It had busy scenes from dawn to dusk and dusk to dawn. Retirement for Washington would not mean repose.

He had become a private citizen two days before Christmas 1783. The last British commanders had folded their flags and sailed out of New York Harbor in late November. Washington bade a tearful farewell to his officers, then rode south to Annapolis to make a final appearance before the Continental Congress. He read his speech with a shaking hand, his voice catching as he commended the interests of his country to God. "Having now finished the work assigned me," he said, "I retire from the great theatre of Action." The general turned in his commission and rode home to Mount Vernon, arriving Christmas Eve.

The estate, Washington discovered, had become "deranged" in his absence. Except for two brief stopovers during the Yorktown campaign, he'd been away for more than eight and a half years, since May 4, 1775—a good chunk of his life, two full volumes in a standard biography. He needed to fix everything, from house to outbuildings to barns. He also needed rest. He needed to sit on his piazza and gaze at his river.

The Potomac had been part of his thoughts for five decades, and he may have felt some sense of proprietorship. He was born on this river, downstream, at Pope's Creek, and for a time he'd been raised on the Potomac, right here at Little Hunting Creek in a wooden farmhouse. Among his happiest memories were the days spent just downriver, at Belvoir, the estate of the Fairfaxes, left a charred ruin by the British.

On this river, Washington suspected, he would soon reach his final hours, journeying to "that Country from whence no Traveller returns." He would meet "the Grim King." He had no illusions on this point. Washingtons died young.

Washington was fifty-two, on the cusp of a period in life when deterioration takes hold, when the power fades from the grip, the joints ache, and a strict daily routine becomes appealing. He had every right to be exhausted and to log many hours of piazza time. Portraitists captured the sagging in his face; Robert Edge Pine painted a Washington who looked not a minute younger than seventy. (Pine later "corrected" the portrait, and the general underwent a miraculous rejuvenation.)

Washington, even in this drained postwar state, had more vigor than the average man. He stood at least 6 feet 2 inches tall, and no one ever looked more like a general, more naturally commanding. A contemporary of Washington observed that "there is not a king in Europe that would not look like a valet de chambre by his side." So much about George Washington deviated from the norm: huge hands, massive feet, narrow shoulders, wide and almost womanly hips. Washington could crack a walnut between his thumb and forefinger. He could bend a horseshoe with his bare hands, by one account. Lesser mortals would quail in his presence, shiver under his icy gaze. No one would be foolish enough to banter with Washington, or slap him on the back as one might a chum. As a young man, he had been a gambler, a carouser, an unbridled spirit, but with age he stiffened and became notoriously aloof to all but his closest friends. Formal, severe, with a keen sense of propriety and personal virtue, he knew that he lived on the stage of history, under the eyes of Argus, as he put it. Often he would astonish his associates with what John Adams called his "gift of silence." He could be a chilly figure, mute, stern, radiating classical virtue. A statue made of flesh.

Now Washington was home, and when he finished riding his land, giving orders to his farm manager and overseers, and dealing with his correspondence, he would escape to his piazza to gaze at the tranquil river and enjoy a glass of Madeira. The piazza was a Washington innovation: a porch, only grander, expanded to neoclassical dimensions and perhaps a bit pompous. Mount Vernon had come a long way. Originally called Little Hunting Creek, the plantation had been in the family for more than a century, but when the master of the house had been Lawrence Washington, George's older half-brother, it was still a modest structure, hardly a mansion. After the death of Lawrence, George Washington inherited the estate, and, flush with money from his marriage to the richest widow in Virginia, doubled the size of the house. He ordered another dramatic expansion just before the war. In the same way that Washington's splintery, rough-hewn country-boy personality had become more polished, the wooden exterior of Mount Vernon had been reshaped, and sand added to the paint, to create the impression that the walls were made of stone. The enlarged piazza became one of the most striking features of the mansion: 96 feet long, running the length of the house, with a flagstone surface and eight wooden pillars, each 18 feet high.

Mount Vernon sat high above the Potomac on a knuckle of land, with the river sweeping around the property. The general could look straight downstream for 5 miles, to a promontory called Mason's Neck. Looking upriver, he could gaze directly into the estuary of Piscataway Creek. The Potomac here was a lazy, tidal river, a finger of Chesapeake Bay. He loved this panorama and took pains to improve it, ordering his slaves to excavate portions of the bluff and hack down any trees that obscured the river below.

"No estate in United America is more pleasantly situated than this," he would write many years later when toying with the idea of renting out much of his Mount Vernon property. "It lyes in a high, dry and healthy Country 300 miles by water from the Sea . . . on one of the finest Rivers in the world."

Washington rarely allowed himself so lyrical an observation. He tended to be a details man, a transmitter of pertinent data. This description of Mount Vernon was simultaneously a real estate advertisement and a statement of identity, for among the general's associates there was nothing more exalted and virtuous than to be a landed gentleman with a view of a river. Washington had Mount Vernon, the Fairfaxes had Belvoir, George Mason had Gunston Hall. Washington as a general had been compared to Fabius; now, in retirement, he had become Cincinnatus, the Roman warrior who returned to his plow. A mansion on a river was essential to the script.

But Washington was also a supremely pragmatic man, and so after exalting the situation of his estate, he pointed out the usefulness of riverfront property in this part of the world: "Its margin is washed by more than ten miles of tide water; from the bed of which, and the enumerable coves, inlets and small marshes with wch. it abounds, an inexhaustible fund of rich mud may be drawn as a manure. . . ."

This was George Washington's America, where even the malodorous muck and silt of a river bottom could be put to good use.

"I am not only retired from all public employments," he wrote Lafayette, "but I am retireing within myself; & shall be able to view the solitary walk, & tread the paths of private life with heartfelt satis-

faction—Envious of none, I am determined to be pleased with all. &
this my dear friend, being the order for my march, I will move gently
down the stream of life, until I sleep with my Fathers."

That was his vision in the winter of 1784.

The months passed, the snow and ice melted, the river rose with the
spring rains. The blue-green river of winter became the milk-
chocolate river of spring, choked with sediment from the denuded
riverbanks. Other than a brief trip to Philadelphia, he stayed close to
home. Spring turned to summer. The general was behaving perfectly,
staying with the master plan. *Stick to the vine and fig tree.*

The grass grew.

Roosters crowed.

Pigs snuffled in the mud.

And Washington made a decision: On the first day of September he
would head west, on horseback, across the mountains, to the frontier
of America, and then would keep going, into the most remote, uncivi-
lized backcountry—a thousand-mile journey into that forest realm
that men of his breed had always called *the howling wilderness.*

"I have come to a resolution (if not prevented by anything, at present unforeseen) to take a trip to the Western Country this Fall," he
wrote in July to his lifelong friend and traveling companion, Dr. James
Craik.

Washington was not a statue after all! As much as he loved Mount
Vernon, he could not sit idle while other enterprising Americans were
racing into the West, carving out homesteads in that primeval terrain
drained by the Ohio River.

It would be something of a business trip, an inspection tour of
Washington's western properties, his personal backwoods empire.
When not supervising his already enormous plantation at Mount
Vernon, or winning a protracted war against one of the great powers
of Europe, Washington had devoted himself with great vigor over the
course of many years to the purchase of spectacular tracts of land,
some many miles on a side, in the remote territories beyond the crest
of the Alleghenies. He owned 4,691 acres in western Pennsylvania. He

possessed a moist tract running along five miles of the Little Kanawha River, in a region of Virginia many days' ride by horseback almost due west of the headspring of the Potomac. Still farther west, so deep in the woods that hardly anyone could be persuaded to settle there, he owned a magnificent piece of real estate extending 17 miles along the Great Kanawha River upstream from its mouth on the Ohio, a tract "abounding plentiously in Fish, wild fowl, and Game of all kinds," as he enthused that spring to a fellow patriot. He might be an absentee landlord, but at least he could say he'd seen these lands, that he'd personally surveyed them in an epic journey by canoe down the Ohio in 1770, with the familiar presence of Craik by his side. Washington had been wildly successful in obtaining fertile tracts of bottomland before anyone else could lay claim to them, but a decade and a half later these properties were generating no income, indeed had fallen out of his control. He needed to go back across the mountains, collect some rents, impose some order, get in the face of some squatters.

But there was something else in Washington's mind, something that had been there for years, decades, a kind of geographical obsession. It involved that river down there at the base of the bluff.

He had an image in his head of the new nation, of the mountains that separated the East from the forests of the Ohio country. As he gazed at the river below, he could see it as a natural passage to the continental interior. The river, he believed, could become the great commercial artery to the West. A highway. A corridor. The Potomac already carried the tide hundreds of miles from the Capes of Virginia, and he had paddled up the river, deep into the mountains, to the flank of the dividing ridge between the western and eastern waters. From the Potomac headwaters it was just a quick jump to the headwaters of the Ohio. The Potomac was clearly the Route to the West. And thus his journey had a secondary function: ". . . one object of my journey," Washington wrote, "being to obtain information of the nearest and best communication between the Eastern & Western Waters; & to facilitate as much as in me lay the Inland Navigation of the Potomack."

This was not something that had popped suddenly into his head.

Washington had been pondering a Potomac project for decades. The Potomac would be akin to the mythical Northwest Passage between Europe and the Orient. Just as Columbus had sought a sea route to China three centuries earlier, and as Lewis and Clark, two decades later, would seek a river passage across the Rockies, so too did Washington dream of a largely navigable route from the Atlantic to the Mississippi Valley through the riverbeds of the Potomac and the Ohio. In an era of grand ideas, this was *his* grand idea.

So here was the plan: Washington and Craik would ride across the Blue Ridge, to the Shenandoah Valley, travel up through the valley of the Potomac, ramble across the Alleghenies to western Pennsylvania, and then switch to canoes and float down the Ohio River for nearly 300 miles, to the junction of the Great Kanawha.

Which was about as far as a Tidewater gentleman could get from his vine and fig tree.

*   *   *

WASHINGTON'S POTOMAC SCHEME has inspired some excellent scholarship, but it is often treated as a sideshow, a kind of eccentric hobby. Most biographers focus on his full-time jobs (plantation owner, warrior, president). Yet sometimes we understand a person best when we see what he does in his spare time, when he is not forced by necessity to dash off into battle or settle a political dispute. Washington, given the chance, high-tailed it to the hinterlands. He saddled up and headed west. We've won the war, he said, now we've got to do something about these mountains that divide us.

The 1784 trip reveals Washington at his most appealing and his most imperious. It affords an unusually vivid look at a man whose personal concerns had a way of becoming national ones. It gives us a glimpse of an infant nation, destiny uncertain, sprawled upon a wild and tantalizing landscape. And it shows some of the first steps in the creation of what would become a continental nation, and eventually the most powerful country on the planet.

This western trek is not exactly obscure, but there are few in-depth accounts of it. Douglas Southall Freeman allots the journey four-teen fine, highly detailed paragraphs in his seminal seven-volume biography. John Marshall, possibly the most ponderous Washington biographer, gives the '84 trip precisely fifteen words. David Ramsay is even more efficient, summarizing the 680-mile frontier adventure in nine words (" . . . he made a tour as far west as Pittsburgh. . . ."). It never became part of the Washington lore.

The trip to the frontier set in motion a series of events that not only altered the landscape of the Potomac corridor but also rippled the po-litical structure of the United States. Washington may have been thor-oughly a man of the eighteenth century, but his schemes were advanced by others well into the nineteenth. His presence is still felt on the river today. The Potomac survives as an unusually evocative stream, a place of intriguing ruins, including an old canal, crumbling mills, stone chimneys, quarries, fish dams, strange walls peeking through the weeds on the riverbank. Any visitor can see that the place has a secret history, a thousand stories long forgotten, eroded by time, buried in silt. The Potomac is a time tunnel, a route to the past, if not to the West. It's a portal to George Washington's America, to a mo-ment when the nation was young, when rivers were highways, when water ruled the planet, when information moved at the speed of a horse, when omens good and bad hung in the air—when no one knew how this experiment in self-government called the United States was going to turn out.

*   *   *

THE POTOMAC PLAN was motivated in part by fear. The general (that is what even his wife called him) feared that the country he had helped create would not long endure. It could easily split right along the line of the mountains—West from East. The Potomac Route to the West might act as a binding agent, a long and winding tether.

The nation in 1784 was still something of an allegation, an assertion, a hypothesis, an aspiration written in the dirt of North America. The United States was—*were*—thirteen loosely connected political units,

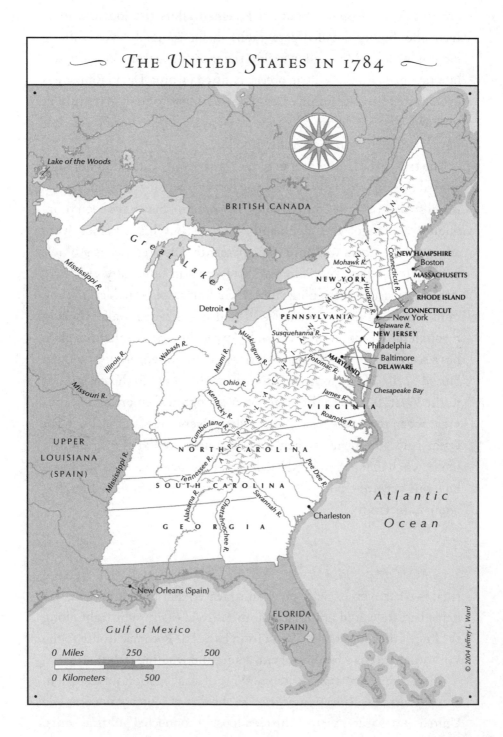

THE UNITED STATES IN 1784

Lake of the Woods

BRITISH CANADA

Great Lakes

Mississippi R.

Missouri R.

Mohawk R.

NEW YORK

Connecticut R.

NEW HAMPSHIRE
Boston
MASSACHUSETTS
RHODE ISLAND
CONNECTICUT

Hudson R.

Detroit

PENNSYLVANIA

New York

Illinois R.

Wabash R.

Muskingum R.

Susquehanna R.

Delaware R.

NEW JERSEY

Philadelphia

Miami R.

Ohio R.

Kentucky R.

MARYLAND

Potomac R.

Baltimore
DELAWARE

Chesapeake Bay

James R.

VIRGINIA

Roanoke R.

Cumberland R.

NORTH CAROLINA

UPPER
LOUISIANA
(SPAIN)

Mississippi R.

Tennessee R.

Pee Dee R.

SOUTH CAROLINA

Alabama R.

Chattahoochee R.

Savannah R.

GEORGIA

Charleston

Atlantic

Ocean

New Orleans (Spain)

FLORIDA
(SPAIN)

Gulf of Mexico

0 Miles   250   500

0 Kilometers   500

© 2004 Jeffrey L. Ward

with "United States" treated as a plural noun. ("The United States of America have terminated their dispute" with Great Britain, the Continental Congress declared in 1784. Under the peace treaty of 1783, "his Britannic Majesty hath acknowledged the United States to be free sovereign and Independent States, that he treated with them as such. . . .") The states had passed the Articles of Confederation, but the Continental Congress had minimal power. It made "humble requests" to the states, some of which still conducted their own foreign policy.

Congress wandered from city to city with no permanent home, an enterprise so itinerant that some foreign dignitaries simply couldn't *find* the blasted thing. (Was it convened in Trenton? Lancaster? York? Philadelphia? Annapolis?) In 1783, while at Philadelphia, the congressmen were besieged by furious continental soldiers demanding back pay, and the sage leaders of the nation responded to the crisis by packing up their papers and hitting the road. They fled to Princeton, 40 miles away, where they crowded into Nassau Hall with the professors and students. It was hard for foreign diplomats to take the government seriously when it was practically on the lam.

One could not simply boast a nation into existence. There had to be some real ties, some binding connections of a commercial, political, legal, and cultural nature. So far, most of these connections were so fragile they might rip apart with the next political wind. The revolutionary leaders could argue that they were forging a new kind of society, one that put the Enlightenment into practice, one that had big ideas galore, but they also knew they had created something delicate, that any postrevolutionary society is subject to chaos, anarchy, spasms of rage and vengeance. A significant minority of the population had been loyal to the Mother Country, and there were still Tory pockets up and down the Atlantic seaboard. The country had no president, no prime minister, no chief executive, no federal judiciary, no federal government apparatus, no central bank, no common currency. In remote communities, currency took the form of whiskey, oxen, or cowbells. When the general kept his books, he had to specify the state in which the money was owed. The pound in Virginia had 1,289 grains of silver, but the pound in Pennsylvania had only 1,031¼ grains. The coinage took the form of Spanish milled dollars, or some other coin, such as doubloons, moidores, or johannes. In Virginia and New England, 6 shillings, or 72 pence, equaled a dollar, while in other states a dollar was 7 shillings and 6 pence, or 8 shillings, or as little as 4 shillings and 8 pence.

A map of the nation revealed a patchwork of overlapping territorial claims—Indian reserves, military bounty lands, wilderness sovereignties, and breakaway republics. There were still British forts on American soil, along the Great Lakes at Detroit, Michilimackinac, Oswego, Niagara, and Oswegatchie. Spain, though not the empire it had been two centuries earlier, still held the peninsula of Florida, all of the American Southwest, Texas, the Louisiana Territory, New Orleans (and thus all traffic to the Gulf of Mexico from the Mississippi), and California. Virginia was itself an empire, for, although it was in the process of ceding to the national government all of its claims to land northwest of the Ohio, it still sprawled from the barrier islands of the Atlantic seaboard to the Mississippi River, encompassing the newly settled land of Kentucky. The Kentuckians might well decide to secede from the Union. A breakaway republic had already formed in the mountains of eastern Tennessee, where the settlers proclaimed themselves citizens of the independent nation of Franklin.

The country was fractured by region, religion, language, race. There were Catholics in Maryland, Anglicans in Tidewater Virginia, Quakers in Pennsylvania, German-speaking Lutherans in the Great Valley of the Appalachians, Scotch-Irish Presbyterians filtering into the hollows and crags of the mountain interior. There were Frenchmen still running the rivers of the Ohio Valley. There were Swedes in the Delaware Valley, and ax-wielding Finns and Danes stomping through the backcountry looking for pine and oak. Many of the street signs in Manhattan were still written in Dutch. There were pockets of Swiss and Jews and French Huguenots. Settlers came from the highlands of Scotland, from southern Ireland and Wales, from ancient villages in Palatine Germany, from the ice country of Scandinavia, from the slums of London. A million Americans were Africans or the descendants of Africans, but this group too was highly mixed, for in addition to the increasing population of free blacks, particularly in the North, the slaves of the South included Guineans, Angolans, Gambians, and so on, with entirely different languages and cultural traditions. There were even microbial divisions, as Washington knew all too well. He had tried during the Revolution to limit contact between New Englanders and southerners in his army, lest they give one another exotic diseases to which they lacked immunity. In America it was dangerous for strangers to touch.

And yet Washington had high hopes for this country. He believed in its possibilities, and knew, better than almost any of his fellow citizens, the texture of its land, the abundance of its resources, the incredible dimensions of its new boundaries. The Treaty of Paris had awarded the United States an empire that was almost beyond imagination. Washington had seen the forest of the West when it was untouched by ax or plow, and now, at the stroke of a quill, it was all U.S. territory. The nation extended west to the banks of the Mississippi, south as far as Spanish Florida, north to the Great Lakes, and as far northwest as the Lake of the Woods. The country ranged from southern piney woods to northern boreal forest. It was obvious to Washington that this was the foundation of an empire, that the United States, with so many resources, could become a global power:

> The Citizens of America, placed in the most enviable condition, as the sole Lords and Proprietors of a vast Tract of Continent, comprehending all the various soils and climates of the World, and abounding with all the necessaries and conveniences of life, are now by the late satisfactory pacification, acknowledged to be possessed of absolute freedom and Independency; They are, from this period, to be considered as the Actors on a most conspicuous Theatre, which seems to be peculiarly designated by Providence for the display of human greatness and felicity.

The language is lofty, even a bit pretentious, but Washington meant every word. The historian Joseph Ellis, citing this passage, says of Washington, "the one big thing he knew was that America's future as a nation lay to the West, in its development over the next century of a continental empire. . . . The future lay in those forests he had explored as a young man." Washington sensed that a new type of human being had been planted on the rich soil of North America. This had all the markings of a providential scheme. The Americans had tremendous, almost explosive energy. They were dynamic and determined, a people who wanted a better life and would stop at nothing to get it. They lived in a time of expanding commerce and, as he put it, "progressive refinement of Manners" and "growing liberality of sentiment." If the Americans did not become completely free and happy, "the fault will be intirely their own."

And here is where Washington's vision turned dark. Perhaps Americans would not, in fact, capitalize on their blessings. Fools would squander their chance at historical greatness. Freedom would turn into chaos. All the suffering and all the money and all the spilled blood of the war would be wasted. Washington believed in order. He believed that men need strong leadership and the confederation needed a more powerful central government. So far, the states had been selfish, refusing to cede authority, sending their second-tier and third-tier citizens to serve in Congress. Washington fervently desired that the American people develop a spirit of "subordination and obedience to government." If things didn't improve, Washington advised a fellow Virginian, "like a young heir, come a little prematurely to a large inheritance, we shall wanton and run riot until we have brought our reputation to the brink of ruin. . . ."

There was so much work to be done. The country was like Mount Vernon, a great sprawling mess. How could America become an Actor on a most conspicuous Theatre when it had hardly any decent roads? It had no bridges! The Potomac had not a one. A traveler in America repeatedly learned the lesson that *you can't get there from here.* This vast tract of continent had rivers choked with rocks, a range of nearly impassable mountains, and a gloomy, dense forest the size of France. The country spanned a thousand miles of the temperate zone of North America and, at approximately 900,000 square miles, was the fourth-largest country in the world by size, smaller only than Russia, China, and Turkey. But the Russians had been Russians and the Chinese had been Chinese and the Turks had been Turks for centuries, even millennia—whereas many Americans were still getting used to the idea that they weren't *British*.

Washington knew that there were interested parties who had never agreed to the peace treaty, that the western Indians had signed no document, did not believe themselves a conquered people, and did not perceive their hunting grounds and villages as a "wilderness" or "virgin land." The Indians hadn't rated a single reference in the Treaty of Paris. They were not going to evaporate suddenly. They were active players in the unfolding drama, a race of men who did not see themselves as objects to be cast aside.

Nor, as it turned out, would the British evacuate the frontier forts along the Great Lakes, as the treaty required. The future of the nation would be decided not by peace treaties signed by diplomats, but on the ground, in the hearts and minds of farmers, woodsmen, hunters, tribal elders, warriors, and all those men and women and children moving through the mountain gaps and down the river valleys.

America was a land of people in motion. They seceded, separated, emigrated, rebelled. The center could not hold amid the centrifugal forces. Things were flying apart, dissolving, disbanding; it was as though geography compelled movement, as though people had no choice but to ramble into new territory. The West would be "a most happy asylum," Washington wrote, for citizens seeking personal independence. The existence of all that land beyond the mountains, all that unsettled wilderness, dimpled the gravity field of the thirteen states. Going west was like falling.

The country had only one anchor, one monumental entity capable of holding the esteem of citizens everywhere, North and South and East and West. And he had just retired.

*   *   *

BY ANY MEASURE he should have been dead already. Washington's ability to survive adventures that would be surely lethal to others had given him the aura of an immortal. He felt he had a special destiny.

Though not particularly religious, he believed that things happened for a reason, that the affairs of men were overseen by the Great Ruler of Events. (The general hesitated in his writings and public speeches to talk of "God"; his Creator was an Architect, "the Author of the Universe," the kind of God who is usually too important to get down and dirty with mortals on a day-to-day basis. His God, in short, was rather Washingtonesque.)

He should have died at twenty-one, on a winter journey to confront the French. In 1753 Washington was a major in the Virginia regiment, dispatched by the governor on a sensitive mission to the western slope of the Alleghenies, to a region coveted by both the English and the French and defended by native tribes. The French were sending troops into areas around the upper Ohio River, establishing fortifications in territory over which the British believed they had sovereignty. The conflict between the two great empires had not yet erupted into a full-scale war, and Washington, as things would turn out, did much to change that.

Washington and his guide, a woodsman and trader named Christopher Gist, traveled north from the Forks of the Ohio, eventually reaching a French fort near Lake Erie, where they delivered the written warning from the Virginia governor. On their return trek they ran into all kinds of trouble. A storm had left the landscape deep in snow and the rivers icy, and the horses they had left behind had nearly starved to death, too emaciated to carry them back to Virginia. Washington and Gist set out on foot, but now their Indian guide proved treacherous, suddenly turning upon them with a gun, firing and missing from fifteen paces away. (Bullets had an uncanny inability to strike George Washington.) The two men subdued the guide, but sensed that the woods were teeming with hostile warriors, and marched all night through the snowy woods until they came to the banks of the Allegheny River, and to yet another dilemma. There wasn't a ferry anywhere in this part of the world, they had no canoe, they weren't about to try to swim across a swollen, ice-choked river in December, so they had to build a raft. That done, they began to pole across, but the raft suddenly lurched and Washington careened into the drink.

They were hurtling down the river now, Gist on the raft, Major Washington in the river, his body rapidly stiffening. No amount of exertion could bring them nearer the shore, but they managed to reach an island in the river, where they spent a brutal night, without a fire, the temperature dropping steadily. At dawn they were not only still alive, but the river had iced over, and the major and Gist could simply walk to the far bank, from which they eventually reached the sanctuary of a trading post.

The most astonishing part of this little adventure is that when Washington wrote up the story, he made only the most passing reference to being *cold* ("The Cold was so extremely severe, that Mr. Gist had all his Fingers, and some of his Toes Froze.") He did not even say that *he* was cold, only that *Gist* was cold and had frostbite. And he didn't indicate any fear. ("He was incapable of fear, meeting personal dangers with the calmest unconcern," Thomas Jefferson wrote years later.) Washington had minimal capacity for complaint of any kind, with the prominent exceptions of situations involving money or real estate (in which case he could be prosecutorial) or his own lofty reputation (which incited a defensiveness of comic dimensions). But he would never write something as irrelevant as "I was cold." Report the relevant data, then move onward—that was the Washington style.

In the spring of 1754, still sniffing out French mischief, he came upon an encampment of French soldiers led by an officer named Jumonville. The French were on a diplomatic mission, carrying a message ordering the English to abandon the Ohio country, but Washington saw them as spies, a hostile force, and thus a legitimate military target. He later pointed out that they had instructions "to reconnoitre the Country, Roads, Creeks &ca to Potomack," which must have struck a nerve for a young man who viewed the Upper Potomac region as his personal stomping ground.

Washington had allied himself with a number of Indians led by an Iroquois warrior named Tanaghrisson, also known as the Half King.

The English crept up to the camp from one side, the Indians from the other. The French awoke and bolted for their guns. Washington gave the order to fire. It was no contest. The French lay bleeding and wounded, captives of the English. Tanaghrisson came up to Jumonville, spoke to him in French—"Thou are not yet dead, my father"—and clove his skull with a tomahawk. Lest his fellow Indians fail to grasp the significance of this gesture, Tanaghrisson then scooped out the contents of Jumonville's skull and washed his hands with them. The other Indians quickly executed the prisoners. The massacre would roil the Great Powers across the sea and trigger what might well be called the first world war, known in America as the French and Indian War, and in Europe as the Seven Years' War, a great tragedy that left more than 800,000 soldiers dead, in addition to hundreds of thousands of civilians. Washington emerged unscathed.

The incident soon led to Washington's comeuppance, the disastrous battle at Fort Necessity, the only time Washington ever formally surrendered to an enemy. In a Pennsylvania field called Great Meadows, Washington and his troops, having built a stockade fort—a ring of timbers, and some earthen embankments—wallowed haplessly in pooling rainwater in a vicious firefight with French soldiers and their Indian allies. Washington was surely doomed, for the French despised him for the recent Jumonville affair (after which the young Washington had enthused in a letter, "I heard the bullets whistle, and, believe me, there is something charming in the sound"). Now the young officer was trapped as surely as a fox surrounded by hounds. The rain kept falling, the meadow began turning into a lake, and the men splashed in the ditches as bullets took them out one by one. They were either going to die of gunshot wounds or simply drown. Two bullets struck one of Washington's unlucky officers, and as the poor man was carried to the surgeon, a final bullet finished him off. Thirty British Americans died, another 70 were wounded, and Washington had no choice but to surrender. For reasons that are no clearer after two and a half centuries, the French showed mercy, requiring merely that Washington sign a document of capitulation, surrender his sad little fort and his modest artillery, march back to his "own Country, "and vow on his "Word of Honour" to build nothing more on the west side of the mountains. The document referred twice to the "Assassination" of Jumonville, but the smudged handwriting on soggy paper could hardly be read by the French interpreter, and Washington later claimed he didn't know he had signed something so incendiary. The affair might have been humiliating, and indeed the retreating British Americans suffered a final indignity when Indians robbed them of their supplies during their retreat, but the simple fact is that Washington once again survived a potentially lethal situation. To walk away in one piece was highly improbable, but that was the Washington way.

The next year, 1755, in the same remote country, with the war now full-blown, Washington, ill and feverish, moved with the British General Edward Braddock and more than 2,000 men toward Fort Duquesne, the French stronghold at the Forks of the Ohio. They marched in European military formation on a primitive road hacked through the forest. From the trees came a storm of bullets. The panicked British began firing wildly, cutting down their own men, unable to see their attackers. Washington, a towering target, felt his horse fall dead beneath him. He jumped on another horse, and it too soon collapsed from enemy fire. Washington mounted a third horse. Braddock took a bullet, mortally wounded, and the feverish Washington, only twenty-two years old, suddenly became the only officer in the field able to carry out Braddock's orders.

Now the death toll had reached 700. Washington galloped away with two scouts, racing back through the mountains to seek help from a reserve force. His actions helped save half the army. Again he survived unhurt, but his cloak bore four unmistakable bullet holes. A legend arose (thanks to Parson Weems, the great hagiographer) that an Indian fired eleven times at Washington from close range, missed every time, and finally gave up. This gigantic young officer, the Indian was said to have concluded, must be under the protection of the Great Spirit.

Meanwhile a dozen captive soldiers, men of a different destiny, were taken back to the Forks of the Ohio and burned at the stake.

During the War of Independence, Washington repeatedly displayed personal bravery on the battlefield, exposing himself to British fire and all the random violence of combat. Legend has it that at the Battle of Princeton, Washington rode his horse directly between the American and British lines, and gave the order to fire. He could not have been more exposed. One of his aides, horrified by the prospect of seeing his beloved commander obliterated, covered his eyes. The gunfire thundered across the meadow, and when the smoke cleared, men were sprawled on the ground, bleeding and dying, but the general was untouched, still majestic on his steed, never in finer spirits. *You could not kill him.* The story goes that Washington pursued the fleeing British, shouting, "It's a fine fox chase, my boys!"

He survived all the other hazards, the accidents and pathogens, that cut down so many men of his generation. Many times he'd been deathly sick but had always pulled through. Tuberculosis killed his beloved half-brother Lawrence but spared George Washington. Smallpox merely left a few scars on his nose and the benefit of lifelong immunity. His sole physical malady was the poor condition of his teeth, which fell out one by one, leading him to turn, in his fifties, to prosthetic teeth (but never made of wood, contrary to American mythology).

*   *   *

MARTHA Washington, who had spent a fair bit of the war in military camps with the general, was clearly thrilled to have "my little family" home again at Mount Vernon in 1784, even if there was an outbreak of measles among her grandchildren. She wrote a friend that "my frequent long Journeys have not only left me without inclination to undertake another, but almost disqualified me from doing it, as I find the fatiegue is too much for me to bear."

The general wanted to tour his farm and plant his crops and drink his wine on the porch, maybe ride to the hounds once in a while, but there were so many interruptions, distractions, vexations. In the months that followed, guests arrived at the mansion like locusts. (Lafayette, who came in August, was a rarity in that he had actually been invited.) Most of these visitors had no claim to the affections of the Washington family, and many showed up unannounced. "It may be compared to a well resorted tavern, as scarcely any strangers who are going from north to south, or from south to north do not spend a day or two at it," the general wrote his mother in an oft-quoted letter advising her not to come live with him. A total stranger might expect to be welcomed to Mount Vernon and given an audience with the general. The combination of southern hospitality and the rigid dictates of republicanism (aristocrats were not supposed to behave aristocratically) required the Washingtons to remove barriers between themselves and whoever might be happening by. Visitors would be brought first to the piazza for a once-over. If they made the grade, they would be invited to dinner, and the better sorts were offered a bed for the night. Dinner guests had to be entertained lavishly, for the republican principles said nothing about modesty in dining. The Mount Vernon Tavern boasted a groaning board for the ages, with wine flowing as if from an artesian well. The servants dressed in finest livery. Washington saw no alternative, and referred to his home as "the expensive mansion in which I am, as it were, involuntarily compelled to live."

Washington rationed his personal warmth. His natural temperament at times seemed to border on the reptilian. This too was part of his script, his creed of proper behavior. Perhaps no American ever mastered so fully the art of remaining dignified and reserved. A gentleman didn't run on at the mouth. Washington certainly knew how to smile, but he had those bad teeth. Smiling invited trouble. One day the sculptor Joseph Wright slathered plaster over Washington's face to make a life mask. Martha Washington came into the room, saw her husband, and shrieked. The general found this outburst so amusing that his face moved in a smile-like fashion, or, as he put it more technically, "Her cry excited in me a disposition to smile, which gave my mouth a slight twist or compression of the lips that is now observable in the busts which Wright afterwards made."

As a teenager, Washington had meticulously copied a translation of the maxims of a sixteenth-century Jesuit. They included such admonitions as "Spit not in the Fire" and "Kill no vermin as Fleas, lice, ticks &c in the Sight of others" and the sweeping, inarguable "Put not your meat to your mouth with your knife in your hand neither spit forth the stones of any fruit pye upon a dish nor cast anything under the table." Washington's stoical demeanor and correspondingly inanimate facial expression may have saved him many times from violating the maxim "Do not Puff up the Cheeks, Loll not out the tongue, rub the Hands, or beard, thrust out the lips, or bite them or keep the Lips too open or too Close." Washington would no sooner loll out his tongue than wear breeches on his head.

Tremendous labor and calculation went into Washington's rise to greatness. A person didn't become the "Father of His Country" by accident or luck. Contingency plays a powerful and underappreciated role in history—a bullet's flight a few inches left or right could have made General Horatio Gates or some other figure the paramount hero of the Revolution—but there was nothing random in Washington's greatness. From early in life, he craved distinction. He was desperate to avoid becoming one of the "common run" of men. Even before the Revolution, he carefully saved all his personal papers, as if he knew that someday the documentary historians would need them. "They are the archives of someone who derived great satisfaction from organizing, setting down, and preserving the detailed record of his own existence," observes the historian W. W. Abbot. "More than most, Washington's biography is the story of a man constructing himself." Historian Gordon Wood writes, "He was obsessed with having things in fashion and was fastidious about his appearance to the world. It was as if he were always onstage, acting a part."

Even his decision to renounce power was driven in part by his desire to elevate himself in the eyes of his contemporaries. His humility formed a thin crust on a deep lake of pride. If he did not literally say "I cannot tell a lie," he came close often enough. He once declared, "I do not recollect that in the course of my life I ever forfeited my word, or broke a promise made to any one. . . ."

So successfully did Washington adopt the manner of a landed gentleman that it's easy to forget his relatively unpromising origin. His father, Augustine Washington, died of gout in 1743, at the age of forty-nine, when George was just eleven. George scarcely mentioned his father in any of his voluminous writings. His family had some money, but not the kind of wealth of the top-tier Virginia planter families, like the Byrds and Carters and Fairfaxes. They did have tenure as Virginians: George's great-grandfather John Washington emigrated to America from England back in 1657 and became known in the Virginia Regiment as an excellent Indian-fighter. Some historians have flatly declared that the Washingtons were a rather undistinguished clan with, in the words of historian W. E. Woodward, "a persistent mediocrity." Unlike his half-brother Lawrence and many of his contemporaries, George Washington never received an education in England. He learned the manners of a gentleman by studying Lawrence, and by loitering in the mansions along the Potomac. The person he became, the personality he hewed and polished, was ultimately decent, honest, cautious, deliberate, but not truly humble. He sought a level of virtue that would never be questioned. So he agonized about whether he could accept a gift and seemed genuinely fearful that someone, somewhere, might question his motives.

The general never bragged about winning the war, and declined to regale his visitors with the kind of war stories they had expected. One houseguest, Brissot de Warville, found Washington to be bizarrely modest: "He speaks of the American War as if he had not been its leader."

After the war the general may have suffered from spells of melancholy, as the biographer James Thomas Flexner maintains. Washington talked a lot about death. One Dutchman who dropped in at Mount Vernon in 1784 was shocked by the general's demeanor: "He is slow of perception; he expresses himself slowly. Transition from one subject to another is difficult for him; he does not consider matters profoundly; he shares the indolence common to Americans who stifle in themselves all inclinations to industry." Or perhaps the general hoped the Dutchman would drop in somewhere else.

He felt burdened by the duties of correspondence, which trapped him at his writing desk. He wrote many letters to people who owed him money, and these letters show that, in financial dealings, Washington tended to be excruciatingly exact. He wrote to a certain John Stephenson, ritually offering his condolence for the deaths of Stephenson's brother William, his brother Valentine, and his brother Hugh. That courtesy out of the way, Washington noted that there is a "Sum of money due to me from your Fathers Estate; which I wish to know when it can be settled & paid, as the situation of my private Affairs makes it absolutely necessary to close my Accounts & to receive payment as soon as possible."

In a letter to a business partner, Gilbert Simpson—who operated a mill that Washington owned in western Pennsylvania—his tone acidified: "How profitable our partnership has been, *you best can tell*; & how advantageous my Mill has been, none can tell so well as *yourself*."

The mill, Washington felt, was the best on the western slope of the Alleghenies.

"I expect something very handsome therefore from that quarter. I want a full settlement of this Account from the beginning, clearly stated. I also require a full & complete settlement of our Partnership accounts, wherein every article of debit is to be properly supported by vouchers."

Vouchers required! So declared the greatest American. He expects . . . he wants . . . he *requires* . . .

Simultaneously, he was generous with his nephews and nieces, his friends, even the children of friends, and he carried out his charity with little noise, seeking no acclaim or thanks. But he could be demanding as well. A dissolute nephew made the mistake of writing Washington with a request for financial assistance, provoking the general to dash off a note declining any help, citing his own financial hardships, and adding in a postscript a couple of chilly questions: "There was a great space between the 23d of Septr 1778 when you were called upon by your Father for a specific list of your Debts; and his death: How happened it, that in all that time you did not comply with his request? and what do they amount to now?" He might as well have added, *And whom do you think you're dealing with?*

The general scrambled for information about his western lands, what tenants he might have there, what rents he might be owed, who might be disputing his rightful title. He needed to "recover my business from the confusion into which it has run" during the war. Was there anyone living on the tract he owned at Great Meadows, site of Fort Necessity? Where could he find paperwork to prove his ownership of the tract called Round Bottom on the Ohio River? Could he perhaps come to terms with the squatters on his large property west of the Monongahela (who, he said, had settled there "ignorantly, or under a mistaken belief, founded on false assertions, that the Land did not belong to him")?

One might imagine other reasons the general became sometimes dour or restless. He had a solid marriage to Martha Washington, and for that could be grateful, but the object of his youthful passion, Sally Fairfax, a beauty married to his neighbor, had long since departed to Europe. Martha Washington had children from an earlier marriage but had never become pregnant by the general. They did, however, have two children to raise: Martha's grandchildren Eleanor Parke (Nelly) Custis and George Washington Parke Custis (called Washy and, later, Washington), whose father had died in 1781. Both the general and Mrs. Washington adored these children. Mrs. Washington referred to them as "my little progeny."

And yet even though the aging warrior and his wife had many lovely times around the hearth with Nelly and Little Washington, the general was acutely aware that he had no biological offspring—that he had, as he put it in a painful expression, "no family."

*   *   *

AS MUCH AS he claimed that his happiest times were spent at Mount Vernon, his most fantastic adventures had been in the hinterlands, the deep woods, where the rivers ran swift and the mountains crumbled slowly and a man was always grateful to live through the night. Washington could never suppress the urge to light out for the territory. He'd been a surveyor as a young man, lugging his chain and his theodolite into the remote vales of colonial Virginia, looking for big trees and boulders and springs and creeks and other landmarks that would help him enclose the terrain with imaginary lines. He always liked to poke his nose into blank spots on the maps, but at 52, those blank spots were growing smaller, the realm of the Delawares and Senecas and the Miamis and Cherokees and all other other Indians rapidly undergoing a radical transformation. Where once there had been Indian villages, there were now outposts of European-American culture, with ranches, farms, sawmills, ironworks, lime kilns, mines of every kind, trading posts, stockade forts, and even some wagon roads.

When Washington was a boy, in the 1730s, there was only a smattering of European-Americans living more than 100 miles from tidewater. There was no one beyond the mountains but Indians, the odd missionary, a few French trappers, and maybe a hopelessly lost botanist.

Though the wilderness was often described by European-Americans as hideous, a realm of ravenous animals and predatory natives ("wild beasts and wild men," in the formulation of William Bradford, the governor of Plymouth Plantation), it held a powerful allure. So much fertile land lay just across those mountain ridges, in what is now Ohio, Indiana, Illinois, Michigan, Wisconsin, Minnesota, West Virginia, western Pennsylvania, Kentucky, Tennessee, Alabama, and Mississippi.

Washington had seen more of America than almost any other prominent figure in his generation. In an era when New England and Virginia were as distinct as France and Spain, he could say honestly that he knew both regions intimately. He'd spent eight years on the move, plotting his next attack or retreat, combing the land for provisions, learning who his friends were and where he could find enough food to feed an army. He knew the cities—Philadelphia, New York, Boston—but he also knew the backcountry, the darkest forests. He'd seen trees as big around as a cabin. He'd paddled down western rivers, hunted bear, passed the pipe with Indian chiefs. Of the men who would someday be known as the Founding Fathers, only Washington had routinely slept under the stars. During much of the Revolution he'd practically lived on the back of a horse. And now he could not resist the urge to explore further.

"I shall not rest contented," Washington wrote to the Chevalier de Chastellux in October 1783, just before his retirement, " 'till I have explored the Western Country, and traversed those lines (or great part of them) which have given bounds to a New Empire."

He had hoped to begin his western tour as soon as spring arrived in the mountains to the west. He wrote to Lafayette:

> I have it in contemplation . . . to make a tour thro' all the Eastern States, thence into Canada; thence up the St. Lawrence, and thro' the Lakes to Detroit; thence to lake Michigan by Land or water; thence thro' the Western Country by the river Illinois, to the river Mississippi, and down the same to New Orleans; thence into Georgia by the way of Pensacola; and then thro' the two Carolina's home. A great tour this, you will say, probably it may take place no where but in imagination. . . .

That was too ambitious an itinerary, as it turned out. The demands of Mount Vernon prevented him from making the full Grand Tour of the country and forced him to postpone his trip until late summer. But even his more modest plan called for two months of travel and would potentially cover a thousand miles round-trip. It would be dangerous, because the Ohio Indians, furious at the invasion of their hunting grounds and recently the victims of white atrocities, were scalping settlers. If the troubles didn't abate, he might not be able to go all the way down the Ohio to the Great Kanawha.

Even in the best of circumstances, the trip would be arduous, for the simple reason that he lived in a country where it was hard to get *anywhere*. Roads in America were often hardly more than trails, choked with stumps, particularly south of the Potomac. Even between Mount Vernon and nearby Alexandria people would routinely get lost in the woods for hours. Travelers in this part of the world would be bewildered by roads that forked promiscuously, that refused to go in a straight line, that seemed utterly overmatched by the rugged topography along the Potomac and its tumbling tributaries. Throughout the United States, bridges over major rivers simply didn't exist. People traveling in coaches often drowned in swollen streams. Travelers had to hope the ferryboat captain had not yet become completely inebriated. These nuisances and travails were intolerable in a 900,000-square-mile republic. Washington's grand idea—his Potomac plan—would speed things up, enhance fluidity, create networks, make it possible for people and products and information to flow from east to west and west to east. The connective tissues would strengthen the fragile union.

For all its geographical virtues, however, the Potomac in 1784 remained inadequate as an artery of commerce. He would need to remove boulders from the riverbed, build skirting channels around the rapids and falls, and construct dams to funnel water to channels that would otherwise be too shallow. And he would need, on this western journey, to find the shortest land portage between the headwaters of the Potomac and the headwaters of the Ohio, out near the tip of the Maryland panhandle. He needed to blaze a trail that would become the prime connection between the settled part of America and that wilderness empire on the far side of the mountains.

Washington subscribed to the idea of Providence: History did not proceed randomly, but rather was progressive, purposeful, reflecting a higher purpose. Divine will was written in the land itself. Providence, the general had written the Chevalier de Chastellux, had "dealt her favors to us with so profuse a hand." He added, "Would to God we may have wisdom enough to improve them."

He would not be initiating something new. He would simply take what was already there, what had been etched on the face of the land—this passage through the mountains, carved by the Potomac—and finish the job.

2

The Race to the West

*W*HEN WASHINGTON looked at a map, he saw that the major rivers between Virginia and New England were like the splayed fingers of his right hand, turned palm-down. The Connecticut and the Hudson and the Delaware and the Susquehanna ran generally north-south, in parallel—but the Potomac was down here, on the left, low on his hand, a curved thumb jutting toward the western frontier. He couldn't miss the obvious message: The Potomac wasn't just a southern river, it was a *western* river.

The seaboard of the mid-Atlantic states didn't run north-south, after all, but rather from northeast to southwest. Georgetown, at the fall line of the Potomac, could claim to be the westernmost port on any of these rivers. Washington had spent his life taking the measure of things, and he could easily see that the village of Pittsburgh, at the Forks of the Ohio—the Gateway to the West—was closer to George-town on the Potomac than it was to Philadelphia. In a logical and or-derly world, the Potomac would unquestionably become the highway between the Atlantic and the Ohio River watershed.

For Washington and many others of his generation, geography was destiny. To know the future you had to study maps. You had to look at the land, follow the rivers in their courses, gauge the difficulty of the mountains and the possibilities of portage. You had to know not only distances and elevations, but also the soils, the annual rainfall, the drainage, the predominant trees, the availability of forage and game, the presence of minerals, the proximity of salt, the date when a river would close with ice and when it would open in the spring—all the practical data embedded in the environment. The enterprising American had to abide faithfully by the commandment of John Adams: "Really there ought not to be a state, a city, a promontory, a river, a harbor, an inlet or a mountain in all America, but what should be intimately known to every youth who has any pretensions to liberal education."

The Potomac's rivals among American rivers had some geographical virtues of their own. The Susquehanna, marred by falls and rapids near its mouth, was nonetheless the largest river system along the seaboard, with a watershed extending from upstate New York to the Chesapeake. The hazardous lower reaches could be circumvented by roads, in theory. The western branch of the Susquehanna, like the Potomac, emerged from deep within the Alleghenies.

The Hudson loomed as an even more formidable competitor. The Hudson is a fjord, splitting the mountains, and carrying the pulse of tide all the way to Albany, 150 miles from New York Harbor. From the west the Hudson is joined by the Mohawk. A traveler moving up the Mohawk would discover some falls and rapids and difficult portages, but no mountains, for the Alleghenies were off to the south and the Adirondacks off to the north. There was a broad gap in the Appalachians, screaming for a commercial artery to the west.

The St. Lawrence River, far to the north, provided another western passage, for it flowed from the Great Lakes to the Atlantic *behind* the Appalachian chain. It gave the French the perfect entry to the fur-rich continental interior in the early seventeenth century. The glaciers that gouged the Great Lakes left only a modest berm along the southern shore of the lakes, and the Indians taught the French how easily they could portage to the rivers flowing into the Ohio and Mississippi.

The Potomac had another competitor on its southern flank, the James, running east-west through central Virginia. Some Virginians had envisioned a link between the James and the New, the river known downstream as the Great Kanawha. The New flows across the mountains in the opposite direction from the other transappalachian rivers, almost as if providing a Newtonian counter-reaction to the flow of the Potomac. But the New is an ornery, vicious mountain river that runs through impassable gorges. Washington gave lip service to the James and the New only to keep his southern Virginia friends happy.

One final river entered the picture, and it was a monster: the Mississippi. Compared with the Mississippi, the Potomac was just a millrace. The Mississippi clearly had the potential to be the major artery of commerce in the West, but for the moment, it wasn't open for business. Spain controlled the Lower Mississippi, including New Orleans, and in 1784 closed the river to American commerce. That move created no distress for Washington, who didn't want Spain to lure the western settlers into its orbit. Keep the Mississippi closed, Washington thought, until we have time to bind the westerners to the East.

And that's where the Potomac came in. It showed a way through the mountains. It blasted through stone. With a little improvement the Potomac would make those westerners forget about the Mississippi and the Hudson and the Susquehanna and every other competing route.

Washington's idea about the natural superiority of the Potomac had grown into something like a faith. He was prepared to gamble a great deal on this river—his time, his money, his reputation. He had bought large tracts of land along the Potomac and Ohio river corridors, and that itself was a gamble, a wager that this was the right strip of America for a rich man's investment. The Potomac route wasn't an abstract issue for him. He'd bet the farm.

*   *   *

WASHINGTON DIDN'T HAVE to rely entirely on his own geographical analysis. He had a crucial ally, a fellow Revolutionary, geographer, surveyor, Virginia planter, and thinker of big ideas: Thomas Jefferson.

The Potomac brought them together in a way that the Revolution itself (and the War of Independence—which was not quite the same thing, as Jefferson and John Adams pointed out in their old age) never could. Though Washington and Jefferson could both boast of being Revolutionaries in a formal sense, Jefferson had made his greatest contribution with his pen. He had camped comfortably by the hearth of Monticello while Washington and his men gnashed their teeth at Valley Forge.

Jefferson and Washington began corresponding about the Potomac in the spring of 1784. In their individual ways, both had spent many years thinking about the West, and now their interests converged. The two men had recently spent time together at Annapolis—Washington's final address to Congress, explaining his decision to retire, may have been partially scripted by the younger Virginian. (When a person needs a speechwriter in a pinch, it's always nice to hear that Thomas Jefferson is in the building.)

They had certain traits in common. Both men knew their dirt. To be a planter in Virginia required an intimate understanding of soil, climate, pests, weeds, and as their land grew barren under the harshness of tobacco cultivation, they kept searching for new ground to cultivate. Jefferson owned 10,000 acres, including a tract at a separate plantation called Poplar Forest, though he was never in the same league as Washington, who by the end of his life would be among the largest landowners in the country. They each had a natural engineering impulse, always thinking of ways to improve their farms and the tools for wringing food from the soil. Washington had his fishing nets, distillery, barns, and fine breed of jackasses; Jefferson invented a new kind of plow.

Jefferson brought to the discussion an Olympian certitude about what was right and wrong in the race to the West. This is the way it must be done, he would say. This is the course that nature dictates. This is what an enlightened and rational person should think.

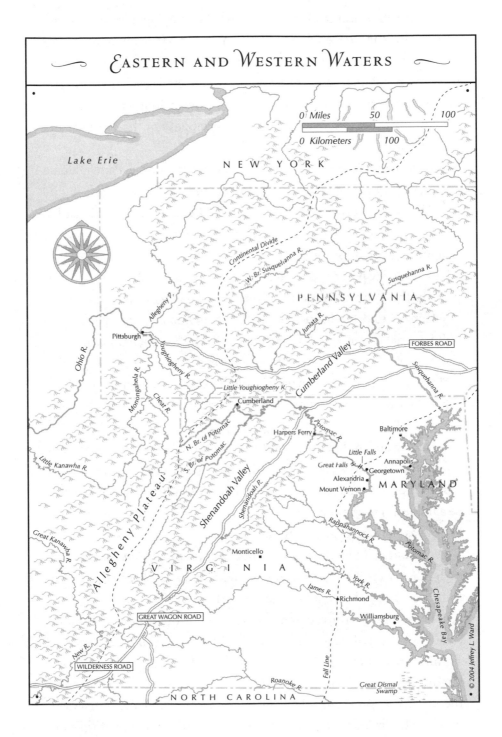

EASTERN AND WESTERN WATERS

0 Miles 50 100

0 Kilometers 100

Lake Erie

NEW YORK

Continental Divide

W. Br. Susquehanna R.

Susquehanna R.

PENNSYLVANIA

Allegheny R.

Juniata R.

Ohio R.

Pittsburgh

Cumberland Valley

FORBES ROAD

Youghiogheny R.

Monongahela R.

Cheat R.

Little Youghiogheny R.

Cumberland

Susquehanna R.

N. Br. of Potomac

S. Br. of Potomac

Harpers Ferry

Potomac R.

Baltimore

Little Kanawha R.

Little Falls

Annapolis

Great Falls

Georgetown

Alexandria

MARYLAND

Mount Vernon

Shenandoah R.

Shenandoah Valley

Allegheny Plateau

Rappahannock R.

Great Kanawha R.

Monticello

Potomac R.

Chesapeake Bay

VIRGINIA

York R.

James R.

Richmond

GREAT WAGON ROAD

Williamsburg

New R.

WILDERNESS ROAD

Fall Line

Great Dismal Swamp

Roanoke R.

NORTH CAROLINA

© 2004 Jeffrey L. Ward

"[T]he Ohio, and it's branches which head up against the Patowmac," Jefferson wrote fellow Virginian James Madison, another Potomac promoter, "affords the shortest water communication by 500. miles of any which can ever be got between the Western waters and Atlantic, and of course"—exact science now giving way to a blunt provincialism—"promises us almost a monopoly of the Western and Indian trade."

Jefferson didn't think Virginia could afford to dawdle. Pennsylvania and New York would seize the trade if Virginia hesitated in the slightest. The resources of the West staggered the mind: inexhaustible minerals, endless trees, dark soil begging for the plow, furs beyond imagination. If those resources could be sent to the world through Alexandria, the port on the Potomac could become a fabulous entrepôt, perhaps the commercial center of the nation—bigger than New York.

Jefferson told Madison that the Pennsylvanians were plotting to build a canal connecting Philadelphia with the Susquehanna, and that the project would cost only 200,000 pounds. "What an example this is! If we do not push this matter immediately," Jefferson wrote Madison, "they will be beforehand with us and get possession of the commerce. . . ."

Jefferson added that the Potomac navigation project would be a fine hobby for General Washington in his old age: "Genl. Washington has that of the Patowmac much at heart. The superintendance of it would be a noble amusement in his retirement and leave a monument of him as long as the waters should flow."

Washington and Jefferson were not friends, exactly, but they found each other useful, at least for the moment, and fed off each other's enthusiasm. They shared a fascination with scientific agriculture. They had no patience with religious pieties and, though not atheists, increasingly steered clear of the church. Both perceived their historical significance and took great care to preserve their personal papers. Jefferson had a more facile brain and far greater eloquence, and he noted the disparity many years later in a rather cold assessment of Washington: "His mind was great and powerful, without being of the very first order . . . when called for a sudden opinion, he was unready, short, and embarrassed."

On March 15, 1784, a few weeks after writing to Madison, Jefferson sent a long letter to Washington that laid out the geographic and economic reasons why Washington should pursue the Potomac navigation project. Although Jefferson idealized the simple life of farming, he acknowledged that the world was changing, that people craved manufactured goods, that they would not be content to wear homespun clothes and eat only the fruits of their own labors:

> All the world is becoming commercial. Was it practical to keep our new empire separated from them we might indulge ourselves in speculating whether commerce contributes to the happiness of mankind. But we cannot separate ourselves from them. Our citizens have had too full a taste of the comforts furnished by the arts and manufactures to be debarred the use of them. We must then in our own defence endeavor to share as large a portion as we can of this modern source of wealth and power. That offered to us from the Western country is under a competition between the Hudson, the Patomac and the Missisipi itself.

The Ohio trade, Jefferson informed Washington, was nearer to Alexandria than to New York by 730 miles (Washington later questioned his math) and was interrupted by only one portage.

> Nature then has declared in favour of the Patowmac, and through that channel offers to pour into our lap the whole commerce of the Western world. . . . This is the moment in which the trade of the West will begin to get into motion and to take it's direction. It behoves us then to open our doors to it.*

---

* The reader will have noticed that these men are unsure how to spell the name of the river. The spelling seems to have varied according to mood or barometric pressure. In the letter to Washington, Jefferson uses two different spellings, and a third in his letter to Madison (and he routinely spelled "its" as "it's"). The word is of Native American origin, and in the original tongue may have had an extra syllable, more like *Patawomeck*. The United States

Nature had chosen the Potomac. This was a powerful idea. Washington, Jefferson, Madison, and their allies had a duty, not only as Virginians, but as men who thought about the dictates of nature and the imperatives of geography, to support nature's decision. Jefferson's words carried weight with Washington, but not so much because they offered new insight—the younger man was telling the older man a lot of things he already knew (indeed there is almost an element of impertinence in Jefferson offering advice to the country's leading Potomac expert). What really struck Washington was that Jefferson had no direct stake in the scheme, that he owned no land along the Potomac or the Ohio. Jefferson lived a full two days' ride on a swift horse south of the Potomac, near the Rivanna River, a tributary of the James. Jefferson's sanction seemed pure.

Washington touched on this directly, and with admirable frankness, when he wrote back to Jefferson: "I am not so disinterested in this matter as you are, but I am made very happy to find that a man of discernment and liberality, who has no particular interest in the plan, thinks as I do, who have lands in the country, the value of which would be enhanced by the adoption of such a measure."

Jefferson had cleared Washington's conscience. A man who wouldn't take a salary as commander in chief certainly wouldn't push a river-

---

Geological Survey reports the following variations on the name: Pataromerke, Patawmack, Patawomeck, Patawomecke, Patawomek, Patawomeke, Patomack, Patomacke, Patomak, Patomake, Patomeck, Patomecke, Patomeke, Patoumak, Patowmack, Patowmacke, Patowmec, Patowmeck, Patowomeck, Patowomek, Pawtomack, Pokomoach, Potamack, Potamak, Potawmack, Potomack, Potomacke, Potomak, Potomeack, Potomock, Potomoke, Potomuck, Potomucke, Powowmac, Potowmak, Potowomek, Pottomock, Powtowmac, Powtowmack. The name Potomac is an Algonquian word that roughly means "place where something is brought," or "trading place," though no two references seem to agree, and one can find such translations as "they are coming by water" and "where goods are brought in." Complicating matters is the fact that the Indians thought of the Potomac, quite logically, as more than just one river. The Indians' "Potomac" was the tidal river below the falls. The river above the falls was called Cohongorootan, roughly meaning "honking geese." A section of the river from Will's Creek to the Shenandoah bore the Shawnee name Ouiriough, meaning "the place of the burning pine, resembling a council fire.")

navigation scheme to enhance the value of his lands. With Jefferson's affirmation of nature's intent, Washington could persuade himself that this was not primarily a personal project, that he had national interests in mind, and the interests of Virginia and Maryland, of Alexandria and Georgetown. He would be tidying up a geological feature already selected for national significance by the Master Designer of the Universe. He could plausibly say, *This isn't about me.*

Washington told Jefferson that local rivalries had stopped his own efforts in the past to put public funds behind Potomac improvements. The Baltimoreans had looked askance at the situation. They worried that the Potomac would draw commerce away from their city. Congress, meanwhile, had been ineffectual in domestic matters—stymied by what Washington called, using a wonderful if rather obsolete term, "inertitude." He warned Jefferson that one group of northern rivals was not wasting time: "I *know* the Yorkers will delay no time to remove every obstacle in the way of the other communication" (via the Hudson). The general had spent a lot of time with the entrepreneurial Yorkers, and knew they were eager to exploit the western trade through the Hudson-Mohawk route. But Washington and Jefferson persuaded themselves that the Hudson and Susquehanna rivers were too far north and too far east. As northern rivers, they would be closed by ice much longer than would the Potomac. And as eastern rivers, they were remote from the Forks of the Ohio and the vast western territory.

If someone wanted to go east from the West, why would they take the long way around?

* * *

POTOMAC NAVIGATION had interested Washington for decades. The river had caught his fancy as a young man, even before the French and Indian War. Between 1749 and 1753, he spent much of his time tromping around the Potomac backcountry, surveying for Lord Fairfax and putting together his initial landholdings in the Potomac Valley. When he was twenty-two years old, Washington canoed from

Patterson's Creek, 13 miles below Cumberland, downriver to Harpers Ferry, a distance of 122 miles in which, as he told a friend, "there is no other obstacle than the shallowness of the water to prevent Craft from passing." The shallowness of the water would turn out, many decades later, to be a significant issue, but his basic point was correct—the river has no falls for that entire distance, flowing smoothly, if sometimes with great swiftness, through what geologists call the Ridge and Valley Province. At Harpers Ferry the river tumbles through a series of rapids, through narrow chutes and over rocky ledges, but Washington believed that these cataracts might be "improved" with a little labor. And in any case, Washington knew from his own adventures over the years that an intrepid boatman with a little guile and brio could simply shoot the rapids.

In 1758, during the campaign against the French, Washington became a vehement Potomac partisan, objecting to Brigadier General John Forbes's plan to construct a road across Pennsylvania to Fort Duquesne at the Forks of the Ohio. Washington argued that a good road already existed, the one traveled by Braddock and his men during the disastrous march three years earlier. To build another road for the assault on the French stronghold would be a waste of time, Washington argued, but what seems to have animated him particularly was his fear that a new road would take commerce from the Potomac Valley. In a letter to the treasurer of the Virginia Colony, Washington cursed "the luckless Fate of poor Virginia to fall a Victum to the views of her Crafty Neighbours."

As Washington amassed huge tracts of western land in the late 1760s, he also began to see clearly the disadvantages of living in the colony of a distant Mother Country. In 1763 the British, believing they could not afford more warfare with the western Indians, had closed the territory west of the Alleghenies to white settlement. The Proclamation of 1763 confounded land speculators such as Washington. He assumed the proclamation would be a temporary measure, and continued to acquire western land by every available means. But the interference from the Crown drove him to reassess the future of the colonies. Until this point, historian John Ferling has pointed out, Washington had been a rather low-key figure in the Virginia House of Burgesses, hardly a revolutionary, and a bit tongue-tied around Jefferson and all the other college-educated lawyers. But by 1769, Washington was chomping at the bit, in part because his western investments would be worthless if the Appalachians continued to serve as an impermeable wall. Thoughts about western land, Potomac navigation, and independence from Great Britain swirled through his brain, and Washington started supporting anti-British measures in the Burgesses.

In 1770, Washington urged Thomas Johnson, who would become Maryland's first governor seven years later, to make the Potomac a channel of commerce "between Great Britain and that immense territory, a tract of country which is unfolding to our view, the advantages of which are too great and too obvious." Washington's efforts inspired the Burgesses to pass a Potomac navigation bill, but a peculiar jurisdictional problem reared itself. Under the original charter of Maryland, carving the colony out of Virginia, the entire Potomac, from bank to bank, belonged to Maryland. Maryland didn't go along with the Potomac navigation plan of Virginia because of the obstreperous Baltimoreans.

Another early Potomac visionary, John Ballendine, took direct action to improve navigation. He lived at Little Falls, where he built a house, grist mill, and bakery, and where sometime around 1770 he constructed a dam and the first primitive canal skirting the falls. (Little Falls is a picturesque set of rapids, roughly half a mile in length, just upstream from Georgetown. Near the beginning of the cataract, a strikingly tall island, appropriately named High Island, rises near the Maryland bank as though it were an anchored cruise ship. Downstream the river narrows, and then narrows yet further, the entire watershed forced to funnel its liquid through a sluice where the river is 70 feet deep.) Ballendine had trouble paying his debts and briefly spent time in jail. He claimed to have reconnoitered the terrain between the Upper Potomac and the Monongahela, but his estimate of the land portage was just "ten or eleven miles," which is hardly the case. He became so taken with the notion of a Potomac Route to the West that he went to England and studied the canals there, and even brought a few engineers back to America to work on Potomac improvements. But he's a forgotten figure, by and large, because his project was subsumed into the dream of a much more powerful figure.

The Revolution soon put all river projects on hold. Washington went to war, and, though he continued to keep track of his western lands via correspondence with various land agents, he had more pressing concerns for eight and a half years.

*   *   *

IN THE SPRING of 1784, Thomas Jefferson hadn't yet become an icon, hadn't yet earned the title of Sage of Monticello. He was forty-two and living in an unfinished house on his little mountain near Charlottesville, surrounded by children, relatives, and more than a hundred slaves, yet fundamentally alone, a widower, and a damaged man.

Though his fellow Revolutionaries had recognized his genius and availed themselves of his masterly pen, his authorship of the Declaration of Independence hadn't yet generated a global reputation for greatness. He was still some months away from his momentous voyage to France to serve as the American envoy. His reputation had taken some blows during the war, for as governor of Virginia he had failed to muster much resistance to British invaders. The legislature investigated his actions, including his notorious, last-second, pell-mell flight from Monticello as the British neared. Technically, his term as governor had expired when he scrambled to safety, but for some critics the incident had the odor of an abdication, and even cowardice. The investigation officially cleared him of wrongdoing, but for years thereafter his political enemies and some war veterans continued to question whether this alleged Revolutionary lacked the courage of his convictions.

After that debacle, Jefferson retired from public life, using the same kind of vine-and-fig-tree sentiment as the general. ("I have taken my final leave of everything of that nature, have retired to my farm, my family and books from which I think nothing will ever more separate me.") Then his world collapsed. His wife, Martha, died soon after giving birth to their second daughter. Jefferson disintegrated. He went into isolation and for many weeks could barely speak. For months it appeared the country had lost forever the talents of one of its most brilliant citizens.

His friends persuaded him to accept election as a delegate to the Continental Congress, and slowly he emerged from his grief, crafting a portentous plan for the West. Virginia had ceded an immense swath of territory to the general government, hundreds of millions of acres northwest of the Ohio River. Congress lacked the power to levy taxes, but it could pay off some of the nation's war debts by selling the western lands. Jefferson proposed to turn the western territories, over time, into ten separate states (or fourteen in another variant of the plan), and envisioned them not as colonies of the original states but as equal members of the Union. Moreover, they would be free states, barring slavery. Jefferson, mining the more exotic realms of his brain, where Indian names and geological terms swished freely about, went so far as to jot down some possible names for the new states: Cherronesus, Metropotamia, Saratoga, Pelisipia, Polypotamia, Illinoia, Assenisipia, Michigania, Sylvania and, finally, Washington. (The reaction to the suggested names was, as you'd expect, widespread bewilderment and vicious mockery.) Jefferson also conceived a surveying scheme in which the entire region would be sectioned off in rectangular townships and counties. He turned the wilderness into a grid. His plan led to the classic heartland patchwork seen today by airline passengers.

Jefferson came into the world at the western edge of white settlement. In 1746, when he was three years old, his father, Peter, surveyed the western boundary of Lord Fairfax's domain, a task that took him deep into the mountains to the seep that spawns the North Branch of the Potomac. In 1751, Peter Jefferson and Joshua Fry completed the *Map of the Most Inhabited Part of Virginia, Containing the Whole*

Province of Maryland . . . , which, with some emendations, remained the best map of Virginia and the Upper Potomac for several decades. Jefferson grew up with maps in his head, and they remained there his entire life and into his presidency, when he began filling in the blank spaces, sending Lewis and Clark up the Missouri. He understood that rivers not only provide an avenue for exploration, and define political boundaries, but their headsprings are geographical markers even prior to their discovery—reference points in the blank spaces of the map. The precise location of a headspring may be unknown, but it definitely exists out there *somewhere,* as opposed to, say, a hypothetical volcano.

In his spare moments in the early 1780s, Jefferson wrote and re-vised *Notes on the State of Virginia,* which included a discussion of the major rivers of the United States. Jefferson used *Notes* to re-fute the notion that colonialism led to mental and physical degrada-tion. The French naturalist Comte de Buffon (Georges-Louis Leclerc) had argued that animals in the New World were smaller and less var-ied because the two continents "remained longer than the rest of the globe under the waters of the sea." This was Buffon's way of smearing the entire American populace, of arguing for a kind of intrinsic, geo-logically enforced degeneracy of everything and everyone in the Americas. Buffon blamed the humidity for much of the New World's inferiority. The place was just too *damp.* Jefferson could not let such a ridiculous notion go unchallenged. He plotted to send Buffon the hide of a moose, a classic that-ought-to-shut-him-up gesture. Jefferson had his own scientifically flimsy notions, including his suspicion that somewhere in the uncharted regions of the continent mammoths still might be found. He could see no theoretical justification for the disap-pearance of a species.

Jefferson's *Notes on the State of Virginia* features a singularly evocative description of the American landscape—specifically, the Potomac's passage through the Blue Ridge. In 1783 he visited Harpers Ferry, and after a short walk through town climbed onto a rock with a spectacular view of the rivers and the mountains. (The crumbling "Jefferson Rock" is still there, a few paces from the Appalachian Trail.

The rock is of a kind of shale that erodes rapidly, and so it has been propped up on steel beams, enabling tourists to enjoy more or less the same view that Jefferson had.) He wrote:

> The passage of the Patowmac through the Blue ridge is perhaps one of the most stupendous scenes in nature. You stand on a very high point of land. On your right comes up the Shenandoah, having ranged along the foot of the mountain an hundred miles to seek a vent. On your left approaches the Patowmac, in quest of a passage also. In the moment of their junction they rush together against the mountain, rend it asunder, and pass off to the sea.

Jefferson offers his theory of how the rivers pass through the mountains, imagining that an ocean formed behind the Blue Ridge, then burst through, creating the passage. He then describes the scene in the distance, contrasting it with the violence in the foreground:

> It is as placid and delightful, as that is wild and tremendous. For the mountain being cloven asunder, she presents to your eye, through the cleft, a small catch of smooth blue horizon, at an infinite distance in the plain country, inviting you, as it were from the riot and tumult roaring around, to pass through the breach and participate of the calm below. Here the eye ultimately composes itself; and that way too the road happens actually to lead.
> . . . This scene is worth a voyage across the Atlantic.

Jefferson is being promotional: Come to America, spend your tourist dollars here, he is saying. But he's also extending a kind of animism to geology. The land is an actor, the mountains and rivers shape our lives, the smooth blue horizon beckons. The calm land in the distance, no doubt blessed with a fertile, loamy soil, invites us to pull up stakes and seek a new and better life far away. The landscape is fraught with raw energy and compels us to move.

*　　　*　　　*

WASHINGTON AND JEFFERSON had vast horizons, but they looked at that western world in different ways. Both saw it as a land of opportunity, but Washington, as the historian Donald Jackson has observed, also saw the West as a series of problems. Washington's "West" extended across the Appalachians to the boundaries of the United States, while Jefferson's "West" kept on going, to the Pacific. Jefferson, more than Washington, seems to have sensed that the Mississippi did not serve as an eternal barrier to the American empire. Jackson notes that, while Jefferson greedily absorbed any information he could about the rivers and settlements of the Far West, Washington in all his letters and documents never mentioned Oregon, the Columbia River, the Rio Grande, the Missouri, the Colorado River, Mexico, the Sandwich Islands, or the mysterious tall mountains rumored to rise far beyond the Mississippi. Though not short-sighted, Washington viewed his country in such a way as to make the Potomac appear a more formidable stream than it would turn out to be just a generation later.

Jefferson had an extraordinary geographic imagination, an ability, as historian John Logan Allen points out, to "view the world at different scales and to work easily up and down the hierarchy from the local to the global and back again." He had to have such an imagination, for in his entire life, he never managed to venture farther west than the Shenandoah Valley. In 1784 he contemplated his own Washingtonesque western tour, a long journey to the Ohio country and back, but he never followed through.

This is one of the enduring Jefferson puzzles: He loved the West, but never saw it. Jefferson knew of the West only from maps, books, travelers' accounts, rumors, and the visions in his head, while Washington, intent on inspecting his world directly, repeatedly rubbed the western soil between his thumb and fingers. Jefferson may have come up with ordinances for the West, but Washington paddled into the heart of that territory, shared meals with Indian chiefs, and paced off individual tracts of forest. Washington knew individual *trees*—"An ash standing on the upper side of a large run . . . a Beech and Hiccory standing in the point . . . Beginning at a large Spanish oak at the Bank of the River . . ." These were the landmarks of his 1770 survey of the rich bottomland along the Great Kanawha River.

For Jefferson the West existed as an element of a broader theoretical view of the world. His American West would be a kind of Utopia, an agrarian society, unpolluted by urban toxins. He idealized the yeoman farmer. "Those who labor in the earth are the chosen people of God, if ever He had a chosen people, whose breasts He has made His peculiar deposit for substantial and genuine virtue," Jefferson famously declared in *Notes*. By contrast, "The mobs of great cities add just so much to the support of pure government, as sores do to the strength of the human body."

Perhaps it was only appropriate that Jefferson and Washington went in opposite directions in the summer of 1784. As Washington prepared for his western journey, Jefferson sailed for Europe to serve as the nation's envoy to France. Washington would be heading into his element as he reached the American backwoods, while Jefferson would take to Paris like a man slipping into a tailored jacket.

Jefferson and Washington believed that if the thirteen states could hang together and overcome any new colonial efforts by the European powers, the nation might someday be a continental power. They did not view this possible expansion as a pure power grab. The American experiment was all about human transformation. They were hastening the emergence of the species from a condition of subservience and degradation. This was *Progress*. History had an arrow. Enlightened men would lead the human species from barbarism and, in the process, if all went well, turn a tidy profit.

There was one lingering problem, however, that refused to go away. The very people who would lift their brothers to a higher state of existence kept one boot firmly on the neck of an entire race of men. Washington and Jefferson had their own individual ways of discussing or, in some cases, avoiding the topic of slavery, but both genuinely loathed the institution, even as they continued to participate in it intimately. Washington in particular wanted to get out, for both economic and moral reasons. He increasingly saw his slaves as more of a hindrance to his personal fortunes than an asset. He'd also commanded black men during the Revolution, seen their heroism, and perhaps could perceive, as few of his white contemporaries could, that it was not the design of nature that one race should keep another in chains.

Washington and Jefferson spoke at various times of abolition, but couldn't see how it would be possible politically, how there could be any resolution that would not split the Union. They felt powerless before an institution that had surrounded them and supported them their entire lives, that dated almost to the founding of Jamestown, and that continued to grow and expand with the rest of American society. As Roger Wilkins has pointed out, Jefferson's first memory was of being carried on a pillow by a slave. Slavery was not peripheral to America; it was the central conflict.

Freedom, equality, liberty, republican government, democracy—these were lofty ideas that had rarely been tested on the ground, among real people in a real place. The issues that Washington and Jefferson struggled with involved questions that are still asked today:

What kind of republic is this?

What kind of people are we?

3

Up the River

*O*N SEPTEMBER 1, 1784, at nine o'clock in the morning, George Washington left Mount Vernon on horseback, riding toward distant waters. He had vowed, nearly two months earlier, to leave on this exact day, and he was certainly a man of his word.

Trotting along at five miles an hour—his preferred speed—he was momentarily unencumbered, free of the concerns of his plantation. He traveled light, with only the provisions that any gentleman would require for a frontier expedition: two kegs of West Indian rum, tea, seven pounds of sugar, a fruity spirit called cherry bounce, Madeira and Port wine, oil, mustard, vinegar, and "Spices of all sorts." Washington didn't drink rum, but it would be ideal for trading with frontiersmen or securing thirsty guides through the backwoods. He also had a horseman's tent, and extra horseshoes and canteens of water. He had fine sheets. He had silver cups and silver spoons. The general might be going into the remote fringe of western civilization, but he didn't intend to live like an animal.

He sent his baggage ahead, along with three servants and three horses. Only James Craik, who had been with him at Fort Necessity and the Braddock disaster, and who had also been his traveling companion for his last major western journey—the trip down the Ohio into the heart of Indian country in 1770—rode with him on the pike to Leesburg. Educated as a surgeon, and two years older than the general, Craik had moved to Alexandria after the Revolution. He had always been with Washington in person or in spirit. In 1777 he warned the general about the Conway Cabal, critics of Washington's leadership of the army. Craik treated Lafayette's wounds at Brandywine and was by the general's side at Yorktown, where he tried to save the life of Washington's ailing stepson, Jacky Custis. He rose to the position of chief physician for the army, and for many years after the war would zealously guard Washington's health. Craik was something special and rare in Washington's life, for he was not really an employee (other than serving as the family doctor) or a business partner or a political ally. He wasn't a distant relative or someone who needed to elevate his self-esteem by hanging around the great man. He was simply a good friend. Even George Washington needed one of those.

They expected to be joined in a week by Bushrod Washington, the general's nephew, and Craik's son, William. For now the stripped-down traveling party was perfectly designed for a serene jaunt across the Piedmont. Washington had come this way many times, for the road led to Leesburg, where he owned property, and then over the Blue Ridge to his Bullskin Plantation in the Shenandoah Valley.

The general had to be thrilled to be on the road again. No man this side of the Asian steppe was more comfortable on a horse. Washington had that broad beam, that low center of gravity. You couldn't have dismounted him with a cannonball. To be a great man in America it was necessary to ride well, and Jefferson called Washington "the best horseman of his age."

The route, on the Alexandria-Leesburg road, roughly paralleled the Potomac but didn't come in sight of the river proper. The valley of the river was to the right, sloping gradually away. There were few people to be seen, for although Virginia had a large population, its inhabitants were thinly scattered. This was not New England, so they would not encounter any neat, orderly, embowered towns with a steepled church at the center, straight-as-string fencing, and gleaming three-story frame houses with a widow's walk at the top. It would be another century and a half before the farmland northwest of Alexandria would turn urban, and the Leesburg Pike, aka Route 7, would be enclosed by a dense forest of retail outlets, with every chain store and fast-food eatery vying for the attention of traffic-jammed travelers. If someone had stopped Washington and Craik and told them that at the beginning of the twenty-first century a single county in this part of Virginia would have a million inhabitants, they would have assumed the speaker did not refer to humans. Spiders, perhaps. Some kind of vermin.

They were not going to see any cities on this trip. Virginia, though a colossal state, had no cities to speak of. Richmond came close, Williamsburg had plenty of history, and Alexandria had the potential to become a bustling port, but the nature of the tobacco culture worked against the formation of cities. Ships traditionally sailed right up the creeks and estuaries to the wharf of an individual planter. The typical avenue of commerce in Virginia was not a Main Street, but a rolling road, essentially a path through the fields, traveled by stout hogsheads of tobacco on their way to the wharf. Washington had seen many exotic things as a young man before he ever saw anything as astonishing as a genuine, densely populated city (at the age of twenty-four, having already done his part to start a world war, he visited Philadelphia, New York, and Boston). On this journey west, the riders would see only a few villages and humble roadside taverns. They'd see no structure larger than a mill.

Most of the homes the riders passed were made of wood, and some were huts with dirt floors. They trotted through a tired land, the nutrients sucked from the ground by tobacco. Abandoned fields were returning slowly to forest. It had been more than a century since the Tidewater planters had reached the fall line of the Potomac, and the tobacco culture wasted no time in ravaging the landscape. As early as 1750, Lewis Evans, creator of an excellent map of the middle British Colonies, had described the erosion of soil in the Piedmont: "[W]hen the country was cover'd with Woods, and the Swamps with brush, the rain that fell was detained by these interruptions, and so had time to insinuate into the Earth, and contribute to the springs and runs. But now the country is clear'd, the rain as fast as it falls, is hurried into the rivers, and washes away the earth and soil of our Naked Fields. . . ."

A late-eighteenth-century visitor, the Englishman Isaac Weld, described the exhausted appearance of the land around the Tidewater Potomac: "Nothing is to be seen here for miles together but extensive plains, that have been worn out by the culture of tobacco. . . . In the midst of these plains are the remains of several good houses, which shew that the country was once very different to what it is now."

Washington and Craik were riding through an old society, one that was already *historic*. Far to their south, the English settlement at Jamestown, founded in 1607, had long since become a ghost town. Human beings had been leaving their mark on this part of the world for at least 11,000 years. They had hunted mammoths at the end of the last ice age, before the rise of the ocean and the formation of the Chesapeake Bay, when this was a grassland environment and not yet overrun with enormous trees. Even before the arrival of the Europeans this was a changed landscape, the flora and fauna coevolving with human beings. The Indians burned the understory of the forest to improve the hunting, and when the first Europeans arrived, they found a park-like setting in some areas, so open and free of underbrush that a coach could roll unimpeded through the woods.

By 1784 the planting of European culture in the "New World" had already been going on for 292 years. George Washington was closer to the early twenty-first century than to the voyages of Columbus. White exploration and colonization in the mid-Atlantic began long before Jamestown. John Cabot may have seen the mouth of Chesapeake Bay as early as 1498; it's possible that Amerigo Vespucci beat him by a year. The Spanish hunted for Indian slaves in the Chesapeake waters in the 1520s, and the Portuguese and French soon thereafter explored the region and traded with natives. The discovery of the enchanting weed tobacco thrilled the English. The smoke of tobacco, they decided, opened pores and prevented diseases. It "purgeth superfluous fleame and other grosse humours," claimed Thomas Harriot, the great English scientist (he made the first telescopic observation of the moon) who in the 1580s visited Walter Raleigh's doomed English colony on the Outer Banks. Harriot was a better astronomer than epidemiologist; he developed a cancer of the nose that ate away at his face and eventually killed him.

The first European to see the Potomac proper may have been the Spanish Admiral Pedro Menendez de Aviles, the founder of St. Augustine, Florida, who apparently sailed up the river in 1571 to within 25 miles of what is now the nation's capital. The Spanish called the river Espiritu Santo. The colonists with George Calvert, Lord Baltimore, who settled in Maryland in 1634, initially called the river St. Gregory. Early descriptions of the Potomac were rhapsodic. When Captain John Smith explored the river in 1608, he was astonished by the wildlife: otters, beavers, martens, sables, "luswarts," and an "abundance of fish lying so thicke with their heads above the water, as for want of nets (our barge driving amongst them) we attempted to catch them with a frying pan."

Nearly two centuries later the tidewater region was a society in flux. The population was growing, but there were also rotting barns and crumbling mills and empty tobacco warehouses. Commerce had evolved in the general's lifetime. Trading vessels had gotten bigger, and no longer would they sail up to every planter's wharf to pick up the hogsheads of tobacco rolling down from the fields.

As much as George Washington believed in Progress, and claimed that this American landscape was providentially designed for the display of *human greatness and felicity,* he could see as well the signs of regression, of societal decline. He had to wonder, in his moments of doubt, if the world would improve over time—if order would eventually trump chaos.

*   *   *

THE GENERAL and the doctor rode 25 miles that first day, and lodged in a tavern on Difficult Run, a "mirey, inconvenient and troublesome" creek that separated Fairfax and Loudoun counties. They were on the road again at dawn. Within a few hours they arrived in the village of Leesburg, where Washington had to endure the usual robust salutations and fawning tributes from local dignitaries.

At dawn the next morning Washington mounted his horse and headed up the road toward the Blue Ridge. He had arranged to meet Craik on the other side of the mountain. After so many years as commander in chief, and then as the owner of a large plantation and the part-time host of a "well-traveled tavern," years in which solitude had been the rarest of pleasures, he had apparently managed for at least one morning to shake free of every encumbrance. He followed the winding road to the crest of the Blue Ridge at a notch in the ridgeline called Vestal's Gap. The mountain here was relatively modest, a 1,000-foot dull blade of rock, easily ascended in a couple of hours. But it gave the general a sublime view of his world. At the crest, the slightest turn of the head offered him a panorama of two geological provinces, the Piedmont to the east, and the Shenandoah Valley to the west. From this height the rolling terrain below, with its irregular assortment of farms and meadows and stands of trees, looked flattened out, and as inviting as a garden.

Washington dropped down from the ridge, took a ferry across the Shenandoah River, and soon reached the home of his younger brother, Colonel Charles Washington. Happy Retreat, as the colonel called his house, was unfinished, like seemingly everything else in the country. It had two wings and no center, just a breezeway where the entrance hall and sitting room would soon be built. The place quickly filled up with acquaintances, local gentry, old friends from the war. There were slaves in this part of the valley, for it was, with the presence of the Washingtons, an island of Tidewater society, a place where men and women spoke English and attended the Anglican Church. Venture beyond the island and the traveler would hear a great deal of German, the language of farmers who had migrated into the valley from Pennsylvania over the previous half century.

The general had known the valley his entire adult life. In 1748, at the age of sixteen, he became employed as a surveyor for Thomas, the sixth Lord Fairfax. His Lordship, a peculiar fellow who had an aversion to women (spurned once, he never recovered) and loved to chase foxes, astonished his contemporaries by moving to an estate in the valley when it was still perceived as beyond the pale. The royal land grant obtained by the Fairfaxes specified that the western boundary of the domain ran from the Potomac headspring to the Rappahannock headspring, but there was much ambiguity in that, because the Potomac had more than one major branch. Lord Fairfax successfully pressed his claim to everything south of the Northern Branch, a ruling that gave him an empire of 5 million acres.

The Fairfax operation had its ancestral headquarters at Belvoir, the estate next door to Mount Vernon. William Fairfax, the cousin and land agent of His Lordship, was the father-in-law of Lawrence Washington. Young George, slipping in and out of Belvoir, became a favorite of Lord Fairfax and soon found himself with a surveyor's tools, taking the measure of the Fairfax lands.

He loved the woods, the mountains, the valleys. He rode through the "most beautiful Groves of Sugar Trees and spent the best part of the Day in admiring the Trees and richness of the Land." The backcountry life peeled away some of his Tidewater veneer. In his first journey to the mountains, in 1748, he realized he had much to learn about the backcountry, such as how to survive the vermin in his bedding:

> . . . we got our Supper and was lighted into a Room and I not being so good a Woodsman as the rest of my Company striped myself very orderly and went into the Bed as they called it when to my surprise I found it to be nothing but a Little Straw-Matted together without Sheets or any thing else but only one thread Bare blanket with double its Weight of Vermin such as Lice Fleas &c.

Two days later he cleaned himself and got rid "of the Game we had catched the Night before." He also had his first significant encounter with Indians, witnessing a rum-fueled war dance:

They clear a Large Circle and make a Great Fire in the middle then seats themselves around it the Speaker makes a grand speech telling them in what Manner they are to Daunce after he has finished the best Dauncer jumps up as one awaked out of a Sleep and Runs and Jumps about the Ring in a most comicle Manner. . . .

He was so much younger then, so easily impressed. Back then he even wrote poetry, the kind of love-struck, melodramatic material that perhaps deserved to be burned rather than archived at the Library of Congress. ("Ah! woe's me, that I should Love and conceal, / Long have I wish'd, but never dare reveal, / Even though severly Loves Pains I feel; / Xerxes that great, wasn't free from Cupids Dart, / And all the greatest Heroes, felt the smart. . . .")

But now he was mature, he was Cincinnatus, he was a man of obligations and responsibilities and duties, he had important things to accomplish, and so he did not pause, in his diary, to discuss the beautiful sugar trees, and he certainly did not write verse. He was fifty-two years old, on a business trip, and well beyond the point where he needed romance in his life.

The success of his western tour would be measured in its utility.

* * *

AT HAPPY RETREAT, Washington collected rent—24 pounds from Thomas Griggs, 50 pounds from Henry Whiting, 10 pounds from David Fulton, and 6 pounds from Samuel Scratchfield. He dashed off a note to Colonel David Kennedy, who had been living at another of the general's properties, the nearby Bullskin Plantation. Please pay me 28 pounds Sterling, the back rent you owe, Washington wrote.

Washington kept a wary eye on his finances and jumped at any chance to obtain cheap land. He once told a friend to "look to Frederick"—the town now called Winchester, just a dozen or so miles southwest of Charles Washington's house,

... & see what Fortunes were made by the Hites & first takers up of those Lands: Nay, how the greatest Estates we have in this Colony were made; Was it not by taking up & purchasing at very low rates the rich back Lands which were thought nothing of in those days, but are now the most valuable Lands we possess?

Washington invested in such land ventures as the Walpole Grant, the Mississippi Company, and the Dismal Swamp Company. Nonetheless, he denied being a land speculator. This was a sensitive point, for in his mind a speculator was a wheeler-dealer, a huckster, someone who snapped up land and sold it on a whim. He was not such a man. He had a gentlemanly relationship with his property and his tenants. He tended not to sell his land, but rather bought and held, and hoped to find tenants who would lease the property and make improvements, such as clearing fields and erecting fences. Despite owning 30,000-plus prime acres along the Ohio and Great Kanawha, among other western properties, he still declared, "It cannot be laid to my charge that I have been either a monopolizer, or land-jobber, for I never sold a foot of Land in the Country, nor am I possessed of an acre west of the Alleghaney (and the quantity comparatively speaking is small) that I do not hold under military rights."

What he wanted to do to his land is what he wanted to do to the entire country: Add value. Fix it up. Improve the infrastructure. Transform raw material into something polished and gleaming. Make something good out of the ragged wilderness. How dare anyone call that "speculation"!

Now, poring over his accounts, he noticed a recurring problem: Many of his tenants didn't pay up, and squatters abounded. There was no respect for the owner of the deed.

The victory in the Revolution destroyed much of the world that Washington had always known. He had turned himself into a Virginia aristocrat, but what place was there for an aristocracy in a republican nation? As the historian Daniel Boorstin puts it, "The Revolution which the Virginia aristocracy did so much to make and 'win' was in fact the suicide of the Virginia aristocracy." Washington was born a British citizen in a quasi-British society, one that received virtually all its manufactured products from London, and existed as a satellite, a dependency, of His Majesty's dominion. Virginia, with its rolling terrain and mild climate, had been a reasonable facsimile of the Mother Country. But now the great plantations were failing or in disarray, and tobacco, the crop which the colony had grown for more than a century and a half, had destroyed much of the farmland. A new society was being birthed all around him—and what role would there be, if any, for a Virginia planter?

*   *   *

WASHINGTON and Craik set out for the town of Bath, or Warm Springs (today's Berkeley Springs, West Virginia), where they would be joined by Craik's son and the general's nephew, Bushrod. John Augustine Washington, the general's brother, hoped to exchange some of his slaves for land in what he called "the new Country," and he had dispatched Bushrod to scout out the soil and climate of the West, as well as the prospects for trade.

Though welcoming the prospect of traveling with his nephew, the general viewed the young man's excursion as too little too late. For years he'd been telling his close relations to follow his example and seize the opportunities in the West, but they'd failed to take seriously the urgency of the situation, the rapidity with which prime real estate was being gobbled up by speculators and land-jobbers. "[T]he golden opportunity I conceive is past," the general told his brother a month before setting out on this journey, "and I own it has been a matter of astonishment to me that all of you should have been so inattentive to it . . . where does my most valuable property lye?—Berkeley—what did it originally cost about—years ago? Nothing, or that which is as near to it as possible." Why hadn't they listened?

The road led from Happy Retreat northwest over the undulating terrain of the broad valley. They soon crossed Opequon Creek, and on the slope above, Washington came upon a prosperous farmer, Captain

James Strode. The captain was surely impressed that the hero of the Revolution had trotted up to his farm. It is possible (departing the realm of documentation) that the two men talked about the recently concluded War of Independence, but all we know from the diary is that they talked about rivers and portages.

"I held much conversation with him," Washington wrote, "the result of which, so far as it respected the object I had in view, was, that there are two Glades which go under the denomination of the Great glades—one, on the Waters of Yohiogany, the other on those of Cheat River; & distinguished by the name of the Sandy Creek Glades—that the Road to the first goes by the head of Pattersons Creek—"

There is a breathless quality to the diary entry, as though the general were too excited to indulge a period: "—that from the accts. he has had of it, it is rough; the distance he knows not—that there is away to the Sandy Creek Glades from the great crossing of Yohiogany (on Braddocks road) & a very good one. . . ."

The normally terse general grew voluble, almost ecstatic, in recounting the conversation. No rumor of a friendly mountain pass or easily portaged cascade was too trivial to be worthy of a diary entry. It was so early in the trip, and Washington was so hungry for information, that he did not seem to mind that Strode was giving him inexact information, bordering on rumor. But Strode also provided a tantalizing piece of data, or at least a nice theory: that it was possible to create an all-Virginia route to the Ohio River, using portages between rivers: "He says that old Captn. Thos. Swearengen has informed him, that the navigable water of the little Kanhawa comes within a small distance of the Navigable Waters of the Monongahela, & that a good road, along a ridge, may be had between the two. . . ."

The general drained Strode of everything he knew.

Washington was clearly having a grand time. This we infer not from anything he says directly in his diary—the geographical data are never interrupted with a digression about his *feelings*—but from the diary's mere existence. He'd given up his diary in late 1781, after Yorktown, and only on September 1 had he started writing again. The diary is a historical treasure, if not exactly a rollickin' yarn. Jefferson had a gift for language, weaving beautiful literary fabrics, while Washington usually approached writing as a farmer would a frozen field. He hacked away with gusto, but with little joy, his language a blunt instrument. Still, he was not wholly incapable of a literary flourish, and now and again he could even be wry, sarcastic, or flirtatious. He could be winningly grave, the most serious writer on Earth. But he seldom showed any delight in the language itself, and on this western journey his descriptions grew vivid only when directed toward a piece of land that might be amenable to tillage.

Many entries in the early years of his life indicate a stenographic intent, with the diaries divided into three categories, labeled "Where & how my time is Spent," "Remarks of the Weather," and "Observations" (or sometimes "Remarks & Occurances"). The combined effect is an account of his minutes and hours; the temperature, wind direction, and precipitation; and the latest bulletin about crops and livestock. At this later point in life Washington joined the three threads into a single narrative. The land is there, the geographical data are there, the rivers and rapids and falls are there, but sometimes the general himself is hard to find. He's the dispassionate collector of information.

When he wrote, on October 31, 1770, during his remarkable journey hundreds of miles down the Ohio River and into the heart of Indian County, "Went out a Hunting & met the Canoe at the Mouth of the big Kanawha distant only 5 Miles makg. the whole distance from Fort Pitt accordg. to my Acct. 266 Miles," we long for more description of this primeval world, more of his reaction to being in a place so remote from Tidewater Virginia. And yet at the same time we must marvel that his estimate of the distance from Fort Pitt to the Great Kanawha is only a quarter of a mile different from modern-day calculations.

Surely now, as he trotted up the Warm Springs road, he felt excited by the prospect of once again seeing the West, of seeing the rivers and forests and battlefields of his youth. But he doesn't tell us this directly. Indeed, he does not mention any of his previous journeys. He'd made significant treks across the Alleghenies and into the Ohio watershed in 1753, 1754, 1755, 1758, and 1770, and from those journeys could have written an epic tale of early American adventure, of the clash of empires in the western country, yet as he writes in 1784, George Washington includes not a single sentence, not a word, about the earlier trips. Washington didn't dwell on the past; he preferred to look ahead, to ponder his next move, to envision a world much different from, and much better than, the one that surrounded him. As the historian Archer Hulbert noted in his 1905 book *Washington and the West*, a person reading Washington's diary would have no idea that he had ever come this way before.

*   *   *

THE GENERAL had chosen a soggy season for his journey, and on the fifth of September, after a night in a tavern owned by a certain Mr. Snodgrass, he and his party rode onward in a "drizling rain." (The road is still there—still winding and dipping and rolling, designed more for wagons than for the speeding sedans of commuters who have made the Shenandoah Valley an outpost of metropolitan Washington.) He passed North Mountain, the boundary of the Shenandoah Valley, and entered a more rugged terrain, what geographers call the Ridge and Valley Province. The valleys were narrow, the mountains jammed together almost shoulder to shoulder. Farmland disappeared for the most part. He was now in the sticks, the deep woods where bear and elk still roamed.

The typical eighteenth-century backcountry road did not have a uniform surface. Often it was just a tunnel in the vegetation. The traveler endured diabolical combinations of holes, mires, and tree stumps. When a state government eventually got around to chartering a road, it would stipulate how high the stumps could be. The more a road was traveled by horses and wagons, the more the surface became chewed up and rutted, and eventually the whole track would be lower than the surrounding terrain, ensuring that water would flow into it. The wheels of wagons would sink to the axle. The situation tended to get worse rather

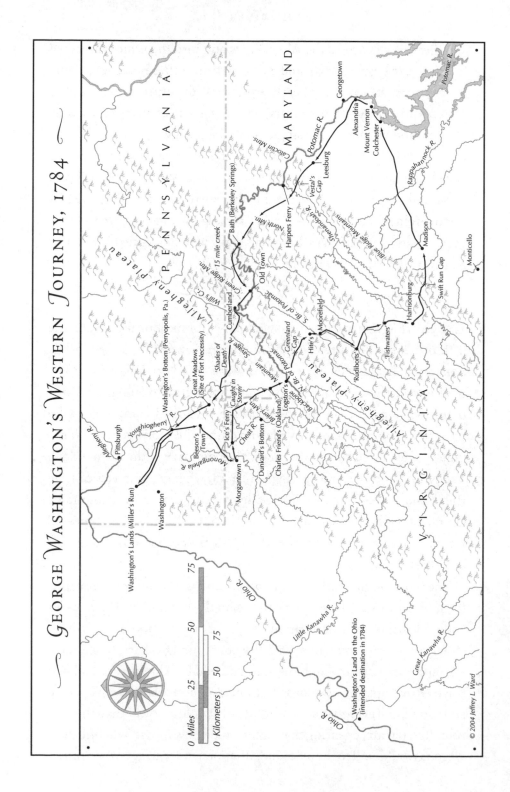

~ GEORGE WASHINGTON'S WESTERN JOURNEY, 1784 ~

© 2004 Jeffrey L. Ward

than better. Roads were not self-healing, and eventually the track through the woods would not really be a road at all, just a linear bog.

Travelers would use turnouts at the worst mud pits, so that travel was rarely in a straight line. Even without turnouts, roads went up the hills and down through the gullies and around the rock outcroppings and into the streambeds and, in general, followed the fine detail of the topography. When we say that technology has shrunk the distances between two points, it is not just a metaphor; by one historical estimate, the average distance by road between two points in the late eighteenth century was at least 10 percent greater than on the straighter roads of today.

To combat the mud, road-builders—often a local farmer seeking a credit on his tax bill—would lay small trees or boards crossways along the track, then cover them with soil that would, naturally, wash away in the next storm, leaving the exposed wood. These "corduroy roads" could easily lame a horse, and they tore up a wheeled vehicle. The only respite from the terror of these primitive roads came when they suddenly ended at the edge of a stream, an entirely different sort of transportation obstacle. Early wagons were waterproof on the bottom and sides, because when crossing streams they had to function like boats. All of which explains why some people chose to spend their entire lives close to home.

At least the traveler didn't have to worry about being robbed by highwaymen. That criminal niche didn't yet exist, for hardly anyone in America at this point carried any money.

Washington's entourage forded Back Creek and skirted the northern tip of Third Hill Mountain. The wagon road passed within three miles of the Potomac. The route led across Sleepy Creek, then descended into a valley where, just before nightfall, they reached the village of Bath. For a wet and weary traveler it was a charming destination, for the cabins of this enclave were clustered around a series of warm mineral pools bubbling from the base of Cacapon Mountain. Washington had visited here often. A man didn't go anywhere near this part of the world without pausing for a therapeutic soak.

*　　　*　　　*

JAMES RUMSEY loomed large in the village. Rumsey was handsome, vigorous, and brilliant. Son of a poor farmer, self-taught, he appears in a portrait by Benjamin West as an almost pretty man, with dreamy eyes and girlish lips. He owned a sawmill and a store and an equity stake in a boardinghouse "at the sign of the Liberty Pole and Flag." He built homes. He invented. Just recently, he had constructed a model of a mechanical boat that, in seeming defiance of common sense and Newtonian physics, could travel against the current of a small stream using the power of the current itself. Naturally, Rumsey had to show this magical boat to the general, who proved to be an enthusiastic audience.

The little craft had a set of geared wheels, and two long poles attached underneath. When Rumsey placed the boat in the shallow stream, the current spun the wheels, which forced the poles to the bottom of the streambed and pushed the boat against the current. The boat "walked" upstream on stilts, one might say. It was ingenious to say the least, since it required no energy other than water power. Would such a boat work at full scale, in a real river, against a strong current, carrying a heavy cargo? Rumsey didn't know.

Washington, like almost everyone in the late eighteenth century not named Benjamin Franklin, had little experience with new technologies. In 1784 the tools of ordinary life were not much different from those of 1684 or 1584. The world certainly changed over time, for anyone could see that empires rose and fell, and people moved across the surface of the Earth and changed their environment, and occasionally a new contraption would appear, like Franklin's lightning rod or his bifocals. Washington himself was an innovator in agriculture, always ready to experiment with a new seed or a new technique for improving the soil. But few were the people who sensed that technology could reshape the world, that Franklin's lightning would not remain forever in his Leyden jar.

Washington had limited knowledge of mechanics or fluid dynamics, but what he saw in the little creek impressed him tremendously. Rumsey's boat worked: It defied the current and went upstream. He raved about it in his diary:

> ... the principles of this were not only shewn, & fully explained to me, but to my very great satisfaction, exhibited in practice in private, under the injunction of Secresy. ... The model, & its operation upon the water, which had been made to run pretty swift, not only convinced me of what I before thought next to, if not quite impracticable, but that it might be turned to the greatest possible utility in inland Navigation ...

Rumsey and Washington were a good match. Both imposed their wills upon recalcitrant nature. Both perceived waterways as the arteries of civilization. Now it appeared that harnessing the power of a river or stream might be easier than anyone had imagined. The very thing that vexed the paddler—a contrary current—could be exploited!

Washington gave Rumsey a letter attesting to the merit of the mechanical boat. The certificate stated that he had "been an eye witness to an actual experiment in running water of some rapidity; & do give it as my opinion (altho' I had little faith before) that he has discovered the art of propelling Boats, by mechanism & small manual assistance, against rapid currents. . . ." (Washington some months later raised the possibility that a model might not "justly represent a greater object in its operation," but he seems to have had no serious doubts that he was witness to an engineering breakthrough. "I chose . . . to see the actual performance of the model in a descending stream before I passed my certificate; and having done so, all my doubts were satisfied. . . .")

Rumsey quickly published the testimonial in regional newspapers. He later informed Washington that the endorsement "Convicts almost Every person that Sees it. . . ."

In optimistic moments the general could imagine that, someday, a person would be able to go almost anywhere by water. Canals would lace the landscape, connecting navigable rivers, linking every state, city, and village. He wrote a letter to a friend describing the most tantalizing of scenarios—that someday, with enough effort, it might be possible to bring water navigation "to almost every Mans door."

The magic boat was a good omen.

4

Ridge and Valley

THE ROAD from Bath took Washington up the side and over the crest of Cacapon Mountain. Washington came to a place he'd been before, a rocky outcrop with a panoramic view of the ridges and valleys to the west. Above every ridgeline in this part of the world was another, fainter ridgeline, on into the distance, where the last and most distant ridge might be only a faint suggestion against the hazy sky (no wonder the Indians in Pennsylvania called them the Endless Mountains). Through the middle of all this flowed the Potomac, defiantly perpendicular to the line of mountains, a vivid geological advertisement for the river's providential nature. This was what it was all about, a river that defied the mountains. *Behold my proof,* the general could have shouted. The river knifed through the parallel ridges as though what flowed in its channel was not water but acid.

In the distance Washington could see the top of Sideling Hill, with a water gap created by the Potomac. The river came into view from behind a ridge in the middle distance, and it barreled straight toward Cacapon Mountain, aiming at a spot below and to the left of the general's perch. From the south came the Cacapon River, giving the Potomac a final burst of liquid energy. At the last moment, just before ramming into the mountain, the Potomac juked north, a sharp turn toward Pennsylvania, out there to the general's right.

Clearly, the river has more than one trick for getting past the mountains. It has to cope with at least ten major ridges and a number of smaller hills that stand between its source and tidewater. Sometimes the river takes on a mountain directly, plowing straight through it, as at Sideling Hill and the Blue Ridge. Other times it makes an end run around a ridge, going many miles out of the way. The river has small turns, loops, and meanders, and big ones as well, and at least twice it seems determined to reach Pennsylvania, only to turn back within sniffing distance. To say that water runs downhill does not give justice to its inventiveness and precocity.

The dramatic water gaps, like the one at Harpers Ferry, had always mystified travelers, and Jefferson had done his best to come up with an explanation (an ocean forming behind the mountain and breaking open a channel through the crest of the ridge). In fact, the gaps were most likely formed by "stream capture." Two streams flowing in opposite directions from the crest of a ridge will each erode a valley. Over time the valleys will merge, and the two streams join, flowing now in one direction.

There's another factor at work. A river such as the Potomac is so old that, in some cases, the entire landscape around it has risen. The river cuts through rising terrain. It's literally older than the hills.

Washington referred to these ridges as the "Apalacheon Mountains." Geologists think the mountains were formed by several distinct tectonic events over the course of 500 million years, a span of time that represents a thick slice of the planet's geological record. The Appalachians once soared as high as the Rockies or even higher. They were most recently thrust upward about 290 million years ago, which makes these mountains older than the bones of the first dinosaurs. They predate the appearance of deciduous trees. They are older than flowers. There were mountains here before the Earth had ever seen anything as fantastic as grass. Some of the rocks were formed in the Precambrian Era, in that gray epoch when life was pondering a wholesale leap from one cell to many. If you could reverse the spreading of the seafloor of the Atlantic, and close up the ocean, you'd see that the Appalachian deformation of the Earth's crust extends from Alabama to Newfoundland, across the northern tier of Scotland, and through the mountains of Norway, to the remote Arctic. Pennsylvania's ruffled-rug topology fits nicely against the hump of northwest Africa.

By the time the general arrived on the scene, most of the great mountain range had been beaten down and blown away, the belts of stone turned into boulders, pebbles, flakes, gravel, and silt. Time pulverized the Appalachians. Only the hardest layers of rock survived, coded messages of what had been. Still, to the eighteenth-century traveler these durable ridges stood like walls.

A forest covered much of this mountain landscape. This was a gloomy world, and a traveler could walk for miles without encountering a sunbeam. The Eastern Forest was nothing less than an ocean of trees. Lewis Evans, who mapped the interior of the country in the early 1750s, may have been one of the first to use the ocean metaphor: "To look from the hills into the lower Lands, is but, as it were, into an Ocean of Woods, swelled and deprest here and there by little inequalities, not to be distinguished, one part from another, any more than the waves of the real Ocean." Nearly two centuries after the first European colonies had been established on the Atlantic Coast, the forest remained largely intact, stretching virtually without interruption across the continental interior to the edge of the Great Plains. Washington may not have been a romantic, but even he could feel nourished by such a view—this was a scene that, to borrow a phrase from F. Scott Fitzgerald, was commensurate with his capacity for wonder.

From a bluff a traveler looking down on the forest would see a surprisingly uniform canopy, with a slash or dip here and there to signify a stream. But rising above the treeline would be a few giants—the white pines, soaring 50 feet higher than everything else, surveying their domain. White pines were prized timber, so beautifully straight, perfect for masts, easily sawed, lightweight, buoyant, a wood so congenial that this tree alone could entice a man halfway across the continent. Sycamores leaned over the creeks and rivers, hollow inside, so roomy that a family could live in the trunk while constructing a cabin. (Washington once found a sycamore that, 3 feet above the ground, measured 44 feet 10 inches in circumference.) When the settlers entered the forest, their swine would forage on the beechnuts, the chestnuts, the walnuts. There was white oak ruling the western slopes of the Allegheny Plateau, and sugar maples, and poplar. The variety of trees was astounding: ash, birch, black gum, black locust, hickory, pawpaw, sassafras. On higher slopes ahead there were vast stands of hemlock looming over an impenetrable understory of mountain laurel.

The agents of change act on different scales. Mountains form over tens of millions of years; animals evolve and become extinct over millions of years; ice ages come and go on the order of tens or hundreds of thousands of years; and the works of human beings take place in decades, years, months, days. As Washington rode across the mountains, he knew the West had changed dramatically since his last visit, fourteen years earlier.

Naturally, he didn't know about plate tectonics, could not imagine that entire continents could move. Jefferson, in his wonderful passage in *Notes on the State of Virginia* about the Potomac's passage through the Blue Ridge, sagely opined that "this earth has been created in time," though even a visionary in the eighteenth century could not grasp the depth of the past. Washington had no inkling that life evolved, that from a single primordial germ a diverse array of organisms could appear, that giant reptiles once roamed the planet, that the flora and fauna that framed his life had not sprung fully into existence at the moment of the Creation.

And yet the general knew much about his surroundings. He knew facts that later generations would forget. He knew the names of the trees, the habits of the animals. He knew the soils and the rocks, the resources beneath his feet. He knew where to find useful mud and fuel for the fire. He knew how to read the sky and measure the wind and smell the coming of a storm. As he stood on the overlook on Cacapon Mountain, Washington had abundant knowledge of the terrain ahead, from personal experience, from a lifetime of exploration and adventure. He knew where he was on the planet.

*   *   *

THE GENERAL wound his way on the mountain road into the valley below, and soon reached the bank of the Potomac. The river was shallow enough to ford. A century and a half later, people would drive cars across the river near this spot. Washington and his companions splashed across the river and into Maryland.

The diary makes only a brief reference to the river crossing. The river, though conceptually central to Washington's trip, barely registers in the written account. It's as though he knew the river so well he didn't need to discuss it. The Potomac goes without saying.

He soon crossed back into Virginia to inspect one of his properties, a horseshoe-shaped tract of about 200 acres with the Potomac on three sides, "which I find exceedingly rich, & must be very valuable. The lower end of the Land is rich White oak; in places springey; and in the winter wet. The upper part is exceedingly rich, and covered with Walnut of considerable size many of them." Good dirt, big trees: This was fabulous backcountry property. When he liked what he saw, he would become as verbally enthusiastic as a man closing a real estate deal. He looked at the world not as it was but as it might someday be. A copse of trees in a remote forest was a fertile farm in waiting. A cabin with a dirt floor and a pig sleeping in front of the fire was a fine manor needing a little attention.

Washington soon found himself on a familiar road, one that ran along the north side of the Potomac. He once described it as "the Worst Road that ever was trod by Man or Beast."

On the eighth day of his trip, Washington arrived at Old Town, also known as Shawanese Old Town. People had been inhabiting this patch of bottomland beneath high bluffs for thousands of years, but the Shawanese, or Shawnees, had been devastated by European diseases and pressure from settlers, and the survivors had relocated to the Ohio Valley over the course of the previous half-century. There was nothing much in Old Town now but the legendary Colonel Thomas Cresap, perhaps eighty-five years old, maybe much older, still sharp but quite blind.

The general had known Cresap since his 1748 surveying trip for Lord Fairfax. Everyone knew Cresap. You couldn't make a journey in the backcountry of Maryland in the mid–eighteenth century without a Cresap encounter, for the Cresap cabin was one of the most famous trading posts between the Carolinas and New England. The Indians would stop to trade furs or to obtain supplies for their own military incursions against other tribes. Cresap sat on the tip of the white man's spear as it pointed toward the Ohio Territory, and more than once he had found himself under Indian attack, driven back down the Potomac or forced to hole up in his makeshift fort with other white refugees from western Maryland.

Cresap was the prototypical frontiersman, a hustler, incapable of fear, foul-mouthed, mean as a rattlesnake. That's one of the things people called him: "Rattlesnake Colonel." Also, "a vile Rascal" and "the Maryland Monster." Born in Yorkshire, England, sometime around the beginning of the eighteenth century, he came to Maryland with his family at about the age of fifteen, and moved at about age thirty to a spot on the Susquehanna River opposite what is now the town of Columbia, Pennsylvania. Cresap took out a patent for 500 acres from the colony of Maryland. Unfortunately for Cresap, he was not, in fact, in Maryland at all, but deep into the next colony up the road. The two colonies were, at that time, family operations, fiefdoms run by the Calverts and the Penns, and Cresap by his lonesome triggered an instant border war. The two sides chose to resolve the border dispute with that most trusted of diplomatic tools, the gun. The Pennites surrounded Cresap in his stone house, set the house on fire, and captured him when he attempted to flee. As a prisoner, he was not on his best behavior. When transferred to Philadelphia, he reportedly told his guard, "Damn it, Aston, this is one of the Prettyest Towns in Maryland." He so annoyed the Pennsylvanians that they let him go, and he wound up selling backcountry lands in Maryland at Old Town.

Cresap became one of the original shareholders of the Ohio Company. This was one of the first and most ambitious efforts to sell land to whites on the west side of the Alleghenies. Powerful Virginians, including Washington's brother, Lawrence, persuaded the Crown to grant the company 200,000 acres west of the mountains and north of the Ohio River (the rights of Indians were viewed as unimportant in the larger competition with France). Cresap was essential to the project, for he knew the backwoods and had good contacts with the Indians. After the company built a storehouse at the junction of the Potomac and Will's Creek—across the river from present-day Cumberland, Maryland—it enlisted Cresap to hack a rough road across the mountains to the tributaries of the Ohio. Cresap joined forces with a chief of the Delaware Indians, Nemacolin, who had already blazed a trail over the mountains. Nemacolin did most of the work in improving the trail.

Washington had used and improved the so-called Nemacolin Trail (or Path) during his trips west in 1753 and 1754—some texts refer to it as "Washington's Road." In 1755 it was further expanded to accommodate General Braddock in his ill-fated campaign against the French and Indians. Nemacolin's Trail thus begat Washington's Road, which begat Braddock's Road.

And now Cresap, a living relic of the heyday of fur-trappers, sat with Washington by his fire in Old Town. They had seen the West raw, had known it as an untrammeled forest kingdom. Washington didn't record their conversations, but we can guess what they talked about. Roads. Rivers. Portages. Falls. Indians and Indian trails and old battles and Braddock's death and their endless war to transform the wilderness. A lifetime of hustling in the backcountry.

*   *   *

MORE RAIN. Rain meant mud. Mud meant impassable roads and rivers. It was the ninth of September and Washington knew he wouldn't be going anywhere. He stayed at Cresap's another day. He got rid of one of his horses, which had a bad back, and hired a new horse to pick up the slack. Otherwise the day was a bust.

The general had promised to reach his mill on the Youghiogheny on September 15, but he still faced the most difficult part of the journey, the long slog up and over the Allegheny Plateau. Realizing he would make better progress without the full entourage, he set forth early on the tenth of September without the Craiks or Bushrod Washington or most of the servants, and without the luggage and the cargo of cookware and tents.

He took, as he put it in the diary, "one Servant only." He did not mention the name of this companion, and documentary historians haven't discovered his identity. It is unlikely the man was Billy Lee, the general's most trusted slave in the War of Independence. Lee was a superior horseman and had accompanied the general on his 1770 western tour. But Lee would have been mentioned by name in the diary, and moreover, he was ailing at this point in his life, and only recently had been reunited with his wife. So the "one Servant" has remained anonymous. The two men rode into the high country, one draped in laurels, destined to be revered, studied, and monumentalized, the other an enigma. The servant was not exactly forgotten by history, because he was never permitted to be known in the first place.

They hewed to the road along the eastern bank of the Potomac, through heavy woods, to Fort Cumberland, a relic of the war with the French, at the junction of the river and Will's Creek. The fort had been abandoned two decades earlier, but a village had grown outside the walls. The Allegheny Plateau rises just west of town. In 1755, camped at Fort Cumberland while commanding British regulars and militia, Washington had fallen in love with the place. The geography clicked for him, just as it had for the Indians, who had long before built a village here, called Caiuctucuc. Cumberland in its brief history had already gone through a slight boom-and-bust cycle. The horsemen didn't linger, but kept going, up the mountain.

Road conditions worsened by the minute. The rain would not abate.

"Crossing the Mountains, I found tedeous and fatieguing," Washington wrote. "From Fort Cumberland to Gwins took me one hour and ten Minutes riding—between Gwins & Tumbersons I was near 6 hours and used all the dispatch I could. . . ."

The Allegheny Plateau can be rather subtle. Today, driving on Interstate 68 west of Cumberland, one notices that the road climbs steadily at a fairly gentle grade. Ten miles west of Cumberland is the town of Frostburg, atop the plateau. The valleys are broader, shallower. The ridgelines are routinely above 3,000 feet, yet not terribly impressive. Thomas Jefferson noted that these mountains don't seem as tall as some to the east, because the country rises "behind the successive ridges like the steps of stairs." (As always, he chooses the perfect simile.) The Allegheny Plateau is the backbone of the Appalachians, and in fact one of the ridges is called Backbone Mountain. From the plateau, rivers flow to all points of the compass. The line that separates the waters flowing to the Mississippi from those flowing to the Atlantic is not a single, easily identified mountain range. The divide sometimes follows the crest of a ridge, but then it will abruptly skip across high, open meadows to a different ridge entirely.

The Continental Divide (what we now call, with our knowledge of the Far West, the *Eastern* Continental Divide) could inspire travelers to literary effusions ("Ideas of immensity swelled and exalted our minds as we contemplated a prospect partaking of so much of infinitude," wrote Thaddeus Mason Harris), but Washington focused on road conditions and their obvious deficits:

> The Road from the Old Town to Fort Cumberland we found tolerably good, as it also was from the latter to Gwins, except the Mountain which was pretty long (tho' not steep) in the assent and discent; but from Gwins to Tumberson's it is intolerably bad—there being many steep pinches of the Mountain—deep & miry places and very stony ground to pass over.

He met travelers heading the other way, carrying salt and ginseng toward the Atlantic ports. These were among the few commodities valuable enough per pound to merit the haul across the high country. Whiskey was another. The travelers, Washington wrote, disabused him of the notion that the creeks he'd heard about so far were in any way navigable. Their general message, passing him on that high road through the woods, seems to have been something along the lines of *Are you crazy?*

Washington was not crazy, though. He was engaged in the grand tradition of overcoming natural obstacles in pursuit of trade. The goal was to render the world fluid. People find a way to expand their influence in time and space, to extend what an economist might call their "action radius." Man is an engineer. He reshapes the world. He knocks down barriers. He invents modes of transportation. He takes the natural gifts around him, the bounty of the rivers and seas and forests, and transforms them into houses, cities, tools, ornaments. He is always mobile. He carries seeds and artifacts and cultural traditions from one environment to another. The fragmented world thus moves inexorably toward homogenization. It is not a smooth or easy process, for there is destruction along the way, there are crimes, tragedies, there are desecrations, there are poisonings, there are people displaced, people murdered, and in some moments the forces of fragmentation reassert themselves, and things seem to be falling apart. Yet over large scales of time the cements of interest prevail. The human dominion increases. The planet shrinks.

Washington had been observing the process his entire life. The hardships and dangers of frontier life were innumerable, and yet people kept going, kept pushing forward, advancing into the forest in pursuit of the mere rumor of free land. Yes, you *could* get there from here, if you had courage and stamina and no great need for the comforts of Eastern society. There was a presumption underlying this forward thrust, a belief that the continental interior was in some fundamental way unoccupied, that although the Indians had lived there for millennia, and knew every trail and stream, every spring and salt lick, and had built villages and raised crops and interred their dead in ceremonial mounds, they still did not own these ancestral lands. They didn't have any use for the concept of private property, and they found bizarre the European belief in imaginary lines that enclosed the natural world. So it was all up for grabs.

The wilderness was not truly wild, for it had been occupied for thousands of years by people who, like the Europeans, had more than a passing interest in commerce. The most remote Indian villages were transformed by trade long before the first whites settled in the western territories. If people couldn't drag their deerskins over the mountains, they would find some other way to sell them. Historian Eric Hinderaker reports that in 1783 a group of Delawares on the Upper Ohio wanted to sell a pile of animal skins and knew it would be too difficult to send them over the Appalachians. Instead, they canoed down the Ohio to the Mississippi, then down the Mississippi to New Orleans, then sailed through the Gulf of Mexico and around Florida, all the way to Philadelphia, and sold their skins. Then they walked home, to the Ohio River.

People find a way.

*   *   *

WHEN WE IMAGINE the frontier of the eighteenth century, we compose a scene informed by the Hudson River School of painting: tumultuous rivers, craggy outcroppings, gnarled and windswept trees, everything raw and unspoiled and kinetic. What the Hudson River School painters didn't include were the squatters, the riffraff, the people whom J. Hector St. John de Crèvecoeur, the Frenchman turned American farmer and author, called the "off-casts" of society, creatures no better than "carnivorous animals." Crèvecoeur wrote, "There, remote from the power of example and check of shame, many families exhibit the most hideous part of our society."

Margaret Van Horn Dwight, a nineteen-year-old schoolteacher who journeyed through this part of the country in the early nineteenth century, fending off drunken wagoners and enduring the filth of the road, gave a rather nifty description of a couple that ran a frontier boardinghouse: "I found the people belong'd to a very ancient and noble family—They were first & second cousins to his *Satanic Majesty*. . . ."

Journals of early western travel indicate that it was not uncommon to find something dead in the middle of the road, and indeed it might be human. "24th. Found a dead Man on the Road who had killed himself by Drinking too much Whisky," the Indian interpreter Conrad Weiser wrote. "The Place being very stony we cou'd not dig a Grave; He smelling very strong we covered him with Stones & Wood & went on our Journey."

Or perhaps one might encounter a man not yet dead, merely slowly perishing in agony from the bite of a copperhead snake, a scene enthusiastically described by Crèvecoeur: "his eyes were filled with madness and rage, he cast them on all present with the most vindictive looks: he thrust out his tongue as the snakes do; he hissed through his teeth with inconceivable strength, and became an object of terror to all bystanders."

Alcohol is a recurrent element of frontier writing. The settlers are drunk, the Indians are drunk, the travelers soon become drunk. Whiskey cost 3 cents a glass. Wagoners would dance to a fiddler, drink all night, and would never repair to their room, since they had no room, only a claim to a few square feet on the barroom floor. They smoked crude cigars that emitted a mephitic stench and were priced at four for a penny. That such twists of tobacco were smoked by drivers of Conestoga wagons gave the cigars their enduring name: stogies.

We can imagine what this world smelled like. But what did it look like? The written record of the eighteenth-century American landscape is contradictory. Some accounts are romantic and effusive; others dismissive, repudiating. The nineteenth-century historian George Bancroft gave the classic romantic description of the land that enveloped the early Virginia colonists:

> There was no need of a scramble; abundance gushed from the earth for all. The morasses were alive with water-fowl; the creeks abounded with oysters, heaped together in inexhaustible beds; the rivers were crowded with fish; the forests were nimble with game; the woods rustled with coveys of quails and wild turkeys, while they rung with the merry notes of singing-birds; and hogs, swarming like vermin, ran at large in troops.

If hogs swarming like vermin are your idea of a nice place, then this was Paradise. A man didn't have to break a sweat to feed his family. Food practically flew in the cabin window and landed on a pewter plate.

Yet Bancroft was rhapsodizing after the fact. He wrote in a time of rapid industrialization, and his words are an artifact of the nineteenth century even as they claim to describe the eighteenth. This is likewise true for the writings of Francis Parkman, who in the second half of the nineteenth century visited an old-growth forest in northern New Hampshire while researching *France and England in North America*. This is what he saw:

> . . . the stern depths of immemorial forests, dim and silent as a cavern, columned with innumerable trunks, each like an Atlas upholding its world of leaves, and sweating perpetual moisture down its dark and channeled rind; some strong in youth, some grisly with decrepit age, nightmares of strange distortion, gnarled and knotted with wens and goitres, roots intertwined beneath like serpents petrified in an agony of contorted strife . . .

By the time one gets to Parkman's description of fallen trunks "bent in the impotence of rottenness" and stretched out like "mouldering reptiles of the primeval world," one is afraid to ever again go near a tree.

When Constantin Volney, a traveler from France, toured Virginia in 1796, he discovered he was not in Paris anymore:

> I always found the roads, or rather the paths, bordered and obscured by copse or forest, whose silence, uniformity, and stillness was wearisome. The ground beneath it was sterile and rough, or encumbered with the fallen and decaying trunks of ancient trees. Clouds of gnats, mosquitoes and flies hovered beneath the shade, and continually infested my peace.

Buggy, pestilential, dark: This was a scary and uncomfortable place. And there were wild animals, testified Joseph Doddridge in his *Notes on the Settlement and Indian Wars of the Western Parts of Virginia and Pennsylvania, from 1763 to 1783:*

> He did not know at what tread his foot might be stung by a serpent, at what moment he might meet with the formidable bear, or, if in the evening, he knew not on what limb of a tree, over his head, the murderous panther might be perched, in a squatting attitude, to drop down upon, and tear him to pieces in a moment.

The constant of early written accounts is the foreboding, tangled, gloomy forest, as well as the strenuous, sometimes inelegant efforts of the settlers to make the forest go away. There were no orderly hedgerows in the back country, no fountains at the end of a garden path. There were thousands of girdled trees and rotting stumps. The savvy pioneer used every means to attack the woods, including the forces of decay. Why cut down a tree and grub out the stump when nature would do most of the work for you? A girdled tree would die, and after three or four years the branches would fall to the ground, and eventually the trunk would fall and, fifteen to twenty years after the original girdling, the entire log would have vanished. Even where the tree became lumber, settlers would often leave the stump alone for a decade or so. A typical backcountry acre might have two to three hundred rotting stumps, plus four or five bonfires. The scene could become rather hellish, particularly at night, far from a village, when the moon and stars backlit the mangled landscape, and when, in the words of the intrepid Sarah Kemble Knight, "Each lifeless Trunk, with its shatter'd Limbs, appear'd an Armed Enymie; and every little stump like a Ravenous devourer." (Madam Knight survived a 1704 journey through still-primitive New England, and gave us perhaps one of the best descriptions of the simple act of crossing a river, as she did near Providence, as a passenger in a canoe, a craft so tippy that she spent the entire time "sitting with my hands fast on each side, my eyes stedy, not daring so much as to lodg my tongue a hair's breadth more on one side of my mouth then tother, nor so much as think on Lott's wife, for a wry thought would have oversett our wherey.")

White explorers had been probing the backcountry beyond the Blue Ridge for more than a century by the time Washington made his 1784 tour. As far back as 1654, Abraham Wood had made a trek from the falls of the Appomattox River, at present-day Petersburg, Virginia, over the Blue Ridge and the Alleghenies, to the New River. John Lederer reached the summit of the Blue Ridge in northern Virginia in 1669, and in 1716, Alexander Spotswood, the colonial governor, crossed into the Great Valley beyond the Blue Ridge, mistaking the Shenandoah River for a tributary of the Ohio (he called the Shenandoah the "Euphrates," which gives a hint of the feelings of explorers upon encountering the resources of the interior).

The French went farther than anyone else, and earlier. In the early eighteenth century and even in the mid-seventeenth, the French could be found a thousand miles farther west than the western settlements of the British colonies. They bypassed the Appalachians by taking the northern route from the Atlantic, up the St. Lawrence River, through the Great Lakes, then up the rivers that flow into the lakes, and across the narrow portages to the rivers that feed the Mississippi. The French took Indian women as wives, were adopted by Indian communities, and learned to hunt like natives. The English aristocrats might be building a simulacrum of England in Virginia, with manor houses sitting on riverside bluffs, and the religious leaders of New England might be building a Shining City on a Hill, constructed around small towns and Yankee ingenuity, but the French were following the fur. As early as the mid-1600s, they'd established trading villages in what is now southwestern Indiana, at Vincennes, and on the Mississippi River, at Kaskaskia, in what is now Illinois. They were in Green Bay, and up in the Lake of the Woods. They made friends with the Hurons and other Indians, learned the languages, and converted whomever they could to Christianity. Robert Cavelier, Sieur de La Salle, had explored a section of the Ohio River in 1672, 112 years before this trip by Washington.

Mysteries remained on this continent, but no one could honestly say that Washington was heading into virgin territory. There was nothing virgin about it. The general knew full well that he didn't live in "early American history."

No, the hour was late.

*　　　*　　　*

HEADING WEST atop the Allegheny Plateau, Washington spent the night of September 10 in the Red House Tavern, built by the Tomlinson family in the 1760s in a meadow that still, in 1784, showed signs of having been a campsite for General Braddock's army in the French and Indian War. The next day Washington reached the "little crossing of the Yohiogany"—the Little Youghiogheny, known today as the Casselman River—and was pleased to see the water smooth and abundant. Even this high in the mountains, the river was clearly navigable! At least that's how he saw it.

He crossed into Pennsylvania on an "exceedingly bad" stretch of road that passed through the gloomy wood called the Shades of Death. After spending a night in a private home, Washington and his servant rode at dawn to the Great Meadows, the site of Fort Necessity, the sad little stockade that had been the scene of his humiliation by the French and their Indian allies. General Braddock lay nearby in his grave. The diary ignores these facts, focusing instead on real estate. The general owned 234 acres here, including a small house, "which appears to have been but little improved, tho capable of being turned to great advantage, as the whole of the ground called the Meadows may be reclaimed at an easy comparitive expence & is a very good stand for a Tavern." Forget the past! What this meadow needed was a place to get some ale.

American romanticism would have to wait for the nineteenth century, for Bancroft and Parkman. Here in the eighteenth century there was work to be done. A man needed to find a way to get somewhere, to move things around, to overcome natural impediments. For Washington the Potomac was a tool, the West a financial opportunity, and the nation itself a potential empire to rival or surpass those of Europe. The forest was a nearly infinite warehouse of masts and boards and shingles. To create a strong nation would require the vigorous application of the ax and the plow. Washington, like virtually everyone of his day, viewed wilderness as abhorrent. He wanted to bring light to that dark world.

There would come a day when Americans would mourn the vanished forests, when they would yearn for a glimpse of a landscape unmarred by human intervention. But for now there was land to clear. As Tocqueville would write half a century later, a frontiersman "will gladly send you off to see a road, a bridge, or a fine village. But that one should appreciate great trees and the beauties of solitude, that possibility completely passes him by."

5

Squatters

ON THE THIRTEENTH of September, 1784, having crossed the Youghiogheny, Washington arrived at the gristmill. *His* gristmill. He had never seen it. Years earlier he had been assured that his mill was the finest west of the Alleghenies, but it hadn't brought him any income, and he knew that it might turn out to be underwhelming.

The structure rose three stories, the ground floor walled in stone, the upper floors made of wood. A steeply pitched roof ended in narrow eaves. The modest wooden wheel, not much wider than a man's forearm, caught the drippings of the millrace. The mill, to the general's dismay, harnessed the might of a feeble stream, a virtual rivulet—a seep! The millrace was essentially dry. The mill lacked its most important ingredient. Perhaps the masters of the place were expecting some other source of power to come along, something more sophisticated than this system that exploited water and gravity.

Washington examined the surrounding land and noted good patches of rich soil, but the level tracts were interrupted by gullies, depressions, rocky outcroppings—"broken" terrain. He owned 1,644 acres of rolling backwoods turf inhabited by people living in humble dwellings. They called this place "Washington's Bottom." What an honor.

I do not find the Land in *general* equal to my expectation of it. . . . The Tenements, with respect to buildings, are but indifferently improved—each have Meadow and arable [land], but in no great quantity. The Mill was quite destitute of Water. . . . In a word, little rent, or good is to be expected from the present aspect of her.

He could not have been entirely shocked, however, for he had been here before. He had visited this very spot, in 1770, before there was any mill. He had been accompanied by Captain William Crawford, the man who had been scouting properties for him. Washington at the time had noted in his diary that the "stream is rather too slight, and it is said not constant more than 7 or 8 Months in the Year." He had praised the "Rich Meadow" and the level nature of the terrain in what is otherwise a region of mountains, hills, knolls, ravines, gullies, and outcroppings. A flat patch of land on the western slope of the Alleghenies was a thrilling sight. And yet the improvements of fourteen years had done nothing but knock the bloom off the rose. The inhabitants struck the general as people of a lower order, and the mill at the heart of their community did not seem capable of handling a single kernel of corn.

Washington knew whom to blame for the mill disaster: Gilbert Simpson, his business partner, the on-site mill manager. Washington had once described Simpson as a man of "extreame stupidity." Simpson knew he'd lost Washington's confidence. A few months earlier Simpson had written a long and not terribly articulate plea to Washington asking him to consider the financial hardships a man faces on the frontier:

I have been here Twelve Years I came into a Howling Wilderness continually apprisd for the first Year of the incursions of a Ravenous and Merciless Enemy which I was Obligd to fortify my Self on the Occasion and having the Mill on hand the same Year it could not be expected that much could be done on Either Plantation or Mill. . . .

Forgive me, he was saying, *for I am but a poor man in the woods, sur-rounded by bloodthirsty savages.*

When the general finished dealing with Simpson, he'd have to cope with another, even more irritating problem. A group of people had journeyed to Washington's Bottom to discuss with the general his al-legation that they were squatting on another of his properties. They were Scotch-Irish Presbyterians who belonged to a sect called Seced-ers (sometimes spelled Ceceders). They lived on Washington's land—or what Washington claimed as his land—about half a day's ride to the north, on Millers Run, just southwest of Pittsburgh.

Pennsylvania had been founded by Quakers, but these Scotch-Irish were a different breed, rougher, more belligerent, and ready to tromp into every remote mountain hollow of the Appalachians to carve out a new life. They did not come to the mill to give the general a parade. The great man wanted to take away their farms. When they had ar-rived in this part of western Pennsylvania, they found a trackless for-est. They'd hacked down trees, burned and grubbed the stumps, built fences, log cabins, barns, and found a way to survive in a world that still knew the howl of the wolf. They'd endured the constant risk of Indian attacks, and indeed, one of their members, Thomas Bigger, had narrowly escaped a massacre that claimed the lives of three families a dozen miles to the west of Millers Run, near Raccoon Creek. And now, years later, they'd gotten word of a visitor, the alleged owner of their land, at best an absentee landlord, and in their view a man with no right to their farms whatsoever.

Washington's claim to the Millers Run land was, indeed, a bit thin legally. He first saw the area around Millers Run in the early 1750s, during his military adventures against the French. Somehow amid the enchanting whistling of bullets he retained an impression of fertile terrain. In 1767, he asked William Crawford, who lived on the Youghiogheny (the "Yock"), to "look me out a tract of about fifteen hundred or two thousand or more acres somewhere in your neigh-borhood," and stipulated that, since such lands were remote from navigation, they should be first-rate, rich, and level. And do it soon, Washington said, for others will soon rush in to grab these lands.

The energetic researchers at *The Papers of George Washington,* and the nineteenth-century historian Boyd Crumrine of Washington County, Pennsylvania, have done heroic work in trying to untangle the legal knots around the Millers Run property, though this may require several more centuries of labor. It appears that in 1763, a war veteran named John Posey, one of Washington's neighbors, obtained a military warrant (as payment for service in the French and Indian War) for 3,000 acres between Millers Run and Raccoon Creek, in the primeval forest southwest of the Forks of the Ohio. Crawford, in turn, told Washington about Posey's land, and in 1770 Washington obtained Posey's warrant (Posey owed him 2,000 pounds sterling; in exchange for the warrant, Washington forgave the debt). That year, while traveling deep into the Ohio Territory, he learned from the Indian trader George Croghan that it was a "body of fine Rich level land," words designed to stir Washington's soul. In fact it is by no means level, but rather a rolling terrain, much like the Virginia Piedmont.

Late that year, or perhaps early in 1771, Washington recalled, Crawford surveyed 2,813 acres near Millers Run in Washington's name. But Croghan, himself a man with aspirations of a western empire, also coveted the land, claimed it as his own, and encouraged a number of settlers to move in, saying he would back them up if Washington put up a fuss.

The situation at that point turned downright devilish. To secure rights to a piece of property, the owner had to improve it somehow, even by proxy. An improvement might be anything—some clearing and fencing, for example, or the construction of a cabin. Crawford, representing Washington's interests, arranged for a man to build a cabin on the Millers Run site. That single, thrown-together dwelling, as lost amid the 2,813 acres as a mollusk at the bottom of a lake, supposedly satisfied the improvement requirement. But then Croghan's people reciprocated, and built their own cabin inches from the first. They simply blocked the door to the first cabin. If there had been someone inside he would have died of thirst.

Crawford by letter regularly updated Washington on the conflict. There are squatters on your land, he told Washington, and they won't budge.

This dispute was, in miniature, the conflict of the continent: Who owned the land? How was that ownership established? Could the rule of law be applied fairly on the frontier? Was the whole game stacked against the common man, the pioneer, not to mention the tribesman? Was this to be a nation run by aristocrats and land speculators and the moneymen of the big eastern cities?

Who had power in this young republic?

*   *   *

THE SECEDERS were part of a great migration of people into the West. For decades European-Americans and African-Americans had been pooling on the eastern side of the Alleghenies, constrained first by the Indians and the French, then by the British proclamation that the western lands would be reserved for the Indians. But the Revolution opened the floodgates. The powers of attraction of the West, which so many times had yanked Washington from the comforts of his Tidewater estate, had an even more powerful effect on landless people. It could compel a man and woman to load their children into a wagon, round up their cows and goats and chickens, gather pots and kettles and knives and axes and of course the long rifle, and set out for the edge of what they considered to be civilization.

(Today, with the United States a geographically static nation, with the wilderness in the Midwest converted to farmland, with the technologies of transportation so advanced and commonplace that Americans routinely fly 7 miles above the Earth from New York to Los Angeles and never look out the window, it is hard to imagine how intoxicating, in 1784, was the existence, the sheer physical reality, of all that unsettled, fertile, lush, forested, seductive, "virgin" land. It's safe to say that no one today becomes atwitter at the mention of the physical existence of this thing out there called Ohio.)

The Scotch-Irish, Germans, and French were in the vanguard of the western assault, along with Finns and Swedes. In addition to families, there were many lone wolves, usually young men fleeing the backbreaking labor of the indigo and rice fields of the Deep South or recently released from debtors' prison. The worst of these, Newgate prison in Connecticut, was something straight out of the Middle Ages, as we are told by John Bach McMaster: "The only entrance to it was by means of a ladder down a shaft which led to the caverns under ground. There, in little pens of wood, from thirty to one hundred culprits were immured, their feet made fast to iron bars, and their necks chained to beams in the roof. The darkness was intense; the caves reeked with filth; vermin abounded. . . ." For many Americans the dangers and deprivations of the West, the terror of Indian raids, the shortage of staples and ordinary comforts, were still a step up in life. They were being pushed by the harsh society of the seaboard as much as pulled by the prospect of free land.

Voyagers to the West had to supply all their own needs as they migrated. For food they would hunt deer, bear, wild turkey, and perhaps the occasional squirrel, raccoon, or groundhog. The earliest settlers were amazed at the abundance of game: Thomas Walker, who traveled through Kentucky in 1750, reported that "we killed in the journey 13 buffaloes, 8 elks, 53 bears, 20 deer, 4 wild gees, about 150 turkeys, besides small game." Settlers traded for salt, to keep their meat fresh. They dreamed of white bread, for their own bread, if they had any at all, would be dark and hard, not exactly the kind of stuff that melted in one's mouth. For breakfast they often ate johnnycakes made of cornmeal and heated on a plank by a fire.

At the end of their journey through the forest would be nothing as coherent as a village or town, just a patch of woods along a river or stream. There wouldn't even be sunshine, just the permanent gloom of a vegetal kingdom. If they were lucky, there might be a few families nearby, and a mill or a small stockade that passed for a fort. Many a family made a clearing in the forest and, using nothing but an ax, built a cabin, complete with wooden hinges, wooden pins, wooden chinking (held in place by clay or mud), even a wooden chimney. Packed clay served well enough for a floor. Eventually, the family would build a proper residence, a log house, with square-hewn logs, sometimes whitewashed on the inside, and a few glassless windows, some sawn lumber for a floor, and a shingled roof. (The general may have found the habitations of western Pennsylvania "indifferently improved" because of the rarity of stone or brick.) Even a town like Pittsburgh had primitive dwellings; when Arthur Lee of Virginia visited Pittsburgh in 1784, he opined, "[It] is inhabited almost entirely by Scots and Irish, who live in paltry log houses, and are as dirty as in the north of Ireland, or even Scotland."

The pioneers didn't rely on maps. To wait for a region to be mapped and divided into neat sections (as would happen soon after Washington's journey) would be to lose precious time. As Daniel Boorstin puts it, America was, for the most part, settled *before* it was explored. "The haze which covered the New World in that age probably covers no part of the world today; America was one of the last places where European settlers would come in large numbers before the explorers, geographers, and professional naturalists," Boorstin writes. Local knowledge proved crucial: From the very beginning of European colonization of the continent, whites would never have survived without the help and guidance of the indigenous cultures. The Indians knew which crops would thrive, where to find game, how to avoid treacherous falls and rapids.

André Michaux, the French botanist who traveled widely in the United States in the late 1700s and early 1800s, felt the settlers had a pathological need for motion. Settlers didn't *settle.* They kept going. They were

> a kind of men who cannot settle upon the soil that they have cleared, and who under pretence of finding a better land, a more wholesome country, a greater abundance of game, push forward, incline perpetually towards the most distant points of the American population, and go and settle in the neighbourhood of the savage nation . . .

The disapproving Michaux raised an important issue: The Americans who went West didn't instantly replace or vanquish the Indians. The two cultures often coexisted, trading with one another. The most common result when two cultures meet is not war, but commerce.

The settlers could never know with certainty what the forest held, and even the silence of the woods did not ensure one's safety, for the hostile Indians had a reputation for stealth. Hundreds of settlers, including many women and some African-Americans, had been taken captive. Many people had read, or at least heard others tell of, the captivity narratives of their countrymen. One of the most famous was that of Mary White Rowlandson, dragged from her home in Lancaster, Massachusetts, in 1675, by what she would call a "company of hellhounds." The Rowlandson captivity narrative became a bestseller; readers would not soon forget the image of this woman carrying her six-year-old daughter, who had been shot in the gut, and who would perish on a forced march through the wilderness. The genre of the captivity narrative flourished and, as the historian Bernard Bailyn puts it, drove these experiences "deep into the American psyche."

Even as Washington was confronting the Seceders, the legend of Daniel Boone began to spread eastward from the bluegrass country of Kentucky. In the 1770s, Boone brought settlers into Kentucky through the Cumberland Gap, a mountain pass in what is now the extreme southwest corner of Virginia, reachable only after a long journey down the Great Valley of the Appalachians. In 1784, John Filson wrote the first biographical treatment of Boone, *The Discovery, Settlement, and Present State of Kentucke*, which is cast as a Boone autobiography. The Filson/Boone biography is a harrowing and picaresque tale in which Boone is cavorting with Indians one day and at war with them the next. His brother dies, his eldest son dies, his second-eldest son dies, and his wife marches back to North Carolina in despair with the remaining children in tow. Boone follows them to North Carolina and drags them back to the wilderness. "Many dark and sleepless nights have I been a companion for owls, separated from the chearful society of men, scorched by the summer's sun, and pinched by the winter's cold, an instrument ordained to settle the wilderness," writes Filson in the voice of Boone. (Boone's own words were probably more along the lines of the famous inscription carved on a tree in Tennessee: "D. Boone Cilled a Bar.") The narrative continues: "But now the scene is changed: Peace crowns the sylvan shade." Filson's message is clear: Providence ordained the spread of European-American civilization. This is Manifest Destiny, decades ahead of its official flowering.

Peace, as a rule, did not follow the settlers as they infiltrated the West. Some frontiersmen took a break from Indian fighting by inventing new ways to maim one another. Eye-gouging became something of a sport, and the countryside had an unusually large number of one-eyed men. Wrote one observer, "The whole society was, with very few exceptions, about as wicked as fallen human beings can be on this side of utter perdition. Female seduction was frequent, quarreling and fighting decidedly customary—drunkenness almost universal." The historian Leland Baldwin reports that a "fair fight" meant the use of fists and nothing more, but the "rough and tumble" was the more common form of frontier combat, one in which "the endeavor of each man was to maim and disfigure the other by gouging out his eyes, biting off his lips, nose, or ears, or kicking him in the groin."

These people did not follow Washington's maxims for gentlemanly behavior.

*   *   *

WASHINGTON EMBRACED the westward course of empire. But he didn't want to be left behind. He feared that hustlers and squatters and speculators and con men and financiers and all sorts of nefarious land-jobbers were snatching the best tracts in the Ohio Valley. He declared that scarcely a single valuable spot northwest of the Ohio lacked a claimant, even though the territory was reserved, by Congress, for the Indian nations. The "rage for speculating," Washington wrote Jacob Read, was such that an ambitious person might talk of acquiring five hundred thousand acres in the same tone that someone in bygone times would have spoken of a thousand acres. It was outrageous. One possible solution, Washington thought, would be to declare all such "Northwest" claims invalid, and all persons who presumed to survey such property "outlaws, but fit subjects for Indian vengeance."

Another possibility would be to create one or two new states, and ration the land, setting a price too high for "monopolizers." He wished Congress could act quickly. "It is much easier to avoid mischiefs, than to apply remedies after they have happened," he wrote to Read.

Some historians do not view Washington as a friend of the western-ers, and his Potomac scheme might be viewed as a dramatic example of that antipathy. If he really cared about helping the western farmers and lumbermen and miners get their products to market, the argu-ment goes, he would have used his influence to try to persuade Spain to open the Mississippi to American commerce. Instead he wanted the western cargo to come directly to the East via the Potomac. Other eastern elites, such as Henry Lee and John Jay, strenuously opposed the opening of the Mississippi. Historian Thomas Slaughter, in *The Whiskey Rebellion*, gives a harsh summary of the situation: "The im-mediate needs of western settlers for markets must be sacrificed to the long-term benefits of eastern merchants, eastern canal investors, east-ern speculators in western lands, and, of course, the nation itself." Under Washington's plan, westerners would be "economic captives of remote commercial and political overlords."

Slaughter takes a sharply critical view of Washington's actions be-yond the Alleghenies ("he lied, broke the law, and betrayed public trusts in pursuit of private gain," Slaughter writes), but he is not the first to sense that the great man was overly aggressive when amassing his western empire, or the first to suggest that easterners did not re-ally have the interests of westerners at heart. Early historians went out of their way to give Washington a pass. Bernhard Knollenberg, in *Washington and the Revolution: A Reappraisal* (1941), noted that the first scholar to compile Washington's writings, Jared Sparks, changed a key phrase in the September 21, 1767, letter from Washington to William Crawford in such a way as to clean up Washington's inten-tions. Washington suggested that Pennsylvania laws against purchas-ing large tracts of land might "possibly be evaded"; Sparks altered the sentence so that the incendiary phrase could be replaced outright with the words "perhaps be arranged." Even so, there is remarkably little tarnish to be mined in the Washington archive. We can be confident that his reputation as an honest man is not the product of a historical whitewash. He was aggressive and rather obstreperous in the West because he felt it was the key not only to his personal fortune but also to the entire American experiment. Those two interests were foremost in his thoughts; the interests of squatters and other backcountry settlers were always going to come in third.

When the general moved among frontier folk, he didn't mix. He passed over these people like a dark nimbus cloud. To be George Washington required an adherence to certain principles and behaviors and beliefs that could properly be described as elitist, and that elitism wasn't superficial; it came from the marrow. Whatever he found common in himself he tried to purge. He once referred to ordinary farmers as "the grazing multitude." He clearly did not subscribe to the Jeffersonian dictum that yeoman farmers were God's chosen people.

Washington's antipathy to frontier folk dated to his teenage years, when he made that first surveying trip for Lord Fairfax and encountered a band of settlers on the South Branch of the Potomac. The sixteen-year-old wrote in his diary: "I really think they seem to be as Ignorant as Set of People as the Indians. They would never speak English but when spoken to they speak all Dutch." During the Revolution, Washington wanted only "gentlemen" to be officers. Earlier, as leader of the Virginia Regiment, he viewed his own men as fairly worthless and the backcountry folk as insolent. In October 1755 he told the Virginia governor that none of his orders had been obeyed except by the threat of a drawn sword, and that relations had gotten so bad that the frontier people wanted to "blow out my brains."

And now he was in the West, repelled by westerners. They were unmannered, uncouth, unclean, a distasteful breed at the social and geographical margin of civilization. ("His heart was not warm in its affections; but he exactly calculated every man's value, and gave him a solid esteem proportioned to it," Jefferson wrote.)

Washington was hardly alone among the Founders in his disdain for the common man. After John Adams met a "wretch" who spoke enthusiastically about the abolition of courts of justice, he wrote, "If the powers of the country should get into such hands, and there is a great danger that it will, to what purpose have we sacrificed our time, health and everything else?" On another occasion Adams lamented the "lawless tyrannical rabble" of Massachusetts. (Abigail Adams likewise declared that man is a natural tyrant, though in her case she was speaking of the masculine sex specifically.) Alexander Hamilton viewed businessmen ("rich and well-born") as the crucial allies of government, and the "mass of the people" as a potential menace, for "the people are turbulent and changing; they seldom judge or determine right." Elbridge Gerry, a Massachusetts conservative, said, "The evils we experience flow from the excess of democracy." As early as 1776, certain Revolutionaries feared that they were inciting a leveling spirit that would bring disaster to the elite. The advance of liberty might lead to demands for *equality*. They were all taking an enormous risk. The people had natural rights, to be sure, but the great men of the nation were not about to trust the rabble to make the important decisions of the world.

In the eyes of the more aristocratic members of American society (who would deny being part of an aristocracy), the West could be penetrated initially only by a rugged, uncouth, semiwild species of person—"men of enterprising, violent, nay, discontented and turbulent spirits," as one congressman put it. Henry Adams, great-grandson of the second president, gave a nineteenth-century historian's view of Virginia's lower and middle classes:

As explorers, adventurers, fighters,—wherever courage, activity, and force were wanted—they had no equals; but they had never known discipline, and were beyond measure jealous of restraint. With all their natural virtues and indefinite capacities for good, they were rough and uneducated to a degree that shocked their own native leaders.

Shocked indeed was Washington. The human detritus, combined with the ragged landscape and the harshness of wilderness travel, removed any romance from the journey among the western waters.

*   *   *

THE GENERAL had to meet face-to-face with these squatters. His diary contains a detailed account of what happened, and one can sense, between the lines, the reddening of the general's visage. They

> came here to set forth their pretensions to it; & enquire into my right. After much conversation, & attempts in them to discover all the flaws they could in my Deed, &ca.; & to establish a fair and upright intention in themselves; and after much Councelling which proceeded from a division of opinion among themselves— they resolved (as all who live on the Land were not there) to give me their definitive determination when I should come to the Land, which I told them would probably happen on Friday or Saturday next.

Both sides explained their positions. The Seceders probed Washington for proof that he owned the land, beyond the deed that he carried, which they viewed as unpersuasive. According to a subsequent memo written by Washington, the Seceders had been told years earlier by William Crawford that Washington owned the land, but when they searched the records of the land office, they found no paperwork to support the general's claim. They had concluded that Crawford was blowing smoke, that he was a land-jobber who wanted to scare off settlers until he could obtain the land himself and later sell it. After Crawford's death in 1782, the Seceders must have felt home free. But any lingering suspicion that Crawford had invented or exaggerated the Washington story had been shattered by the arrival of the general.

The two sides resolved nothing in the meeting at the mill. They decided to have a second meeting in a couple of days, this time back on the Seceders' home turf (or what they perceived as such).

The next day, September 15, while still at Washington's Bottom, the general attempted to sell his gristmill to the highest bidder. A crowd formed. That much seemed promising. But Washington quickly realized that the people had come not to bid on the mill, but rather to gawk. They were there to see the show, to see him, the great man, the famous George Washington. It was utterly confounding. He had serious business to conduct, and they seemed to view the whole thing as an entertainment. (Washington was the country's first celebrity, according to one modern scholar of popular culture. At the very least, on this September day in 1784, he was the most interesting thing to look at for hundreds of miles.)

He called for bids.

No one answered.

The great man waited. Still no bids.

At some point it became obvious that no one was going to buy his mill. The general had all this wealth on paper, but what was it worth if you couldn't make it liquid?

Doing his best to salvage the situation, the general announced that he would rent the farm on which Gilbert Simpson had been living. He would not even ask for cash, merely a payment in wheat. Five hundred bushels a year would cover it, he said.

Again, no one in the crowd showed any interest. Only one man wanted to rent the farm: Gilbert Simpson, again. The vile Simpson! Washington wanted to end all connection with him, but he was trapped in a land where hardly anyone had two shillings to rub together, where a man of extreme stupidity and timorousness such as Gilbert Simpson was nonetheless at the pinnacle of the social hierarchy. He agreed to keep Simpson as a tenant.

The general always had a good instinct for when to retreat.

*   *   *

THE NEXT DAY Washington made the rounds of several more farms on his land, visiting his tenants, trying to collect rent and impose some new leases. It could not have been a pleasant day for either the general or the farmers; Washington's diary entry for this day, the sixteenth, is an enervated two sentences, and perhaps he sensed that a paper agreement to transfer money from this remote province of the world to his manor at Mount Vernon would be difficult to enforce (and in fact, the tenants would later balk at paying the back rent due).

A "settled Rain" fell the next day and kept the general once again at the Simpson farm, giving him plenty of time to close all his accounts with this difficult person. Ending a business partnership in 1784 was no simple matter, and the transaction involved livestock, Virginia currency, a bond in Pennsylvania currency, and an African-American woman, supposedly a slave, given by Simpson to Washington even though, as it turned out later, she was entitled to her freedom.

The next day Washington and Craik and the rest of their traveling party hit the road again, north and west, traveling by ferry across the Monongahela River, and riding onward to the home of one of the local elites, a certain Colonel Cannon. This would be Washington's base of operations for his final assault on the squatters at Millers Run.

The general wasn't in a rush to confront these people. He arrived on a Saturday afternoon, and on Sunday morning decided to postpone the reckoning. "Being Sunday, and the People living on my Land, *apparently* very religious, it was thought best to postpone going among them till tomorrow. . . ." There's a rare whiff of sarcasm there. *Apparently* very religious—his italics.

The next day Washington made a tour of the thirteen farms that had been carved out of his land. The general knew as well as anyone alive how to eyeball a farm on horseback. He examined the soils, the trees, the houses, the barns, the fences. He took notes, recording the names of the squatters and the number of acres cleared and under cultivation:

James McBride. 3 or 4 Acres of Meadow . . . Pretty good fencing—Land rather broken, but good—white & black oak mixed— A dwelling House and barn (of midling size) with Puncheon roofs . . .

Brice McGeechen. 3 Acres of Meadow . . . Arable—under good fencing. A small new Barn good . . .

John Reed Esquire. 4 Acres of Meadow . . . A Small dwelling

House—but Logs for a large one, a still House—good Land and
fencing . . .

And so on, a complete inventory.

That night the settlers showed their visitor a modicum of respect,
hosting him for dinner at the home of one of their leaders, David
Reed. They announced that they would be willing to buy the land outright from the general—a sign that, as much as they doubted his legal
right to the properties, they feared that they might lose their farms
should Washington prosecute his claim. They made clear to the general that they weren't conceding that he owned the land, but merely
wanted to avoid a nasty fight. Washington said he had no inclination
to sell. The squatters talked of their hardships, their history, how
they'd come together, their religious beliefs, and so on. The steel in
Washington's resolve softened ever so slightly. He would consider
selling, he said.

Now they talked price, and Washington said he would accept no less
than 25 shillings an acre, paid in three annual installments, with interest. Otherwise they could sign a 999-year lease. No one was interested
in the lease, but the squatters asked if the general would sell the land
for his asking price but over a much longer period of time and without
any interest. He said he wouldn't. That ended the negotiations. The
squatters formally declared that they did not recognize Washington's
ownership, and that he would have to sue them.

There is a bit of local lore about what happened next. Supposedly,
Washington declared rather dramatically that he would have the land,
and accompanied this vow with a curse. Squatter John Reed, who
served as a justice of the peace, promptly fined Washington 5 shillings.
The general paid up on the spot and apologized for violating the laws
of God and man. This anecdote obviously does not emit the resounding peal of truth. Boyd Crumrine dismisses the story, noting that the
son of one of the squatters later denied that Washington made any
such oath. But Crumrine endorsed the son's account of what Washington told the squatters in this testy moment. The general, the son

said, pulled out a red silk handkerchief, held it by one corner, and said: "Gentlemen, I will have this land just as surely as I now have this handkerchief." Again, what we know of the general and his personality leads us to doubt that he would taunt the squatters in such a flamboyant fashion. Usually an icy stare served his purposes well enough.

Washington now found himself in an uncomfortable position. The squatters believed that they'd called his bluff. He knew it wasn't a bluff, but he also knew that his various documents had become deranged during the war, and that a local court might side with the Seceders rather than an absentee landlord with incomplete paperwork. He held out hope that somewhere in the motley bunch there might be men willing to abandon their stance, and he decided to resort to a little theatricality. As commander in chief of the Continental Army, he had managed to quell rebellions through the force of his personality. (The most famous incident happened late in the war, when his officers, furious at Congress for failing to provide money or support, threatened to stage a military coup. Washington made a surprise visit to a meeting of the officers, and after rebuking them, pulled out a pair of glasses to read an otherwise inconsequential letter. "Gentlemen, you will permit me to put on my spectacles," he said, "for I have not only grown gray but almost blind in the service of my country." The mutinous atmosphere evaporated. Blind in the service of his country! Tears ran down the faces of the officers, and Washington had won again.)

So now Washington had to stage a little more theater. He asked each of the settlers if they would stand up individually to attest an intention to go to court over the land dispute. The general said he would call out the names of the settlers one by one. He wanted to break up this gaggle of Seceders into its constituent parts. It was time to fight man to man.

"James Scott," the general said.

James Scott rose to his feet.

"William Stewart."

William Stewart stood.

"Thomas Lapsley . . . Samuel McBride . . . Brice McGeechin . . .

Thomas Biggar . . . David Reed . . . William Hillas . . . James McBride . . . Duncan McGeechin . . . Matthew Johnson . . . John Reed . . . John Glenn."

One by one, they all stood. Thirteen backwoods settlers were defying Cincinnatus.

6

A Darker Wood

*W*HAT BAD LUCK for the Seceders: They had squatted on the wrong man's land, and worse, he was a details freak. He kept track of every shilling he was due, every acre he owned. The war hero doubled as an accountant. Even so, they might have gotten away with it, for frontier law tended to be squishy, and there had always been in Pennsylvania a general presumption that settlers who improved land had priority over an absentee landlord with only a paper title.

The Seceders had heard, moreover, that Washington had a bogus title, that the land hadn't been properly surveyed, that the surveyor, William Crawford, lacked proper credentials, and that the whole area had been off-limits to patents at the time that Crawford began amassing lands for his Virginia friend. And where had Washington been, anyway? Far away, on the tidewater Potomac. The Seceders, when they began clearing land and burning stumps and building fences and raising barns, assumed that they had found their own little place in the world, that they were beyond the reach of moneymen. They would grow their corn and wheat, raise their cows and pigs, hunt wild game, and worry only about the weather and the threat of Indians, wolves, and panthers. That was the plan, until the grave, frowning, humorless George Washington himself came riding up. Who could imagine?

Washington saw himself as the victim, not as a feudal lord showing up to slap around some lowlifes. He felt abused. These people had taken advantage of him. He hadn't been around for the past decade because he'd been busy *winning freedom for the nation.*

He insisted that he was not a land speculator or "monopolizer": "Indeed, comparatively speaking I possess very little land on the Western Waters," he wrote. "To attempt therefore to deprive me of the little I have, is, considering the circumstances under which I have been"—*fighting for liberty!*—"and the inability of attending to my own affairs, not only unjust, but pitifully mean."

Archer Hulbert, in *Washington and the West,* offers a savvy analysis of Washington's attitude in the case. The general had more than just the Millers Run land on his mind. He feared that a loss of this one parcel would have a cascading effect, and that he might lose all his lands in the remote backcountry. Being lenient "would certainly result in the establishment of a precedent that would be ruinous to him; and if Washington could not keep his land how would the less influential and less powerful fare?"

He would fight this battle on behalf of *all* absentee landlords. It would become more than a passing legal skirmish, occupying him for more than two years, the figures of James Scott and William Stewart and the Reeds and McBrides and McGeechins never far from his mind as he pondered the fate of his country.

*   *   *

WASHINGTON'S TESTY ENCOUNTER with the squatters destroyed his western momentum. He had intended, of course, to keep going, down the Ohio, to his huge tracts of land on the south side of that river, but he changed his mind. He told his fellow travelers, the Craiks and his nephew Bushrod and their servants, that he wanted to go home. The Grand Tour of America had already been downsized into a mere business trip to his western properties, and now even that was turning into a bust.

He'd been thinking of turning back even before he'd run into the Seceders. He had been told that the Indians had started a new campaign of resistance, and had recently killed a number of white settlers who had encroached on Indian lands north of the Ohio. Washington didn't want to push his luck. Discretion is different from cowardice. "The Accts. given by those Whom I met of the late Murders, & general dissatisfaction of the Indians, occasioned by the attempt of our people to settle on the No. West side of the Ohio, which they claim as their territory; and our delay to hold a treaty with them, which they say is indicative of a hostile temper on our part, makes it rather improper for me to proceed to the Kanhawa agreeably to my original intention," the general had written. Later he elaborated, saying it was "better to return, than to make a bad matter worse by hazarding abuse from the Savages of the Country."

Thomas Freeman, his land agent, subsequently informed him that the Indians knew Washington was headed to his Ohio River lands, and they were preparing to greet him with an ambush. "The Indians by what means I can't say had Intelligence of your Journey and Laid wait for you," Freeman informed the general.

Washington in his reluctance to go further west surely had in mind the fate of William Crawford, the surveyor who'd obtained these Pennsylvania lands for him. In a gentler world, Crawford would have been on hand at Washington's Bottom to greet the arriving general, and would have been a handy witness for Washington in his ejectment suit against the Seceders. But Crawford was a warrior as well as a surveyor. In 1782, just two years before Washington's western trek, Crawford led an expedition of armed men into the Ohio country to fight Indians. He would discover directly the price of the settlement of the West.

Earlier that year, as frontier conflict intensified, a band of Shawnees had massacred a family named Wallace, leaving the mother of the family impaled on a sapling. The western Pennsylvanians sought revenge. An expedition of militiamen encountered a group of Christianized Indians known as Moravians (from the Protestant missionaries who had converted them). They were considered friendly Indians.

They had adopted many of the ways of white farmers. But to the settlers of western Pennsylvania, they were still a suspect class. The Moravians had traded with the hostile Indians for pewter dishes and branded horses that had been stolen from the whites. Worse, they had a bloody dress—Mrs. Wallace's dress, purchased from the Indians who had attacked the family.

The militiamen rounded up the Moravians—women and children included—and led them, with ropes around their necks, to two huts that the whites called their "slaughter houses." A debate broke out among the whites: How, exactly, should they kill these Indians? They chose scalping. The Indians asked for a moment to prepare their souls for death.

Then the militiamen scalped them—42 men, 20 women, and 34 children.

The campaign continued months later with another expedition, this time led by Crawford. The men headed for the Sandusky village of Indians, intending to destroy it with fire and sword. Crawford and his men camped initially in the ruins of the Moravian village, where orphaned corn still stood in the fields. They were being watched.

Wyandot, Delaware, and Shawnee warriors, accompanied by a white compatriot, Simon Girty, were well aware of the movements of Crawford's men. Meanwhile another player entered the field—the British (the peace treaty ending the Revolution was still a year away). British horsemen came down into the Ohio country from Detroit, ready to help the Indians repulse the Pennsylvanians.

The battle with the Indians quickly went against the white militia, and Crawford's men took flight. During his retreat, Crawford was captured by Delawares and taken to the headquarters of Pomoacan, the grand sachem of the Wyandots. A Delaware chief named Wingenund, who had met Crawford previously—had been entertained, in fact, by Crawford at his house on the Yock—painted the white man's face black. He told Crawford he would be adopted as an Indian. But Crawford knew otherwise: The black paint meant he would die.

Because another captured man, a surgeon, witnessed the ensuing events, there is an elaborate narrative of what took place. According to the surgeon, the Indians found the most flamboyant means of putting an end to Crawford's earthly existence. They stripped him naked, beat him, cut off his ears, prodded him with burning sticks, made him walk on coals, tied him to a stake, scalped him, fired gunpowder into his body, and poured hot coals on his head. He begged Girty to shoot him, but Girty just laughed. Instead, the Indians built a hot fire in a circle about 15 feet from the stake. That was far enough to ensure that he wouldn't burn to death quickly. They slowly roasted him.

Washington knew the tale of Crawford all too well, and was, in his clipped phrase, "particularly affected" by it. He had relied so heavily on Crawford in his quest to obtain western land, and then had gone adventuring with him, plunging down the Ohio River in 1770 through an ancient world of Indian mounds and lonely campfires that few white men had ever seen. But Washington could not say he was truly surprised by what happened to Crawford: "no other than the extremest Tortures which could be inflicted by Savages could, I think, have been expected, by those who were unhappy eno' to fall into their Hands," he wrote after the story reached him. He was a realist, and now, given everything he knew about the latest Indian troubles, he decided that the better part of valor would be to stay far away from those who did not subscribe to the white man's plans for the West.

*   *   *

WASHINGTON, like most white men of his time, regarded the Indians as savages. After spending a great deal of time with Washington in 1754, the Half King (Tanaghrisson) complained that the young major treated his Indian allies as though they were his slaves. But Washington also conceded that Indians had natural rights that could not be blandly waved away for the sake of convenience. Washington over the years held many meetings with Indian chiefs. He shared the pipe with them. He ate their food. He learned from them. His victory in the War of Independence might not have happened had he not studied in the school of Indian warfare, had not seen up close the tactical advantages of surprise and deception. He had a wary respect for their intelligence, and he warned his colleagues that they knew much more English than they let on. But it appears that his major sentiment about the Indians was that they were obstructions. He wished to create a powerful Anglo-American nation on this continent. The Indians, like the mountains, were simply in the way.

Washington represented the antithesis of the Indian approach to the world. He was a man who would change nature rather than adapt to it. He would reconfigure his world, alter the rivers, and hack through the mountains. He promoted European science and philosophy. In his personal life he was always a man in a hurry. He may have been willing to learn from the native people of the continent, but at his core, George Washington was the quintessential un-Indian.

Both Washington and Jefferson believed that Indians could survive only if they changed their ways. They had to abandon their traditional culture and adopt the agrarian practices of white civilization (not that this did any good for the Moravians). The American leaders assigned to the Indians at least the theoretical possibility of becoming full-fledged members of Anglo-American society, a status they couldn't imagine for African-Americans. The Indians simply needed to be reengineered. They were like rivers: They could be improved!

Benjamin Franklin didn't agree. He was in Paris at this point, and had recently authored a short article on Indians that told of an exchange, possibly apocryphal, between Virginia leaders and representatives of the Six Nations at the treaty negotiations in Lancaster, Pennsylvania, back in 1744. The Virginians made a dramatic offer to educate six Indian youths at the College of William and Mary and bring them into the fold of white civilization. The speaker for the Six Nations responded politely—any other form of response would be unthinkable from an Indian chief—but he made it clear that his people were not interested in the white man's offer:

> Several of our young People were formerly brought up at the
> Colleges of the Northern Provinces; they were instructed in all

your Sciences; but, when they came back to us, they were bad Runners, ignorant of every means of living in the Woods, unable to bear either Cold or Hunger, knew neither how to build a Cabin, take a Deer, or kill an Enemy, spoke our Language imperfectly, were therefore neither fit for Hunters, Warriors, nor Counsellors; they were totally good for nothing. We are however not the less oblig'd by your kind Offer, tho' we decline accepting it; and, to show our grateful Sense of it, if the Gentlemen of Virginia will send us a Dozen of their Sons, we will take great Care of their Education, instruct them in all we know, and make Men of them.

The Indians were not a monolithic presence in the Ohio country, but rather a far more unpredictable factor in western travel and commerce. They had their own chaotic history in the region. In the mid-1600s the Iroquois, largely based to the north in what is now the state of New York, dealt a series of blows against the Algonquians who had been living between the Great Lakes and the Ohio River. As the Algonquians fled west, toward lands closer to the Mississippi, the Iroquois stayed primarily east of Lake Erie, and thus a vacuum appeared, an area of relatively low population, a "middle ground." Much of that forest in the upper Ohio River valley was virtually empty when the whites started to drift into the area. This helped create the more general illusion that America was a vast empty continent, that it just needed people to show up with their axes to start making it into something worthwhile.

In the mid-1700s, at the very time that European-Americans were starting to filter through the mountains from the east, groups of Indians began repopulating the area. It was hard to say who was truly "native" to this part of America. The Iroquois came from the north, and the Delawares and Shawnees came from the east. Along with other Indian groups, such as the Miamis and Mingos, they were collectively known among whites as "the Ohio Indians." In 1744—when Washington was on the cusp of adolescence—the Shawnees established

Logstown, which became the key trading center of the upper Ohio River. No single Indian group, however, dominated the region west of the mountains.

Indians were constantly menaced not only by white settlers and soldiers but also by "strange Indians." They formed alliances and confederations; the so-called Five Nations of the Iroquois (Cayuga, Oneida, Mohawk, Onondaga, Seneca) became the Six Nations in 1722 with the admission into the Confederacy of the Tuscarora, and gave some sense of a unified front during treaty negotiations. In general, however, the Indians kept their options open. "Indian policy" varied from village to village. In any general discussion such as this one, there is an inevitable tendency, out of convenience (if not intellectual laziness) to refer to "the Indians" as a single category of people. But they didn't think of themselves that way any more than a Swede considered himself the same thing as a Greek. Until they met white people, and learned of Columbus's mistake about where he had landed, the native peoples of the continent had no idea that they were "Indians." They had distinct languages, traditions, beliefs. They saw themselves as Hurons, Eries, Senecas, Caddos, Muskhogees, Susquehannocks, Piscataways, Sioux, Mohawks, Mingos, Chippewas, Potawatomis, Winnebagos, Menominees, Fox, Sauk, Illinois, Delawares, Shawnees, Miamis, and so on.

Whites and Indians were almost continuously engaged in commerce in the eastern region of the continent. Indians started wearing cloth instead of skins; they had access to iron, to firearms, to brass kettles. They had glass and silver, artifacts of personal wealth. Instead of hunting for subsistence, native peoples were more likely to stockpile furs and skins and sell them in bulk to European traders. Portions of the forest became overhunted. By the end of the Revolution the area around the Upper Ohio had a scant fraction of the deer and beaver of just a few decades earlier. The "wilderness" west of the Alleghenies had already been changed by historical events in which the Indians were active participants. The Indians weren't inert figures on the landscape. They weren't a bunch of cornstalks waiting to be blown over by the windstorm of European-American culture.

In 1763, at the close of the war with France, the British couldn't enforce the Proclamation Line that marked the western boundary of legal settlement. The war so taxed the British that they couldn't afford to monitor the western settlers, and at one point pulled back even from Fort Pitt, at the Forks of the Ohio. It was a free-for-all in the West. "By the 1770s, chaos reigned in the Ohio Valley, and aggressive opportunism was the rule," writes historian Eric Hinderaker.

The Indians for the most part held their ground until 1774, when the Virginia Regiment clashed with Shawnees, Delawares, Mingos, and their allies in the Battle of Point Pleasant, fought near the land, at the junction of the Great Kanawha and the Ohio, that George Washington had surveyed four years earlier. The Shawnee leader, Cornstalk, rallied his warriors with the cry "Be strong, be strong," but they were outnumbered and overwhelmed. It was the key engagement of what is known as Lord Dunmore's War, after the Virginia governor. (Today there is a historical pillar that informs the tourist that on this site "was fought the most important battle ever waged between the forces of civilization and of barbarism in America.")

Soon, settlers poured into Kentucky through the Cumberland Gap, and George Rogers Clark began waging his Indian wars in what is now Ohio, Indiana, and Illinois. But many Indians continued to press a fierce resistance. Washington received new evidence of the difficulty of western settlement when he tried to establish a small community of farmers and slaves on his Great Kanawha land. Washington had hoped that some of his people would eventually make their way back up the Ohio, to the Millers Run site, and improve that land, too, rather than leave it for the machinations of squatters. But the slaves tended to disappear into the forest, and the Great Kanawha community essentially evaporated.

The colonists warned the Indians not to join the British during the War of Independence, but many tribes didn't heed the advice. The Six Nations fractured: The Oneida and half the Tuscarora supported the Americans, while the rest supported the Crown. At the negotiation table in 1783 the British sold out their Indian allies. Although the British insisted to the Indians that they would not lose the western lands under the terms of the peace treaty, the Americans viewed the situation differently, claiming that the "right of conquest" gave them full sovereignty of the Ohio Territory. The Indians were aghast. They had not lost these lands in battle. Why should a Miami chief give up his hunting grounds simply because the British had been trapped and defeated in some obscure, distant place called Yorktown?

The Americans pressed their advantage, leaning on the most pliable Indian leaders to acknowledge the dominion of the United States. Feigning generosity, the Americans said they would let the Indians remain on portions of their traditional hunting grounds, but without sovereignty. The official policy of the Continental Congress was to make peace with the Indians as a matter of self-interest, with a dollop of morality thrown in as an afterthought. "Generosity, Clemency and Mercy ought to appear in the Transactions of the Grand Council of the United States with a people who live in a lamentable state of ignorance and error," stated a report on Indian affairs in the South, produced in Congress by Thomas Jefferson in May 1784.

For Washington the Indian claim to the West represented not so much a moral conundrum as an obstacle to easy and fluid commerce. Bad roads, few bridges, unreliable ferries, decrepit towns and taverns, hustlers, squatters—all these things made the West a difficult place, and to top it off there were all these . . . *savages.* The Washington plan for the West would be one of temporary mollification and permanent containment. He wanted the Indians respected, but only to a point. To Washington and the other leaders of the new nation, the Indians were a temporary hazard, like trees fallen across a river, or wolves. Washington believed the Americans had the right to expel the Indians beyond the Great Lakes, "but as we prefer Peace to a state of Warfare, as we consider them as a deluded People . . . we will . . . draw a veil over what is past and establish a boundary line between them and us beyond which we will *endeavor* to restrain our People from Hunting or Settling. . . ." He had no illusions on this score. Settlers would inevitably drive the Indians from the West. "[T]he gradual extension of our Settlements will as certainly cause the Savage as the Wolf to retire; both being beasts of prey tho' they differ in shape. In a word there is nothing to be obtained by an Indian War but the Soil they live on and this can be had by purchase at less expence. . . ."

The master plan was taking shape. This would become the realm of the white man. *Westward the course of empire takes its way.*

*   *   *

HE RODE SOUTH AGAIN, back toward Gilbert Simpson's, and along the way received assurances from some of the local gentry that they would hunt up more documentation of his ownership of the Millers Run land. The next day he rode south to Beeson's Town (now Uniontown, Pa.), where he found himself a good lawyer. In fact, he found a great one: Thomas Smith, a Scotsman who had emigrated to America and had become one of the leading land lawyers in the state, a kind of traveling salesman of legal services. In a single year, by Smith's calculation, he'd ridden 4,000 miles on horseback, all over the craggy Pennsylvania terrain. He'd seen a lot of different characters in his day, and when George Washington came calling, Smith had to use all his legal and psychological skill to guide the case toward a positive outcome.

Washington was almost too eager to sue. He had steam coming out of his ears. Had it not violated his maxims on personal deportment, he would have been literally hopping mad. But Smith quickly detected the shortage of documentation behind Washington's claim. This would not be an easy case.

The general told Smith he'd return to western Pennsylvania to testify against the squatters, but he knew it would be no minor matter to make yet another trip over the mountains. Events might easily detain him elsewhere. This was only the second time since 1758 that he'd managed to venture to the West. He might never see this part of the world again.

While in Beeson's Town, Washington met a certain Captain Hardin, an accomplished Indian fighter who had served with William Crawford and who would someday himself be on the wrong end of a tomahawk. In his diary Washington turned enthusiastic again:

At Beason Town I met with Captn. Hardin who informed me, as I had before been informed by others, that the West fork of Monongahela communicates very nearly with the waters of the little Kanhawa—that the Portage does not exceed Nine Miles and that a very good Waggon Road may be had between—That from the Mouth of the River Cheat to that of the West Fork, is computed to be about 30 Miles, & the Navigation good—as it also is up the West fork. . . .

And so on. The geography buff had returned to his element. Forget squatters, what about rivers and portages?

It appears that the conversation with Hardin got Washington's juices flowing again, for he decided suddenly that he wouldn't go home after all. Nor would he head west. He would simply explore. He would go off-road, into the backcountry of the backcountry, to places even an old woodsman like himself had never been. He'd go where there were no people.

He put much of his baggage in the care of Dr. Craik, who along with his son headed back east, toward the Shenandoah Valley. The general, load lightened, and accompanied now by his nephew Bushrod and their servants, set an entirely new course, this one south, into the Virginia backwoods, the region drained by the Monongahela, Cheat, and Youghiogheny rivers, west of the Allegheny Ridge. He intended to visit a survey office where he thought he might find a document proving his title to the disputed Millers Run land (Smith had made it clear that some additional paperwork would be quite helpful to the general's cause). He also wanted to reinvigorate his search for the best portage between the Potomac and the Ohio headwaters.

On September 23 the general rode to the mouth of the Cheat, where it flows into the Monongahela, near present-day Morgantown, West Virginia. Local officials frantically apologized for not having prepared a formal address and homage, but at this point Washington cared only for rivers, roads, the data of the American landscape. The Cheat looked to him a rather fine river, more navigable than he'd expected: "[T]he Cheat River had been passed with Canoes thro' those parts which had been represented as impassable."

After staying at the home of a Colonel Phillips, Washington on the morning of the twenty-fourth forded the Cheat. His description of the confluence of the two rivers is striking:

> The colour of the two Waters is very differt., that of Cheat is dark (occasioned as is conjectured by the Laurel, among which it rises; and through which it runs). The other is clear; & there appears a repugnancy in both to mix, as there is a plain line of division betwn. the two for some distance below the fork. . . .

He went to the surveyor's office but could find no record of his purchases of the Millers Run land.

It so happened that in these very woods a young man of great destiny had spent the year surveying property. His name was Albert Gallatin. He was twenty-three years old, small and birdlike, one of those unprepossessing little men, in the mold of James Madison, who would become giants on the American landscape. Gallatin had only recently immigrated to western Pennsylvania from Switzerland (had he been born in America, he might well have become president). He had no way of knowing that a river in Montana would someday bear his name, especially since no man of his society had ever heard of a place called Montana. For now he was speculating in land and trying to establish a store in southern Pennsylvania.

As Gallatin later recounted, Washington and his nephew arrived at the office of a land agent, a cabin 14 feet square, where Gallatin and a number of backwoods surveyors and hunters had been awaiting the great man. The confined space forced everyone to stand, except the general, who sat at a pine table and methodically recorded everything he learned about possible routes for a road across the Alleghenies. Gallatin stood near the table and listened attentively, growing increasingly frustrated at what seemed to be the obtuseness of the old man. The general seemed so indecisive! Finally, Gallatin did something unthinkable: He interrupted George Washington.

"Oh, it is plain enough," he said, and cited a specific route that would be "the most practicable."

Everyone turned and stared. Washington lay down his pen, and looked up from his paper.

He glared at the pipsqueak, and neither said a word.

Then the general went back to the work of grown men, interrogating the visitors. After a few minutes he suddenly dropped his pen and turned to Gallatin.

"You are right, sir," the general said.

The lad had figured it out! There was a logical, obvious place for a road, and although the general was not about to pay him any more compliments, he did have an obligation to acknowledge the young man's accuracy. *You are right, sir.*

* * *

BY THIS POINT the general was fully in the throes of a geography frenzy, his brain whirring with data. In his diary he set down his new intelligence, part of a scheme for a portage between the eastern and western waters:

> That from the fork of Monongahela & Cheat, to the Court House at Morgan Town, is, by Water, about 11 Miles, & from thence to the West fork of the former is 18 More. From thence to the carrying place [land portage] between it and a branch of the little Kanhawa, at a place called Bullstown, is about 40 Miles, by Land—more by Water and the Navigation good.

From Morgan Town, Washington had to figure out where to go next. The route to the south was impassable with briers, the path "very blind." He couldn't follow the Cheat upstream, which would take him in the right direction, because the river had carved a deep and forbidding gorge. He decided to go along a new road and find McCulloch's Path, an old bison trail that he'd been told about way back in Bath. This meant going east and then southeast through the forest and across the accurately named Briery Mountain. He left Morgan Town before dawn.

Washington and his nephew came again to the Cheat and crossed on a ferry kept by a man named Ice. He drained Ice of information about the river, which, though not as large as the Monongahela, had the virtue of being farther east. Looking at a map, and reading left to right (west to east), one sees three major tributaries of the Ohio that flow from the south: the Monongahela, the Cheat, and the Youghiogheny. The Yock is the closest to the Potomac, but Washington knew that it had a major set of falls in southern Pennsylvania and other rapids and riffles that could destroy a boat. The Monongahela was deep and navigable but just a bit too far of a hike from the Potomac. So Washington kept a close eye on the middle of the three, the Cheat.

Large rocks "choak the river," Washington wrote in his diary. There were three sets of rapids. Nonetheless, Ice claimed to have passed down the river in both rafts and canoes, and Washington, buoyant, declared that it would surely be possible to open navigation on the Cheat.

He traveled up a gradual slope, ascending Laurel Hill, the westernmost major mountain of the Alleghenies. The path grew rockier in the white oak forest atop the mountain. On the downslope it improved a bit, and 15 miles after he left Ice's Ferry the general found himself at the home of James Spurgeon, on the banks of Sandy Creek. There was no ferry here, just a ford. Beyond, he found McCulloch's Path—"which owes it origen to Buffaloes, being no other than their tracks from one lick to another & consequently crooked & not well chosen. . . ."

He rode on, southeast, into higher country and gloomier forest. Eventually he met a man named Lemon, who agreed to be his guide. They plunged into what seemed to be an absolute wilderness. The woods were every bit as dark as the Shades of Death on the old Braddock Road, the only difference being that they were more remote, and not yet blessed with such a formal, frightening name.

He crossed Briery Mountain. He'd reached the high country, the land rocky, steep, the path "intolerable," yet even as he recorded this harsh judgment in his diary, he immediately added, with the pluck of the eternal optimist, that these ascents and descents "might be eased, & a much better way found if a little pains was taken to slant them."

Switchbacks: That's all this path needed.

The general and his nephew and their guide Lemon soon found themselves on the edge of a glade. There was not a house for miles, not another living soul as far as they knew.

A storm blew in.

Where was the general's tent? Gone, sent ahead with Craik a few days earlier. His diary entry is a classic: "At the entrance of the above glades I lodged this night, with no other shelter or cover than my cloak; & was unlucky enough to have a heavy shower of Rain. Our horses were also turned loose to cator for themselves having nothing to give them."

The most powerful man in the nation, the greatest American, the hero of the Revolution, huddled on the ground under his cloak in a pelting September rain. As when he fell in the freezing Allegheny those many decades earlier, he did not dwell on personal discomfort. In reporting the fact of his soggy night, the general added yet another bit of data to his burgeoning file: "It may not be amiss to observe," he wrote, "that Sandy Creek has a fall within a few miles of its mouth of 40 feet, & being rapid besides, affords no navigation at all."

And so he went to sleep, thinking of geography.

*   *   *

THE SITUATION did not improve the next morning. The path remained an atrocity. Vines grabbed at the travelers, mud sucked at the hoofs of their mounts. The rain continued to fall. The general registered a rare complaint:

> Having found our Horses readily (for they nevr. lost sight of our fire) we started at the dawning of day, and passing along a small path much enclosed with weeds and bushes, loaded with water from the overnights rain, & the showers which were continually falling, we had an uncomfortable travel to one Charles Friends,

about 10 Miles; where we could get nothing for our horses, and only boiled Corn for ourselves.

(Even in this rare expression of discontent, he did not go so far as to write "I was hungry.")

Somehow, he still saw wondrous possibilities for a road through this land. The ground, he wrote, "would admit an exceeding good Waggon road with a little causeying of some parts of the Glades; the ridges between being chiefly white oak land, intermixed with grit & Stone."

There were a few German families living in the glades, which he noted were already suffering frost in the morning, though it was not yet the end of September. He saw walnut trees and crab apples amid the oaks, and small streams meandering across the uneven terrain. He came to the Youghiogheny, which was about 25 yards wide. He was now in western Maryland, on land owned by the governor. The Yock flowed north, tumbling, with a series of rapids and falls, and Charles Friend, a squatter and hunter who had lived in the area for two decades, assured the general that the river could not be navigated by any kind of vessel carrying cargo. Washington didn't believe him. "[T]hese difficulties, in the eyes of a proper examiner might be found altogether imaginary," the general wrote. If you look at a problem with the right attitude, it might disappear.

Friend opined that perhaps it would be possible to build a road across his land between the North Branch of the Potomac, near the place where McCulloch's Path crossed it, and a place called Dunkard's Bottom, on the Cheat River. The road would be only 22 miles long. The general liked that idea. He proceeded to Archy's Spring, 3 miles away. From the spring he crossed Backbone Mountain, the divide between the western and eastern waters, and reached Ryan's Glade. The spring and the glade were a scant two miles apart—Washington estimated 1.5 miles—but one was in the watershed of the Ohio (and thus the Mississippi), the other in the watershed of the Potomac. The roads ranged from bad to very bad to, as Washington put it, "infamous."

The general now reached the Potomac again, high up the river from Fort Cumberland, where not a soul could be found other than a hunter, Joseph Logston. Logston told Washington that a road from the Potomac to Dunkard's Bottom would not be 22 miles long, but merely 20—if, that is, the general would blaze it across the high country a couple of miles to the east of Mr. Friend's property. Washington by now had become savvy about the ulterior motives of his informants. "[T]heir accts. are to be received with great caution," he wrote. The roads in this part of the world "seem calculated more to promote individual interest, than the public good."

The next day, September 27, Washington and his companions traveled from dawn to dusk, 35 miles on horrible roads in a still-pounding rain, the brush threatening to swallow them at every turn. They rode from the North Branch of the Potomac on a generally southeast trajectory, up and across one mountain, and down a "very steep and bad" road to a major Potomac tributary called Patterson's Creek. They crossed that creek, then another creek, then climbed another mountain, steadily moving onward in a realm where the danger of being slowed down by public tributes and fanfare was nonexistent. They were in a region that had scarcely a privy, much less a tavern or public house. They rode all the way to the South Branch of the Potomac, fully 35 miles from their starting point on the North Branch, perhaps the most vigorous display of horsemanship on what had already been quite the backcountry ramble. There, at the home of Colonel Abraham Hite, they rested, utterly drained.

> Remained at Colo. Hite's all day to refresh myself and rest my Horses, having had a very fatieguing journey thro' the Mountains, occasioned not more from the want of accomodation & the real necessaries of life than the showers of Rain which were continually falling & wetting the bushes—the passing of which, under these circumstances was very little better than swimming of rivulets.

From here Washington had originally planned to shoot straight across the mountains to the Shenandoah Valley, where he hoped to rendezvous with Craik and all his baggage, but he changed his mind again. He'd heard that, with only an extra day's ride, he could detour to the south, into even more remote country, eventually reaching Staunton, Virginia, where he believed a land agent might have documents that would help him in his legal battle against the Seceders. The detour would mean going through a region that even two centuries later is still rugged and undeveloped, so far from a city that radio astronomers have chosen it for the construction of huge telescopes that listen to the stars. It's so far in the boondocks, the only radio waves come from outer space.

Washington now dismantled the last remnant of his original traveling party. He sent Bushrod to meet with Craik, and took off instead with the son of Colonel Hite. They rode up the South Branch for 24 miles, found someone ("Rudiborts") to give them a meal, and then headed to higher terrain, scrambling along a "very confined and rocky path" that followed a tumbling stream. They reached another mountaintop and clomped down the other side, where, after 36 miles of tough travel, they found refuge in a private home, the general retaining enough energy to record all the pertinent geographical facts of the day.

The next day the younger Hite went home, and Washington resumed his backcountry trek, still deep in the mountains and heading east toward the Shenandoah Valley. For a guide he had only the sun, moon, and stars, and his own residual memory of the texture of the Virginia mountains and the directions of the rivers. He had zigzagged his way to exquisite isolation. The diary mentions no servants or any other traveling companions (though it is possible and perhaps likely that he retained at least one servant). Twice before in this journey he had ridden either alone or with a pared-down retinue of a single servant, but then he had been on familiar, well-trod routes. Now he was in the middle of nowhere. So much of his life had been lived under the gaze of others, his every word carefully regarded, his clothes scrutinized, his expression interpreted, but out here, in the remote Virginia woods, he did not have to perform for anyone, didn't have to worry about a violation of one of his maxims. For the moment, Washington had escaped the demands and pressures of being the singular public figure in a nation poised to become an empire. He had won his freedom.

He rode for 40 miles, and spent the night in another private home. The following day he conferred with a one-eyed country lawyer named Gabriel Jones, well known in the Shenandoah Valley, full of geographical wisdom. They talked about the Potomac, the Yock, the Cheat, the James, the Great Kanawha, about cataracts that are not quite the same thing as a "perpendicular tumble," about rivers "closely confined between rugged hills," about the navigational implications of, as Washington put it, "the ascension of the Fish."

The day after, having met with the Staunton land agent about the Seceders suit, Washington started back to the northeast, crossing the Blue Ridge and pausing for a meal at what he bluntly called a "pitiful house." But then he was hospitably entertained, he wrote, at the home of a certain Widow Yearlys. He was now in the Piedmont, getting close to his home turf, but the roads had decayed during the war, and after all those days in the mountains he managed out here in the rolling farm country to get lost, not once but twice, going many miles out of his way and finally seeking shelter with a certain Captain John Ashby. The final morning of the trip, October 4, he ate breakfast by candlelight as the rain continued to fall, and, with Ashby guiding him on intricate roads weaving through the fields of Fauquier and Prince William counties, crossed the final 30 miles to Mount Vernon.

Washington had been gone thirty-four days and had traveled, by his precise calculation, 680 miles. He was bursting with enthusiasm. Everything he believed about the Potomac had turned out to be true!

"The more then the Navigation of Potomack is investigated, & duely considered," wrote the man who had seen almost nothing but rapids, rocks, low-life squatters, land-jobbers, speculators, broken-down taverns, boggy roads, gloomy forests, and nearly impossible portages, "the greater the advantages arising from them appear."

7

Skirting the Falls

WASHINGTON HAD BEEN SCRIBBLING in his little leather-bound notebooks for the past five weeks, often by candlelight, amid interruptions and the logistical vexations of backcountry travel, but now, in the comfort of his study, he could sit at a proper desk and describe precisely what he'd seen. For years he'd been talking to friends and comrades (perhaps to the point of tediousness) about the Potomac, the West, the problems with the weak national government, the importance of binding together the fragments of the Union, and so on, and now, energized by his trip, he decided to put it all down on paper. This wouldn't be just a dissertation on the Potomac, packed with geographic data. He would include a broad assessment of the destiny of Revolutionary America. This would be the ultimate synthesis of his grand idea.

In the decades to come, as historians pored over his papers, this particular document—a long diary entry for October 4, 1784, with no particular title—would never get quite the attention that it deserved. It surely was not as significant as his Farewell Address of 1796, but it was more purely Washingtonian, a clearer glimpse into the workings of his mind. The document doesn't have anyone else's fingerprints on it (as is the case of the Farewell Address, drafted in part by James Madison and Alexander Hamilton).

Washington declared that almost every significant tributary in the Potomac basin could be rendered navigable. Weeks of fresh air had returned him a Potomac booster. (Melancholic? Thinking of an early death? That Washington vanished somewhere out in the mountains.) The Shenandoah was navigable upstream from the Potomac for 150 miles, he wrote; the South Branch of the Potomac was navigable, with minor effort, 90 miles upstream from the confluence with the North Branch near Old Town. Patterson's Creek, the Cacapon River, and Opequon Creek were all "more or less Navigable." The rivers flowing north into the main branch of the Potomac could provide navigation for an immense area between the Blue Ridge and the Allegheny Plateau—the entire Ridge and Valley Province—but even that area, Washington wrote, trilling with enthusiasm, is "trifling when viewed upon that immeasurable scale which is inviting our attention!"

Anyone looking at a map could see that there was a relatively simple portage between the eastern and western waters: A road could be built between the Potomac and one of the western rivers. In fact, such roads already existed—Braddock's Road, the route of the fatal campaign, was such a land portage. But Washington had to deal with the annoying political considerations, all the Pennsylvania-versus-Virginia problems. Braddock's Road crossed state lines, and was surely not the shortest route between the Potomac and the Ohio tributaries. He came up with an exceedingly elaborate scheme, one that only a man freshly oxygenated and adrenalized by travel could possibly entertain.

Start with some cargo on the Ohio River. Take it up the Little Kanawha, heading southeast into Virginia. At Bulls Town, carry that cargo over land for 9.5 miles to the west fork of the Monongahela. Float it downstream, to the junction with the Cheat. Take it back up the Cheat (south), to Dunkard's Bottom. Haul it by portage road over the mountains, through the Allegheny highlands, to the North Branch of the Potomac. Float it down the Potomac to tidewater. That would work, in Washington's mind. Ohio River cargo could easily roll into the holds of oceangoing ships docked at Alexandria, Virginia.

In fact, such a route might even connect Alexandria to the Great Lakes. Washington envisioned cargo carried from Detroit to Lake Erie and on to the mouth of the Cuyahoga, then 54 miles up that river, across a short land portage to the Muskingum River, down that river 192 miles to the Ohio, back up the Ohio for 12 miles to the Little Kanawha, up the Little Kanawha—and so on, across hill and dale, from river to river, eventually reaching Alexandria after a journey of, he calculated, precisely 799 miles.

By his reckoning, the Potomac Route was clearly the best corridor to the West. This was not something he had deduced from looking at the backcountry maps of Thomas Hutchins or Lewis Evans—he'd seen it with his own eyes. He'd gathered the data personally. This was not rumor and speculation and self-interested hype. He wasn't Jefferson, speaking Olympian verities about the West without ever bothering to go there.

Washington, still writing furiously, turned to the larger political issue, the reason that his scheme had national significance:

> No well informed Mind need be told, that the flanks and rear of the United territory are possessed by other powers, and formidable ones too—nor how necessary it is to apply the cement of interest to bind all parts of it together, by one indissolvable band—particularly the Middle States with the Country immediately back of them. For what ties let me ask, should we have upon those people; and how entirely unconnected [would] we be with them if the Spaniards on their right, or Great Britain on their left, instead of throwing stumbling blocks in their way as they now do, should envite their trade and seek alliances with them? . . .
>
> The Western Settlers—from my own observation—stand as it were on a pivet—the touch of a feather would almost incline them any way.

This last is an oft-quoted line, and it is vintage Washington. He worries about the intrigues of other parties. He smells schemes and betrayals in the offing. He trusts the settlers only as far as one of his servants can throw them. The slightest puff of wind from Spanish or British intriguers could separate the West from the East. If that happened, the United States would never become the continental empire that Washington thought it could be. It would be a quaint Atlantic seaboard republic. It might someday be dwarfed and dominated by whatever great nation arose in the Mississippi Valley. The United States might become the North American equivalent of the Low Countries.

This was hardly paranoia. The general was onto a powerful fact of American life: Many people didn't consider themselves Americans. Many of them truly weren't: They were from somewhere else, far away, and had never paused long enough in the eastern United States to feel connected to those who called themselves patriots.

One passage in this treatise jumps out when viewed in the context of what happened nearly eight decades later. When Washington insisted that the country had a particular need to bind "the Middle States with the Country immediately back of them," he showed not only his provincial thinking (for this was the terrain he'd spent much of his life traversing) but also his latitudinal orientation. His eyes read a map from east to west. He thought horizontally. He viewed the East-West political divisions (particularly those more or less along the 40th parallel) as the most threatening to the Union. He had little interest in the migration of Georgia farmers into Choctaw country, for example. As if by reflex, he tended to look more or less due west from Mount Vernon. The need for connections, for the cement of interest, between North and South did not seem to trouble him particularly. And in truth, the North and South already had a fantastic transportation link: the Atlantic Ocean. The lack of good overland routes between North and South would persist for the better part of a century.

In writing his Potomac treatise Washington deftly combined his personal interests with loftier national goals. The imperatives of the

Union effectively carpeted the underlying pecuniary motives. This virtually absolved him of any charge of self-interest. Who could argue with his central point? The nation needed massive amounts of that cement of interest, great globs of it all over the map. Benjamin Franklin had tried as far back as 1754 to put together a functioning Union, and the Articles of Confederation had made the Union a paper reality, but no one truly believed that the states were bound inextricably. Sectional rivalries and talk of secession would dominate politics in the decades to come. Washington realized, quite correctly, that the country might split asunder—West from East.

*   *   *

IN THE ENSUING months, Washington aimed his considerable powers of persuasion at his friends and fellow patriots. To Virginia's governor, Benjamin Harrison, he sent a more polished version of his treatise, suggesting that support for the Potomac plan would make Harrison's administration one of the most important in the annals of American history. To Jacob Read he opined that if the westerners formed connections with the Spanish or British, they'd become "as unconnected with us, indeed more so, than we are with South America." To Secretary of War Henry Knox he warned that the westerners might "become a distinct people from us—have different views—different interests, & instead of adding strength to the Union, may in case of a rupture with either of those powers, be a formidable & dangerous neighbour."

The general tried to communicate both the tantalizing possibilities of "what we might be"—a great and powerful nation—and the realistic facts about human nature. He offered James Madison the distillation of his economic philosophy: "[T]he motives which predominate most in human affairs [are] self-love and self-interest."

Washington didn't want anyone to perceive that he had provincial or personal interests in mind, and so he made clear that he didn't oppose river-improvement efforts in Pennsylvania and New York. The more connections to the West, the better, Washington assured

George Plater, president of the Maryland Senate. But he said the geo-graphical facts shouldn't be ignored. "[A]ll I would be understood to mean therefore is, that the gifts of Providence not be neglected, or slighted," Washington wrote. To fail to improve the Potomac corri-dor—obviously the best route to the West—would be tantamount to insulting the Supreme Architect of the Universe.

As he sought support for his plan, he ignored the Continental Con-gress, which continued to show only a feeble pulse, and which he re-ferred to as "a half starved, limping Government, that appears to be always moving upon crutches, & tottering at every step." Washington traveled to Richmond, to meet Lafayette and lobby members of the Virginia House of Delegates, including James Madison. He wanted the Virginia delegates to charter a private stock company that would raise money for improving the river. It would be what is now referred to as a public-private partnership. The state would throw in a chunk of money and let private citizens pay for the rest.

As always, provincial interests complicated the process. The dele-gates from central Virginia could not bear to see the James River ig-nored. The legislators decided to compromise, and fund two separate river-improvement companies, one for the Potomac and one for the James.

To honor the war hero the delegates awarded shares in both compa-nies to Washington, a decision that gave him sleepless nights. The general had a number of core principles, and one of them was that he didn't take public money, other than expenses. This was an essential element of the Great Man Plan. He had vowed to "shut my hand against every pecuniary recompense." The slightest misstep would in-vite his political enemies, particularly the ones abroad who viewed the entire American project dimly, to accuse him of self-enrichment. But neither did he want to make an "ostentatious display of disinterested-ness," Washington told Jefferson. Jefferson, gentle, diplomatic, was nonetheless firm: Washington had to decline the shares. Washington, not wanting to offend the legislators, decided to accept the shares, but said he would eventually donate them to a college (as, in fact, he ulti-mately did).

Support grew for the Potomac plan. On December 2, 1784, an anonymous article appeared in the *Maryland Gazette*, published in Annapolis. Penned in Alexandria, it could have easily come from Washington's publicist if such a creature had existed. Or perhaps the general himself was the author—it certainly has his touch:

> The opening of the navigation of Patowmack is, perhaps, a work of more political than commercial consequence, as it will be one of the grandest chains for preserving the federal Union. The western world [beyond the mountains] will have free access to us, and we shall be one and the same people, whatever system of European politics may be adopted. In short, it is a work so big, that the intellectual faculties cannot take it at a view.

Mind-blowing stuff. To make this noble project all the more enticing, it would also make everyone rich: "The commerce and riches, that must of necessity pour down upon us, are too obvious to mention."

(Note the echo of Washington's 1770 letter to the governor of Maryland, cited in Chapter 2, in which he talks of "a tract of country which is unfolding to our view, the advantages of which are too great and too obvious, I should think to become the subject of serious debate. . . .")

Lafayette, meanwhile, had to return to France. Washington rode with his friend to Annapolis. Washington let down his guard and admitted to himself, and to Lafayette, how difficult it was to say farewell. The reader can become frustrated with Washington's bland farm narratives and strangely impersonal travelogues, but there are moments when he suddenly turns flesh, when his heart beats as does that of any other man. There is genuine anguish in the letter he sent Lafayette a week after his departure:

> I often asked myself . . . whether that was the last sight, I ever should have of you? And tho' I wished to say no—my fears answered yes. I called to mind the days of my youth, & found they had long since fled to return no more; that I was now descending the hill, I had been 52 years climbing—& that tho' I was blessed

with a good constitution, I was of a short lived family—and
might soon expect to be entombed in the dreary mansions of my
father's—These things darkened the shades & gave a gloom to
the picture, consequently to my prospects of seeing you again.

The dreary mansions of my father's. The gloom had descended
with winter. The next, heartbreaking line of the letter might have
come from an 80-year-old man: ". . . but I will not repine—I have had
my day."

*   *   *

THE GENERAL must have slapped himself a few times, and pulled
himself together, for he continued to promote the Potomac project,
journeying to Annapolis shortly before Christmas. This time he
needed to get the Maryland legislators signed onto the plan. None of
his fellow Virginians came with him, and Washington felt the entire
project on his shoulders. On December 28 he reported to Madison, "It
is now near 12 at night, and I am writing with an Aching head, having
been constantly employed in this business since the 22nd without assistance from my Colleagues."

Despite the usual reservations from Baltimore merchants, Maryland officials this time affirmed the charter. Now he had the two
key states backing the Potomac project. A visitor to Mount Vernon,
expecting to hear tales of the Revolution, reported, "He modestly
waived all allusions to the events, in which he had acted so glorious
and conspicuous a part. Much of his conversation had reference to the
interior country, and to the opening of the navigation of the Potomac. . . ." (A guest expects Yorktown or Valley Forge or the crossing
of the Delaware, and instead gets something called the "Youghiogheny.")

When Robert Hunter, Jr., son of a Scottish merchant, visited in
1785, he had the good luck of arriving with one of Washington's old
friends, Richard Henry Lee, whose presence inspired the general to
launch into a long talk about the river:

The General sent the bottle about pretty freely after dinner, and gave success to the navigation of the Potomac for his toast, which he has very much [at] heart, and when finished will, I supposed, be the first river in the world. . . . He is quite pleased at the idea of the Baltimore merchants laughing at him and saying it was a ridiculous plan and would never succeed. They begin now, says the General, to look a little serious about the matter, as they know it must hurt their commerce amazingly.

The general had become a Potomac navigation *bore.* He seems to have approached his Potomac plan with every bit of the psychic energy that he had employed during the war. James Madison wrote Jefferson: "The earnestness with which he espouses the undertaking is hardly to be described, and shows that a mind like his, capable of grand views and which has long been occupied with them, cannot bear a vacancy."

*　　　*　　　*

IN MAY 1785, George Washington became president of the "Patowmack Company." The company's charter required it to create a navigable channel in the river at least 1 foot deep throughout the year. Washington was, in effect, chairman, president, CEO, business manager, personnel director, design consultant, chief spokesman, and in-house canoeist.

He would draw a nominal salary of 30 shillings a year. He didn't really have enough time to devote to the job, and worse, he didn't have the expertise, however much he tried to think like an engineer. But he had the vision, and any enterprise in America in 1785 would be pleased to have, as its chief visionary, General George Washington.

Serious money poured into the Patowmack Company coffers, and fed other entrepreneurial ventures along the river. Near the mouth of the Monocacy, a Patowmack Company investor, John Frederick Amelung, built a glassworks called New Bremen, after his hometown in Germany, and a colony of workers sprang up on the bank of the Potomac. The New Bremen glassworks, as Frederick Gutheim reported in his classic book *The Potomac* (published in 1949 as part of the Rivers of America series), produced the best glass in America, lots of it, from window glass to bottles to jelly jars to mirrors to goblets. Amelung built himself a twenty-two-room mansion called Mountvina. Never mind that the business would collapse in a decade and cows would soon be grazing in what had been the formal gardens of the mansion—for the moment the Potomac was the place to be.

By late spring of 1785, the Patowmack Company had sold 403 shares of stock, raising 40,300 pounds. Washington himself invested 2,400 pounds. He had an entrepreneur's certainty of financial success, writing to Lafayette that, if he could, he'd sink all of his money into shares of stock in the two river companies: "[M]en who can afford to lay a little while out of their money, are laying the foundation of the greatest returns of any speculation I know of in the world." To George Plater he wrote: "To describe the usefulness of water transportation, would be a mere waste of time. [E]very man who has considered the difference of expence between it, & land transportation, and the prodigeous saving in the article of draught cattle, requires no arguments in proof of it."

In America, no one knew how to build canals. Did they need locks? Stephen Sayre, one of Washington's correspondents, said no: "[N]othing is more practicable than a good, safe, & convenient navigation thro the great & Little Falls, without a *single Lock*—to my understanding, all Idea of Locks ought to be renounced & exploded forever." But Washington and his fellow directors of the company—George Gilpin, John Fitzgerald, Thomas Lee, and Thomas Johnson—wanted canals with locks.

They decided to hire two teams of men, each 50 strong, one to work on the lower stretches of the river, between Harpers Ferry and Great Falls, and the other to work on the upper river, from Harpers Ferry upstream as far as navigation could possibly proceed. The directors declared that they would pay "liberal wages with provisions and a reasonable quantity of spirits." This would later be detailed: Three gills of rum a day. The men would be given abundant salt pork, salt beef, and fresh beef or mutton. Men acquainted with explosives were eagerly sought: "Encouragement will be given such as are dextrous in boring and blowing Rocks."

Washington couldn't find anyone with experience in building canals. Advertisements in Baltimore and Philadelphia newspapers failed to turn up a qualified engineer. In July, desperate, the general turned to that interesting character he had met back in Bath, the guy with the magic boat—James Rumsey.

Rumsey had continued to improve his current-defying boat, but the magic seemed to work only in a miniature format, as a tiny model in a creek. When he put a full-scale boat in a real river, the craft lurched and yawed and bucked and tilted as the poles alternately jammed into and then slipped on the river bottom. But Rumsey began developing a new idea: steamboats. Steam had already been harnessed in England to power machines used in mining. Before Rumsey could make much progress on a steamboat, Washington lured him away to work on the Potomac project.

The Patowmack Company appointed Rumsey "principle superintendent," at an annual salary of 200 pounds. He quickly dispatched laborers to three places: Shenandoah Falls, next to Harpers Ferry; Seneca, a set of rapids, roughly halfway between Harpers Ferry and Georgetown; and Great Falls. The first two sites were challenging; the last, with its 87-foot fall, was daunting. But Rumsey was not a man to back down from a difficult, or even an impossible, assignment.

*   *   *

ON AUGUST 1, 1785, Washington took another trip up the river, a shorter one. The general and the other directors of the Patowmack Company, after meeting in Georgetown, ascended the river to inspect the ongoing work at Seneca and Harpers Ferry.

On the third day of the journey Washington found himself in a canoe, bumping his way through the rapids at Seneca. The river was

wide in this section, several hundred yards from bank to bank. He canoed 4 miles downriver and 4 miles back, by his estimate. "The principle difficulties lye in rocks which occasion a crooked passage," he
wrote. One option would be to use a skirting canal, for there was, in
fact, a natural channel along the Virginia bank, but Washington at this
time wanted to keep the navigable channel right in the middle of the
wide river. The side channel, he believed, "would probably be frequently choked with drift wood, Ice, and other rubbish." A channel in
the middle of the river, he reckoned, would be self-clearing, thanks to
the current. Obviously, there could be no towpath if the channel were
so far from the bank, but there could be chains, anchored to rocks, and
floated with buoys, with which boatmen could haul themselves up the
river.

He went canoeing again on the seventh, this time at Harpers Ferry,
through what is known as Shenandoah Falls, a rather more violent
and longer cataract than the one at Seneca, "greatly incommoded with
rocks, shallows and a crooked channel," in Washington's words. Washington, Colonel Gilpin, and Rumsey descended the river by canoe
with full intention of running the "Spout," a chute about half a mile
below Harpers Ferry, but handwringers on shore (unaware, perhaps,
that Washington could not be killed) persuaded them to try a safer
channel to the left. Several miles downstream, Washington and his
fellow directors held a council and decided that, once again, they could
make the river navigable without locks.

But company records in the National Archives reveal Washington's
doubts. At one point he wrote: "The President and Directors have no
doubt could they personally attend the work in its progress and see
the River at those places in its different Situations they might in
many Instances depart from their present Opinions."

The river had many "different Situations." Just as Washington
knew, as a veteran Potomac observer, how easily a side channel might
become choked with drift logs after a flood or become a craggy landscape of ice after a few cold days, he also knew that almost any stretch
of the river changed from week to week, that the whole thing was

wondrously mutable. The river was not a static player in the drama. The Potomac's latitude is one of sharply fluctuating temperatures and precipitation, and a blizzard, depositing two feet of snow on frozen ground as hard as marble, might be followed suddenly by a 60-degree day and yet more rain, a perfect recipe for a flood. One morning the river will be shrouded in fog; another morning a freezing rain will render every surface treacherous. Drought is routine. Ledges of rock will suddenly jut across what had seemed to be a navigable stretch of river. The paddler has to be on constant alert for the Potomac's latest surprise. When Washington said the river didn't need locks at Shenandoah Falls, he had to interject a note of doubt. He knew better than most people that the Potomac was many different rivers inhabiting the same valley at different times of the year.

On August 9, Washington and two of his colleagues, Gilpin and Fitzgerald, canoed through the treacherous Spout and down the river for 25 miles. The general once again saw a congenial river, amenable to improvements that would require only moderate exertions. There seemed to be enough water in the river, and the surface was generally smooth. There were a few ripples here and there. The big problem was the fish dams, the "Fish pots," as he put it—stones placed on the riverbottom to funnel fish toward a central chute, where they could be easily caught.

Washington arrived home after ten days. Reading his diaries, we detect that his energy starts to dissipate. He becomes old again, sad again. One senses that, in surveying the river, running the rapids, plotting to change the geology bequeathed to the United States, he felt exhilarated, but perhaps he also saw how slow and difficult would be the imposition of order upon an unruly natural world. And then, coming home, he found a dry, barren landscape, parched by drought. His mood plummeted.

"In a word nature," he wrote, "had put on a melancholy look—every thing seeming to droop."

*   *   *

THE COMPANY DIRECTORS gave wide discretion to Rumsey, but Rumsey, for all his ingenuity and zeal, did not know how to smooth out a river. He hired ex-convicts just off the boat from England, and they drank oceans of rum. Rumsey had to figure out how to tame the Potomac with a crew of rapscallions and drunks. During a company meeting in September 1785 in Alexandria, Washington somberly reported that the workers employed in the opening of navigation of the Potomac "are irregular and disorderly in their Behavior." The board, desperate for good laborers, decided to hire slaves (compensating their masters) and indentured servants. The labor of such men, opined Thomas Johnson, "will be more valuable than that of common white Hirelings."

Indentured white servants had been an important source of labor in the South since the early days of the Virginia Colony. These men were not so oppressed as slaves, but they could not come and go as they pleased, and were fated to spend years serving out their indentures in conditions that could be cruel and degrading. Some chose to run away. William Fee, an Irishman working for the Patowmack Company, took flight, only to be captured. To punish him his supervisors shaved his eyebrows and cropped his hair on top in the shape of a cross.

The work was exceedingly dangerous. The blasters used black powder. (Dynamite would not be invented for another eight decades, and even something as simple as a safety fuse would not appear until 1831.) It took a great deal of finesse to drill a hole in solid rock, pack it with powder, insert a hollow iron rod, tamp some clay on top, insert a fuse, light it, and somehow get out of the way before the explosion launched boulders into the air. Premature ignition had grisly results. That September a worker had "both his hands most horridly maimed," Rumsey reported. Another worker was loading powder into a hole when it exploded; a local newspaper reported, "His situation is scarcely to be described, having had the fore part of his head blown to pieces, one of his eyes blown out, and his breast and limbs shockingly bruised and mangled."

Washington went to Seneca in a rainstorm on September 21, hoping to examine the work in progress, but he arrived after the workers had quit for the day. The next morning he passed by boat down the falls to the point where workers were trying to remove rocks from the riverbed. What with the continued rain, the river was high and muddy, and the general hadn't the foggiest notion of what had really been accomplished. Indeed, he could discern hardly any changes in the riverbed whatsoever: "To me it seemed, as if we had advanced but little, owing to the fewness, and sickliness of the hands, which it appeared ought to be increased and their Wages raised in order to obtain them."

The general did everything he could to stay in touch with the river at the most intimate level. One day he went to Great Falls, got in a canoe with Colonel Gilpin and one other man, unnamed in the diary, and proceeded through the gorge of the Potomac to Little Falls, a bumpy ride in the best of conditions, and dangerous when the river is high.

The project proceeded miserably. Floodwaters repeatedly drove the hands from the bed of the river. The Patowmack Company would need an extension from the legislatures of Maryland and Virginia; three years would not be enough to finish the job. Meanwhile, Rumsey had internal problems, a dispute with his deputy, Richardson Stewart, who Rumsey claimed was incompetent and deceitful. The deputy allegedly had built several machines for lifting stone and, knowing the contraptions to be pitiful, had buried one to hide it from General Washington. (It must not have been the most imposing piece of heavy industrial equipment if it could easily fit in a hole.) Stewart had also been cruel to the slaves, had driven off two overseers, and had sparked animosity with the neighbors of the project along the river. But the board did not heed Rumsey's warnings and declined to terminate Stewart.

Slowly, the Patowmack Company laborers began carving out what would someday be a 1.3-mile canal on the Virginia bank of the Potomac at Great Falls. Only after work had begun did Rumsey and his crew discover that the lower end of the canal would need to be cut through solid rock. No one had ever used so much blasting powder before on an American engineering project. It was dangerous work, and tedious. Months passed, and in the battle of canal versus natural geology, the ancient rocks seemed to be winning.

Nearly a year after he began the job, Rumsey wrote a grim report to the company treasurer:

> Great Falls potowmack July 3rd 1786. Sir We have been much Imposed upon the last Two weeks in the powder way (we had our Blowers, One Run off the other Blown up) we therefore was Obliged to have two new hands put to Blowing and there was much attention gave to them least Axedents should happen yet they used the powder Rather too Extravagent, But that was not all they have certainly stolen a Considerable Quantity. . . . Our hole troop is such Villains.

He'd reached the end of his rope. He wanted more money to stay on the job, and when the directors refused to give him a raise, he quit. His incompetent deputy, Stewart, took over.

Rumsey had only a few years left to him, but in that time he would help change the world. He moved to Shepherdstown, on the Potomac about 70 miles upstream from Georgetown, and scraped together enough money to build a steamboat. On December 3, 1787, in front of 100 spectators, as Rumsey attended to the boiler and machinery, he and Captain Charles Morrow piloted the boat upstream at about three miles an hour. General Horatio Gates, watching from the bank through an eyeglass, shouted, "She goes, by God, she goes!"

Rumsey spent the next several years trying to secure his priority as the inventor of the steamboat, a claim challenged by another inventor, John Fitch of Connecticut. In a country so scattered, with no federal government to speak of, an inventor had to go state to state to establish his rights. Rumsey ended up going to London to form a company there for steamboat navigation.

One evening in December 1792, after delivering an extended explanation of the principles of steam navigation to a society of scientists and mechanics, he suddenly put his right hand to his temple and complained of a violent pain. Those were his last words. He collapsed and died in a matter of hours. An autopsy seemed in order, and John Brown Cutting wrote to Thomas Jefferson with the conclusion of that procedure:

"Overplied with energies of thinking some of the vessals of the brain were fairly worn out."

8

Trial and Tribulation

ASHINGTON SETTLED into the active life of a gentleman farmer. He supervised the cutting of wheat and hay and wild grass. His farm was a biological riot: cows and sheep and pigs, of course, but also guinea hens, bulls, rams, foxhounds, the jackasses and jennies, plus the fish from the river, and all the representatives of the vegetable kingdom, the wheat, rye, barley, flax, hemp, corn, cabbages, carrots, beans, turnips, apples, pears, peaches, plums—all of it under his careful scrutiny. At night he recorded the relevant data from his five farms, as well as the level of the mercury at morning, noon, and night. Sometimes he jotted his daily account in the blank pages of a farmer's almanac. The reader of these diaries glimpses a straightforward, prosperous, industrious man of the soil, one who has an unusual hobby involving river navigation and who seems to entertain a staggering number of overnight guests. His diaries (unlike his letters) are almost entirely apolitical; the only storms and tempests are literally that:

> Clear & warm, with very little Wind till about 2 oclock, when a
> black & extensive cloud arose to the westward out of which much

139

wind issued with considerable thunder & lightning and a smart shower of Rain.

Rid to the Plantations in the Neck—Muddy hole, Dogue run & Ferry. At the first began to cut the ripest of the Oats, but thinking them in general too green quitted after breakfast and set all hands to pulling flax the doing of which was completed about Sun down. . . .

Examined the low, & sickly looking corn in several parts of this field, and discovered more or less of the Chinch bug on every stalk. . . .

Quite calm and exceedingly Sultry. Very clear.

Every so often a painter or sculptor would arrive at the mansion to preserve the countenance of the great man. He no longer resisted these efforts. He told a friend that sitting for a painter once made him as restive as a colt under the saddle, but his flouncing had decreased, he said, and now "no dray moves more readily to the Thill than I do to the painter's chair."

Throughout this retirement he continued to take good care of his reputation. A rumor reached his ear, *fourth-hand*, that the governor of Maryland had been displeased by the "officiousness" of a letter from Washington. Washington could not let this allegation of officiousness (which seems, in retrospect, a fairly mild perjorative, given that Washington was, indeed, officious) go unanswered, and so he wrote to the governor, and coldly asked "what foundation there is" for such a remark. The governor assured him that the rumor had no basis.

Though Washington continued to worry about the ineffectual government of his nation, he saw much to admire in the muscularity of the American people. Where the British had ravaged the countryside, the Americans had rebuilt quickly. There were fences going up, new land under cultivation, cows fattening. Surely no country on the entire planet had such immense potential. "The arts of peace, such as clearing of rivers, building of bridges, establishing conveniences for traveling &c., are assiduously promoted," he wrote to one of his foreign correspondents. "In short the foundation of a great Empire is laid, and I please myself with a persuasion that Providence will not leave its work imperfect."

*   *   *

THE GREAT MAN'S CRUSADE to impose order on a ragged and uncooperative world led him over the years to question the foundation of the planter society. He grew to despise slavery. He'd known slavery all his life, and had been a slave-owner since the age of eleven, when he inherited ten slaves upon his father's death. Over the decades, first through purchases, later through natural reproduction, his slave population had risen to more than a hundred, not including the so-called "Custis slaves" inherited by his wife from her first husband, Daniel Parke Custis.

In 1786, nearly three years after his return from the war, Washington told an associate that he would never purchase another slave, "it being among my first wishes to see some plan adopted by the legislature, by which slavery in this Country may be abolished by slow, sure, & imperceptable degrees." This dramatic statement turns up often in contemporary discussions of Washington's attitude toward slavery, but like many items in the archives, it is a bit ambiguous. The word "abolished" is a powerful one, and seems bluntly declared, especially since such abolition is among his "first wishes." But Washington was no revolutionary when it came to attacking slavery. He wanted abolition to be "slow," so slow that the dreadful institution would vanish by "imperceptable degrees." He wanted slavery to disappear without any fuss.

He became so uncomfortable with slavery that he often could not bear to refer to it except through euphemism. At one point he referred to slaves as "a certain species of property which I possess, very repugnantly to my own feelings. . . ." Slaveowners such as Washington and Jefferson could not have gone through life without finding a way to rationalize, through the presumption of white supremacy, the systematic brutalizing of their fellow human beings. (Jefferson did so explicitly in *Notes*, speculating wildly about biological differences between the races.)

Washington was not, by the standards of his day, a cruel master, but he was demanding, expecting his field hands to work long hours, sunrise to sundown. He wanted his slaves to be "at their work as soon as it is light—work till it is dark—and be diligent while they are at it." His wishes were seldom met to his satisfaction; a person deprived of the profit of his or her labor might find a greater reward, and a small measure of dignity, in refusing to go along with the Master's agenda. Some slaves learned trades and rose in stature around the plantation; the majority of his overseers in this portion of his retirement were black. But the slaves were still, to Washington, a constant source of disorder, chronically recalcitrant, the likely culprits when something mysteriously disappeared. Some of the most talented simply vanished on him. When one of Martha Washington's personal slaves, Oney Judge, a seamstress, ran away from the family and escaped to New Hampshire, Washington was offended by "the ingratitude of the girl, who was brought up and treated more like a child than a Servant."

He had a policy of never selling a slave, for that struck him as immoral, since it would mean splitting up slave families, husband from wife, parent from child. Stories about Washington's possible fathering of a mulatto child are not very persuasive.* In Flexner's words, "Nei-

---

* Henry Wiencek's *An Imperfect God: George Washington, His Slaves, and the Creation of America* (New York: Farrar Straus & Giroux, 2003) offers a smart, fair analysis of Washington's checkered history as a slave-owner, capturing the harshness of the daily life of a slave and showing the evolution of the general's view of slavery in the 1780s and 1790s. In one rather speculative chapter, Wiencek explores the possibility that Washington sired a mulatto child, West Ford, who lived at Mount Vernon for many decades after the general's death, and inherited from Bushrod Washington 160 acres adjacent to the plantation. There is oral tradition among some of Ford's descendants that George Washington was Ford's father, but Wiencek points out that there is also an oral tradition assigning paternity to Bushrod. The story lacks any documentary support. It's not even clear when Ford was

ther lust (despite legends to the contrary) nor sadism beckoned him on to his slave quarters." Washington insisted to his plantation manager that his slaves be treated humanely:

> [I]t is foremost in my thoughts, to desire you will be particularly attentive to my Negros in their sickness; and to order every Overseer *positively* to be so likewise; for I am sorry to observe that the generality of them, view these poor creatures in scarcely any other light than they do a draught horse or Ox.

There was an obvious solution, at least obvious to modern Americans: He could set them free. But that was a difficult move for a man of his time to make, and not simply because the slaves represented a significant portion of his wealth. Like most white southerners, he couldn't imagine them becoming full members of society. If he freed them, what would they do? Where would they go? His fellow planters would not look kindly on a wholesale manumission of slaves. They feared insurrections. It did not escape the notice of the masters that they were outnumbered by the men and women they kept in bondage. Slave-owners believed that only rigid enforcement of slave laws could keep black men and women from seizing control.

Something dramatic and portentous was happening to the former colonies in this last quarter of the eighteenth century. Slavery was dwindling in the North even as it expanded in the South. There were

---

born, but Wiencek believes it was sometime prior to November 1785. Wiencek notes an archived letter that hints that Venus, the enslaved mother of West Ford, who normally lived 95 miles from Mount Vernon, might have accompanied her mistress, Hannah Washington, to Mount Vernon at some point in the fall of 1784. Wiencek, inferring the timing of the visit from a reference in the letter to someone borrowing a coat, writes, "They might have arrived in early October just when Washington had returned from a five-week trek through the Virginia outback. He returned to find Martha sick and confined to her bed. If Venus arrived at that moment the opportunity for an encounter was there" (p. 308). Wiencek ultimately finds such an event unlikely. Given the evidence, it is safe to stick with the story offered by the documentary record: that upon arriving home, Washington immediately turned his energies to writing about rivers and mountains and portages and the future of the nation.

still slaves in every state, but north of the Potomac there was a pro-nounced increase in the number of free blacks. The country was grad-ually becoming a "society with slaves" in the North and a "slave society" in the South, to use the formulation of historian Ira Berlin. Washington felt trapped in the slave society. But he didn't know what to do other than register an ominous breeze:

> Were it not then, that I am principled agt. selling negros, as you would do cattle in the market, I would not, in twelve months from this date, be possessed of one, as a slave. I shall be happily mistaken, if they are not found to be a very troublesome species of property 'ere many years pass. . . .

*   *   *

WASHINGTON HADN'T FORGOTTEN about those infuriating Se-ceders. They were still rooted on his land at Millers Run, still growing crops and raising livestock and acting as though they weren't the shameless squatters that Washington knew them to be. The lawsuit had dragged on for two years. After Washington's western trek in 1784 he regularly corresponded with Thomas Smith, his savvy Penn-sylvania attorney. The general might have been a master of delegation in certain arenas of combat, but in this lawsuit he intended to lead the charge personally. Not even Cornwallis had faced such rage.

Washington vigorously compiled a packet of information for Smith's scrutiny. The general made it clear that the only acceptable outcome of the case would be the total surrender of the enemy. He was rankled by all the paperwork he needed to obtain to support his case, which he believed was self-evident. "I think nothing more is neces-sary but to state facts," he wrote. He said he would ride out to western Pennsylvania to make his argument directly if he could be "morally certain" of the date of the trial. In a later letter he told Smith that he'd heard a rumor that the squatters might voluntarily leave before the suit went to trial. He requested of Smith that, even if the Seceders did abandon their homes and relinquish their claims, "you will sue them respectively for Trespasses, rents or otherwise as you shall judge best & most proper to obtain justice for me." The general wanted his lawyer to chase these people through the American backcountry and punish them. He was not about to forgive and forget. (He'd been winning freedom! And to be treated like this. . . .)

Smith wrote back with gentle words to cool the litigious ardor of his client. Any move that seemed designed to punish the squatters might backfire, Smith informed Washington. Juries in similar cases had sided with the defendants. To bring trespassing suits against the squatters "may produce a bad effect, in the minds of the jury who are to try the Ejectments—their modes of thinking may lead them to believe the Defendants rather unfortunate, then blameable, and that as these double actions will well nigh ruin most of them; will not the jury be willing to lay hold of every point however trifling which may make against your title or in favour of the Defendants."

Washington replied in the tone of a man recognizing that he'd momentarily lost control of his passion (a maxim violation). He didn't intend, he said, for Smith to file additional suits for trespassing, but rather believed they might be pursued after the main ejectment cases had been settled. But now that he'd heard about other cases that had not gone well, he wrote, he would leave such suits entirely to Smith's discretion.

"I never should have thought of this mode of punishment, had I not viewed the defendants as willful and obstinate Sinners—persevering after timely & repeated admonition, in a design to injure me," Washington wrote, and then added, incredibly, "but I am not at all tenacious of this matter."

The general separately prepared a long legal brief that laid out both sides of the case as Washington saw it. Washington had never prepared a legal argument, but demonstrated such a grasp of the adversarial nature of the courts that one might have assumed him a member of the bar. Giving his own side of the story would clearly not be sufficient: He first would prepare the most persuasive arguments in favor of the defendants, and only then, Socratically, demolish them one by one. To make this point-counterpoint legal brief all the easier to follow, he wrote down the squatters' "Pleas" side by side with his "Answers."

PLEA: Supposing (they may say, because they have said it) that my Patent was originally good, yet, my right is forfeited for want of that cultivation and improvement which was required by Law, and which is conditional of the Grant.

ANSWER: It may be asked how I could improve or cultivate the Land when they had taken possession of it & violently detained it from me? . . .

PLEA: That one of the Defendants, in behalf of the rest had been sent to the Land Office of this State to ascertn the truth of the Report of my having a Grant of the Land;—but finding no Record of the Patent or Survey, the presumption was, that none had ever been made. . . .

ANSWER: Whether this search was really made, or not, is not for me to determine; but admitting it, it can be no reason why I should loose my right, because they did not, or even could not, discover a record of it . . .

PLEA: Under these circumstances, and this conviction, they took possession; and at great expense have improved the Land; and ought not in Law or equity to be deprived of it.

ANSWER: [T]hey knew this Land was reputed to be mine. That as soon as they set down upon it, they were so informed, and repeatedly warned off, and admonished of the consequences thereof. . . . [If the law did not protect absentee owners], no one could be secure in Lands at a distance—as possession & occupancy wd. set aside the best title, and put legal Right at defiance.

The legal brief ran pages and pages, covering every conceivable point of law and, more importantly, every shade of right and wrong.

*　　　*　　　*

IN OCTOBER 1786, Pennsylvania Supreme Court Justice Thomas McKean, riding circuit in western Pennsylvania, presided over the

J AM BECOME a private citizen on the banks of the Potomac, & under the shadow of my own Vine & my own Fig tree…" From the piazza of his mansion at Mount Vernon, George Washington (seen here in a 1780 portrait by Charles Willson Peale) saw the tidal river below as an arm of the sea, reaching deep into the continent. With a little improvement it would surely become the premier commercial artery of the young republic. (*Top: Courtesy of The Mount Vernon Ladies' Association. Above: Library of Congress*)

*H*E KNEW the wilderness, the western rivers, the way of the Indian. In this nineteenth-century engraving of a famous incident in 1753, a young George Washington and his guide Christopher Gist, fleeing hostile Indians, pole across the swollen Allegheny River on a homemade raft, moments before Washington would take an unexpected plunge. (*Library of Congress*)

*H*E SUPERVISED a plantation of 8,000 acres (facing page, top) and, at its peak, more than 300 enslaved African Americans, whose lives were hardly the pastoral reverie seen here. His 1784 farewell to Lafayette pained the general and brought on thoughts of an early death: "I was now descending the hill, I had been 52 years climbing. . . . But I will not repine—I have had my day." (*Library of Congress*)

*T*HE REVOLUTION unleashed a free-for-all in the West, as thousands of people streamed though the mountain gaps and floated down the Ohio. Washington's plan to transform the Potomac into a route between West and East required a heroic canal around the Great Falls, seen below in a romanticized 1802 drawing by George Beck, an earlier version of which was owned by Washington. (*Library of Congress*)

*T*O THE POTOMAC promoters, the pastoral landscape around Georgetown in the late eighteenth century (seen in an 1801 George Beck drawing) offered the perfect place for the seat of government. Detractors declared it a
wilderness, far from civilization, a veritable swampland, along the lines of the
1839 August Kollner drawing below. (*Library of Congress*)

Capitol at Washington D.C.

$\mathcal{T}$HOMAS JEFFERSON (left) saw the possibilities of an Empire of Liberty and encouraged Washington's Potomac scheme. As a congressman in the 1780s, James Madison (right) pushed for a Potomac capital and decades later, as president, fled the city in the face of a British invasion. Albert Gallatin (below), secretary of the treasury, put together the blueprint for a great nation linked by roads and canals. (*Library of Congress*)

THE POTOMAC ROUTE to the West became a reality. In a photograph (top) taken circa 1910 near Hancock, Maryland, the arteries of commerce are side by side: from left to right, the Western Maryland Railroad, the Chesapeake & Ohio Canal, the mountain-sundering Potomac River, and the Baltimore & Ohio Railroad. However, by the Civil War era the Potomac had become not a binding agent but a fracture line. In an 1864 *Harper's Weekly* illustration (below), Confederates sabotage the C&O Canal. (*Library of Congress*)

*T*HIS PHOTOGRAPH, taken in 1953, shows the seat of government grown from a muddy village to a world-class capital. A president standing on the balcony of the White House (extreme upper left) had a clear view of the Washington Monument (upper left) but was directly lined up with Jefferson's statue in the memorial (center), built on a former Potomac mudflat. The great liquid highway to the West is now a notorious traffic obstacle. (© 1953, The Washington Post. *Photograph by Tom Kelly. Reprinted with permission.*)

trial in the town of Washington, a few hours by horseback south of Millers Run. Because the record of the trial is extremely sparse, it is impossible to know if anyone involved asked for a change of venue to a community that had not been named after the plaintiff.

A flamboyant Pittsburgher represented the Seceders: Hugh Henry Brackenridge, the leading literary figure west of the mountains, a title for which, admittedly, there were few rival claimants. Brackenridge started the first newspaper in the West, having contrived, with a partner, to haul a printing press over the Alleghenies. He also wrote plays, pamphlets, and a novel called *Modern Chivalry.*

Washington wanted to travel to western Pennsylvania for the trial, but pleaded illness. Possibly he couldn't stomach another encounter with the western rabble.

Smith, Washington's attorney, took the case to trial with great anxiety. He'd never been more agitated, he later told Washington. He was a successful man, elected to public offices, but to represent such a client was clearly the pinnacle of his career. (No doubt he told his associates: Yes, *the* George Washington.) It could not have been a palliative to his nerves to be reminded with each letter from Mount Vernon precisely how much the client cared about the suit. Failure was not an option.

Smith had spent months figuring out how to get a friendly jury and the best possible judge. He personally served many of the subpoenas to Washington County residents who had been named to the jury. He decided to "take the Bull by the Horns," as he later told Washington, and brought the first suit against James Scott, Jr., the group's ringleader and the man with the strongest claim to ownership of the land. It was a smart move, because Smith would smoke out all the best arguments in favor of the Seceders' claim, but risk only the solitary defeat, reserving the chance to try the other cases with knowledge of what to expect. Smith called as a witness Charles Morgan, who'd been with William Crawford when he had surveyed the land, and who had seen Crawford pay 5 pounds to a man named Thomas Crooke to build a cabin on the property. Smith had many more witnesses as well, including another surveyor and several prominent members of the community.

Smith had one tremendous handicap: Washington's warrant to the land, as the general himself discovered unhappily in the summer of 1786, showed a date of November 25, 1773—"posterior," as Washington put it, to the arrival of the Seceders in October 1773. The date on the warrant was simply a bureaucratic mistake, but on paper, it appeared that some of the Seceders had been on the property before Washington officially owned it. Under a resolution passed by the Virginia Convention in 1776, settlers on unclaimed land had a preemptive right to purchase it.

Washington had hoped to dig up the original survey by Crawford, which would have showed a date of 1770 or 1771, but he learned that the survey and many other public documents had been destroyed by the British during their 1781 romp through Virginia.

The jury learned about the complex history of the land, the shifting jurisdictions (when Washington obtained the land, Virginia still claimed the area, and only later did it become part of Pennsylvania), the missing paperwork, etc. Smith won an important ruling from the judge, who barred any evidence about improvements to the land. This meant that the jury didn't learn about the dueling cabins on the property, or, more importantly, about the building of houses and barns and fences, the clearing of land, the plowing of the soil, and all the other things that the Seceders had accomplished over the previous thirteen years.

The trial began the afternoon of October 24, 1786, and lasted through the next day and until 11 o'clock in the morning of the twenty-sixth. There is no record of how long the jury deliberated, but Smith perceived that the jury wanted badly to give verdicts in favor of James Scott. "We had very strong prejudices, artfully fomented, to encounter," he told Washington. Yet as Smith steeled himself for defeat, the jury came back with a verdict in favor of the general. It is not entirely clear why a jury with natural sympathies for settlers sided with an absentee landlord, even one as famous as Washington. There were limited means in America for turning anyone into what would later be called a celebrity, and Washington himself hadn't appeared; the jury had to render a verdict in favor of someone far away and against James Scott, who was right there in the courtroom. Perhaps Smith, a lawyer of considerable talents, destined to be on the state Supreme Court, had managed to show beyond any doubt that the general had legitimate title to the land and had been unable to pay more attention to it because of his service to the country. Or perhaps the verdict was just another example of the Washington magic. Bullets couldn't hit him, and squatters couldn't defy him. After winning the Scott case, Smith persuaded Justice McKean to consolidate the other twelve cases. That trial ended quickly, again with a verdict for Washington. The Seceders would be evicted from their farms.

"You have now *thirteen* plantations—some of them well improved," Smith informed the general, and then delicately raised the possibility that now would be a good time to back off and show these frontier families some mercy. "[They] are now reduced to indigence; they have put in Crops this season, which are now in the ground—they wish to be permitted to take the grain away—to give this hint may be improper in me—to say more would be presumptuous."

Smith advised Washington to employ an agent to take possession of the land immediately, because the squatters were likely to burn down all the houses and barns and even the fences. Washington turned to John Cannon, a major landowner who'd hosted the general in 1784, and asked him if he would handle the matter, ideally by demanding rent from the Seceders. Washington went so far as to indicate that he didn't require the back rent from the past twelve years.

But the Seceders wanted nothing to do with George Washington. They would not be his tenants. They would own their own land. The Mount Pleasant Township Warrantee Map, compiled from early plats, shows a kind of splatter effect from the explosive visit of Washington in 1784. Several of the Seceders obtained warrants for land adjacent to, or near, Washington's land. They pulled out their axes once again, hacked down trees, burned the stumps, broke the ground. For years, settlers had been pulling up stakes and moving toward deeper wilderness to start anew, and perhaps, as they scouted nearby land to settle, they could pretend they were another band of restless Americans. But just as surely a few of them thought of George Washington as they swung their axes at the oaks and pines and hemlocks of the Pennsylvania forest.

One of the defendants, John Glenn, surveyed 285 acres just north of his former plantation on Washington's land. Glenn gave his new estate a forlorn name: "Remnant."

Washington would never again see his land at Millers Run. He would manage to rent it to new tenants until 1796, when he would finally sell it at a bargain price, $12,000, to a certain Colonel Matthew Ritchie (still a profit, factoring in the value of the 2,000-pound debt he'd forgiven in exchange for the original land warrant). Even so, it would not be a lump sum payment, but rather a mortgage, and Ritchie would fail to make the proper payments, ensuring that the property would revert to the Washington heirs upon the general's death. From beginning to end, this "body of fine Rich level land" would be vexatious.

Brackenridge many years later jotted down a postscript to the case: Washington, he thought, should have compensated the Seceders for the buildings and cultivated fields they were forced to abandon. Strictly as a matter of law, Brackenridge wrote, Washington did not have to pay them anything. "He could not be considered as under more than an imperfect obligation," he concluded. Washington may have thought that the State of Pennsylvania would compensate the Seceders, since their land had been taken from them in deference to Virginia's claim to sovereignty, in the 1770s, over what became southwestern Pennsylvania. But it was all moot, Brackenridge said.

"It remains now, not a matter of legal discussion, but of history."

*   *   *

THE GENERAL KEPT BUSY. The king of Spain wooed Washington with the gift of a fine jackass. The creature, called Royal Gift, discombobulated by his journey, initially showed little promise as a stud. Soon the animal got his footing and managed in a single winter to earn the general more than 600 dollars in stud fees.

Farming presented constant dilemmas. He had more than 100 head of cattle, but found, to his profound disbelief, that he still had to buy butter for his family.

The general kept an eye on the river:

> The Ice on the river began to break this morning and move with the tide, for the first time since the river closed.

> The River, which had opened very much yesterday and promised a free Navigation was entirely closed again to day, in all the malignancy of the frost.

Perhaps, as he sat on the piazza on warm days, drinking tea or Madeira and enjoying the view, he saw the river through a romantic haze. There were, after all, many Potomacs, and the one below his house was placid and delightful, seductively smooth, plenty deep, flanked by gentle hills. He knew as well as anyone the rages of the upper Potomac, but in his mind he could calm them. The man who had stood up to the king of England would not be intimidated by some rocks or rapids or even that 3,000-foot Allegheny wall blocking the way to the West.

He struggled to find funds to keep the river-improvement project going, yet somehow he kept seeing progress. At one point he wrote to Jefferson that only the bad luck of heavy rains had kept the river from being navigable all the way from Cumberland to Great Falls. And the big picture remained the same:

> There remains now no doubt of the practicability of the Plan, or that, upon the ulterior operations being performed, this will become the great avenue into the Western Country; a country which is now settg. in an extraordinarily rapid manner, under uncommonly favorable circumstances, and which promises to

afford a capacious asylum for the poor and persecuted of the Earth.

At this point he was proselytizing the already converted.

*   *   *

WASHINGTON'S POTOMAC scheme culminated in something entirely different from, and far more important than, a navigable river. In the pursuit of his goal, Washington set in motion a series of meetings that would lead to the creation of a document that would endure long after the skirting canal at Great Falls had been abandoned.

On March 20, 1785, amid a heavy snowstorm, a group of commissioners appointed by Maryland and Virginia gathered in Alexandria to talk about cooperating on the governance of the Potomac. At the suggestion of James Madison, they had come together to deal with a lingering jurisdictional problem that dated to the antiquity of the tobacco civilization—Lord Baltimore's 1632 royal grant that put his colony's boundary on the *southern* shore of the Potomac. The entire river belonged to Maryland. But the charter also allowed Virginia a vague right to free navigation and use of the Potomac.

If the grand Potomac scheme of General Washington had any chance of succeeding, the two states needed to sit down and hash out their interests and try to work together. After four days of discussions, the commissioners accepted Washington's invitation to reconvene at Mount Vernon. Once in the general's mansion, drinking his wine, the commissioners made great progress, agreeing on tolls, tariffs, the common valuation of currency (no more of this craziness where a coin changed value when you crossed the Potomac), and shared naval protection of the river. The two states realized this was not a zero-sum world after all. Inspired, perhaps, by Washington's vision of a powerful empire, they opened their eyes to the possibility that interstate cooperation could be extended beyond the parochial concerns of the Potomac. Why not bring in the other neighboring states? Maryland bordered on Pennsylvania and Delaware, Virginia on North Carolina.

Shouldn't they *all* form a compact to unify their commercial regulations and economic interests?

They were not, after all, separate nations. As Washington once said to James Madison, "We are either a United people, or we are not." If not, he said, "let us no longer act a farce by pretending to it." The Mount Vernon Compact, as it came to be known, ended with a call for another meeting, a larger one, in Annapolis, with representatives of all thirteen states.

The attendance of the Annapolis Convention in September 1786 proved a bust, but a glorious one. Only five states managed to get delegates to the convention. Historian John Ferling points out that the organizers made a fatal mistake in not inviting George Washington, the one figure who could have given such a conference an aura of national significance. Two more delegations were on their way to Annapolis, and that would have given the meeting a quorum, but the delegates on hand decided to call it off and try again within the year, with an even broader agenda for adjusting the Articles of Confederation. The delegates adopted a statement urging a continental convention to be held in May 1787, in Philadelphia.

That meeting is now known as the Constitutional Convention.

The Potomac has a way of interjecting itself into key moments in the republic's history. (Today, in our cinematic age, we could refer to this propensity to pop up unexpectedly as Zelig-like.) It would be a reach, however, to claim that the discussions about governance of the Potomac led to the Constitution. A country growing rapidly and covering more than half a billion acres had no national government to speak of. Something had to be done.

Historians will often allow a cameo role for the Potomac in the story of the making of the Constitution, but a more prominent role is typically given to Captain Daniel Shays. A farmer in western Massachusetts who had fought at Bunker Hill, he and his fellow citizens were furious at the increase in taxes even as farm prices dropped. Banks were foreclosing on one farmer after another, and many once prosperous tillers of the land were thrown into debtors' prison. It was a class conflict: yeomen farmers, many of them veterans, against the moneymen of eastern Massachusetts. The farmers crowded around the country courthouses and tried to prevent judges from hearing cases. The state sent more than 4,000 troops to quell the rebellion. At the high point of the conflict, Shays led a thousand men to seize the arsenal at Springfield. The general commanding the troops loyal to the government gave the order to fire, and four rebels suffered mortal wounds. The rebels fled into the countryside, and over the course of many weeks the militiamen tracked them down and killed or wounded more than thirty of them.

Thomas Jefferson, in Paris, was astonished at what seemed to him an overreaction. But the Shays Rebellion put Washington in a lather. "Good God!" he said when he heard about it. Washington demanded of his former aide, David Humphreys, "[F]or Gods sake tell me, what is the cause of all these commotions? Do they proceed from licenciousness, British influence disseminated by the Tories, or real grievances which admit of redress?"

In the fall of 1786, after the failure at Annapolis, Washington came near to despairing of his country's future:

> The want of energy in the foederal government; the pulling of one State, & parts of States against another; and the commotions among the Eastern people, have sunk our national character much below par; & have brought our politics and credit to the brink of a precipice. A step or two more must plunge us into inextricable ruin.

He'd spent all this time trying to improve the Potomac; now he needed to try to improve the government.

With George Washington as the presiding officer in Philadelphia, the leaders of the young nation—55 men meeting behind closed doors, deliberating secretly—momentarily reversed all the centrifugal forces of the past two decades. The process might not have been the acme of government-in-the-sunshine, but the delegates succeeded in creating a more perfect union. Washington presided for four months, and, with a Valley Forge–like demonstration of willpower, remained magnificently silent throughout the debates. When not focused on the constitutional questions, he thought of his farms back home. "How does the grass Seeds which were Sown with the grain, & flax, seem to come on?" he wrote to George Augustine Washington, his nephew. "How does those which were sown in my little garden advance? And how does the Crops which are planted in drills between the Corn, come up, & progress?"

During a break, he wrote to Jefferson in France to discuss—what else?—the Potomac. Washington said he had investigated the possibility that Alexandria, of all the major ports along the Atlantic (including Baltimore, Philadelphia, and New York), would be the ideal place to handle the fur trade of the West. He said he had left "as little room for partiality and prejudice to operate as possible" as he made this geographical inquiry. His conclusion: Alexandria would indeed be the best place. It was as plain as day. A mere "glance at the Map must decide Alexandria in point of distance to be the most convenient spot." Even without the Patowmack Company improvements on the river, his hometown port would be the right choice. He noted that much of the fur trade had been passing from Pittsburgh to Philadelphia, a blatant contravention of the logic of the landscape. Eventually the natural order would be restored, for no amount of machination by the Pennsylvanians could withhold from Alexandria "the advantages which nature has bestowed on her."

The Constitution required that the new federal government be headed by a president, and of course there would have to be a presidential election. The nation would have to choose its preeminent leader. The decision would be, to use a term from a much later era, a no-brainer.

9

A Capital Idea

*G*EORGE WASHINGTON never ran for the presidency. He ran *from* it. The job stalked him from the moment the Framers conceived it. As the presiding officer of the convention, he knew that the position of chief executive had been tailored for him down to the last buttonhole.

It was essential to the entire enterprise that he would be the president, for the states would be unlikely to trust anyone else with such a potentially monarchical position, and they had the option of rejecting the Constitution outright. As Washington observed the ratification debate (his endorsement of the Constitution was powerful even if he remained silent), he made no public comments about the presidency. He told his friends, however, that he reserved the right to decline the job. He didn't yearn to ride forth once again into the Great Theater of Action.

Today we are accustomed to false modesty in politics, but Washington was not simply playing hard-to-get. The surveyor knew the boundaries of his talents. He suspected he would make a mediocre president. Worse, the position would put his legacy in jeopardy. His return to private life had been so masterfully staged and so fundamentally astounding—with a single gesture he'd separated himself from every despot, every mandarin, every Caesar in the history of the world—and he didn't want to scramble the narrative. You could say his reputation was his palace, handcrafted over many years. He'd fired every brick, hammered every nail. He'd eyeballed every beam and joist to make sure they were on the level. It didn't need any more work, this reputation. Didn't need another wing.

His presidential campaign consisted entirely of private agonizing. "But how can I know what is best, or on what shall I determine? May Heaven assist me in forming a judgment: for at present I see nothing but clouds and darkness before me," he wrote his wartime aide Jonathan Trumbull.

He imagined what people would say if, after all his lofty talk about being a simple farmer, living under his vine and fig tree, he were to gallop back into public life. Might he not, he asked Henry Lee, "be chargeable with levity and inconsistency; if not with rashness & ambition?" (And not just chargeable; wouldn't there be some *truth*, he added, to the levity and inconsistency part?)

It would be some years before presidential aspirants would dare to do anything so vulgar as ask for votes, but Washington set a standard for not campaigning that no one else in American history will ever match. Modern candidates who will pander to any audience and grovel for any campaign contribution might recall that Washington stayed on his farm and rued his cruel fate. Admittedly, this strategy wouldn't work for everyone.

For Washington the presidency would not really be a step up in political or cultural status. Gods do not toil in the fields of mortals. But Hamilton played to the general's vanity, telling him that a refusal to serve would harm his reputation. Washington had always answered the call of duty. Virtue and honor required that he take the job. And so Washington by the spring of 1789 began using the language of a condemned man: "[M]y movements to the chair of Government will be accompanied by feelings not unlike those of a culprit who is going to the place of his execution."

Jefferson wrote sympathetically from Paris: "[N]obody who has tried both public & private life can doubt but that you were much happier on the banks of the Patowmac than you will be at New York . . . I am sensible of the immensity of the sacrifice on your part. Your measure of fame was full to the brim: and therefore you have nothing to gain. But there are cases wherein it is a duty to risk all against nothing. . . ."

The Electoral College voted on February 4, 1789, and everything went as planned. The electors, to a man, voted for Washington, and a smaller number awarded the vice presidency to John Adams, whose candidacy for that somewhat enigmatic post had been sanctioned by the general. That was the easy part. Much harder would be assembling a quorum of congressmen to count the votes in New York City on March 4. Nothing in early America, not even the howl of the wolf, was as terrifying as a quorum call in Congress. And then when the votes were counted, someone would still have to deliver the information to the winner down in Mount Vernon, which would require days of slogging through the slush and snowmelt of the late-winter countryside, fording swollen streams, booking passage on ferries across raging rivers, and so on.

Information traveled only as fast as animal muscle-power— human, horse, whatever—could propel it. The situation created a kind of relativistic society in which two events at distant points could not truly be said to have happened simultaneously, since there was no way that any observer could perceive them as simultaneous. (Einstein would understand this point even if Washington couldn't.) In the late 1780s the delay could be days, weeks, or months. Washington had no way of knowing on February 4 that he'd been elected president. For the next twelve days he remained aware only of the overwhelming probability that he was the president-elect. In a long letter to Jefferson, dated February 13, Washington made no mention of the presidency, and instead launched into another dissertation on inland navigation, the Potomac, the Ohio country, etc. He said he'd received an excellent map of the country between the Potomac and western waters, and had concluded that linking East and West would be surprisingly simple: "I enclose you such a rough sketch, as my avocations would permit me to make: my principal object therein being to shew, that the distance between the Eastern & Western Waters is shorter, and that the means of communication are easier, than I had hitherto represented or imagined."

Eight miles, he reckoned, was the entirety of the land portage between the two sides of the Eastern Continental Divide (the rough sketch, sadly, has never been found). That's about the distance between Mount Vernon and Alexandria. This route would presuppose some locks on the upper Potomac, above the Savage River. Some people—"not professional men I should add"—doubted that the Potomac could be rendered navigable that far into the mountains, Washington told Jefferson, but he was optimistic on that point. Indeed, when he closely scrutinized the map, he saw that the Little Yock River, when it had enough water, offered a possible endpoint for a land portage from the Potomac watershed of only *five* miles.

Eventually he learned that he had been called to the presidency. The message came in a roundabout manner. Washington had previously written Secretary of War Henry Knox with a request for some "superfine American broadcloth" that had been advertised in New York City (the general was already thinking of using an American fabric for his inaugural coat). On February 16, 1789, Knox wrote to inform the general that the cloth had not yet arrived, adding casually that the general had, according to the latest election returns, been selected unanimously as the first president of the United States. It was one of those "By the way, you're the president" letters.

Members of the Senate and House of Representatives began trickling into New York City, the capital, to count the ballots on March 4. But there was no quorum. Days passed. Still no quorum. The days became weeks. Congressmen straggled in, one by one, as Washington cooled his heels at Mount Vernon. To make the situation all the more absurd, Washington had no money, and didn't think he could afford to travel to New York to become the first president of the United States.

He started asking around, seeing if there was someone who would give him a loan. Eventually, he found a neighbor in Alexandria who was willing to lend him 500 pounds, then another 100 pounds for good measure.

On April 6, two months and two days after the Electoral College voted, Congress finally achieved a quorum, tabulated the results, and dispatched Charles Thomson, the congressional secretary, to Mount Vernon with the official notification. Thomson clattered up the general's drive on the fourteenth and delivered the momentous news. Washington pulled out a piece of paper—had he been on television he could not have been more conscious of the eyes of his countrymen—and read his acceptance: "Sir, I have been long accustomed to entertain so great a respect for the opinion of my fellow citizens, that the knowledge of their unanimous suffrages having been given in my favour scarcely leaves me the alternative for an Option. Whatever may have been my private feelings and sentiments, I believe I cannot give a greater evidence of my sensibility for the honor they have done me, than by accepting the appointment." Historians can only wonder what he would have done if a rogue elector had declined to vote for him.

Martha Washington, reluctant to leave home, did not accompany her husband on the inaugural journey. She couldn't bear to see him pulled from his retirement. "I think it was much too late for him to go in to publick life again," she wrote a nephew, "but it was not to be avoided, our family will be deranged as I must soon follow him."

The president-elect's trip to New York, slowed in one town after another by tributes, celebrations, feasts, and parades—a kind of running coronation—required ten days of exhausting carriage travel even though Washington insisted on starting out every day at the first glimmer of light. The general would not return to the banks of the Potomac for seventeen months.

*   *   *

IN THE CAPITAL TODAY the presidency is a twenty-four-hour operation, the subject of a relentless publicity apparatus. It's a conspiracy of sorts: The White House markets the president at every opportunity, and the media transmit his every utterance, grateful for a dependable newsmaker who puts a human face on the sometimes inscrutable functions of the enormous federal government. TV news organizations film the president's most routine walks from door to limo on the off chance that something terrible might happen, an assignment known, perhaps indelicately, as the Deathwatch. The president is said to live in a bubble, but that's too organic a metaphor; he's really inside a machine, tooled and retooled over two centuries, partially automated, and designed to inflate the head of government into a nearly omniscient figure who can command the military, oversee the economy, supervise the federal bureaucracy, appoint judges, and yet somehow remain a regular fellow.

When George Washington became president, no one knew precisely what an American president was supposed to do, what he was supposed to *be*. He would have to do a lot of improvising. No wonder the Europeans doubted the durability of the American nation: Everyone seemed to be winging it.

Vice President John Adams openly struggled with such delicate questions as how the president should be addressed. "His Majesty," perhaps? "His High Mightiness," maybe? During one of the initial sessions of the U.S. Senate, Adams said, "I feel great difficulty how to act." He noted that he was the president of the Senate, and thus should be addressed as "President" when presiding. But, he added, "when the President comes into the Senate, what shall I be?" At least one senator, the dyspeptic diarist William Maclay of Pennsylvania, had to stifle a snicker. *What shall I be?!*

Washington took office nervously, bearing little resemblence to the rigid figure of popular iconography. The calm he experienced in battle did not extend to public speaking. He stood with one hand shaking as he held his speech, the other hand jammed in his pocket. He switched the text back and forth, hand to hand, always with one hand pocketed. Maclay wrote: "This great man was agitated and embarrassed more than ever he was by the leveled cannon or pointed musket. He trembled, and several times could scarce make out to read, though it must be supposed he had often read it before."

With every action Washington set a precedent that would reverberate across the ages. He knew he had to set a tone of dignity and command. Given his physical stature and regal bearing, he made the presidency a highly ceremonial, even theatrical office. He would travel the country roads in a beautiful carriage, with a crest he'd personally designed. When preparing to enter a town, he would get out of the carriage and mount Prescott, his majestic white stallion. Increasingly, he wore velvet and satin outfits. He looked as if he'd come from the womb wearing a ceremonial sword.

The tradition of southern hospitality required an open door, but he could not easily uphold that code in New York City, rapidly turning into a teeming metropolis of more than 30,000 people. Pigs ran freely in the streets—in most American cities they were the garbage collectors—and were by no means the lowest life forms. Here, as on the frontier, Washington was surrounded by people of all levels of income, status, education, and hygiene. The president was a visible figure, if not exactly approachable in the usual meaning of the word. He would bow to common folk in the street and greet visitors in a receiving line at the President's House, but he felt most comfortable with the society people. He could never be king, but sometimes he could do a fair impersonation of one.

As for his duties, the Constitution sketched some specifics but left room for interpretation. No one can accuse the Constitution of being unambiguous. The Framers thought in the negative: how to limit the reach of any one element of government, how to play one branch off another, how to divide the legislature into one chamber that represented states on an equal footing and a second one that gave more representation to the larger states, and so on. The goal was to reduce the risk of tyranny or its polar opposite, mob rule. The Framers must have felt they were threading a needle.

They had a deep skepticism about the motives and morals of the human race. Men, wrote Hamilton, "are ambitious, vindictive and rapacious." He viewed himself as a realist. People could not be fully trusted. To say otherwise was to live in a dream world:

> Is it not time to awake from the deceitful dream of a golden age, and to adopt as a practical maxim for the direction of our political conduct that we, as well as the other inhabitants of the globe, are yet remote from the happy empire of perfect wisdom and perfect virtue?

Madison made the point that there's a difference between a democracy and a republic. A republic delegated power to a small number of citizens elected by the rest. Madison saw the size of the country as the nation's best defense against the rise of diabolical factions. In a large republic, it would be harder for men to "practise with success the vicious arts by which elections are too often carried." But no one knew for sure if the government would work, if the system of checks and balances would function properly. Would the chief executive control foreign policy or would Congress? Who had the final right to interpret the meaning of the Constitution? Was the Constitution organic and evolving, or something rigid and unchangeable? *What kind of republic is this? What kind of people are we?*

With these difficult questions in the air, two powerful factions formed, howling different answers. We refer to them now as Federalists and Republicans (or Anti-Federalists; they soon became Democratic-Republicans, and founded what became the Democratic party), but in their inaugural moments they had no official names, no membership list, and only the feeblest sense of who was on which side. They were not yet parties. As a general rule, the Federalists wanted a strong central government, the Republicans a much weaker one. The Federalists were accused of being monarchists, the Republicans of being democratic zealots who would destroy anyone with wealth. The Federalists wanted America to be allied with England, the Republicans with revolutionary France. The Federalists had most of their power in the North, the Republicans in the South. Federalists supported cities and manufacturing; Republicans idealized the agrarian life. Hamilton provided the intellectual firepower for the Federalists, with Washington his stealth advocate; Jefferson led the Republicans, seconded by Madison. It's all rather quaint and formulaic in retrospect, but at the time, the political situation bordered on riotous.

We think of the Founders as cool, collected, preternaturally serene, issuing long-winded declarations on liberty and equality, and always displaying exquisite penmanship and an undue affection for Latinate words, but they tended to be a yeastier bunch of folks, chronically obstreperous, difficult, sometimes paranoid. The polemics of that generation may seem mildly amusing, but it's worth remembering that politics in the late eighteenth century had a lethal edge. The French Revolution turned increasingly fanatical and violent, and conservatives in America feared that French ideas would inspire a form of the Terror here at home. Meanwhile the mulattoes in the French sugar colony of Saint Domingue, now known as Haiti, overthrew the French authorities and provided a reminder to American slave-owners that their own slaves might revolt. The leaders of America didn't know for certain if they would make it to the next century without being beheaded, jailed, or killed. (Hamilton made it all the way to 1804 before being gunned down in a duel by the vice president of the United States.)

Soon after Washington took office, the factions were raging back and forth about "Assumption," Hamilton's proposal that the federal government assume the war debts of the states. Jefferson believed Hamilton dreamed of consolidating power and establishing a monarchy. Meanwhile, Congress and the Cabinet grappled with the seemingly intractable question of where to put the permanent seat of government. The so-called Residency debate didn't seem to lend itself to compromise. One place would win this contest, and everywhere else would lose.

*   *   *

WAS THERE A HAMLET in all America that hadn't been mentioned as a candidate for the construction of a federal town? Was there a field somewhere, a vale, a glade, a sunny glen in the great Eastern Forest, that hadn't been offered as the perfect site? The federal government might have little experience with what future generations would call porkbarrel politics, but this was the rare case in which Congress could point to a spot in the vast American landscape and make houses and buildings and wharves appear almost overnight. Now that the government had some bone and fiber, the seat of government might someday become a true *capital*, a grand city.

Everyone had an opinion about where the seat should be, and the consensus seemed to wander across the land like a dowser. Back in October 1783, at the end of the war, Congress had discussed a long list of possible locations, including Kingston (N.Y.), Elizabethtown (N.J.), Newark, New Brunswick, Princeton, Trenton, Germantown (just northwest of Philadelphia), Wilmington, Annapolis, Georgetown, and Williamsburg. The Virginians, in offering Williamsburg, threw in an alternate suggestion: somewhere on the Potomac.

"The Potomac" might mean Georgetown, or someplace just up the river around Little Falls, or further up the gorge, at Great Falls, or perhaps way up at the mouth of the Monocacy, or even near Bath, where the Potomac briefly flows within a couple of miles of Pennsylvania. James Madison made notes about the relative merits of the contending sites: The "Falls of Potowmac" had the advantage of geographical centrality, proximity to the West, and "remoteness from the influence of any overgrown commercial city." That was a key criterion: to keep the government pure of the corruptive influence of cities.

The Residency debate was fraught with complex political and geographical calculations. Putting the capital in the South, northerners thought, might induce the southern states to follow the lead of Virginia and cede western lands to the general government. Slavery lurked over the debate; a southern capital, between two slave states, would imply that the government would not try to quash the peculiar institution.*

---

* In *"Negro President": Jefferson and the Slave Power* (Boston: Houghton Mifflin, 2003), the historian Garry Wills advances the provocative thesis that Washington wanted the government securely fixed in slave territory. Wills notes the extreme distress that President Washington felt in 1791 when, living in Philadelphia, he feared that his most trusted

The geographical virtues of a Potomac site were not obvious to many northerners, who imagined the river as the habitat of wild beasts and Indians, and who believed that a kind of Potomac Fever had become epidemic among the Virginians. Echoing this view today is Joseph Ellis, who insightfully sorts through the Residency debate in his bestselling book *Founding Brothers: The Revolutionary Generation*, coming down hard on the Potomac partisans and what he describes as the "grand Virginia illusion" that the Potomac was the only direct water route to the Ohio valley. The "myth of the Potomac," he writes, derived from Virginia's vast expanse in the colonial era, when its western boundary was considered to be the Mississippi or perhaps even the Pacific, and when Virginians began to see the Potomac as the gateway to the West. This is all true, and the river did have a mythical quality, but it also had something else: a witness. It had this highly influential figure at Mount Vernon, a man who had paddled nearly two hundred miles of the upper river, who had seen its water gaps, had navigated its rapids and spouts, had fought wars from its banks, had even blazed a road from its headwaters to those of the Ohio River. The Virginians had direct testimony about the Potomac from a man who had won independence for the nation and didn't seem capable of telling a lie. The Potomac's virtues didn't seem the slightest bit illusory.

In 1783 the Solomons of Congress reached a compromise: They'd build *two* federal towns, one at the falls of the Delaware River, and the other at or near Little Falls on the Potomac. In the meantime Congress would spend six months at Annapolis and six months at Trenton. In other words, Congress would continue to be a jumping bean, or maybe two jumping beans. The New Englanders liked the idea of a rambling, decentralized, two-sited Congress. As historian Kenneth Bowling has

---

slaves would be freed under a Pennsylvania emancipation statute. But Washington's 1791 distress tells us nothing of his thoughts in 1790 and earlier, when the Residency debate raged. Washington's conspicuous public silence about the location of the seat of government makes all theories possible, and certainly many Southerners associated a Potomac capital with the perpetuation of slavery, but the simplest explanation for why Washington would want a Potomac capital is that he always believed in the providential geography of the river and its potential as a commercial corridor (and it was right in his backyard).

explained, the New Englanders felt that a single and permanent seat of empire would lead to concentration of power and eventually monarchy. Two capitals seemed more in keeping with republican virtue.

Nothing happened to resolve the issue. Eventually, Congress moved to New York City, which is where the debate on the permanent seat intensified in the early summer of 1790.

*　　　*　　　*

HENRY LEE had aggressively, almost fanatically, pushed Great Falls on the Potomac as an ideal capital. "Light-Horse Harry," who'd attended the College of New Jersey (Princeton) with Madison and Aaron Burr, and had studied under Hugh Henry Brackenridge, had been a dashing commander in the South during the war. His cousins William Lee, Richard Henry Lee, and Arthur Lee had distinguished themselves as leaders of the Revolutionary generation. Henry Lee had every reason to expect that glory would follow his every move, that his future would be as brilliant as his past. But then he started buying land.

He was entranced by the Potomac, which was visible from his majestic family estate, Stratford Hall, downriver from Mount Vernon. He was, writes historian Charles Royster, "in the fifth generation of a family that for one hundred-fifty years had looked at the Potomac and seen wealth." Lee believed that a grand federal city might rise at Great Falls, which, with his military mind, he saw not as a scenic environment nor even as a necessary transfer point for cargo, but as a kind of refuge, a place far enough up the river to be free from attack by enemy warships. The British navy had easily dominated the navigable waterways during the Revolution, and Lee imagined that someday the British might return, and—who knows?—try to burn down the seat of government.

Lee bought 500 acres at Great Falls, including the land where the Patowmack Company had started digging its canal. In 1788 he lured Madison to join him as an investor. "The advantages infinitely exceed that of any spot of ground in the U. States," Lee wrote Madison. "Mr.

Fitzgerald one of the directors of the potomac company says that the navigation of the river will be used next summer indubitably, as far as the Great falls. This event will render the property invaluable."

Madison asked Washington, still a retired farmer, for his opinion. Conceivably, the old man was not the most unbiased counselor, having spent so much energy and zeal on the Potomac, but Washington sprinkled his response with caveats (his opinions, Washington conceded, "may be too sanguinely dilated"). Washington admitted that the canal at Great Falls was "the *most* doubtful part of our Work," but said that, even so, a tremendous amount of water-borne produce would be funneled through the site, and a town would have to be established to handle the commerce. Moreover, the Shenandoah River would soon be opened for navigation for at least 150 miles, and all the produce of "that rich and extensive vale between the Blue Ridge and the Alligany Mountains" would soon be coming down the Potomac to Great Falls. Throw in the cargo from the Western Waters, "and it opens a field almost too extensive for imagination."

That persuaded Madison. The young Virginian scraped together enough money to join Lee's venture. Lee promoted the Potomac even more fervently than his friend George Washington. Washington didn't have to persuade Lee that his grand idea about the Potomac would potentially bring riches to a man of foresight. Lee believed. He felt in his bones the explosive energies of his young nation. The secret to success would be to think big, on a scale that matched the country itself. "No dealer he in idle farm lands, no petty gambler in crossroads ordinaries. His every scheme was grandiose, and his profits ran to millions in his mind," writes Douglas Southall Freeman. Lee had Washington's expansive vision without his discipline. He was Washington unbound.

Lee imagined that at Great Falls there would be a city with all manner of mills, forges, houses, taverns. He laid out on paper a town he called Matildaville, in honor of his wife. But Matildaville would never be a great city. Matilda Lee died that very year in childbirth. The town at its peak would be a cluster of six structures, all of them destined to rot and crumble. Light-Horse Harry Lee's feverish land speculation would eventually bring him financial ruin and two stints in a debtor's jail.

*　　　*　　　*

THE DEBATE over the siting of the national government touched on the central question of what kind of country America would become. Were we to be a nation of commerce and financial maneuvering, or one of green pastures and haystacks? Would we be a nation of free labor, or one inextricably tied to chattel slavery? *(Who are we?)*

President Washington obviously favored a Potomac capital, but his conflict of interest forced him to remain silent in public. Whatever he had to say, he said it in private, discreetly, ensuring that the documentary record would reveal no sign of him, not even a partial fingerprint. Historians face a serious challenge when their protagonist decides to don a cloak of invisibility. Meanwhile the secondary figures, such as Jefferson and Madison, may have felt the need to tell the president what he wanted to hear. An idea that appears, in the record, to be Jefferson's, might merely be an echo of something Washington had already decreed. Further complicating the matter is that the prosecution of the matter required stealth and intrigue, since no faction in the debate wanted the other factions to know what they were thinking. All of which is a reminder that history is not an exact science and at moments is more like a séance, a desperate attempt, in the mist and fog, to channel the voices of the dead.

Washington, in thinking about the seat of government, certainly kept his grand Potomac navigation project in mind. What, he wondered, would a Potomac capital mean for his river plan? And what would his river plan mean for a Potomac capital? The situation reeked of synergistic possibilities. In a 1792 letter, he acknowledged the connection between his Potomac plan and the Residency question:

> There is such an intimate connection in political and pecuniary considerations between the federal district and the inland navi-

gation of the Potowmac, that no exertions, in my opinion, shou'd be dispensed with to accomplish the latter. For, in proportion as this advances, the City will be benefited. Public and private motives therefore combine to hasten this work.

At least one erudite biographer, John Ferling, reads this as a confession of Washington's self-interest—his "pecuniary considerations" and "private motives." But as a confession it is rather austere. Certainly, there is no hint of guilt here, nor even the use of first person. The gist seems to be: Onward with our Potomac scheme!

*   *   *

MADISON, using the kind of statistics that would have made Jefferson and Washington proud, calculated that the distance that congressmen would need to travel, collectively, to reach a capital on the Potomac from points south was 12,782 miles. Congressmen from the north would have to travel only 12,422 miles. This was Madison's way of arguing that the Potomac wasn't really a "southern" site. He also reminded his compatriots that the Potomac was the westernmost river in contention, and that the West would soon be home to "an astonishing mass of people" who, if not connected to the Atlantic states, might become "an alien, a jealous and a hostile people." He did not mention that he owned some property at Great Falls.

The Potomac promoters didn't say where, exactly, they would put the capital, but they raised the idea of putting it at Williamsport, where Conococheague Creek flows into the river. The New Englanders reacted to the suggestion with hoots of derision. Imagine, a capital stuck out in the boondocks, on something called the Conococheague, where bears and snakes would easily outnumber government officials! Even though the Conococheague idea was just one of many suggested, the northerners adopted "Conococheague" as a kind of code word for all things Potomac, remote, vermin-infested, and inscrutable. Some referred to it simply as the place with "the long Indian name."

The famous compromise that ended the Residency and Assumption debates will be forever associated with the chance encounter of Jefferson and Hamilton one night in June 1790. The story, as told by Jefferson years later, is that he was on his way to the President's House when he came upon a dejected, disheveled Hamilton.

> Hamilton was in despair. . . . He walked me backwards and forwards before the President's door for half an hour. He painted pathetically the temper into which the legislature had been wrought; the disgust of those who were called the creditor States; the danger of the secession of their members, and the separation of the States. . . . I proposed to him . . . to dine with me the next day, and I would invite another friend or two, bring them into conference together, and I thought it impossible that reasonable men, consulting together coolly, could fail, by some mutual sacrifices of opinion, to form a compromise which was to save the Union. . . .

The dinner became legendary. Jefferson invited Madison to join them, and over a wine-soaked meal, they came up with a swap: Hamilton would modify Assumption to take into account Virginia's minimal debt, and would lobby his fellow federalists to support a Potomac capital; Madison, in turn, would lobby a few southerners to back down in their opposition to Assumption (and indeed, four Potomac congressmen, Alexander White and Richard Bland Lee of Virginia, and Daniel Carroll and George Gale of Maryland, voted for Hamilton's legislation). As one guidebook to the capital puts it, "the savory viands and mellow Madeira proved softening influences upon the guests."

History is full of contingencies, moments where, to borrow Washington's metaphor, the touch of a feather could alter the course of human events. What if Jefferson had not seen Hamilton in the darkness? A better question might be: What if Jefferson had fully grasped the details of Assumption and what it meant for Hamilton's vision of the nation? Jefferson would eventually say of the Assumption deal, "I was duped into [it] by the Secretary of the Treasury and made a tool for forwarding his schemes, not then sufficiently understood by me; and of all the errors of my political life, this has occasioned me the deepest regret." The idea that these men needed only a little wine to take the edge off their differences is a stretch: Jefferson and Hamilton grew to hate one another with a passion rarely seen before or since in world politics. "Hamilton was not only a monarchist, but for a monarchy bottomed on corruption," Jefferson shrieked in the secret diary known as the *Anas*. Washington, in Jefferson's view, lacked the ability to detect Hamilton's scheming, because he was "Unversed in financial projects and calculations and budgets," a questionable allegation from a man who would die bankrupt.

The Senate approved the Potomac seat on July 1, by a vote of 14 to 12. Over the next eight days, the House debated the bill ferociously, at one point voting down an amendment to change the words "Potomac, at some place between the mouths of the Eastern Branch and Conogocheague" to "Delaware, at a place not more than eight miles below the Falls thereof," which was perhaps not the most trivial tweaking of the language. Other amendments were put forward to put the capital in Pennsylvania or somewhere between the Susequehanna and the Potomac, or simply in Baltimore. There was, almost ritualistically, talk of disunion. Again some members invoked the mystery of Conococheague, and one congressman said he would vote for Baltimore because he thought "a populous city better than building a palace in the woods." Mr. Livermore, having heard that the Potomac was navigable 200 miles to the foot of the Alleghenies, asked how that could be to the advantage of Congress. "I can conceive none," he said, "except that it may be to send the acts of Congress by water to the foot of the Allegheny mountains."

There were attempts to change the date of occupancy of the permanent seat. There were desperate efforts to undermine the act by stipulating that all federal buildings had to be ready by 1800. There was a move to postpone the vote, a move to adjourn. All amendments were voted down. Finally, the congressmen voted on the bill itself.

By a smidgen, 32 to 29, the Potomac won.

*   *   *

THERE REMAINED some major uncertainties about the future capital. The government wouldn't quit New York for the Potomac just yet, but rather, under the Residence Act, would spend the next ten years in Philadelphia. That raised the possibility that the government would stay permanently in Philadelphia, simply due to inertia. Not that it had ever shown the ability to remain in one place very long.

The legislation called for a capital on the Potomac, but that left a lot of wiggle room. Where on the Potomac would it be? The legislation stipulated that it could be anywhere on the river between the Eastern Branch (now called the Anacostia River, thanks to Jefferson's decision to restore the original Indian name) and the maligned Conococheague Creek, 100 miles upriver from Georgetown.

The act said the federal government would be in "a district of territory not exceeding ten miles square." The slightest nudge of the word "square," to a position in the sentence before "miles," would have made the district a tidy little place, but everyone seemed to understand that the district would be 100 square miles. But did such a district need to be literally a *square*? Washington thought so. Jefferson, with his more elastic mind, concluded that such a parcel could be in any shape whatsoever. And even if it was a square, would the boundaries follow the lines of latitude and longitude, or could they deviate from the cardinal points of the compass? Could the district be, for example, a diamond?

Someone had to make all these decisions. Someone had to say, "Here is where we are going to do it and how we are going to shape it." The Residence Act directed that the president appoint three commissioners to select the site. But Jefferson believed that Washington himself should pick the site, and the president did not shy away from the suggestion. Jefferson gave Washington a memo saying that the appointed commissioners would be "subject to the President's direction in every point."

The president did not look far to find the three commissioners to

oversee the new capital. He picked three fellow investors in the Patowmack Company. One, Thomas Johnson, was a director of the company. Another, David Stuart, was Washington's relative by marriage.
The third, Daniel Carroll of Rock Creek, had changed his vote in the
House on Hamilton's Assumption plan, making the Potomac capital
possible. The commissioner post was a fine reward.

As the president thought of the commercial potential of the new
federal city, Jefferson thought about its aesthetic qualities. He kept
pulling out the city plans of European capitals that he'd obtained during his Paris posting. He made an observation that would determine
much of the character of the capital in the decades and centuries to
come: "In Paris it is forbidden to build a house beyond a given height,
& it is admitted to be a good restriction. It keeps down the price of
ground, [keep]s the houses low & convenient, & the streets light &
airy. Fires are much more manageable where houses are low."

At the end of August, the president, Jefferson, and Madison all left
New York, bound for their home state. Washington spent four days at
the new, temporary capital, Philadelphia, and later lectured his secretary, Tobias Lear, on the proper way to pack material for shipping.
Washington liked order in all things, and broken china did not suit
him. Even with so much happening, he dictated a firm packing policy:

> . . . upon unpacking the china ornaments which accompanied the
> Mirrors for the Tables; it was found (notwithstanding they were
> in Bran) that many of the delicate & tender parts were broken;
> occasioned I believe by the Bran not being put in & settled down
> by little at a time. To press the Bran around the images (you have
> to remove with the Plateaux) will not answer; still, it must be so
> compact as to prevent friction, in moving; and this can only be
> done by putting each image or figure in a seperate box, with
> Bran by little & little, shaking & settling it by degrees, as it is
> added.

Heading south again, Washington survived another "upset" of his
carriage, and on September 11 arrived in Georgetown, where he

quickly received a briefing on the glacial progress of the Patowmack Company projects. That night the president reached Mount Vernon and slept in his own bed for the first time in a year and a half.

Jefferson and Madison, following in the president's wake, were delayed for a day while trying to get a ferry across the Chesapeake, and spent the time well, meandering around in rowboats and feasting on crabs. When they finally reached Georgetown, they met with local landowners, then found themselves inspired to take a boat trip up the river, to Little Falls. To this day it is a sublime journey, a passage from tidewater to the first rapids of the Upper Potomac, the river curving gently, the Virginia bank rising dramatically in a 150-foot palisade, notched by tumbling creeks. The Maryland bank has a wide, wooded floodplain, periodically scoured by floods, and beyond that another series of bluffs. Jefferson and Madison enjoyed the romantic scenery. Jefferson took note of Ballendine's old canal from the 1770s running along the Maryland bank, recently upgraded by the Patowmack Company and now skirting the cataract for roughly 2 miles. The federal district's boundary, Jefferson decided, should be just north of the entrance to this canal, right about the point where the river begins its descent through the falls.

Jefferson and Madison reached Mount Vernon the next day. Jefferson had been bubbling over with plans, had already sketched the federal town, and was eager to see construction begin on public buildings, boarding houses, and half a dozen taverns. Whatever was said at Mount Vernon failed to enter the historical record. The next day Jefferson and Madison eased downriver to Gunston Hall, home of patriot George Mason, the owner of much land and a large island within the projected federal district. Jefferson later briefed Washington on the many reasons Mason favored Georgetown over other sites:

> 1. . . . it's being at the junction of the upper & lower navigation where the commodities must be transferred into other vessels: (and here he was confident that no vessel could be contrived which could pass the upper shoals and live in the wide waters

below his island.) 2. The depth of water which would admit any vessels that could come to Alexandria. 3. The narrowness of the river & consequent safeness of the harbour. 4. It's being clear of ice as early at least as the canal & river above would be clear. 5. It's neighborhood to the Eastern branch, whither any vessels might conveniently withdraw which should be detained through the winter. 6. It's defensibility, as derived from the high & commanding hills around it. 7. It's actual possession of the commerce, & the start it already has.

Though not a disinterested observer, Mason (via Jefferson) surely buttressed Washington's conviction that the terrain should dictate national policy. Forget self-interest: The rivers, the river channels, the harbors, the hills, and the creeks all pointed to a logical place to put the government.

Washington's philosophy about the Potomac had been consistent all along. Great cities should be built at the fall line, that reef of rocks where the Piedmont gives way to the Coastal Plain, and where cargo has to change from one form of transportation to another (from a deep-water ship to a canoe or flatboat or wagon, for example). As he looked at the land around Georgetown, he saw the perfect nexus of transportation: a place where the Potomac, slashing in from the northwest, met the Post Road, bumping along from the northeast. There was practically a giant "X" on the map.

Just to the east of Georgetown was a bowl of land, formed by high, ancient river terraces, and covered with pastures and woods. More than a century earlier, in 1663, tobacco planters began clearing this part of Maryland. George Thompson received a grant of 1,000 acres and built Duddington Manor; Robert Troope patented a tract he called Scotland Yard, north of what is now Capitol Hill; north of the Troope land was Rome, patented by Francis Pope. In 1696, William Hutchinson patented a tract in the Georgetown area that he called the Vineyard. In 1703, Colonel Ninian Beall bought the land that would someday give rise to the White House.

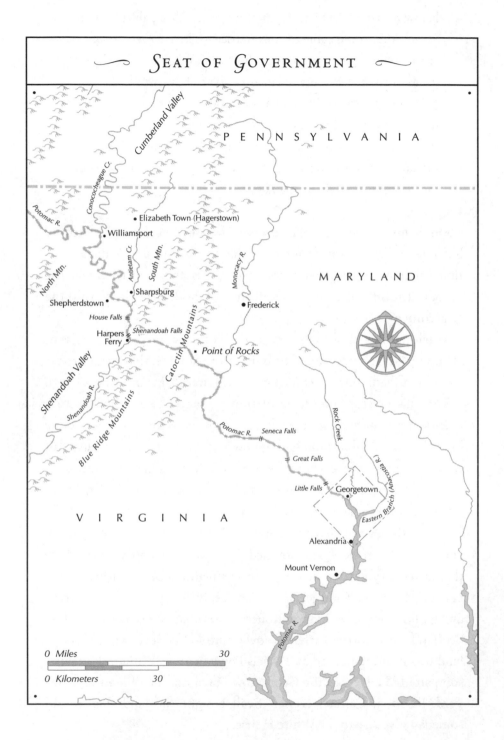

PENNSYLVANIA

MARYLAND

VIRGINIA

Cumberland Valley

Conococheague Cr.

Potomac R.

Elizabeth Town (Hagerstown)

Williamsport

Antietam Cr.

South Mtn.

Monocacy R.

North Mtn.

Shepherdstown

Sharpsburg

Frederick

House Falls

Shenandoah Falls

Harpers Ferry

Point of Rocks

Catoctin Mountains

Shenandoah Valley

Shenandoah R.

Blue Ridge Mountains

Potomac R.

Seneca Falls

Great Falls

Little Falls

Georgetown

Rock Creek

Eastern Branch (Anacostia R.)

Alexandria

Mount Vernon

Potomac R.

0 Miles 30

0 Kilometers 30

An escarpment, forming an arc from Georgetown to the Eastern Branch and continuing into what is now the Southeast section of the District of Columbia, served as the sides of the bowl. There were soggy patches down in that basin, though historians argue about whether the site was truly a swamp. Kenneth Bowling is a leader of the no-swamp school of thought, saying that, although there were some wet areas, including near the White House site and at the foot of what would become Capitol Hill, and there were tidal marshes along the rivers, there was certainly no place where trees grew in standing water. Concrete, sewers and culverts transform a landscape so dramatically that modern scholars and amateur historians are forced to peruse old maps and travelers' diaries in a desperate attempt to figure out what something looked like. In any case, the capital-as-swamp is a powerful political metaphor and is likely to endure for all time.

A good description of the place can be found in *Quebec to Carolina in 1785–1786: Being the Travel Diary and Observations of Robert Hunter, Jr., a Young Merchant of London:*

> You ride through some delightful corn and tobacco fields, with neat farmhouses situated in the middle of them. Now and then a thick wood will intercept the sight, for a little while, of the beautiful river Potomac. We forded Rock Creek, and the tide being up the wagon almost swam. There is a most tremendous steep hill here, which obliged us all to get out of the stage. Excepting that, the road is charming to George Town and the country richly cultivated.

As late as October, Washington still hadn't tipped his hand about where he wanted to put the city. He'd already chosen the site next to Georgetown, but he didn't want the landowners to know that the decision had been made. He needed to put on a show of considering other possibilities along the Potomac. On October 12, Washington left Mount Vernon with his secretary, William Jackson, for a rather epic, if fundamentally insincere, surveying trip up the river.

He stopped in Georgetown, met with the local businessmen, and spent a day riding around the enticing land east of town. Perhaps, due to the breadth of his vision, his genius for imagining the transformation of his world, he could see how the isolated wooden homes would be replaced by massive government structures, how trails through the woods would become broad thoroughfares, how in place of an old oak or poplar or maple there would be an equestrian statue or some monument to the glories of the Revolution. Perhaps he could imagine a farmer's pasture transformed into a luxuriant lawn behind the president's house. Meadows would be parks. Fords would become bridges. Where lime kilns smoldered, prosperous shops would sell the latest fashions. Perhaps he could see this thinly populated tract as a great city of hundreds of thousands of people. But even so, he couldn't have imagined everything that he was setting in motion. The future has surprises that not even the greatest visionary can anticipate. Washington fundamentally was a pragmatic man, and he may well have thought: The first thing we'll do is put a bridge over this creek.

The next day he left Georgetown and rode northwest along the river on a winding, dipping trail that had long guided travelers to the Great Falls of the Potomac. Washington so admired the falls that he later bought an especially romantic drawing of them by George Beck, but the terrain around the falls did not lend itself to a federal town, for there was no level ground, only hills and gullies and tumbling creeks, and the kind of vertical cliffs that would someday be striped with the ropes of recreational climbers. What the president thought as he passed through this area we can only imagine: He kept no diary on this trip, told us nothing of the changing of the leaves and the opening up of the views, and indeed left remarkably few clues about his route and his actions. No one along the way seems to have realized he was coming. Perhaps Washington felt no need to record his observations since he had already made up his mind that the seat of government would be in that bowl of land next to Georgetown.

He didn't linger at Great Falls, but kept going to the mouth of the Monocacy, a lovely, placid little river that flows into the Potomac from the north, draining the Piedmont in and around the town of Frederick.

Amelung had already staked out the place for his glassworks. A "ten mile square" on the site would have encompassed some of the 10,000-acre estate of Charles Carroll, a signer of the Declaration of Independence, and one of the key Senators to change his vote in favor of Assumption after learning about the compromise on Residency. The area was guarded by a picturesque mountain, named Sugarloaf, rising abruptly from the pastures just four miles from the bank of the Potomac, and looking from the river like a perfectly symmetrical mound, something that might have been designed by a child.

Washington kept trotting onward. He left the riverbank and headed north, past the Carroll estate (we could depart the documentary record and imagine Washington delivering some kind of special reward to Carroll for his role in the compromise, or at least giving him a secret handshake, but it's not clear that the two men saw one another at all), and then, through Frederick, veering west into a notch in the crumbling Catoctin mountain. Washington continued onward, through a wide, pleasant valley, and then over South Mountain, the geological rampart that is known on the south side of the Potomac as the Blue Ridge.

At this point he becomes even more of a historical blur: He may have visited Shepherdstown, the community of mills and iron furnaces where James Rumsey had only three years earlier demonstrated his steamboat to much applause. Washington may have stopped in Sharpsburg, a humble village on Antietam Creek, where the Union would be saved decades later on the bloodiest day in American military history. The local businessmen in Shepherdstown and Sharpsburg, grasping the fact that the ten-mile square could encompass them both, as well as the ironworks at the mouth of Antietam Creek, aggressively lobbied to become the seat of government, but only after Washington made his surprise visit. The Maryland officials offered to donate 475 acres of land and scraped together $4,839 to help pay for construction. Shepherdstown pledged $20,000.

Washington rode onward, to the north, to Elizabethtown, later named Hagerstown, a village perched between the Potomac and the

Pennsylvania state line. Perhaps this was the general's way of saying that the Pennsylvanians had not been forgotten, even if, at the crucial moment, the Virginians had prevailed in the Residency debate. Finally, on October 21, he arrived in Williamsport, on Conococheague Creek, where the Great Wagon Road from Pennsylvania met the Potomac, and where ferrymen had been carrying pioneers and migrants across the river for generations. The northerners who had feared that Washington would put the government deep into the woods would have been aghast had they known he was now checking out the place with the long Indian name. Washington met with local officials, made a few bland pronouncements, and headed back home. It's unclear how he traveled, though one report, second-hand, had him paddling down the Potomac, giving him yet another chance to survey the Patowmack Company improvement projects. In any case, the trip lasted twelve days, and did nothing to change his mind about the correct place for the future capital of the United States. The "X" would still mark the spot.

*   *   *

IN LATE NOVEMBER the president and First Lady left Mount Vernon, returning to Philadelphia. The coachman was drunk. The carriage turned over. Only the dignity of the presidency suffered any harm. Then the drunken coachman turned the carriage over a second time. Sometimes traveling by coach was harder than poling a raft across an ice-choked river.

Washington told Congress where he wanted to put the federal city. In the next few months, while dealing with other major political crises (Indian-fighting in the West, Hamilton's proposal to create a Bank of the United States, etc.), he found time to negotiate with the Potomac landowners. He also decided to shift the federal district (the ten-mile square) toward the south, to include Alexandria and other terrain below the Potomac's junction with the Eastern Branch, even though that would require an amendment to the original act. The Pennsylvania interests began scheming once again to change the law and keep the capital permanently in Philadelphia.

But Congress on March 3, 1791, agreed to Washington's plan. The District of Columbia, as it would become known, would encompass one of the president's properties, near Falls Church, Virginia, in addition to the town of Alexandria, with the southern point of the federal diamond only a few miles from the driveway at Mount Vernon. By now it was clear that Washington could have simply declared his house the capital. He was not a king, but neither was he a backbencher in Parliament; with his index finger he could command a city to rise from the American dirt.

Washington hired Pierre-Charles (Peter) L'Enfant, a French-American living in New York, to draw a plan for the federal city. L'Enfant arrived in Georgetown in March, and immediately began designing a city far more magnificent, more breathtaking, than the humble republican village that Jefferson had envisioned. Jefferson's sketch for the capital showed a rectangle of city blocks, a town not that much bigger than a neighborhood. But Washington and L'Enfant wanted to create something that would cover the entire bowl encircled by the ancient river terraces. L'Enfant's plan called for a city of 6,110.94 acres, dwarfing Philadelphia, New York, and Boston. It would become the largest city in North America, L'Enfant thought—a metropolis of 800,000 people.

First they had to find people to buy plots of land. They needed investors, residents, developers, some capital coming in. When they held the first auction of city lots, the sky opened up and drenched the proceedings. Washington, Jefferson, and Madison attended, but the public response was muted at best. Only thirty-five lots sold. The auction raised less than $2,000. L'Enfant was furious, but Washington never lost his optimism. He knew that, for a time, the seat of government would be largely a conceit more than a real city, that the spacious plan devised by L'Enfant would mean that the capital would be, for decades, spread out, seemingly empty.

But wait, Washington thought.

Wait a century.

10

The Final Measurement

PRESIDENT WASHINGTON kept moving. In the spring of 1791, even as he was scratching out a national capital in the dirt near Georgetown, he decided to take a tour of the Deep South, a part of the country he'd never quite gotten around to exploring. The Virginian had seen New England many times but had hardly set foot in North Carolina. Early in his presidential term he had rolled his way by carriage across New England, marveling at the industriousness of the Yankees, their rapid adoption of manufacturing, and the cleanliness and bustle of their towns. But he would not find such sights in the South, a region of desolate fields, shabby homes, scenes of poverty. He would be taken aback. To a degree he couldn't quite grasp, he had become, over the years, less and less of a southerner.

The tour would last three months and take him 1,816 miles over roads even more miserable and mirey than those he'd been accustomed to in Virginia and points north. Bays and rivers provided their own special hazards. Early in the trip, on the afternoon of March 24, 1791, the president's traveling entourage, including his meticulously groomed horse, Prescott, boarded a ferryboat on the Chesapeake Bay, hoping to reach Annapolis before dark. The boat's crew proved incompetent, and struggled with a light headwind. Darkness fell. A gale kicked up. "I was in imminent danger," Washington wrote in his diary. About eight in the evening the boat finally reached the mouth of the Severn River, but ran aground on a mud bank amid "constant lightning & tremendous thunder." The crew managed to float the boat again, but it soon ran aground a second time. The night grew late, the storm continued, and in the darkness, no one had the slightest notion where they were, other than grounded in the middle of a tidal river with an extremely important passenger aboard. The president of the United States spent the night in his greatcoat and boots, jammed into a berth too small for a man his size, while the storm raged outside. It was a rather inauspicious beginning to the tour.

Two weeks later the president nearly met catastrophe again when one of his horses panicked at the crossing of Occoquan Creek, just north of Fredericksburg. The horse, hitched to the other horses and to Washington's coach, plunged off the ferry and nearly pulled everyone, including the president, into the creek. All this served to remind the president that when you traveled by road in America you ran the risk of drowning.

The president did not have what a modern executive would call an advance team, and so there were a few glitches in the itinerary. One morning in North Carolina, Washington stopped at what he believed to be a public house, one of the roadside establishments that functioned as the eighteenth-century equivalent of a motel and diner. The president ordered breakfast. The owner, Colonel John Allen, obliged, even though this was not, in fact, a public house, but rather a private home, unprepared for guests, much less for feting the president of the United States. It is a hallmark of the American people that they respond well to a crisis. They are also taught from an early age the importance of sharing. Colonel Allen and his family threw together the kind of feast you could imagine rendered in a Renaissance fresco, a truly heroic meal, with turkey, ham, chicken, sausages, waffles, eggs, and on and on. It was as if the entire farm had been suddenly harvested or butchered. Only when the president prepared to depart and asked for the bill did he discover his error. (Colonel Allen did not mind, and managed to tag along with the president the rest of the day.)

One afternoon, caught in a tempest, Washington wanted to call a halt to the day's travel, but the only inn had no stables, and the beds had "a dirty appearance." So he kept going. He tried to be diplomatic even in his diary, noting, at one point, that a town had given him "as good a salute as could be given with one piece of artillery." He passed through some desolate terrain, sandy and barren, but eventually reached Charleston, where his scrutiny of rivers and pastures and crops shifted abruptly to an appraisal of the female population: "Was visited about 2 oclock, by a great number of the most respectable ladies of Charleston—the first honor of the kind I had ever experienced and it was as flattering as it was singular."

He attended a dance, and approvingly noted the presence of "256 elegantly dressed & handsome ladies." He did not reveal how he ascertained that number, but undoubtedly he got it precisely right.

*   *   *

WASHINGTON'S FIRST TWO YEARS in office went about as smoothly as anyone could have expected, given that such a government had never before existed on the planet. He brought dignity to the presidency, committed no major political blunders, and kept his disputatious Cabinet members from reaching across the table and throttling one another. Factionalism hadn't turned into fratricide. Washington had characteristically survived a nearly fatal illness. The country had entered a prosperous phase. The contagion of liberty had spread to France. Surely, Americans were leading civilization to a glorious destiny. At the very least, they had a few more coins jingling in their pockets.

The good times for Washington didn't last. By 1792 two military expeditions to subdue the Ohio Indians had met with complete disaster. Josiah Harmar's expedition of 1790 set out to destroy the villages of the Miamis, but his forces, militiamen working for two-thirds of a dollar a day, were routed by Shawnees led by Little Turtle. The 1791 campaign led by Arthur St. Clair was a Braddockesque calamity, with 630 Americans killed and hundreds more wounded in an ambush on the Wabash River.

The master plan of the United States required either the removal or the complete submission (and cultural transformation) of the Indians. They had no intention of complying. Washington knew that the rights of the Indians had been trampled time and again by the chaotic inrush of settlers in the West, a process that refused to stick to the orderly pace the president desired. As much as anyone in his era, Washington had always anticipated, encouraged, and banked on the westward spread of what we generically call the Americans (an inexact term for those who were foreign-born and hardly identifying with the United States), and now as president he heard directly from Indian delegations about the consequences of that migration. One day John Baptist de Coigne, chief of the Wabash and Illinois Indians, told Washington and Jefferson, via a French translator, about the depredations of the Kentuckians, who he said had been stealing his horses and killing his game:

> I am a friend to all, and hurt none. For what are we on this earth? but as a small and tender plant of corn;—even as nothing. God has made this earth for you as well as us: we are then but as one family, and if any one strikes you, it is as if he had struck us. . . . Father, we fear the Kentuckians. They are headstrong and do us great wrong. They are not content to come on our lands to hunt on them, to steal and destroy our stocks, as the Shawanese and Delawares do, but they go further and abuse our persons. . . . Father, you are rich, you have all things at command, you want for nothing. You promised to wipe away our tears.

The government did not wipe away Indian tears. What angered the settlers in the West was the government's failure to wipe out the Indians entirely. The westerners were angry that, instead of sending an army that could make the frontier safe, the government sent tax collectors to enforce the 1791 excise tax on whiskey. There were ominous rumblings of discontent in western Pennsylvania. This could easily turn into an episode like the Shays Rebellion, only instead of flinty New Englanders, these settlers were half-wild, crusty, and mean, independent by necessity, with no sentimental attachment to the government back east.

Meanwhile, Washington faced more vexations in his grand plans for the federal city. His fussy surveyor, L'Enfant, drove everyone crazy with his exacting and uncompromising design. Local landholders refused to acknowledge his genius. When it came time to sell city lots at auction, L'Enfant refused to produce a map of the city. And when Daniel Carroll, Lord Duddington, one of the most powerful men in town (and not to be confused with Daniel Carroll of Rock Creek), began to build a new manor house, L'Enfant declared that it blocked a view and had to be torn down. Carroll refused. L'Enfant then ordered his own workers to raze the house. The president had no choice but to fire L'Enfant. Sales of city lots continued to go slowly, even when the president himself purchased some of them to set a noble example. This idea of a federal town on the Potomac still seemed rather far-fetched.

The president also had to deal with the intensification of factionalism, of political vitriol. Jefferson and Hamilton were hardly having wine-soaked dinners together anymore. Both wanted to quit. Washington wanted to quit, too. He felt himself a "slave" to the public. The political climate revolted him, and he had become a target for criticism in the press. People dared to question his actions, to assign him monarchical tendencies. He told his friend Henry Lee that the barbs could never reach "the most vulnerable part of me," because he had the eternal consolation that "neither ambitious nor interested motives have influenced my conduct." Jefferson knew the truth: Washington "feels those things more than any person I ever yet met with."

The president once again sang his favorite melancholy tune, that he would be happy only as a farmer under his vine and fig tree. He would not accept—much less "run for," as we say today—a second term.

Yes—said the others—you will. You must. Otherwise the nation is doomed.

This was a familiar refrain for the Indispensable Man. *You have no choice.*

He won reelection unanimously. His second inaugural speech, three paragraphs long, still holds the record for rhetorical economy. He slipped away almost immediately to Mount Vernon, but soon heard the disturbing news that the French revolutionaries had guillotined Louis XVI and Marie Antoinette. France and England were now at war. Washington had to find a way to steer a course between those two Great Powers, even as, out in the American backcountry, the centrifugal forces were building yet again.

An incident in August 1793 revealed the temper and genius of Washington the politician. The Cabinet assembled to discuss the new envoy from France, Edmond Charles Genet, who seemed determined to stir up as much controversy and enmity as possible. French privateers were being outfitted in American ports and seizing English ships in American waters, putting the country's neutrality at risk. Genet made the president and Hamilton extremely nervous, for they feared that French revolutionary fever would spread across the United States. The president and his federalist friends were also alarmed by the simultaneous rise in "democratic societies," political clubs that followed the Jeffersonian and Madisonian line of thought and lent vocal support to the French radicals. So the situation was quite tense when Jefferson, Hamilton, Secretary of War Henry Knox, Attorney General Edmund Randolph, and Washington gathered to discuss the execrable Genet.

Hamilton wanted Washington to publish his reasons for asking for Genet's recall, rather than handle the matter more privately, through diplomatic channels. Knox must have wanted to provoke Washington, for he presented the president with a cartoon that had been recently circulated. It showed Washington dressed as a king and placed on a guillotine. The sudden eruption of Mount Washington inspired a vivid description from Jefferson:

> The Presidt. was much inflamed, got into one of those passions when he cannot command himself. Run on much on the personal abuse which had been bestowed on him. Defied any man on earth

to produce one single act of his since he had been in the govern- ment which was not done on the purest motives. That he had never repented but once the having slipped the moment of re- signing his office, and that was every moment since. That *by god* he had rather be in his grave than in his present situation. That he had rather be on his farm than to be made *emperor of the world* and yet that they were charging him with wanting to be a king.

And so on.

Finally the tempest passed. The Cabinet members sat mute. "There was a pause," Jefferson deadpanned in his memo of the meeting. No one knew how to resume the discussion. In the presence of the great man one did not dare crack a joke to break the tension.

And then Washington calmly suggested that they consider the issue another day. He was a rational actor again, deliberate, cautious, unwilling to be goaded into a rash policy. Totally in command.

*   *   *

WHILE IN PHILADELPHIA, Washington managed to direct opera- tions at Mount Vernon via frequent letters. When his farm manager, Anthony Whitting, died unexpectedly in the summer of 1793, the president intensified his supervision. To his nephew Howell Lewis, then living at Mount Vernon, and to his overseers and new manager, William Pearce, he sent commands so detailed that one would think the president could observe his farm through a direct satellite feed.

Build a new rail fence along that property line; mix small seeds with sand so the servants won't be able to sell them on the black market; use manure heavily on one field rather than lightly on two; bury thorn berries for a year before they are sown so that they may fer- ment; plant corn in some of the fields reserved for buckwheat; stop leaving the corn harrows on the ground where they are damaged by the elements; make sure to plow in the buckwheat when it is "green & succulent," because "it is from the juices of this plant that the putrefaction & fermentation proceeds"; fill the Ice House with ice during the next freeze; keep a watchful eye at all times on the slaves. ("There is no other sure way of getting work well done and quietly by negroes; for when an Overlooker's back is turned the most of them will slight their work, or be idle altogether.") When an overseer asked for a raise, the president grudgingly gave it, adding that any further requests for a raise would be futile, that the salary would be precisely 40 pounds per annum "whether the winds blow high or blow low, whether the ground is deluged with rain, or laid waste by a parching drought." A year later, believing the overseer lazy, he fired him.

He told his nephew that he could find a cask of clover seed just to the left of the door in a storehouse, and that if it wasn't there, Mr. Butler, a servant, either stole it or allowed others ("the roguest people about the house") to steal it, and should therefore be responsible for the full value of the seed. He upbraided his nephew for flaws in his reports, which the president viewed as insufficiently detailed. You're just a young man, the president lectured him, and you need to learn "the importance of giving attention, and doing whatever you undertake, well."

In 1794, Washington came to a difficult decision: He would liquidate his real estate empire. He would sell his western lands and either sell or rent four of the five farms at Mount Vernon, reserving only the mansion farm for his retirement. The years of keeping ledgers and monitoring every row of peas had worn on him, and he hoped to lead a simpler and more serene life in his final years. But he also had another motive, he told his secretary, Tobias Lear. He didn't want to own "that species of property" anymore—his slaves.

Washington faced a serious moral, legal, and financial dilemma with the slave population at Mount Vernon. Even though he hoped to free his slaves, he owned fewer than half of the slaves at the plantation. Many others were the Custis, or "dower," slaves, legally the property of the heirs of Daniel Parke Custis, including Martha Dandridge Custis Washington. The two slave populations had intermarried. They had children and grandchildren. Washington had a moral objection to any action that would tear apart slave families (Virginia law didn't recognize a slave marriage as legitimate, but Washington did). Historian Dennis Pogue has contended that Washington wanted to use the revenue from the sale of his land to pay the Custis heirs for the manumission of the Custis slaves. It would be a hefty sum of money, many times the plantation's annual profit in a typical year.

The plan came to naught. Washington advertised the availability of his lands, but few people inquired. The tired soils around Mount Vernon enticed no one, and the western lands were, for the most part, still too remote. He was, for the time being, trapped in the world he had made for himself: the master of a large community of African-Americans and the owner of many dispersed and still-wild tracts of the American backcountry.

*　　*　　*

JUST AS SO MANY THINGS were going badly for George Washington, just as the democratic societies were stirring up outrageous opposition and ill faith in government, just as his own estate was going downhill and who knows how many of his possessions stolen and destroyed in his absence, along came the most serious crisis of his tenure: a rebellion. Citizens of the United States, refusing to pay the 1791 excise tax on distilled spirits, had taken up arms against officers of the federal government. These rebels were a species familiar to the president. They lived in four counties in western Pennsylvania—Allegheny, Fayette, Westmoreland, and Washington.

Those people again.

First the Seceders had tried to steal his land; now the same sort of lowlifes were trying to destroy his Union!

The westerners had legitimate complaints. The Mississippi, for example, remained closed to American commerce. The westerners blamed Chief Justice John Jay, now negotiating a treaty with England (in an experimental republic the chief justice could double as diplomat), for allowing Spain to keep the river closed during his earlier negotiations with the Spanish envoy. "The temper of that country is roused to an extreme," Secretary of State Edmund Randolph told Washington. "They entertain suspicions that it is not the wish of every state in the Union that they should enjoy the Mississippi, or should continue members of the Union." This was half-crazy. Of course Washington wanted them to stay in the Union. That's why he didn't want them gallivanting down the Mississippi to Spanish New Orleans. Washington, unsentimental about the allure of his new republic, assumed that nothing but economic dependency could keep the westerners loyal to the eastern government.

With roads so inadequate and the Mississippi closed, the grain of the westerners had been effectively cut off from the market. Instead of shipping grain as cargo, the farmers distilled it. Whiskey became currency. By Hugh Henry Brackenridge's estimate, the westerners distilled ten times as much whiskey as their countrymen on the eastern side of the mountains. In the *National Gazette*, Brackenridge demanded an exemption from the tax, on grounds of the hardship of the western country, the scarcity of cheap labor, the bad roads and rugged country, the expense of lawsuits due to competing land claims (he did not give as an example his own experience defending the Seceders against General Washington), and most of all the Indian wars, which had drawn men from their families. His people were "hewers of wood and drawers of water"; they were the bed of true republicanism, a necessary balance to the monied interests and would-be aristocrats of the East.

A horse could carry two kegs of 8 gallons each. The spirits were worth 50 cents a gallon on the western side of the Alleghenies, and a dollar a gallon on the eastern—and yet the tax was the same per gallon on both sides of the mountains. Sometimes the pack horses would return with iron or salt. Every farm had a still. The westerners had opposed the excise tax for three years and were prone to tarring and feathering the tax collectors who dared try to enforce it.

On July 16, 1794, about 100 men, armed with rifles and, in some cases, clubs and sticks, surrounded the palatial home of John Neville, the collector of the federal excise tax in western Pennsylvania and a

veteran of the Revolutionary War. Neville had wealth and good connections, and that didn't make him any more popular among the
farmers. He feared for his life, but he was well armed, and exchanged
fire with the attackers for about twenty-five minutes. Five of the attackers were wounded; one later died. Neville, his wife, and his daughter were uninjured, despite fifty bullets fired into the house.

The mob dispersed, but returned the next day, now 500 strong, and
demanded that Neville resign his post and turn over his records.
Neville by this point had wisely found a place to hide. In his place, a
friend, Major Abraham Kirkpatrick, and 11 men from the garrison of
Fort Lafayette had holed up in the house. Another gun battle broke
out, this one lasting nearly an hour. One attacker died, and several
people on both sides were wounded. The attackers set the outbuildings
on fire, and Kirkpatrick and his men finally surrendered. The rebels
burned down Neville's house.

The westerners now talked openly of separation, of establishing
their own government. The ringleaders called for a massing of forces
at Braddock's Field, site of the massacre four decades earlier. They
wanted to march on Pittsburgh and seize the arms of the federal
troops. Torching the city seemed another viable option. Plunder ap-
pealed to many. Anything might happen. They were pretty much
making up the insurrection as they went along.

"The whole country was [an] inflammable mass; it required but the
least touch of fire to inflame it," Brackenridge later recounted. He
briefly thought of dashing through the woods, back east, to the territory of the rational and calm. Along with Albert Gallatin, Senator
James Ross, and a few other politicians and local elites, Brackenridge
had more to lose than gain in an insurrection. These leading citizens
now weighed in as a heavy force of moderation. Brackenridge urged
the rebels at Braddock's Field to march in an orderly fashion upon
Pittsburgh, to demonstrate that they were not simply a bloodthirsty
mob. The march became a kind of parade. Brackenridge was a genius.
He helped turn a revolution into a theatrical spectacle. It was a classic
American call to action: *Let's put on a show.* At another meeting he

managed to persuade the hotheads to defer all decisions on secession to a "Committee on Safety" that would meet later. Send it to a committee! This was hardly a battle cry, but Brackenridge et al. somehow persuaded the whiskey rebels to turn their war into a procedural matter. The rebellion died in committee.

But in Philadelphia, across many mountains, in a different informational environment, the president was in an extreme state of alarm. He reacted to the Whiskey Rebellion as he had to the Shays Rebellion eight years earlier. Washington saw the insurrection as nothing less than a threat to the entire government. If allowed to continue, "there was an end to our Constitution & laws," in the paraphrase of Hamilton.

It is easy today to make the case that Washington overreacted, though we know things he didn't know in August of 1794, such as the persuasiveness in western Pennsylvania of cooler heads, including Brackenridge and Gallatin. We have a sense, too, of the Union as something made of hardy stuff, incapable of disintegrating simply because some country boys have gotten rowdy. But that wasn't the Union of Washington's presidency. He had no way of knowing if his nation would endure for centuries or explode before his eyes. At a basic level, and thanks to personal experience, he respected the ability of the people to pull off a revolution.

Washington felt he had the authority under established law to quell a rebellion by calling out the militia from several states. Hamilton urged him to go full bore, with a force so "imposing" that the rebels would offer no resistance. In military circles today this is known as "overwhelming force." Hamilton calculated that there were 16,000 males aged sixteen or older in the four rebellious counties, and that 7,000 were likely to be armed (he didn't reveal his rationale for this second figure). Armed men might join that group from other counties as well, Hamilton said, and so he recommended that Washington call out no fewer than 12,000 militiamen. Washington ultimately called out 15,000, and appointed as the commander of this massive force his old Revolutionary War comrade and Potomac River true believer

Henry Lee, who was still solvent for the moment despite his zealous land speculation.

Washington and Hamilton would ride with the army as well—back in the saddle again. The president and his friends were ready to fight a civil war. The reaction may seem gung ho, but they were just being cautious, prudent, conservative in their own way—eliminating any and all threats to the Union. Washington had another motive for personally supervising the suppression of the western rebellion: He wanted to keep an eye on the militia, which he knew, from his experience in the Revolution, did not always behave in a gentlemanly manner. He didn't want a bunch of gun-toting wild men terrorizing the locals in the name of the federal government. His paramount goal was loyalty to the Union, and that would be undermined if the militia ran riot.

Washington thought the western insurrection the first "ripe fruit" of the democratic societies. He knew they wanted him to retire, and he wanted to do the same permanently—to "sink into the profoundest retirement," as he told Lee. He believed that the societies were making "the most diabolical attempts to destroy the best fabric of human government and happiness, that has ever been presented for the acceptance of mankind."

Weeks passed while the proper forces were called up and outfitted. Not until the end of September did Washington depart for the West in his carriage. On the road to Carlisle, Pennsylvania, he saw the way the farmers had cut their buckwheat and left it in small cocks, drawn to a point, to let the seed ripen and the straw cure. He jotted off a note with that observation to his farm manager at Mount Vernon. Only a couple of days into his journey, he received a letter from the citizens of Washington County stating their total submission to the laws of the government. They couldn't have been more unambiguous about their loyalty to the United States, reserving only their basic First Amendment rights. ("Resolved unanimously, that we will submit to the Laws of the United States, that we will not directly nor indirectly oppose the execution of the Acts for raising a revenue on distilled Spirits and

Stills and that we will support so far as the Law requires the civil authority in affording the protection due to all Officers and other Citizens reserving at the same time our Constitutional right of Petition or remonstrance.") No matter: The campaign would proceed against them, despite their protestations of submission.

In Carlisle, the citizens greeted him as a conquering hero. "The sword of justice, in the hands of our beloved President," they wrote, "can only be considered as an object of terror by the wicked, and will be looked up to by the good and virtuous, as their safeguard and protection."

Washington answered, "Let us hope that the delusion can not be lasting; that reason will speedily regain her empire, and the laws their just authority. . . ." Washington did not enjoy even the suggestion of popular discontent. His aim, he told the Carlislians, was to establish "the authority of the laws in the affections of all rather than in the fears of any."

His carriage took him south, into Maryland, along the Great Wagon Road to the Potomac River at Williamsport, on Conococheague Creek, where four years earlier he had declined to place the nation's capital. He took a ferry across the river, and after rolling for 20 miles across the Shenandoah Valley, reached North Mountain. At that point the campaign to save the country took a momentary detour, for the entourage became lost on an old road. Soon, however, the presidential party emerged from the wilderness and reached the town of Bath. Washington's diary does not mention anything as indulgent as a soak in the hot springs, nor does it mention the late James Rumsey and the magic boat.

The next day—October 15, 1794—he retraced his journey of a decade earlier, and many times before that. Once again there was no hint that he'd ever seen this part of the world, or had found it, on previous occasions, every bit as rough and tumble as he found it now. He crossed the Potomac again and lodged in Old Town, where the ancient Thomas Cresap had finally passed away. In 1748 he'd called that road from the Potomac crossing to Old Town the worst ever trod by man or beast, and his opinion hadn't changed. He noted "the extreme badness of the Road."

The next day, with artillery booming, three companies of troops escorted the president into Cumberland, where he bowed to all the officers and reviewed the army. He estimated their number at 3,200, with another 1,700 at nearby camps or on their way.

The only hitch in the entire battle plan was that the enemy had already quit the fight. The local leaders had already handled the problem. Most people had taken advantage of a general amnesty offered in exchange for an oath of allegiance; a few rabble-rousers had taken flight. It was over. Washington wasn't satisfied, however, by this latest intelligence. Surrender wasn't enough. These insurgents had to change their ways: "[T]hough Submission is professed," he wrote gravely, "their principles remain the same; that nothing but coercion, & example will reclaim & bring them to a due & unequivocal submission to the Laws."

Washington traveled north, to Bedford, Pennsylvania, this time noting in his diary that the route had been "opened by Troops under my command in the Autumn of 1758"—a rare admission that he had a past.

At this point the president abruptly turned back to the east. He didn't charge ahead to the scene of battle. Perhaps he had no desire to see those irritating western Pennsylvanians up close again. He stated that he was needed in Philadelphia. Lee and Hamilton, however, went forth with the Army, rounded up and arrested some rebels, and turned all of western Pennsylvania into a military zone.

As it happened, none of the Seceders who had caused Washington such problems in the past were prominent in the Whiskey Rebellion, but several felt the blowback. John Reed and Samuel McBride, two of the defendants in the ejectment suit pressed by the general, had stills seized by the government (first Washington takes their farms, then he takes their stills!). James McBride was jailed for a night.

Hamilton suspected that Brackenridge had secretly orchestrated the rebellion, and this was by no means an irrational thought, since Brackenridge had indeed attempted to control events. It occurred to the law-yer that his true intentions could easily be misinterpreted, since that's what he had intended—to fool people into thinking he was in favor of the rebellion when in fact he merely wanted to transform it into some-thing less combustible. He feared the federal dragoons would assassi-nate him. Surely he would be arrested. Strangely enough, General Lee insisted on staying in Brackenridge's house. They had many memo-ries, for Brackenridge had studied alongside Lee at Princeton more than two decades earlier. Dining together now proved awkward, since Brackenridge anticipated that at any moment he would be hauled away in irons and charged with treason.

Eventually, Hamilton decided that Brackenridge was innocent. Some citizens were not so fortunate and found themselves marched out of town, penned up in a wet stable, and thrown raw meat, an un-ambiguous message if there ever was one. But as wars go, this one fiz-zled spectacularly. Ultimately, only two people were convicted of treason, and Washington pardoned them both.

The cause of nationalism had now taken a great leap forward. Not only was the Western Insurrection crushed, but General Anthony Wayne, in the Battle of Fallen Timbers in the northern portion of what is now Ohio, had routed the British-backed Indians. In 1795, in the Treaty of Greenville, the Indians surrendered most of the Ohio Valley. Jay's treaty with England passed the Senate, and the British finally left their forts on American soil at the Great Lakes; Spain opened the Mississippi to American commerce.

There was no stopping the American juggernaut.

*   *   *

JEFFERSON, appalled by the president's handling of the rebellion, now saw Washington as the agent of the "monocrats." What possible justification had there been to arm one part of the population against another? How could Washington be "so patient of the kicks and scoffs of our enemies, and rising at a feather against our friends"?

Jefferson had been holed up at Monticello, insisting that he was retired from politics. When still secretary of state, he had declared, "The motion of my blood no longer keeps time with the tumult of the world." He had hated his job:

> . . . worn down with labours from morning to night, and day to day; knowing them as fruitless to others as they are vexatious to myself, committed singly in desperate and eternal contest against a host who are systematically undermining the public liberty and prosperity, even the rare hours of relaxation sacrificed to the society of persons in the same intentions, of whose hatred I am conscious even in those moments of conviviality when the heart wishes most to open itself to the effusions of friendship and confidence, cut off from my family and friends, my affairs abandoned to chaos and derangement, in short, giving every thing I love, in exchange for everything I hate. . . .

So he returned to his farm, to a vigorous phase of his life in which he never strayed more than a few miles from Monticello—even during the 1796 presidential election, when he narrowly lost to John Adams. Washington felt the siren song of his farm as well. As Washington's presidency wore on, he stole back to Mount Vernon more frequently. The farmer-president retained his zeal for agricultural experimentation, and he bristled at the intransigence of his managers, who, given the chance, would simply plant Indian corn wherever they could. To Jefferson, Washington offered a full report of the successes and failures of his latest crops, and his technique for plowing buckwheat back into the soil not once but twice. He shared his belief that potatoes were an ameliorating crop, turning the soil darker, making it richer. Farmer to farmer, Washington had much to say: "The Albany Pea, which is the same as the field Pea of Europe, I have tried and found it grew well; but it is subject to the same bug that perforates the garden pea, and eats out the kernel; so it will happen, I fear, with the pea you propose to import. . . ."

Beneath the surface of this breezy correspondence lay all those festering political tensions. Jefferson thought Washington had been brainwashed by Hamilton. The Federalists had seized his mind. Washington had even grown a bit dim of brain, Jefferson believed: "His memory was already sensibly impaired by age, the firm tone of mind for which he had been remarkable, was beginning to relax, its energy was abated, a listlessness of labor, a desire for tranquillity had crept on him, and a willingness to let others act, and even think for him."

Jefferson, Madison, and their Republican (Anti-Federalist) allies in government were loath to criticize Washington directly, for any direct challenge to the great man tended to end badly for the assailant, and he remained the most popular figure in the land, by far. (Washington's aura would not dissipate even after his retirement. Albert Gallatin, after dining with Washington in 1797, reported to his wife that the old man was "more than usually grave, cool, and reserved," but pleaded with his wife to keep that opinion private, "for I hate treason, and you know that it would be less sacrilegious to carry arms against our country than to refuse singing to the tune of the best and greatest of men. . . .")

The rift between Washington and his former friends Jefferson and Madison became a yawning chasm in 1796, even as Washington was polishing his Farewell Address. In April, Jefferson wrote a private letter to his former neighbor Philip Mazzei, who had moved to Italy. Jefferson's language had never been more elegantly eviscerating. He described to Mazzei the rise of an "Anglican, monarchical and aristocratical party," led by the Executive and the Judicial branches, most of the legislature, all of the officers of the government and "all timid men who prefer the calm of despotism to the boisterous sea of liberty"—British merchants, American traders, speculators, etc. Then, in a line that would haunt Jefferson thereafter, he made a thinly veiled reference to his former friend, the greatest American: "It would give you a fever were I to name to you the apostates who have gone over to these heresies, men who were Samsons in the field and Solomons in the council, but who have had their heads shorn by the harlot England."

Mazzei copied the incendiary paragraphs to two friends, and eventually these portions of the letter, with additional material written by Jefferson in different contexts, were reprinted in France, and finally wound up, more than a year after the original letter was written, in the Philadelphia newspapers.

Washington had known as early as June 1796 that Jefferson had been speaking ill of him. That month, the *Philadelphia Aurora* published an attack on Washington that exploited a confidential document shared by Washington with his Cabinet in 1793, during a debate on how to deal with France. Jefferson, seeing the report, knew that he would be presumed to have leaked the information. Jefferson quickly wrote to Washington to disavow being the source, though at the same time admitting that it was possible that he had read the document to Madison. Jefferson's assurance of his probity then turned into a kind of confession, for he said he'd never concealed his political sentiments during private conversations. As we read this letter today, we can almost see Jefferson squirming in his chair as he pens the words. Finally, Jefferson himself could stand it no more, and changed subjects: "I put away this disgusting dish of old fragments, and talk to you of my peas and clover."

Washington wrote back, politely but firmly, indeed with a kind of ascending pitch of remonstration.

"As you have mentioned the subject yourself, it would not be frank, candid, or friendly to conceal, that your conduct has been represented as derogatory from that opinion *I* had conceived you entertained of me," Washington wrote. He passionately reminded Jefferson that his political agenda had always been "truth and right decisions," that he'd often sided against Hamilton (not named, but referred to as "the person evidently alluded to"), and that "I was no party man myself, and the first wish of my heart was, if parties did exist, to reconcile them." The letter, on its face, absolved Jefferson of blame for the published insults to Washington, and the president even went off on another agricultural digression about crop rotation, Albany peas, winter vetch, and so forth, but Jefferson had to have been shaken to the core.

Jefferson in his letter had asked Washington for a document on an unrelated matter, and Washington promised to send it. Several weeks later Washington did just that, enclosing a brief note. This was the polite thing to do—but there was no more chatter about peas. In fact, there would be no more letters whatsoever between the two men, no more discussions about the federal city still taking shape, no more strategizing about the Potomac Route to the West.

Their correspondence, and their friendship—and their long, fruitful partnership that in so many ways had changed their world—was over.

*   *   *

WASHINGTON'S FAREWELL ADDRESS, which is still read annually on the floor of the United States Senate, boldly proclaimed America to be a "distinct Nation" that need not, and should not, enlist itself under the banner of any other nation. In his first draft, Washington wrote that he wished "every citizen would take pride in the name of an American," and said that, if it could remain at peace for another twenty years, "such in all probability will be its population, riches, and resources, when combined with its peculiarly happy and remote Situation from the other quarters of the globe, as to bid defiance, in a just cause, to any earthly power whatsoever."

Remain independent, he said; remain neutral if possible in international conflicts. May this Union be "as lasting as time; for while we are encircled in one band, we shall possess the strength of a Giant and there will be none who can make us afraid." He closed with a defense of his motives and an assurance of his incorruptibility. He admitted to having been wounded by partisan attacks. He reminded his countrymen that he had not sought the office of president, and that he was a man who had spent—and this he underlined in his handwritten text—"All the prime of his life, in serving his country." He asked to "be suffered to pass quietly to the grave."

*   *   *

RETIRED AGAIN, Washington resumed his old habits: riding his farms, gazing at the river, trying to be polite to his innumerable houseguests and sycophants, and thinking about the West.

As the historian W. W. Abbot, who edited Washington's retirement papers, has pointed out, he was something new on the American land-scape, an ex-president. What did such a creature do? The political dilemma in 1797 was worse for John Adams, who felt obliged, as the second president, to continue the policies of the first. Adams retained all of Washington's department heads, a decision he would later rue. Washington kept channels open to his old friends in power and of-fered counsel on the growing threat of war with revolutionary France. As Abbot puts it, "for all his talk of longing to sit undisturbed under his own vine and fig tree, Washington was not yet quite ready to watch the world pass him by without giving it a nudge or two."

Given the extreme political tensions of the late 1790s, Washington might well have abandoned his provincial belief that the destiny of the country would turn on the improvement of the modest river flowing by Mount Vernon. There were so many other forces in play. President Adams had to lead the nation past the precipice of war. The Federalists in their ascendancy overreached disastrously with the Alien and Sedi-tion Acts; the crackdown on free speech and freedom of the press made the Federalists resemble the heavy-handed dictators and monarchists the Republicans claimed they were. Sometimes it is the fate of men at the height of their power to turn into their caricatures. The tide turned. The Republicans, led by Jefferson, began to ride a wave of pop-ular revolt. Washington now found himself alienated from his fellow Virginians, not only from his former friend Jefferson, but from Madi-son and James Monroe, whose attacks on the Adams administration struck the ex-president as borderline treasonous. In July 1798, with war against France seemingly inevitable, Adams turned to the old man at Mount Vernon to save the day, to saddle up again at the head of the army.

Washington dutifully accepted the commission as commander in chief, but made it clear that he'd leave home only if war really broke out. The appointment quickly turned into something of a fiasco, as Adams and Washington had their own brief, nasty little war over the appointment of officers. The tale turns into something rather sad at this point, for Washington, meeting with his officers in Philadelphia, became enamored of the details of his new uniform, and carried on a vigorous correspondence with his tailor. Should the cuffs turn up or have a slash through them? Should the flap be embroidered? A good American wants to look away at this point, to give Washington some polite inattention.

Adams managed to stave off war. The friction with the French went into the history books as the Quasi-War.

In the whirl of all these dramas, Washington never forgot his great idea, his Potomac Route to the West. The project lagged, to be sure. But this was not the fault of the river, or of nature. The problem was a lack of due diligence, a failure of will. Washington faithfully attended meetings of the Patowmack Company and, in February 1798, learned that the company needed another $40,000 to finish the locks at Great Falls. He loaned the company $3,498.

In a letter written in the summer of 1799, Washington said, "Much is it to be regretted, that a work of such public utility and (if executed) of such immense advantage to the Undertakers, should be forcd to go limpingly on. . . ."

In his last extended iteration of the Central Dogma of the Potomac, written in a letter dated August 11, 1799, he implored the treasurer of the State of Virginia to help raise money for the venture:

> To dilate on the benefits which would result from improving the great *high way* which nature has marked out as the easiest, and most direct communication with the Western World (maugre all the endeavours of Pennsylvania and new York to divert it into other Channels) would be a mere waste of time; because every one who is disposed to investigate the subject must see them at the first glance.

If, he said, the western trade were to go instead to the East via Pennsylvania or New York, it would require a great deal of time and effort "to bring it back into the course which nature has ordered."

*   *   *

THE GENERAL had been working for several years on his will, and he finished it in the summer of 1799. He had a lot of land to distribute among many heirs and those who had served him so loyally for decades. He detailed each tract, down to the acre, and no doubt could imagine the surveyor's line, the white oak here, the hemlock there, the edge of the creek, the rocky outcropping. He had 240 acres on the Potomac in Hampshire County, 300 acres at Difficult Run, 2,481 at Ashby's Bent, 1,600 on the south fork of Bullskin Creek, 2,341 on the Little Kanawha, another 2,448 about 16 miles downstream on the same river, 10,990 acres on the west side of the mouth of the Great Kanawha, and 7,276 on the east side, 1,000 acres on the Mohawk, the 234 acres at Great Meadows where he'd surrendered to the French— and on and on. He had several thousand acres in three tracts north of the Ohio along the Little Miami. He had 5,000 acres in Kentucky. The total amount: 49,083 acres. He was one of the largest landowners in the country. He put a value on all that real estate of $428,395.

He bequeathed the Patowmack Company stock given him by the Virginia legislature to the endowment of a national university. This had long been another of his dreams: to establish a university in which the youth of America would be educated about liberty and republican government, saving them from the "dissipation and extravagence" so common in colleges overseas.

He also owned 123 slaves (not including the 153 Custis slaves, or 40 other slaves who had been hired to work on the plantation). This was a crucial moment for Washington and for those people he held in bondage.

It is possible he was moved by compassion, and the realization that the future of the country depended not upon river navigation and road-building but upon extending the principles of liberty to everyone. Or maybe he was thinking of his reputation. He saw where things were headed. He wanted to get on the right side of history. This is something people can argue about until the end of time. The simple fact is that he freed his slaves. Washington stipulated that his former slaves be provided for if they wished to stay at Mount Vernon, that they be given jobs and cared for in their old age by Washington's heirs. Children without parents to care for them would be supported on the plantation until they could attain the status equivalent of a white apprentice, and would "be taught to read and write," and "brought up to some useful occupation. . . ."

But manumission of his slaves would be delayed. They would become free, Washington decreed, only upon the death of his wife. Washington had failed to find a way to free the entire Mount Vernon slave population—the will offered no hope of freedom for the Custis slaves—and he knew that his actions might result in "most painful sensations, if not disagreeable consequences"—the ripping apart of slave families as some went free and others remained in bondage. The decision to delay manumission was an attempt to put off the painful moment until neither he nor his wife would be around to witness it. Martha Washington would never be comfortable with the provision (she was unnerved by the thought that all the Washington slaves were waiting for her to die) and would choose, a year after the general's death, to free them. But the Custis slaves would not be so fortunate. Bushrod Washington, the primary heir of the Mount Vernon estate, did not have his uncle's compunction about slave auctions or the sundering of families, and many of the Custis slaves would be sold, sent to the Deep South to work the cotton fields.

Near the end of the will is a striking passage. He gives each of his five nephews a sword:

> These Swords are accompanied with an injunction not to unsheath them for the purpose of shedding blood, except it be for self defence, or in defence of their Country and its rights; and in the latter case, to keep them unsheathed, and prefer falling with them in their hands, to the relinquishment thereof.

*   *   *

ON DECEMBER 12, 1799, Washington surveyed his farms. At sixty-seven he was an old man, perhaps somewhat fuzzy at times in his thinking and not so physically commanding. But he had endured. He was looking forward to the arrival in a few weeks of the 1800s. He had big plans for Mount Vernon, laid out in a memo to his plantation manager. He wanted to rent out two of his farms, simplify all his operations, and move many of his slaves to his lands on the Ohio River. That would certainly mean that he'd go west himself in the near future. Back up the river!

The weather was ominous—the mercury at 33 degrees in the morning, and clouds gathering. Around ten in the morning the snow began to fall, and then it changed to hail, and then to a "settled cold Rain," as Washington put it in his diary. Washington had experienced countless such miserable days, and made his usual rounds of the farm. He spent fully five hours outside, and when he returned to the house for dinner, he didn't change clothes. His secretary, Tobias Lear, noticed snow in his hair. You've gotten wet, Lear said. No, said Washington, my greatcoat kept me dry. Lear noticed moisture on the president's neck. The two men went about their business.

The next morning, the thirteenth, Washington complained of a sore throat. Still, he went outside in the afternoon to mark some trees for cutting. That evening he was croaking. As best he could, he read some of the newspaper to his wife and Lear. When Lear suggested that he take something for his cold, Washington demurred: "You know I never take any thing for a cold. Let it go as it came." In his diary he said nothing of his illness, relaying only the standard meteorological report: "Morning Snowing & abt. 3 Inches deep. Wind at No. Et. & Mer. at 30. Contg. Snowing till 1 Oclock and abt. 4 it became perfectly clear. Wind in the same place but not hard. Mer. 28 at Night." His final piece of writing: a measurement.

In his body, a microbial storm raged unabated. Cartilage at the base of his tongue apparently swelled to the point that Washington could barely speak or swallow. At about two or three o'clock in the morning of December 14, Washington woke his wife and said he was very sick. He was having trouble breathing. He was in great distress.

Attempts to give him a mixture of molasses, vinegar, and butter were unsuccessful, because he couldn't swallow. Doctors began racing to Mount Vernon. Dr. James Craik showed up by midmorning. Washington had known Craik longer than he'd known his own wife. So many memories they shared! Fort Necessity, the Braddock massacre, the Virginia Regiment . . . the long trip by canoe down the Ohio in 1770, deep into the realm of the Indian and the wolf . . . the endless scenes of battle and endurance in the long war against the Mother Country . . . the trek to western Pennsylvania in 1784. Craik needed to be here now.

He and the other doctors did what they knew to do, which was bleed the patient. Martha Washington, increasingly distraught, begged them to stop. But the president said "More, more."

Craik gave him purgatives, emetics. Washington did not complain of the pain, the discomfort, or the indignities. He now knew he would die. "Let me go off quietly," he said. At four-thirty in the afternoon he asked his wife to bring him two wills he kept in his desk. He looked them over: One was old, the other new. Burn the old one, he told Martha. She did, and resumed her bedside vigil.

Late in the day he realized that one of his slaves, Christopher, had been standing in the room all day. Washington told him to take a seat.

He informed Lear that his ailment would be fatal, and gave the secretary instructions to arrange his military letters and papers. To his final breath he made sure that the documentary record of his life, the proof of his virtue, the evidentiary base of his reputation, would be carefully preserved.

Washington, who characteristically uttered not a single complaint, asked if there was anything else he needed to do before he died. Lear could think of nothing, adding that he hoped Washington was not so near the end. Washington smiled. This is the debt we all pay, he said.

"I die hard, but I am not afraid to go."

In the final minutes he asked Lear to wait three days before burying him. Washington had few fears, but being buried alive was one of them.

"Do you understand me?" Washington demanded.

"Yes."

"'Tis well."

Suddenly, Washington's spirits improved. The lack of oxygen had put him into a state of euphoria. He calmly withdrew his hand from Lear's and put it to his own wrist. He felt his pulse—the surveyor's final measurement.

His expression changed, and his hand fell to the bed.

11

The Second
American Revolution

*T*HE NEW CENTURY opened with the United States government camping on the bank of the Potomac. But the citizens of
Washington City knew their community would never amount to
anything as just a *government* town. To thrive, a city needed an economic base built with the tangible elements of commerce, solid things
that people could eat, wear, pound with a hammer, burn, spin, weave.
That's why Washington City needed this Patowmack Company river
plan to succeed. The city needed more coal coming down the river
from the mountains. More pig iron. Lumber. The trickle of politicians
and diplomats into Washington and the drip of federal money in the
form of new buildings were insignificant compared with the potential
flood of commerce—grain, milled flour, whiskey, furs, hides (things of
real value)—that a navigable river might provide.

In the early nineteenth century, work meant labor. No one could
have imagined a day when several hundred thousand people would
occupy themselves by sending memos, peddling influence, analyz-
ing information, cultivating sources, talking across great distances
through magical handheld contraptions, sending digital packets of

data to one another on an almost invisible communications network, etc. It's almost unimaginable even today.

Fortunately, the Patowmack Company had recently found its footing after so many years of stumbling and bumbling. The 1799 infusion of capital from the State of Maryland had allowed a renewal of the blasting at Great Falls, and the company received permission to start collecting tolls. And although the mastermind of the canal lay entombed at Mount Vernon, he became, in a strange way, an even more formidable advocate for the canal, a commanding voice from beyond the grave. His cult of personality did not require his presence in the first decade of the nineteenth century. Orators sang his virtues. Biographers sanctified him. Henry "Light-Horse Harry" Lee correctly called him "first in war, first in peace, first in the hearts of his countrymen." Parson Weems invented the story of Washington and the cherry tree. In this climate people wanted to see the great man's Potomac scheme work out. There was a distinct notion in the air: *Do it for the general.*

The directors of the Patowmack Company announced in the summer of 1801 that they were ready to start building lock gates in the canal at Great Falls. The mood changed dramatically. Workers furiously put the final touches on what had once seemed an impossible dream. On February 2, 1802—nearly seventeen years after the start of construction—the Great Falls canal locked through its first boat.

The Potomac could now be traveled, if the water was not too high or too low, for about 200 miles above the fall line, possibly even 220 miles if the boatman could handle the rambunctious upper river. A boat could start at the mouth of George's Creek, high in coal country, and plummet downstream for about 25 miles, to Cumberland, the old jumping-off point to the West. Then it could float in a more leisurely fashion past the Cresap House at Old Town, through the Paw Paw Bends, past Hancock and Williamsport and Shepherdstown, through the improved channels at Harpers Ferry and Seneca, through the canal with five locks at Great Falls, down the gorge of the Potomac, through the Little Falls canal—and finally dump its cargo at Georgetown or Alexandria. It wasn't an easy journey, but it was doable. Some boatmen would pole back up the river, though more often they'd bust up the craft, sell the scraps, and walk all the way home.

In the summer of 1802, the Patowmack Company declared its first dividend.

It was also the company's last dividend.

Three hundred five boats paid tolls in 1802, carrying 1,952 tons of flour, whiskey, tobacco, iron, and other cargo. This was a fairly impressive haul considering the lack of rain in the summer, the low water levels, and a recurring problem with mill dams and fish weirs (those V-shaped piles of stone that had irritated Washington) imperiling the flatboats. By 1803 the number of boats had risen to 493, carrying 5,549 tons. But in keeping with what seemed to be company tradition, revenues never matched expenditures. The project revealed itself for what it was: a guaranteed way to lose money. In 1805, for example, it would manage to collect $5,213 in tolls against $19,447 in expenses. Such was the norm, year after year. Technological success refused to translate into commercial riches.

There was an obvious culprit. It was right in front of everyone. The river.

The river simply could not adapt itself to a business model. It was, by nature, diabolical and contrarian. The river had a compulsion to overrun its banks. It also had a tendency to dry up. It was constantly changing form. It metamorphosed precociously. The river was like *weather*. One season it might be a frothing, raging torrent, swift and deep, brown with silt, hurling logs like torpedoes, surging into the tributary creekbeds and across the sycamore-studded floodplains, driving all the snakes to higher ground. But in a few months it would be an entirely different sort of thing, parched to within an inch of its life, full of sun-bleached boulders.

Boatmen would try to take advantage of the river after a heavy rain, but then would watch in dismay as the water level dropped drastically in just a day or two, exposing the boats to rocks lurking beneath the rippled surface. The revenues of the Patowmack Company fluctuated dramatically; in 1805 the company locked through 405 boats at Great Falls, but in 1806 only 203 showed up.

When the French naturalist Constantin Volney visited the "Needles" at Harpers Ferry—a section of the river where parallel ledges protrude from the river in low water—he wrote a grim assessment:

> The waters fret and boil up around these obstacles, which, for two miles, form dangerous falls or rapids. They were covered, when I saw them, with the fragments of a bateau, which had been wrecked a few days before, by which sixty barrels of flour had been lost. . . . The temerity of the American navigators renders accidents of this kind as frequent in their rivers as on the ocean.

Temerity had its virtues. The American experiment was something of an exercise in temerity. The Americans had the temerity to defy their British masters. They had the temerity to tame rivers and turn forest into farmland. They were not timid. Consider that at Great Falls the river tumbles 76 feet through a madhouse of stone, and yet the Americans had blasted and grubbed and scoured a passage around it, a monumental feat in service of the humble task of transporting some coal from the mountains to tidewater.

The canal at Great Falls would never pay off for the Patowmack Company, and would someday be an overgrown ditch—something of a palimpsest of Washington's eighteenth-century scheme—but it was still a technological marvel. Travelers from abroad would stomp through the woods, up and down the hills, across the gullies and creekbeds of the river valley, to get a look at this engineering triumph. It managed to lock through boats for twenty-eight years.

*   *   *

WASHINGTON CITY in the early nineteenth century could be described generously as eccentric. A word that visitors tended to use was "muddy." In 1800, a decade after the passage of the Residence Act, and after all the disappointing auctions of city lots, the town could boast of 3,100 scattered residents. Small clusters of houses popped up here and there like thistles in a cow pasture. The town lacked the tidy, coherent quality of neighboring Georgetown on the far side of Rock Creek, or Alexandria a few miles down the Potomac. It lacked the organic quality of a town that grows from a good harbor, gradually radiating outward. This was a synthetic city, and for years to come, the houses and government buildings would be distributed across the terrain as though dropped randomly from an airship.

The enormous Capitol, with only the Senate wing complete, soared incongruously on a grapevine-entangled rise previously known as Jenkins Hill. The President's House, palatial by the standards of American homes, and cavernous in the view of Abigail Adams (who lived there at the end of her husband's single term), stood in a vacant field more than a mile away, near the mudflats of the Potomac. A broad, ruler-straight, stump-lined thoroughfare, alleging itself to be Pennsylvania Avenue, linked the two major landmarks.

Visitors found the capital incredible, in the literal sense. They thought: There must be some mistake. Some congressmen shared that dim assessment. Washington City was a hardship post, a physically uncomfortable place in which there was almost nothing to do other than argue about politics. If there hadn't been a constitutional crisis in the winter of 1801, they would have had to invent one, simply for sport.

Congressman Albert Gallatin of western Pennsylvania stayed at Conrad & McMunn's boardinghouse, one of seven on the Hill. Gallatin could count on two hands every commercial establishment: a tailor, a shoemaker, a printer, a washing-woman, a grocer, a pamphlets and stationery shop, a dry-goods shop, and an oyster house. Gallatin certainly had no trouble discerning swampland at the foot of Capitol Hill. "A small stream," Gallatin wrote to his wife, "decorated with the pompous appellation of 'Tyber,' feeds without draining the swamps, and along that causeway (called the Pennsylvania Avenue), between the Capitol and President's House, not a single house intervenes or can intervene without devoting its wretched tenant to perpetual fevers." He would have to get used to it, for soon he would become secretary of the treasury, with plenty of time to add up precisely the demerits of the capital.

Not far from his boardinghouse, on the Eastern Branch of the Potomac, stood a government warehouse, immaculately empty. And there was a wharf, Gallatin noted, "graced by not a single vessel."

Perhaps, in time, the town's wharf would be visited by a ship, and the warehouse would fill with supplies, and houses would sprout along the desolate avenues, and the sinews of commerce would exert themselves, and this weird little place would be transformed into a mighty world capital. But to see that in 1801 would require an imagination bordering on the delusional. A rational observer would instead wonder if the place was a conceit, a vanity. Perhaps it was conjured up by Washington and Jefferson and Madison after a few too many bottles of Jefferson's fancy French wine. Gallatin's wife, Hannah, declared that even if the government stayed in Washington, it would never become—never!—a place of consequence.

The bold idea of building a capital from scratch, as Peter the Great had built St. Petersburg in 1703, had run headlong into the budgetary reality of the government. The United States could afford to build only a handful of structures. Private homes had been built so slowly that Jefferson had warned during the latter part of the 1790s that the relocation of the government was in jeopardy, for the congressmen were not likely to "lodge, like cattle, in the fields."

But perhaps the new seat of government was just what the country needed. Joseph Ellis sagely notes that Washington City was the perfect republican capital: barely a city at all. The emptiness carried political content. James Madison had made clear over the years that remoteness from big cities would be a crucial attribute of the seat of government. The problem with this reasoning is that it forced the inhabitants of Washington City to endure what would be a prolonged phase of camping, of trying to maintain a sense of order and decorum in an environment more suited to hunting. As the historians Stanley Elkins and Eric McKitrick put it, "The nation's capital, in being removed from the scene of any of the nation's major activities, had been stripped to an abstraction."

When John Adams's Treasury secretary, Oliver Wolcott, arrived in 1800 and took a look at the federal city, he saw "small, miserable huts" and declared that the inhabitants "are poor, and as far as I can judge, they live like fishes, by eating each other." When Abigail Adams traveled to the capital in 1800, her coachman managed to get lost on the outskirts, and the party wandered for two hours in the woods, "holding down and breaking bows of trees which we could not pass," until finally a black man with a horse and cart led them to the post road. "The country around is romantic but a wild, a wilderness at present," Mrs. Adams wrote.

The English traveler and author Isaac Weld said of the Potomac site, "To be under the necessity of going through a deep wood for one or two miles, perhaps, in order to see a next door neighbour, and in the same city, is a curious, and, I believe, a novel circumstance."

John Randolph, the famously fragile congressman from Roanoke, recounted to a friend the travails of a late-evening journey from Capitol Hill to Georgetown. He couldn't find a hack and had to borrow a horse from a fellow member. The horse summarily dumped Randolph onto the road. "Although in the heart of the capital of the United States I was out of hearing of any person or habitation," Randolph wrote. "After some time, a coach passed which I entreated in vain to take me home. At last, a gentleman changed horses with me, and I reached this place (Georgetown) in great torture." (Residents today might note that it is still sometimes hard to get a cab.)

The early inhabitants loved the huge trees, but some citizens preferred them to be horizontal. Margaret Bayard Smith, the Founding Socialite of the capital, considered the city quite enchanting, and was outraged that poor people were girdling the tulip poplars and other magnificent trees, assassinating them for later lumbering. She tells the story of the night that Jefferson, then vice president, suddenly declared, "How I wish that I possessed the power of a despot." Such an outburst from the nation's leading republican shocked Smith and the other guests. Jefferson quickly explained: "Yes, I wish I was a despot that I might save the noble, the beautiful trees that are daily falling sacrifices to the cupidity of their owners, or the necessity of the poor."

The Potomac might yet lose the capital. The seat of government had moved before, both on political whims and to spare the Congress the wrath of its constituents. For years to come, the government didn't seem to be permanently rooted. Move it someplace more habitable, people would say. Move it to the West, toward the future center of population. It wouldn't cost much to move, since it was such a small-time enterprise. The government upon moving to the Potomac had only 131 federal clerks. Certain plantation owners had bigger work-forces.

*   *   *

LIKE THE CAPITAL, the country looked pretty good on paper. The country might be raw and unfinished, overrun with hustlers and vagrants and rapscallions and roughnecks, knotted up with human bondage, prone to eruptions of frontier violence, etc., but at least it had some marvelous *documents*. The Declaration, the Constitution, the *Federalist Papers*, Washington's Farewell Address, Jefferson's *Notes*, Franklin's *Autobiography*—these and many other texts provided a rich intellectual loam for the cultivation of a brash new society.

Its leaders were learned men who took ideas seriously, who read the classics, who would casually mention Locke and Hume and Montesquieu and Newton and Bacon as though they might come into town on the next stage. The country possessed much that other nations might envy. A great many citizens were energetic, supercharged, compelled by some irresistible itch to improve their surroundings. They were determined to subdue the Earth, to *extend their action radius*. They were going to make George Washington's vision a reality. This was probably the country's singular asset: Human energy. Zeal. The courage—and the arrogance—to reengineer the world. Future generations might question to what degree this was truly a virtue; there is a fine line between industriousness and rapaciousness. But at this moment, the dawn of the nineteenth century, the drive of ordinary Americans was a kind of fuel, a natural resource, seemingly inexhaustible.

The United States might not have enough people at the moment to occupy all the fertile ground out there in the hinterlands, even if the Indians weren't defying that ambition, but the American citizens did their best to solve the population deficit. They demonstrated heroic fecundity. Girls had few social options other than to marry young and start having babies, and they did so, prodigiously. The census of 1800 showed an average age in America of sixteen. Four out of five people lived on farms, scattered across the land, far from anything like a city, and even something as common in the Old World as a village was relatively scarce. (Albert Gallatin said simply, "We have no villages in America," which was not literally true, but got his point across.)

The question of union that had so preoccupied George Washington remained unresolved. Was it not true that whole sections of the country, particularly in the West, might go their separate ways "at the touch of a feather"? Was the United States a nation in any real sense? (Or *were they* a nation?) A nation requires more than documents. It needs cultural and social and economic glue.

Many Americans had by now adopted the goal of living in a continental nation, extending from sea to sea, but that remained explicitly contrary to the desires of the Great Powers of Europe. The opening of the Mississippi to American navigation in 1795, under the Treaty of San Lorenzo (better known as Pinckney's Treaty), had spurred western settlement and repressed some of the secessionist sentiment in Kentucky, but even so, the principal port on the river, New Orleans, remained in Spanish hands. Napoleon, meanwhile, had new designs for a North American presence. The Spanish in 1800 had secretly retroceded the huge Louisiana Territory to France. Napoleon envisioned Louisiana as the source of raw materials for the sugar colony of Saint-Domingue (now Haiti), which he planned to retake from Toussaint L'Ouverture.

Americans at the opening of the nineteenth century still hadn't figured out how to overcome natural obstacles and the immense distances of its territory. Infrastructure had improved, but not dramatically. A stage road now linked Washington with Boston. A privately built canal had been opened between Boston and Lowell, and another in South Carolina from Charleston to the Santee River. A private company had built a set of locks at Little Falls, New York, to connect the Mohawk River with Wood Creek. More than seventy turnpike companies had sprung into existence. The Lancaster Turnpike between Philadelphia and Lancaster set a new standard for road construction (a "turnpike" was so called because the tolls were enforced with sharp pikes that jutted into the road, and had to be turned back by the toll collector). The busy Pennsylvanians had extended a few rough roads to Pittsburgh, and intrepid wagoners could keep going as far west as Louisville and as far south as Nashville.

Jon Kukla, in *A Wilderness So Immense*, describes the astonishing array of merchandise bouncing and splashing on those backwoods roads from Philadelphia to the Ohio River and then down the river to Kentucky: linen, muslin, tea, brandy, wine, snuff, china, wool, alum, sugar, coffee, shoe polish, ginger, indigo, brimstone, cotton hose, men's gloves, buttons, shaving boxes, razors, steel spurs, pen knives, teapots, cups, saucers, spelling books, writing paper, playing cards, flannel, *Morse's Geography*, bed ticking . . . and on and on. This level of commerce demonstrated that the American people had the energy and gumption to obtain what they wanted. *People find a way.* But it was all slow, all difficult.

It was possible to haul a wagonload of goods from Maine to Georgia, but the journey took four months. Many inland farmers could barter their produce locally but were effectively exiled from the larger market that exploited navigable waterways. For all practical purposes, New York City was closer to London than to Buffalo.

Because people and cargo moved slowly, so did information. The news of George Washington's death had taken six days to reach New York City, eleven days to reach Boston, and three and a half weeks to reach Cincinnati.

"Even after two centuries of struggle," wrote Henry Adams, "the land was still untamed; forest covered every portion, except here and there a strip of cultivated soil; the minerals lay undisturbed in their rocky beds, and more than two thirds of the people clung to the seaboard within fifty miles of tide-water, where alone the wants of a civilized life could be supplied."

All this was about to change with extraordinary rapidity. The land would be tamed; the forests would be cleared; the minerals would be disturbed in their rocky beds; enormous numbers of people would let go of the seaboard and race to the West. The country would double in size, then expand further still. "Ordinary life" would be radically altered. Dress, social habits, sexual relations, religiosity, architecture, transportation, the speed of information—it would all change in the span of two generations. The country would grow larger and yet seem smaller. It would be possible, finally, to get somewhere. The distant provinces would no longer be beyond the pale. The mountains would seem less lofty.

Americans were going to use Washington's Potomac Route to the West—and every other route they could find. The conquest of the interior would not be orderly or organized, and it would take a heavy human toll. Washington's Potomac project still looked like a grand idea, but in a few years it would be in danger of becoming something quaint, a bit antiquated—a bark canoe in the age of the steamboat.

*   *   *

JEFFERSON HAD CAMPAIGNED in 1800—if letters to friends can be considered campaigning—on his usual Republican argument that the states were fully independent sovereignties on domestic matters and united only with respect to foreign nations. Jefferson planned to get rid of the army and navy. A republic didn't need such things, since state militias could always be called out in an emergency. He planned to obliterate one layer of the federal judiciary created by the accursed Federalists. He would "sink Federalism into an abyss from which there will be no resurrection."

The land, once again, informed his politics, for he perceived that the vast dimensions of the nation required state and local control of domestic governmental matters. "Our country is too large to have all its affairs directed by a single government," he told a supporter. Public

servants at a distance will do an inefficient job and be susceptible to
"corruption, plunder and waste." He concluded, "Let the general government be reduced to foreign concerns only . . . our general government may be reduced to a very simple organization, and a very
unexpensive one—a few plain duties to be performed by a few servants."

A few plain duties by a few servants: This was the plan. Strip everything down to the essentials. Eliminate government waste. The government that governs best is the one that governs least. Jefferson
would ensure that the new federal apparatus on the Potomac would
remain a boutique operation. This would be government by store-
front, a Mom and Pop business where everyone knows you by name
and kids get free candy. Nay, scratch the Mom and Pop metaphor—the
Widower Jefferson could run things by *himself.*

This idea of severely limited national government had a perverse
audaciousness. It was grandiose, in its own way. Jefferson believed his
fruit-stand government could somehow supervise an expanding Empire of Liberty. He would balance an elephant on a jar of marmalade. If
it is a mark of genius to maintain contradictory ideas, then Jefferson
was one of the smartest men who ever lived. He would conquer without war, rule the land and sea without an army or navy, retire the national debt without levying taxes. He had the blessing of conviction, of
knowing that his was the true republican philosophy. He saw himself
as the keeper of the Spirit of '76; his election would be the Second
American Revolution.

Any assessment of Jefferson today is necessarily provisional, because in a few years a new Jefferson will seem to appear, almost magically, from the archival record. As Merrill Peterson has pointed out in
The Jefferson Image in the American Mind, Jefferson is a shape-
shifter, his image remade with each succeeding generation. He's conservative, radical, liberal, anarchic; he's lofty and yet base, powerful
and yet fragile. He's an aristocrat who spoke of democracy, an egalitar-
ian who owned slaves. This simple farmer could not resist fine clothes,
fine wines, fine everything, even if it meant going into heavy debt.

One of his harshest critics, Paul Finkelman, writes, "Jefferson could not maintain his extravagant life style without his slaves and, to judge from his lifelong behavior, his grand style was far more important than the natural rights of his slaves." He warned of the evils of miscegenation even as countless mulattoes inhabited Monticello, many looking remarkably like the Master.

But to Jefferson's eternal credit, he had something that Washington and Hamilton and Adams and so many others lacked: a basic faith in the people, in the ordinary folks of America, particularly the farmers. Men with plows do not form mobs, and can be trusted with self-government. They do not require a paternalistic master to rein in their worst impulses. The yeomen farmers of Jefferson's vision might be common folk, with dirty fingernails and heavy calluses and weather-beaten faces, and they might not be book-smart, but they have a vested interest in remaining free from tyranny. Jefferson might not know many such people personally, but he revered them in theory.

In his first inaugural address, delivered on March 4, 1801, in a tense and awkward ceremony in the unfinished Capitol after the election fiasco of 1800 (the Constitution unwisely instructed presidential electors to vote for two people, leaving Jefferson tied with his ambitious running mate, Aaron Burr, and throwing the election to the House, where the usual partisan hysteria and fears of mob rule, secession, and assassination finally came to an end when Jefferson was elected on the thirty-sixth ballot), Jefferson laid out a powerful description of a rising, expanding nation:

> . . . separated by nature and a wide ocean from the exterminating havoc of one quarter of the globe; too high-minded to endure the degradations of the others; possessing a chosen country, with room enough for our descendants to the thousandth and thousandth generation . . .

The chosen-country language sounded familiar, and the invocation of geographical good fortune echoed Washington in 1783 ("placed in the most enviable condition, as the sole Lords and Proprietors of a vast Tract of Continent," etc.), but in the final rhetorical burst, Jefferson showed the range of his mind, his ability to imagine the world in every spatial and temporal dimension. He took the situation into deep time. Our grandeur is not temporary, he said. This could be an empire for the ages.

*   *   *

THE LOUISIANA PURCHASE in 1803 accelerated the movements of a people already prone to hitting the road. Virginia planters raced to the Mississippi Valley, where the soil and climate permitted the cultivation of short-staple cotton, only recently turned into a cash crop by Eli Whitney's cotton gin. Jefferson, meanwhile, had the idea that the Indians of the Ohio country could be exiled west of the Mississippi.

Upper Louisiana remained a mystery to Jefferson and his fellow seaboard Americans. The president knew of the sketchy reports of mountains in the West, known as the Stony Mountains, or the Mountains of Bright Stones, or the Shining Mountains (an early explorer, Jonathan Carver, learned of the Rockies during a voyage through the Mississippi Valley in 1766–67, and wrote, "Among these mountains, those that lie to the west of the River St. Pierre, are called the Shining Mountains, from an infinite number of chrystal stones, of an amazing size, with which they are covered, and which, when the sun shines full upon them, sparkle as to be seen at a very great distance"). Alexander Mackenzie had made his epic 1793 trip across the continent through Canada, and Jefferson knew that Mackenzie had found a relatively easy portage between the eastern and western waters, a pass only about 3,000 feet above sea level. What Mackenzie hadn't found was a navigable water passage.

Jefferson believed in "continental symmetry." He assumed the western mountains would be the same size as the Appalachians. Mackenzie's discoveries seemed to support that equivalence. Just as the eastern tributaries of the Mississippi (in Pennsylvania, for example) were relatively close to the headwaters of rivers that flowed to the

Atlantic—a fact that had so beguiled George Washington—so too must the western tributaries of the Mississippi be close to the headwaters of rivers flowing to the Pacific. If someone were to go up the Missouri, he presumably would face a day's trip over the mountains. (It couldn't possibly require, for example, a land carriage of 340 miles, 140 of which would be over "tremendous mountains").

Even before the Purchase, Jefferson devised a plan for an exploratory mission to the Pacific, something he'd been pondering since the end of the Revolution, in the days when George Washington had dreamed of making his own Grand Tour of the United States. Jefferson's instructions to Meriwether Lewis focused on the need to find "the most direct & practicable water communication across the continent, for the purposes of commerce." Jefferson told Lewis to learn everything about the Indians of the West, their culture, their languages, as well as everything about the animals, the soil, the vegetation, the minerals, the waters, the volcanoes—the list went on and on. Jefferson found everything in the world, every blade of grass, every seed, to be fascinating. He wanted Lewis to be his eyes and ears and nose and skin. Find out, Jefferson said, about the climate:

> . . . as characterized by the thermometer, by the proportion of rainy, cloudy, & clear days, by lightning, hail, snow, ice, by the access & recess of frost, by the winds prevailing at different seasons, the dates at which particular plants put forth or lose their flower, or leaf, times of appearance of particular birds, reptiles or insects.

And don't get yourself killed, he added.

A little-known fact of the Lewis and Clark expedition is that Meriwether Lewis used the Potomac Route to the West. The tale of Lewis and Clark is often told as though the explorers magically appeared one day on the Mississippi River near the mouth of the Missouri, but even reaching the Mississippi from points east (Clark started from the falls of the Ohio, Lewis from the seat of government on the Potomac) would prove adventurous, and fraught with its own perils and frustrations.

After his final conference with Jefferson, Lewis rode to Harpers Ferry. President Washington had put a federal armory there, exploiting the falls for water power. Lewis obtained rifles, uniforms, and a small iron boat that he planned to use later in the voyage. He then headed northwest, up the Potomac, following Washington's 1784 route, across the Shenandoah Valley and along the winding and dipping country road that hadn't gotten much better since a certain young surveyor in 1748 had called it the worst road ever trod by man or beast. Lewis traveled on "extreemly dusty" roads from Cumberland across the Alleghenies to Pittsburgh, which everyone knew as the Gateway to the West.

Pittsburgh had become a thriving industrial town full of shipyards, hardly the outpost it had been in the 1780s, when Hugh Henry Brackenridge had served as the all-purpose writer, newspaper publisher, and defense attorney for outraged squatters. Lewis knew Pittsburgh well from the days of the Whiskey Rebellion, when he had served with federal forces under William Clark, and he spent much of the summer of 1803 pacing about the city as he waited for a hard-drinking boatbuilder to finish the keelboat. The river level kept dropping. The epic journey to the Pacific seemed to be stymied on the western flank of the Appalachians. Clark had accepted the offer to be co-captain of the expedition, but for a few weeks it seemed questionable whether Lewis and Clark would ever find a way to inhabit the same spot on the planet. This was America in 1803: You couldn't *get* anywhere. Lewis briefly considered paddling down the Ohio in a flotilla of canoes.

On the final day of August, Lewis finally got his 55-foot keelboat, and immediately shoved off for the West. Three miles downriver, while briefly stopping to check for leaks, Lewis demonstrated for some of the local gentlemen a new piece of technology he had obtained at Harpers Ferry: an air rifle, an ingenious thing that required no gunpowder. A man named Blaze Cenas asked if he could see the gun, and as Lewis handed it over, the gun discharged, sending a lead ball careening off the head of a lovely lady standing 40 yards away. She crumpled to the ground, gushing blood.

"[W]e were all in the greatest consternation," Lewis wrote.

The woman revived. The horrifying head shot proved to be a mere grazing of the scalp. Lewis sagely interpreted this as his cue to get back in the boat and get on down the river.

The rest of the story is American lore. At first the expedition seemed to be something of a failure, for Lewis and Clark failed to find the continuous water route across the continent, and the Stony Mountains certainly showed no symmetry with the Appalachians. But something more important had happened: The scale of the nation and its ambitions had radically increased. Among other things, this would put the river that flowed by Washington City into a new perspective. When George Washington and Thomas Jefferson had decided, back in the spring of 1784, that nature had chosen the Potomac to be the artery to the West, and when they had joined with James Madison and other Virginians in putting the seat of government at the fall line of the Potomac, they were thinking of America as a seaboard nation with a dazzling backcountry tract just a short hike across the Appalachians. Two decades later, the country had doubled in size and the very idea of "the West" had to be recalibrated. As the country grew, each constituent part seemed to shrink. For Washington, the Potomac had been a national river, but with the Louisiana Purchase and the Lewis and Clark expedition, Jefferson had taken steps that would turn the Potomac into a regional river in the East, a tributary of the Chesapeake.

The center of geographical gravity had shifted, and clearly the dominant river would now be the Mississippi. The Mississippi shamed every other river on the continent. In the words of James Madison, "The Mississippi is . . . the Hudson, the Delaware, the Potomac, and all the navigable rivers of the atlantic states formed into one stream."

12

The Progress of Man

*A*S THE UNITED STATES EXPANDED, and Jefferson's intrepid explorers scrambled across the Bitterroots, the ambitions of the Patowmack Company seemed to be reciprocally narrowing. The company directors didn't focus on western trade so much as on navigation in the Potomac watershed. Let's work on the Shenandoah River, they said, and the Monocacy, and Antietam Creek. Let's improve navigation on the (fabled) Conococheague. They lacked George Washington's sweeping vision and, instead of seeing great river highways, became lost in the fine-grain details of streams and creeks.

One man kept alive the dream of a highway to the West. Albert Gallatin, Jefferson's Treasury secretary, knew how shabby the roads were between his home turf of western Pennsylvania and the nation's capital. He proposed the construction of a "National Road," linking the Ohio country with the Atlantic seaboard, and "cementing the bonds" between rival states ("cement" remained the favorite active verb of this generation of nation-builders). The Senate approved the plan, and in December 1805 selected a route that might well have been called the George Washington Memorial Route to the West. They would build the road from the Potomac at Cumberland to the Ohio River, more or less following Braddock's Road, which, of course, had been an improvement on Washington's Road, which had been a widening of Nemacolin's Trail. It would come to be known as the Cumberland Road.

The Constitution, however, didn't say anything about the federal government building roads or digging canals or dredging harbors or starting a national university or doing anything else in the category of "internal improvements." The nation's leaders liked the idea of these improvements, but they feared the implications of the federal government getting into that line of work. Things might get out of hand. A road here, a canal there, a national university over here, a lighthouse yonder—then there might be no stopping the government's consolidation of power, until finally the country would be back to square one (monarchy, tyranny, absolute despotism, etc.). So the leaders wrung their hands and agonized and searched their souls. They asked themselves: *Dare we build a road?*

The historian John Lauritz Larson points out that some southern planters feared that any increase in federal power would lead to the abolition of slavery. If Congress could establish banks, and make roads and canals, one congressman wrote, it could free all the slaves. Jefferson had been too persuasive over the years in creating a fear of federal consolidation. The Republicans were paralyzed.

The Senate, however, asked Gallatin to draw up a general plan for internal improvements (when politicians are afraid to act, they appoint a task force or ask for another report). Gallatin responded with the brilliant *Report of the Secretary of the Treasury on the Subject of Roads and Canals,* probably the closest that any government study of infrastructure has ever come to being a work of literature. Gallatin's view of the country is sweeping, as if he's studying the topography from low Earth orbit. In the spirit of George Washington, he sees an expansive theater of potential commerce interrupted by a stone rampart, the Appalachian mountains, rising not far from the Atlantic coast.

The Potomac is prominent in the Gallatin report, for it is something of a test case for internal improvements. Gallatin notes all the work already in progress to make the river—the most "rapid" of all the major rivers of the Atlantic seaboard—navigable deep into the mountains. If the wild Potomac can be tamed, presumably so could the less obstreperous rivers. Like Washington, Gallatin sees the American terrain as needing just a little fix here and there, some tweaks and nudges, to complete a providential design. Only "four necks of land," the report states, obtruded into what would otherwise be a continuous inland waterway from Massachusetts to southern Georgia. Cut those necks with canals, and the country would have a new north-south artery, an intracoastal waterway. The report also proposes a turnpike from Maine to Georgia, and a matrix of canals and roads in the backcountry.

Elements of the Gallatin Plan would come to fruition many years later, which is why yachtsmen can now tool from Florida to New England with rarely a venture into the Atlantic surf, but in 1808 this vision for elaborate improvements on nature fell victim to larger events: conflict with England, an embargo, an economic collapse. When Jefferson retired in 1809 and James Madison became the latest Virginian to hold the presidency, the nation did not have the luxury to build roads and canals and fix the deficits of the natural terrain, but rather had to steel itself for another war with the Mother Country.

*   *   *

THE LOW MOMENT of the War of 1812 (which infamously lasted until 1815) came in August 1814, on the Potomac, and briefly called into question the decision of the First Congress to side with President Washington and his fellow Virginians and place the seat of government at a remote river crossroads. The British did not sack New York City during the war, did not sack Philadelphia, did not sack Boston. But they quite flamboyantly sacked the peculiar village called Washington City.

Decades earlier, in the protracted debate over where to place the capital, defense against invasion had been a recurring concern, and the fear proved prescient. The problem with having a government in a small village at the geological fall line is that the enemy could simply sail right up to it waving torches, and quickly overpower the local inhabitants. The English weren't about to march on burgeoning New York City or Philadelphia, each of which had roughly 100,000 inhabitants. Washington City in the most recent census, in 1810, had fewer people (8,200) than Salem, Massachusetts (12,600).

The Americans had a republican defense, as Garry Wills has pointed out, which meant a scattered command structure, a trivial military apparatus, and a reliance on militiamen who, at a crucial moment, might be sorely tempted to scamper back to the farm. The government had built little in the way of forts to defend the nation's capital. No scouts had been deployed on the Chesapeake to watch for the approach of British ships. As Irving Brant has recounted in his biography of James Madison, Secretary of War John Armstrong couldn't imagine why the British would want to trifle with the village on the Potomac when fatter targets were not so far away. Just prior to the assault, Armstrong said, "[W]hat the devil will they do here . . . Baltimore is the place, sir; that is of so much more importance."

On August 21, 1814, some fifty-one British warships and transports, carrying about 4,000 soldiers, arrived at the mouth of the Patuxent River, on the Chesapeake Bay. Among the invaders were African-Americans who, as during the Revolution, found freedom only by enlisting with the British. The British began marching immediately toward Bladensburg, the village on the Anacostia River (the Eastern Branch of the Potomac) where a bridge carried the Post Road and where, even if the bridge were destroyed, the British could ford the river and then veer southwest toward the Capitol, about six miles away. The American forces, including about 7,000 militiamen and 2,000 army regulars, hastened to Bladensburg for what should have been an epic battle. President Madison himself, at great risk to his life, rode from Washington City to Bladensburg and came within shooting distance of an advance British party not wearing uniforms. Congreve rockets burst near him and whistled over his head. Madison wisely retreated. Unfortunately, so did almost all of his countrymen. They seemed jangled by the approach of trained, professional British soldiers, and even the army regulars, Brant reports, "melted away without firing musket or cannon." Madison had no choice but to flee to Washington, and then keep going, crossing the Potomac on a ferry, seeking refuge in Virginia, a dash to safety not so dissimilar to Jefferson's notorious gallop from Monticello in 1781. The British, so unimpeded they might as well have been greeted with a key to the city, a marching band, and a banquet in their honor, walked into Washington and started putting the best buildings to the torch. British warships sailed up the Potomac and sacked Alexandria, plundering the warehouses before slipping back down the river.

The British burned the Capitol and the White House and the ships in the Navy Yard, and every government building except the post office and the patent office. In the President's House they had plenty of time to stack up the furniture before ignition. In the Capitol they took pains to immolate the contents of the Library of Congress. (Jefferson would later sell Congress his own collection. The republic was fortunate to have as one of its citizens a man so learned, with so many books, and so many financial difficulties.)

The knowledge that the capital wasn't much of a city to begin with may have softened the blow. Dolley Madison emerged a hero, having saved Gilbert Stuart's famous painting of an old, humorless, puffy-mouthed George Washington, an image that probably more than any other has enforced the notion of Washington as a stiff. The British left most of the houses in town untouched, a gesture that seemed to say, *this place is so lowly, it's not worth burning.*

President Madison, traveling at night through the rolling, broken terrain on the Virginia side of the Potomac, could see the glow of the fires of his ruined government. He spent one night in a private home a few miles from Chain Bridge, unaware that the First Lady had found refuge in another home a mile away. They reunited the next morning, and, with an entourage of guards and government officials, tried to transport their miniature government-in-exile back across the Potomac, into Maryland. But at midnight, when the group arrived at Conn's Ferry, just upstream from Great Falls, indeed so close that they could all hear the roar of the river plunging 87 feet off the shelf of the

Piedmont, the ferryman would not take them across. Not in the dark, he said. At this spot the river was wide and shallow, with sharp boulders crouched like assassins just beneath the surface. A sycamore or black walnut battering ram might appear suddenly, and too late, in the ferryman's lantern light. It would not do to have the nation's leader launched into the Potomac and dispatched over the falls like a stray barrel of wheat. And so the Madisons spent a thoroughly republican night in the ferryman's humble farmhouse.

The fate of the nation was still linked to its rivers and bays, its roads and bridges and ferries, which was why the British spent the night in Washington, D.C., enjoying themselves, warming their feet by the burning wood of the President's House and the Capitol, and the president of the United States slept in a poor man's hovel.

The next day Madison & Co. crossed the Potomac, and after a day in the Maryland countryside, having learned that the British had retreated, Madison rode back into the federal town, in advance of his own army. He saw that the oversized, grandiose Capitol and President's House, already starkly set against the humble structures of the local inhabitants, presented themselves all the more dramatically, having become charred, hollow shells.

The disaster led, reflexively, to more talk of disunion. At a convention in Hartford in the fall of 1814, radical New Englanders pushed for secession, while more moderate voices wanted only to present a list of demands for constitutional amendments that would in effect create a separate confederation of states in the Northeast, with its own military and taxing authority. Outright secession, the convention declared, was not necessary quite yet, but it might be preferable to "an alliance by constraint, among nominal friends but real enemies, inflamed by mutual hatred and jealousy, and inviting, by intestine divisions, contempt and aggression from abroad." George Washington had always feared that the westerners would disavow allegiance to his nation; now the Yankees in the Northeast were trying to go their own way.

But even as the Hartford malcontents were gathering, the war had come to a diplomatic resolution. Twenty years after he helped bring the Whiskey Rebellion to a halt, Albert Gallatin, still as savvy as he'd been in that cabin with George Washington in 1784, had sailed to Europe with Henry Clay and negotiated the Treaty of Ghent. The treaty was a monument to the virtues of the status quo. The war had ended without an inch of territory changing hands. It was a tie. Even the initial source of the conflict, the British impressment of American sailors, went unresolved. The informational time lag, however, gave the American side a final shot at post-peace military glory. In early January, unaware of the treaty, Andrew Jackson pummeled the British in the Battle of New Orleans.

America decided it had won the war. It sure *felt* like a victory.

＊　　　＊　　　＊

AFTER THE WAR, everyone suddenly wanted to build roads and canals. Even the leading Republicans, Henry Clay and John Calhoun, had the roads-and-canals bug. During the war it had been so hard to move troops from one place to another. It was time to speed up the country's metabolism.

Nationalism had never been a major element of the American psyche. It had been viewed suspiciously. The Jefferson formula had always proved persuasive: The states were sovereign in all domestic matters. But the war had forever changed that conceit, and the Union no longer was merely an allegation on paper. John Marshall, the chief justice, would soon declare, "The United States form, for many, and for most important purposes, a single nation."

But he still used "the United States" as a plural.

With the passing of the presidency to another Virginian, James Monroe, the Republicans were so ascendant they could talk of the end of partisanship altogether. No more invective, no more hysteria, no more frothing and spewing about monocrats and Jacobins and besotted atheists. This would be the "Era of Good Feeling."

Across the country, per capita income steadily increased, exports boomed, and in the little touches of life many people felt more dignified. Something as authentically American as getting drunk to the gills on rum or cider had become less socially acceptable. Many people began importing fine ceramic chamber pots. The filth and muck of daily life were gradually abating. The country didn't stink as badly. The march of Progress is to some extent merely the organized suppression of odors.

Commerce required better transportation networks, and better transportation networks led to increased commerce, and soon the whole system was heating up like a steam boiler. Major rivers now had bridges. In 1809 the Long Bridge, emerging at the base of Fourteenth Street, had given the federal town a direct connection across the Potomac to Alexandria. The first Potomac bridge had gone up in 1797 just below Little Falls, a short span made of wood that took advantage of the narrow sluice a few hundred yards inside the District of Columbia line. It had rotted and collapsed by 1804, replaced with another wooden bridge that washed away in a flood six months later, and then by a bridge suspended by heavy chains strung between two towers. The "Chain Bridge," 136 feet long, lasted all of two years before high water flushed it down the river. A fourth bridge went up, and eventually a fifth, a sixth, and a seventh. It's a story of failure, redeemed by the willingness to try again. In America you had to keep moving ahead. Build and rebuild.

The booming population gave the country a critical mass, more of a *market*. The United States ceased to be an economic dependency of the temperamental Great Powers across the sea. Cotton from the South found its way to northern textile mills. People who wanted to make money managed to find one another.

And yet a map of all the new transportation ventures in the eighteenth century would reveal something peculiar: The country was better at creating East-West connections than North-South connections. For the moment, that didn't seem to matter much.

*   *   *

RUMSEY'S AND FITCH'S EXPERIMENTS in the 1780s laid the foundation for the appearance of the first commercial steamboats two and a half decades later. The western rivers, notwithstanding the pirates, the masses of driftwood, collapsing riverbanks, and the boat-impaling sunken trees (called "sawyers" if they bobbed up and down, and "planters" if they didn't budge), were now navigable. The current could be conquered. A steamboat was a scarier and more dangerous contraption than Rumsey's magic boat that walked upstream, but it had the redeeming quality of working in an actual river. Steamboats began plying the Potomac in 1815. The first was, naturally, the *Washington.*

Meanwhile the Cumberland Road took form, despite all the *dare we build a road* agonizing by Congress. Construction had started in 1811, and by 1818 the road reached the Ohio River at Wheeling. The road had a remarkable feature: a raised surface of stone, earth, gravel and sand, sloping gently to ditches on either side, at no point at an angle greater than five degrees with the horizon. As a result, the road didn't instantly turn into a muddy ditch. Water drained to the sides. The Age of Progress!

The road instantly became a genuine Route to the West. But was it a *Potomac* Route to the West? Eastward from Cumberland, the road led through the Maryland panhandle to Baltimore, not to the nation's capital. This would become a problem again in just a few years: It was the sort-of Potomac Route.

A rancher in Indiana could now drive his stock to market in Baltimore. Conestoga wagons, carrying flour, whiskey, wool, tobacco, and entire families, bounced along the road until late in the evening, passing hogs, sheep, mules, and the ubiquitous cows. The wagon floor of a Conestoga sloped sharply upward on either end to prevent people and cargo from spilling forth on steep slopes. The road became an instant artery for an adrenalized nation.

The American people, unfortunately, quickly pounded the road into a state of decrepitude. Ruts deepened. Resourceful farmers decided to mine clay right from the roadbed. Congress in 1822 voted to erect toll gates to pay for repairs, but this triggered the usual federal-consolidation, brink-of-monarchy alarms, and President Monroe reluctantly vetoed the act, calling it a constitutional violation. Internal improvement went on hold again. After all these years, the federal government had managed to build precisely one road—one!—and now could not muster the nerve to repair it.

Meanwhile, the New Yorkers got busy. Back in 1784, George Washington had feared the energy and ambition of the "Yorkers," for he could tell they were a different sort of American, quicker to hustle, make a deal, find an edge. For years, Boston had been in relative decline, its position in the American hierarchy slipping noticeably, the smartest minds fleeing to New York, where fortunes could be made. The Yorkers were going to transform the town on the tip of Manhattan Island into a commercial and financial powerhouse. One of their key assets would be that gap in the mountains, up there in the Mohawk Valley.

In 1817 men began digging a ditch to link the Hudson with Lake Erie. The canal engineers had to improvise almost every step of the way. They used "bogtrotters" (many of them Irish, though the percentage is a subject of debate) to do the dirty work. The bogtrotters dug by hand, with shovels. They built bridges, aqueducts, locks, culverts. There was nothing modest about the scheme. The canal would be, in the end, 363 miles long, 4 feet deep, with 83 locks carrying flatwater nearly 600 feet above the tide.

Every day, as the bogtrotters jammed their shovels into the earth of central New York State, the Potomac fell further behind in the race to the West.

*   *   *

TECHNOLOGY CHANGES how people perceive their surroundings. If boats become larger, they need deeper rivers. George Washington had supervised the removal of rocks in the bed of the Potomac, because in shallow water they were a hazard. But now boats needed an even deeper streambed. And if commerce requires reliability, then a river like the Potomac seems wilder, moodier, more tempestuous.

The timeless stream emerging from the mountains looked a little bit different with each passing year, and Washington's grand plan now started to seem too modest. His canal at Great Falls and the other river improvements along the Potomac took on a quaint air. In the eighteenth century this river was up to contemporary standards, but in the nineteenth it would have to be upgraded, somehow.

In fact, it might have to be replaced entirely—by a parallel, artificial waterway.

The Potomac elites certainly could no longer depend on the Patowmack Company (which now, mysteriously, called itself the *Potowmack* Company, and would soon call itself the Potomac Company) to make the river competitive with, much less superior to, the New York route. By 1817 the company had managed to spend $650,000 on its river improvements while collecting only $162,380 in tolls. At least the company was consistent, with its annual expenditures so reliably and steadily exceeding its revenues. An investor hates uncertainty, and the Patowmack Company had always offered a surefire method to turn four investment dollars into one.

The time had arrived for a new approach. In 1822 the governors of Maryland and Virginia appointed a team of commissioners to inspect the Potomac and see to what degree the Patowmack Company had made the river navigable. The commissioners left in canoes from Cumberland, and floated 185 miles downstream. By their calculation they ran into some kind of obstruction to navigation on average every half-mile.

Their conclusion was remarkable: The Potomac simply was not a navigable river under normal circumstances. The only time it was truly navigable was during minor floods. These encompassed only thirty-three to forty-five days in a calendar year. George Washington was simply wrong (though no one had the gall to say it). Washington had canoed the river many times, but perhaps he'd failed to take into full account how rarely the river had the right level of water, and in any case his idea of "navigable" did not meet nineteenth-century standards. The commissioners declared that the Potomac was fraught with "evils." These included:

. . . its dangerous character, arising from the wildness of the torrent, and the suddenness of its courses and meanders—having
worn its devious way, in the lapse of ages, through countless
ridges of rocks and mountains; and, in consequence of huge fragments of rocks and large loose stones, the remains of the wasted
mountains, scattered thickly, and in some places rising over the
entire bed of the river, and leaving no passage for loaded boats,
impelled by the rapid and impetuous current, but what may be
found by warping and winding, with the utmost exertion of
strength, agility, and watchfulness, on the part of the crew,
through a most irregular course.

And so on. There was way too much warping and winding out there
on the Potomac. But there was a potential solution. "Providence . . .
has placed the remedy within our reach," the report stated. There
were glades high in the mountains—luxuriant meadows. They could
be transformed by dams into lakes that would serve as reservoirs for a
canal that could parallel the river even in the high country. The brilliant thing about a canal is that it is flat. There are no rapids. There are
no falls. A canal is an utterly denatured river. If the Potomac was in-
nately demonic, a canal would be a kind of exorcism.

The commissioners proposed that the new canal would hug the
river all the way up to Cumberland, and then beyond, far up the North
Branch, up onto the Allegheny Plateau, continuing *over the crest.*
There might have to be a short tunnel in there somewhere. The vi-
sionaries conceded that water ran downhill. The canal would be 360
miles long. It would make flatwater navigation possible from the entire Mississippi River system to the Atlantic, via the Potomac. With
nothing more than the steady tug from a mule, a boat could simply
float across the Appalachians.

This wouldn't be a narrow, modest little canal like the Erie. It would
be broad and deep. It wouldn't be something built for the present day
or century, but something constructed to endure for all time. It would
be a monument to the Age of Progress, and a monument, obviously, to
George Washington.

*   *   *

CHARLES FENTON MERCER, congressman from northern Virginia, and chairman of the House Committee on Roads and Canals, led the charge. Mercer was an orator of the first rank. He had an aversion to moderation. His ideology cannot easily be condensed to a simple label. "Liberal Congressman" is what it says today on the roadside plaque outside his white frame mansion on a hill in the charming little village of Aldie, Virginia, but his liberalism was not of the twenty-first-century variety. He advanced free public education, and promoted an expansion of suffrage, but he had his limits, which over the years would contract, until finally, late in life, he would become an ardent foe of the unwashed masses, "the idle, worthless, ignorant and corrupt mass of population," denizens of a caldron of filth that "throws up its ebullitions of dregs and froth," and so on.

On November 7, 1823, an ailing Mercer appeared in the Capitol at a convention of delegates from Virginia, Maryland, Pennsylvania, and Ohio who had assembled to discuss this new canal scheme. Gray eminences from George Washington's 1784 tour, including Daniel Morgan and Bushrod Washington, and even Albert Gallatin, were on hand, along with Francis Scott Key and George Washington Parke Custis, Martha Washington's grandson, who had been raised at Mount Vernon and no longer was called Washy. Here were men with names long known in the mid-Atlantic: Tilghman, Fitzhugh, Lee, Forrest, Law, Mason, Carroll.

Mercer's stemwinder of a speech abided by the era's fashion for stentorian oratory. He proclaimed that it would not be sufficiently ambitious to build the canal along the Potomac to the foot of the Alleghenies and then stop. That would be unthinkable. He wouldn't even have made the journey to Washington if such a spineless proposal were to be adopted. The creation of a 200-mile canal past the Little Falls and the Great Falls and past the cataracts at Seneca and Harpers Ferry, past Shepherdstown and Williamsport and Hancock and Little Orleans and Old Town and Cumberland, and all the way up through the rugged valley of the North Branch to the mouth of the

Savage River, must necessarily comprise only the eastern third of the canal, Mercer declared.

The canal—which he wanted to call the Union Canal, in homage to the cement of interest long ago mentioned by Washington—would use locks to carry boats up and across the Allegheny Plateau, and then down through the headwaters of the Ohio, to the Ohio proper, and then perhaps would *keep going*—an unstoppable canal!—until it reached Lake Erie, thus creating a single waterway that bound to-gether the Great Lakes, the Mississippi and Ohio watersheds, the Gulf of Mexico and the Atlantic Ocean, and not incidentally the seat of government on the Potomac. The canal would be, as he described it, an artificial Northwest Passage.

To drive home his point, Mercer played the Washington card. The great hero had become such a secular god that Mercer seemed reluc-tant to utter his name. The allusion, however, was unmistakable:

> For its prime mover, it claims a name, illustrious over the earth: of a statesman, a patriot, and hero; of whom, every object around us, recalls to us the affecting recollection. Under this hallowed influence, we are about to combine all our energies, in fulfilling the early suggestions of his wisdom; in rendering imperishable this proud monument of his glory.

Mercer wanted the new project to assume the debts of the Patow-mack Company and make whole its investors. He delicately suggested that this might be necessary to protect the reputation of Washington. "It has even been whispered," he said, "that a failure of this [Patow-mack Company] enterprise, if followed by the total loss of the capital embarked in it, might cast, in some remote corner of the globe, a shade upon his immaculate character."

That could not be allowed to happen. Washington could not be per-mitted to be a real man with many ideas, not all of them perfect. He had to be a supernaturally blessed being, even if it meant, decades after his death, bailing out the bankrupt river navigation company he founded.

Do it for the general.

The convention ended with a proposal to form a joint stock company, one in which public funds could mingle with private investments. The delegates decided to name the new waterway the Chesapeake & Ohio Canal. But even though President Monroe converted to the cause, the canal scheme would need another five years to get off (or into, perhaps one should say) the ground. In the meantime, the Yorkers finished the Erie Canal. The cost of shipping produce from the West dropped almost twentyfold. New York City boomed, and there was no more doubt about the center of commerce in America.

*   *   *

IN HIS OLD AGE Thomas Jefferson didn't dwell on the lack of progress in Potomac navigation, or the distance from the headwaters of one major river to those of another. He had bigger issues to attend to. He had to tidy up the history of the Founding Generation, make clear who did what, why it all happened. The old man on the mountain insisted that *this is the way it really was.* He was writing for the ages. There was not a lot of grit in his language; he'd become more of a pure theoretician.

He stopped reading newspapers, but when a congressman sent him a letter mentioning that Congress might outlaw slavery in the Missouri Territory, the republican rage boiled over. Jefferson may have sought an abolition of slavery as a young man, but as an old man he pledged his allegiance foremost to the rights of the states to determine their own destiny. The attempt to stop slavery in Missouri, "like a fire-bell in the night, awakened and filled me with terror. I considered it at once as the knell of the Union."

His reaction bordered on the hysterical: "I regret that I am now to die in the belief, that the useless sacrifice of themselves by the generation of 1776 . . . is to be thrown away by the unwise and unworthy passions of their sons, and that my only consolation is to be, that I live not to weep over it."

Despite moments of despair, he never lost his faith in Progress. At the age of eighty-one, sickly, plagued by intestinal problems and rapidly nearing his death, he laid out on paper a remarkable vision of the spread of civilization on the North American continent:

> Let a philosophic observer commence a journey from the savages of the Rocky Mountains, eastwardly towards our seacoast. These he would observe in the earliest stage of association living under no law but that of nature, subsisting and covering themselves with the flesh and skins of wild beasts. He would next find those on our frontiers in the pastoral state, raising domestic animals to supply the defects of hunting. Then succeed our own semi-barbarous citizens, the pioneers of the advance of civilization, and so in his progress he would meet the gradual shades of improving man until he would reach his, as yet, most improved state in our seaport towns. This, in fact, is equivalent to a survey, in time, of the progress of man from the infancy of creation to the present day. I am eighty-one years of age, born where I now live, in the first range of mountains in the interior of our country. And I have observed this march of civilization advancing from the seacoast, passing over us like a cloud of light, increasing our knowledge and improving our condition, insomuch as that we are at this time more advanced in civilization here than the seaports were when I was a boy. And where this progress will stop no one can say. Barbarism has, in the meantime, been receding before the steady step of amelioration; and will in time, I trust, disappear from the earth.

This was the American myth. It is never clear to what degree Jefferson is merely channeling the American psyche and to what degree he's doing surgery on it. But this idea—that the land and its conquest reflect the ascent of man from a state of nature—would prove durable. This is what many Americans believe still, in some form or another (perhaps with caveats and provisos and to-be-sure exceptions). Americans are steeped in the belief that history is progressive and deterministic. Washington's life and Jefferson's life and the lives of so many other Founders were built around the belief, or at the very least the *hope,* that they were part of an inexorable process that was good and right and natural. Westward the course of empire takes its way! The passage by Jefferson compresses American history into a perfect formula. He cites no specific individuals, no cities or towns, no events. Jefferson the scientist does not find it necessary to invoke a guiding hand, a divine Driver on the road to human felicity. The process unfolds naturally, Newtonian in its mechanics. To defy the advance of Jefferson's civilization would be like defying the Second Law of Thermodynamics.

(Nearly three-quarters of a century later, speaking to his fellow historians in Chicago in 1893, Frederick Jackson Turner made his landmark speech on the significance of the frontier in American history. The Frontier Hypothesis included a memorable image: "The United States lies like a huge page in the history of society. Line by line as we read this Continental page from West to East we find the record of social evolution." This is Jefferson's idea, slightly rephrased. An American was, in the Turner equation, *a European transformed by wilderness.* Historians eventually realized that the Turner version of America was a whites-only district, that it turned the Indians into props and pretty much ignored the French and the Spanish, as well as the cities and the common laborers and the women and the blacks and the big land-speculating companies and the missionaries and all the other folks on the continent who didn't happen to be white men wearing buckskins and toting a long rifle.)

Progress may exist, at some very abstract level, but people don't live their lives abstractly. Nor is Progress smooth and efficient and reliable. There are relapses, regressions, side effects. Jefferson could not possibly have imagined the horrors that would befall the planet even as his civilization marched forward. He did know, however, that his own civilization had a fatal flaw. He lived on the battlefield of what he had called, in his youth, a "cruel war against human nature itself." Jefferson was so indebted that he had no hope of keeping his estate intact upon his death. He could not bring himself to free one of his most valuable assets, his human property. He freed only five of his slaves.

Jefferson died on the fiftieth anniversary of the Declaration of Independence, and Adams died some hours later the very same day, a stunning coincidence that told the nation that it was, indeed, providentially blessed. They were great men who had done great things. Adams would have to wait a long time to get his full due from historians, but Jefferson would become an unrivaled icon, in large part because of his authorship of the lines that form the American creed. No one could take from him those words: *We hold these truths to be self-evident, that all men are created equal, that they are endowed by their Creator with certain unalienable rights, that among these are Life, Liberty, and the pursuit of Happiness. . . .*

But the creditors took what they could. On January 15, 1827, Jefferson's estate, including "130 valuable negroes," went on the auction block to settle his debts.

13

A Heroic Age

July 4, 1828

*T*HEY WERE REALLY GOING TO DO IT. They were really going to build this fantastic, borderline-preposterous canal from the tidewater Potomac to the navigable headwaters of the Ohio. They'd raised capital from government and private sources, they'd sent surveyors into the mountains, they'd drawn up plans, and now, amazingly, George Washington's vision of a Potomac Route to the West was going to become a reality. Almost.

Early in the morning, the president of the United States, John Quincy Adams, led an entourage of canal promoters and government officials by steamboat up the Potomac from a wharf at Georgetown. It would be a short but geologically evocative trip, for just upstream from Georgetown the placid Potomac becomes a different sort of river, one with banks instead of shores. It's no longer a river valley but a gorge, one inspected by Captain John Smith in 1608, by Jefferson and Madison in their September 1790 tour of possible sites for the federal district, and by George Washington countless times by both horseback and canoe. The steamboat soon reached a small cove on the

Maryland bank, the site of a prehistoric Indian fishing camp, where shad seem to boil from the water during the spring spawning run. This was Lock Cove, the outlet of the Little Falls skirting canal dug half a century earlier by the forgotten Ballendine and then improved by the Patowmack Company.

Switching from river to canal, the entourage moved up the gorge another couple of miles, past Chain Bridge, to the head of Little Falls, where a boulder dam funneled water into the canal. The Marine Band led the way. Two companies of riflemen fired a salute as the president arrived. Several thousand people dotted the hillside like wildflowers.

The sun came out from behind a cloud. Charles Fenton Mercer took a spade in hand and addressed the crowd:

> Fellow Citizens: There are moments, in the progress of time, which are the counters of whole ages. There are events, the monuments of which, surviving every other memorial of human existence, eternise the nation to whose history they belong, after all the other vestiges of its glory have disappeared from the globe. At such a moment have we now arrived. Such a monument we are now to found. . . .

Those who could hear must have sensed that the speakers were going to make this an epic battle of verbs and nouns and adjectives— oratory to the death. Mercer turned portentously to the president of the United States, extended the spade, and said that here, on a spot where, little more than a century earlier, "the painted savage held his nightly orgies," the chief magistrate of the most powerful country on Earth would initiate the most noble project ever conceived by man. Mercer presented the president with "this humble instrument of rural labor."

President Adams took the spade. He did not have a knack for theater, but he played his role as best he could. He began with a quotation from Bishop Berkeley: "Time's noblest Empire is the last." The last empire was the United States, Adams said, and it was the noblest, because unlike the Assyrian, the Persian, the Grecian, and the Roman, which were empires of conquest, of the dominion of man over man, the American empire was an empire of learning and the arts—"the dominion of man over himself, and over physical nature."

Perhaps this was too elaborate a concept, but Adams kept going. Even more arduous than achieving independence, he said, was the process of improving the nation through academies, schools, and the internal projects "to improve the bounties, and to supply the deficiencies of nature; to stem the torrent in its course; to level the mountain with the plain; to disarm and fetter the raging surf of the ocean."

Adams was not about to let Mercer outexaggerate him, and his listeners may have expected that, at some point in this speech, the president would say the canal would be a rival to the pyramids of the pharaohs. Adams took it to that level and beyond:

> The project contemplates a conquest over physical nature, such as has never yet been achieved by man. The wonders of the ancient world, the Pyramids of Egypt, the Colossus of Rhodes, the Temple of Ephesus, the Mausoleum of Artemisia, the Wall of China, sink into insignificance before it . . .
>
> Friends and Fellow-laborers: We are informed by the Holy Oracles of Truth, that, at the creation of man, male and female, the Lord of the Universe, their maker, blessed them, and said unto them, be fruitful, and multiply, and replenish the Earth, *and subdue it.*

The president then took the spade, aimed it at the ground, and bounced it off something impenetrably hard.

The newspapers called it a root. In his diary the president described it as stump just below the surface. Indisputably, the Earth remained unsubdued.

Adams tried a second time to break the ground, but again the blade bounced. The president threw down the spade and pulled off his coat. He would have to go at it like a true canal digger. He rammed the blade down into the ground with all his might. Success!

The crowd on the hillside had heard none of the speech, but, upon seeing the elaborate pantomime below, cheered lustily.

*   *   *

THERE WAS ONLY ONE PROBLEM with the inauguration of the Great National Project. It had a rival. And the rival had chosen this very same day to announce its appearance on the nation's stage, in a ceremony only 40 miles away, near Baltimore.

This time the audience didn't number in the several thousands, but rather in the tens of thousands. Estimates ranged as high as 70,000, which would mean essentially every living soul in the city had come out to see the spectacle. Baltimore, boosted by the Cumberland Road, had grown into the third-largest city in the nation and had dreams of overtaking New York City. The citizens had come to see Charles Carroll, ninety-one years old, the last surviving signer of the Declaration of Independence, dedicate a symbolic stone. Carroll's gesture would signal the start of construction of something called the Baltimore & Ohio Rail Road.

The celebration began at 7 A.M. with a grand procession along Market Street, toward the first Turnpike Gate two miles from the center of town. The Masons led the way, 400 of them. In due order came Revolutionary War veterans, members of Congress, farmers, planters, carpenters, plow-makers, millers, bakers, brewers, distillers, tailors, and blacksmiths. What an industrious city this was! In the midst of this was a great ship, the *Union*, a magnificent vessel. "So perfect was the symmetry of her form, and show of the strength which her timbers presented," sighed the *Baltimore Gazette*, "so beautiful were the proportion of the height and rake of her masts, to those of the dimensions of her hull. . . ." More tradesmen came down the road: weavers, bleachers, dyers, stonecutters, tin-plate workers, coppersmiths, printers, bookbinders, booksellers, painters, sugar refiners, glasscutters, steam-engine makers, rollers of copper and iron, millwrights, coachmakers. They kept coming: coopers, saddle-and-harness makers, pilots, sailmakers, ship captains. The parade had 5,000 participants.

Gawkers lined both sides of the road. Many of the marchers weren't walking, but rather were performing on floats, or "moving stages," the dairymen churning butter, the blacksmiths pounding their anvils. A printer's float featured a complete "printing establishment," churning out copies of the Declaration of Independence. This was much more elaborate than the president's goofy routine with the shovel down at the Potomac.

General Washington would have been astonished. The Baltimoreans were stealing (what would someday be called hijacking) his idea of a Potomac Route to the West. They were going to exploit much of the mountainous portion of the Potomac corridor, all those providential water gaps leading the traveler toward the West. But they would do so with a new technology, a road on rails. The promoters called it the Great Road.

Washington had presumed that any true commercial highway would be liquid. He made a second assumption: A Potomac Route to the West would benefit the ports on the *Potomac.* That seemed logical enough. A Potomac route would boost the fortunes of Alexandria, Georgetown, and (as he hoped in his final years) the new seat of government that bore his own name. And yet here was Baltimore, 40 miles northeast of the capital, on the Chesapeake, at the mouth of an unimportant river called the Patapsco, threatening to siphon away all the Potomac trade. It was almost like the geological process known as stream capture. Mount Vernon would be left high and dry above a worthless stretch of tidal river.

The Baltimoreans even had the gall to steal General Washington's cement-of-interest rationale. According to the *Baltimore Gazette,* the Great Road would "make the East and the West as one household, in the facilities of intercourse and the feeling of mutual affection." The stone that Carroll dedicated stated that the new road would perpetuate the "happy Union of these Confederated States." It was thievery through and through!

*   *   *

THE EVENTS of this Independence Day exemplified the Age of Progress and all its presumptions and ambitions and astonishing vigor. Both the canal and the railroad were akin to what we would today call a moon shot: Their builders sought to do something that only a generation earlier would have seemed incomprehensible. The Chesapeake & Ohio Canal would make the Patowmack Company project look trivial, even silly. Just the first third of the projected waterway (the part that Mercer said would be too modest by itself) would eventually be 185 miles long, and require (though no one yet realized the dimensions of the engineering challenge) the construction of 11 aqueducts across rivers and creeks, a 3,118-foot tunnel through a mountain at Paw Paw, feeder dams, turning basins, hundreds of culverts, and 74 locks. It would fully deserve the lofty designation of the Great National Project.

Unless the railroad turned out to deserve it more.

There were massive engineering projects underway all across the country. The Pennsylvanians labored on their own route to the West, a creative and perhaps overly complex enterprise that would combine canals with portage railroads. The canal boats would, when meeting a mountain, be lifted on cradles onto a track and pulled by stationary steam engines over the mountain.

Americans were innovators of necessity. They had to have many different skills, and exploit many types of tools, to survive in a frontier republic. New technologies didn't scare them. (Steam had already proved itself on rivers: By 1829 there would be three daily steamboat packets departing Washington for Alexandria—9 A.M., noon, and 5 P.M.—plus another two leaving the wharf at Georgetown.) There were fears that a railroad wouldn't work in America, because the terrain wasn't as flat and as easily traversed as that of England, where the first railroads were already in operation. Railroads in America had previously been used primarily in mining, as a way of taking minerals out of the mines, then downhill using nothing more than gravity. The longest railroad in the world, England's Stockton & Darlington Railway, was only 25 miles long when the planning began for the B&O.

The first commercial railroad in America had gone into service only two years earlier, and it was really just a tramway.

The railroads didn't use steam locomotives at first, but rather horses, which would pull wagons along the rails. The promise of the railroad was not the power source, but the ability to smooth out the landscape, to put everything at a fairly level grade, to enable a wagon to travel across the country without bobbing on rutted roads. Rails offered wheels minimal resistance. Presumably this would be an ideal way to transport people, while canals handled the heavy freight.

Steam locomotives seemed fanciful at first, surely not as reliable as a horse. In a famous race between a primitive steam locomotive and an old gray mare, the machine took an early lead, malfunctioned, and broke down. The mare rumbled dependably onward to victory.

This was clearly going to be an age of burly national projects. The builders of railroads and canals were ready to make things happen, to conquer nature, to create the kind of empire that George Washington and Thomas Jefferson had dreamed about. They were leveraging the nation's raw assets, imposing their will on the landscape, believing in their ability to achieve the nearly impossible. Which was not quite the same thing as knowing how it would all turn out.

The self-aggrandizing rhetoric of the age now reads comically. As we look back upon these moments, we're conscious not only of the technological triumphs but also of the tragedies that accompanied them. The Progress of Man was a grand conceit that had dire consequences for many Americans. For the indigenous people of the continent it led directly to the Trail of Tears. It fueled the expansion of slavery. One could make a long list of sins that emerged from the belief that the Manifest Destiny of the United States was to create a nation from sea to sea.

But perhaps we see a different set of sins in our own time: a reluctance to take on any new Great National Projects, a general self-indulgence, a culture built on consumption, whole generations raised in an environment where dreams are purchased at the mall. If we could somehow select the virtues of early Americans from amid their

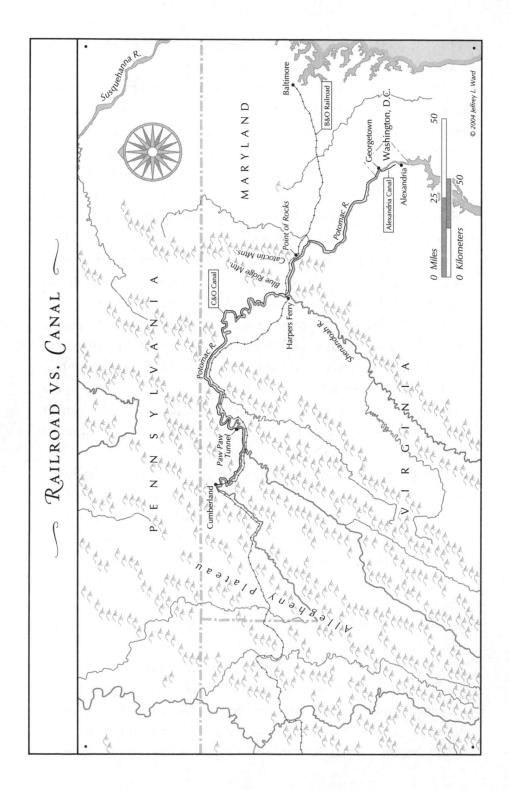

~ RAILROAD vs. CANAL ~

PENNSYLVANIA

MARYLAND

VIRGINIA

Susquehanna R.

Baltimore

B&O Railroad

Washington, D.C.

Georgetown

Alexandria Canal

Alexandria

Point of Rocks

Potomac R.

Catoctin Mtns.

Blue Ridge Mtn.

C&O Canal

Harpers Ferry

Shenandoah R.

Potomac R.

Paw Paw Tunnel

Cumberland

Allegheny Plateau

© 2004 Jeffrey L. Ward

0 Miles 25 50

0 Kilometers 50

failings, we might choose their optimism, their endurance, their inventiveness, their willingness to do something big and difficult—like dig a canal across the mountains or build a new kind of road on rails. These people took on challenges that a more sober and settled populace might consider too ambitious, if not downright insane.

*   *   *

THE RAILROAD and the canal eyeballed pretty much the same route to the West, coming from different starting places and converging at Point of Rocks, where the Potomac cuts through the Catoctin Mountain, east of Harpers Ferry. Both claimed the right of way at Point of Rocks on the narrow bank beneath the coal-black cliff topped by a precarious boulder. Lawyers got busy. Each rival obtained an injunction against the other. After several years the court battle ended in a compromise that, among other things, required the railroad to build a high fence to prevent the noise of the trains from scaring the bejabbers out of the canal mules. The court also recognized the canal's priority in claiming the right of way all along the north bank of the river. Score one round for the canal.

Point of Rocks became a teeming, smoking work camp. The railroad's chief architect, Benjamin H. Latrobe, described this prized slice of American real estate as "a horrid hole, the habitation of a set of sharpers who assemble there to make money by a swindling sort of commerce." The B&O used a combination of slaves and free laborers for the monumental task of building a level road across the mountains. The canal relied primarily on Irishmen who had been lured to America by the promise of $10 a month and a daily ration of meat and liquor. The identities of most of these workers are unknown—they were illiterate, hired by private contractors, and many wound up in unmarked graves in churchyards not far from the Great National Project. Some of those private contractors may have used slave labor as well. The immaculate stoneworking of the canal tells us of the mastery but not the names of those who made the artificial river.

The workers lived in shanties in villages that came and went as quickly as a spring freshet. They had no skills in the formal sense: Theirs was "common labor." They used black powder, just as had those unfortunate workers of Rumsey's on the Patowmack Canal at Great Falls ("we had our Blowers, One Run off the other Blown up").

The canal workers were a piece of a global phenomenon. As capital accumulated, men raised on farms were going to work in factories and on industrial projects. This was a Jeffersonian nightmare. Whatever happened to his agrarian republic? The people were increasingly turning into *the masses,* faceless and exploited. Many were thrilled at the chance at upward mobility and made the best of the harsh working conditions, but others were ground down by industrialization like wheat at the millstone. "[C]anallers were miners and sappers digging the earthworks of North American capitalism, agents of change burying the past and digging the trenches of a future world of industrial production with every spadeful of earth removed," the historian Peter Way has written.

For millions of Americans, industrialization meant only the intensification of pain. The young women who worked in the textile factories were virtually inmates, as James MacGregor Burns has put it. The miseries intensified for slaves in the Deep South as the cotton trade boomed. The work under the southern sun was longer, hotter, more brutally enforced by the lash. Nat Turner's rebellion in 1831 incited a crackdown from slave-owners across the South. George Washington had wanted his younger freed slaves to get educations, but Virginia made it illegal to teach a slave to read and write. Slavery was never a static institution, but one in which the slave codes evolved over time. As Frederick Douglass said of his mistress, who didn't want him to learn to read, "It was at least necessary for her to have some training in the exercise of irresponsible power, to make her equal to the task of treating me as though I were a brute."

Visitors still saw America as a land of beauty, industry, and unlimited potential. Tocqueville toured the country in 1830 and prophesied that one day 150 million people would live in North America, "all equal one to the other, all belonging to the same family . . . and it is a fact new to the world, a fact that the imagination strives in vain to grasp."

That same year, Fanny Trollope got a taste of the Cumberland Road as she traveled by stagecoach up and down the steep mountains. She stayed at an inn that smelled of tobacco and whiskey, and learned that the linens had been used "only a few nights." Mrs. Trollope also saw the plight of the free laborers and black slaves. The slaves, at least, would be cared for when sick, "as a valuable horse is watched and physicked; not so the Irishman; he is literally thrown on one side, and a new comer takes his place."

Working conditions were even worse in the coal mines. In the 1820s and 1830s the coal industry boomed along George's Creek, a tributary of the Potomac west of Cumberland. The miners, mainly Scottish, worked all day underground with only a few vents to the outside world. Children as young as eight and nine scrambled around the mines, opening and closing ventilation doors and, when a bit older, hauling out coal themselves. The miners found a Big Vein, 14 feet across, and it would produce tens of millions of tons of bituminous coal by the end of the century.

Industrialization had another lethal consequence, for as people and products moved across the surface of the Earth, so did pathogens. The organism causing cholera took full advantage of the hideous sanitation of the camps. In 1832, hundreds of canal workers died of cholera near Shepherdstown. So many died, and the burials were so hasty, that no one could keep track of them.

Sometimes the Irish workers went to war with one another. They held ancient enmities from their home counties. There were Longfords, Corkmen, Fardowns, and Connoughtmen. On January 18, 1834, the Corkmen and Longfords squared off in a "disastrous battle," reported *Niles' Weekly Register*. The battle had aspects of Napoleonic warfare:

> A party of Fardouns of Longfords, consisting of about three hundred men, headed by intrepid leaders, were announced as approaching from below. . . . they met the enemy in battle array, drawn up on the top of a hill, about three hundred in number, and armed, in part, with military weapons. . . . Persons who tra-

versed the field after the battle was over, observed five men in the
agonies of death, who had been shot through the head; several
dead bodies were seen in the woods, and a number wounded in
every direction. . . .

Riots broke out annually at the Paw Paw Tunnel. The tunnel, more
than three-fifths of a mile long, bored through a ridge called Devil's
Eyebrow. Men blasted from both directions. At night they blasted
each other, unless they found better game in Welsh miners or German
masons. In the summer of 1839, as workers threatened to strike, they
went berserk, bludgeoned several Germans to death, and heaved one
of the corpses into a fire. The militia marched through the mountains,
obliterated the Irish shanties, destroyed their guns, and threw dozens
of ringleaders in the Cumberland jail.

That summer, stockholders of the C&O took a trip up the canal to
Cumberland and published a lengthy account in the *National Intelligencer*, full of romantic descriptions of the landscape ("The Canal
sometimes passes along the rocky cliffs of the mountain, on the de-
clevities of which were seen shanties adhering like swallow's
nests . . ."). The anonymous author showed an unflagging optimism
about the pace and quality of the Great National Project; there are no
warring workers or backcountry hellholes, only industrious men and
flourishing villages.

The stockholders at one point passed a curiosity: the ruin of a fort. It
was Fort Frederick, a massive stone structure built in the late 1750s during the French and Indian War, when the Indians had managed to push
back the white settlers and even hardy, crusty Thomas Cresap needed
refuge. The scale of the fort is impressive to this day: not some wooden
stockade, as the Seceders later built on Washington's lands, but a virtual
walled town, with two acres of land inside the ramparts. But now, in
1839, the visitors found it bewildering. The history of the place had
been lost: "I have not been able to ascertain when, or by whom, it was
built . . . It is on a tract of land belonging to a Mr. Johnson, who resides
near it, and who, I understand, is himself ignorant of its origin."

The old fort had become an American Stonehenge, a relic from the mysterious depths of time.

*   *   *

THE BUBBLE BURST. The heroic age nearly ended with the Panic of 1837, as the country fell into an economic depression that would last well into the 1840s. By 1840 the C&O, still struggling to dig that tunnel through the mountain at Paw Paw, had run out of money. It had used money raised from bonds to pay off interest on its debt rather than for new construction. It had issued its own scrip to pay its bills, but now no one would accept it.

And the demon river proved uncooperative still. Every flood damaged the canal, choked it with mud, and required extensive repairs. Droughts kept water too low for navigation. Boulders fell into the canal. Hillsides slid into the water. Boats sank and blocked the way, as did floating carcasses. At the end of the canal, in the turning basin at Rock Creek, canal boats clotted, blocking the final short passage to tidewater. The creek filled with silt, the runoff from the denuded terrain of the federal city.

On November 3, 1842, the first B&O locomotive steamed into Cumberland. The railroad had won the race to the heart of the mountains.

The B&O kept going, toward the Ohio, even as the canal crawled along, a few steps forward, a step back. The railroad, though not immune from calamity, could generally operate all year round, in any weather. The canal froze in winter. A flood smashed it in 1847.

The completion of the Paw Paw Tunnel in 1850 finally opened the canal all the way to Cumberland. Though derided in later years as a failure, as a *loser*, as utterly obviated by the railroad, the canal was in fact a technological triumph, just like George Washington's canal at Great Falls. The year it reached Cumberland, the C&O transported 101,950 tons of freight. ("Cumberland," predicted Horace Greeley, "is destined to become one of the largest inland towns in America, a rival of Pittsburgh and Lowell.")

Industry did nothing for the health of the river proper. As Cumberland boomed and the George's Creek mines made fortunes for a few, the Upper Potomac became a lethal brew, so poisoned with mine drainage that for decades no fish could survive.

In 1852, a Potomac flood crested six feet higher than the flood of 1847. For four months no cargo traveled on the canal as the company spent $100,000 on repairs. In 1857 the river flooded four times, including a particularly nasty phenomenon called an *ice freshet* that chewed up the valley that February. The company edged close to bankruptcy. The true believers had a crisis of faith.

The canal would never make it to the West. Cumberland would always be the terminus. The Chesapeake & Ohio Canal became, in effect if not in name, the Georgetown & Cumberland Canal.

*   *   *

THE TRIUMPH of the railroad was a dire portent for the nation's capital. It had bet on the wrong technology. The empire's seat of government had never been Rome, and at the rate it was growing, it didn't look like it would ever be much of anything. Visitors mocked it. Congressmen loathed it. Time and again, debates broke out over the possibility of moving the capital somewhere else, perhaps to the West. Defenders of Washington could make the excuse that it was still a relatively new city, but so was Cincinnati, way out on the Ohio River, and it already had more people than the nation's capital.

Just up the road, Baltimore thrived.

When Charles Dickens visited Washington in 1842 he found a strange, dispiriting place:

> Spacious avenues that begin in nothing, and lead nowhere; streets, mile-long, that only want houses, roads, and inhabitants; public buildings that need but a public to be complete; and ornaments of great thoroughfares, which only lack great thoroughfares to ornament—are its leading features. One might fancy the season over, and most of the houses gone out of town for ever

with their masters. . . . It has no trade or commerce of its own: having little or no population beyond the President and his establishment. . . . It is very unhealthy. Few people would live in Washington, I take it, who were not obliged to reside there; and the tides of emigration and speculation, those rapid and regardless currents, are little likely to flow at any time towards such dull and sluggish water.

Visitors made pilgrimages to Mount Vernon, and were dismayed by what they saw. The mansion had become a ruin. Weeds choked the fallow fields. The barns leaned, except the ones that had already disintegrated. After the deaths of the general and Mrs. Washington, the estate had passed to Bushrod Washington, who gave it to his nephew, who passed it on to his wife, who gave it to her son, John A. Washington. This last in the chain tried to muster the funds to keep the estate in repair, but he failed. When tourists pulled up at the wharf, they met hustlers selling knickknacks and whiskey.

The Chevalier de Bacourt, minister from France, in *Souvenirs of a Diplomat*, wrote of a visit in 1840: "All is as shabby as possible; the park is grown over with weeds; the house tumbling down; everything dirty and in a miserable condition."

Finally, a certain Ann Pamela Cunningham published a letter in the *Charleston Mercury* that ignited a movement to save the general's estate:

Ladies of the South! Can you still stand with closed souls and purses, while the world cries "Shame!" on America—suffer Mount Vernon, with all its sacred associations, to become—as is spoken of, and is probable—the seat of manufacturers and manufactories? Noise and smoke, and the busy hum of men, destroying all sanctity and repose around the tomb of your own world of wonder! Oh, it cannot be possible! What?—such sacrilege, such desecration, while you have hearts to feel the shame, and the power to prevent it?

The Ladies of the South came to the aid of the old plantation, which is why, to this day, the estate is owned not by the federal government or the State of Virginia, but by the Mount Vernon Ladies' Association.

*   *   *

GEORGE WASHINGTON'S POTOMAC ROUTE to the West never quite materialized in the way he had envisioned. Washington had the big picture right, in that the Potomac's water gaps and its general geography (a western river!) made it a workable path to the Ohio country. His personal experience in the backcountry, including his major western excursions in 1753, 1754, 1755, 1758, 1770, and 1784, had given him an unusually vivid impression of how readily accessible the Ohio River tributaries were to someone jumping off the Potomac's North Branch. And in a very real sense, the Potomac Route existed in several forms by the middle of the nineteenth century: the National Road, the B&O Railroad, and, though it didn't make it all the way to the Ohio, the C&O Canal.

But it was not the ideal water route to the West. The mountains were too tall. The Erie Canal route had the geographical advantage, despite being farther north and farther east, and it also had all those entrepreneurial New Yorkers behind it. The continued backwater status of the nation's capital, the shabby fate of Mount Vernon, the struggles of the canal, and the comparative efflorescence of other places in the nation all demonstrated that Washington on his piazza had wished too much for his river, had banked on it too heavily.

John Lauritz Larson writes, "Washington's dream of harmonious interests, centered on the Potomac, shattered within a generation, partly because his friends and countrymen had independent visions of their own, partly because his class of 'monied gentry' lost the political authority to impose design, and partly because his own vision (like everybody else's) was far more local and self-serving than he ever was able to admit." There are several lessons racked up there at once, not least of which is that Washington's geographical vision, sweeping though it was, still lingered around the river below his mansion. Other people had their own schemes, their own grand ideas.

Washington had more influence than anyone in America, and surely worked harder and more diligently than anyone else to create and then sustain the Union. But the fate of a nation is not controlled by any one person. History is like that river below Mount Vernon, fundamentally unpredictable, prone to overflowing its banks, finding new channels, backing up into sidestreams, forming whirlpools and eddies in unfamiliar places. No wonder Washington struggled to find serenity and peace in the years after the rupture with Great Britain: He knew that the whole experiment was fundamentally chaotic.

There were things that Washington couldn't have known. No one in the eighteenth century could have realized that water would not remain forever the dominant mode of transportation. The Potomac specifically, with its tempestuous and devious behavior, would not be well matched to a growing modern market economy that needed year-round, all-weather transportation, that didn't want to shut down on account of too much or too little rain. Obviously Washington had no way of foreseeing the eventual dominance of the railroad, since such things didn't exist in the eighteenth century. A person in 1799 could no more have anticipated the technology of 1850 than we can today anticipate the intergalactic wormhole-subway of the 2050s. Washington lived his life in the age of wind, water, and muscle power, when mountains and rivers seemed certain to shape the destiny of society. He could not have imagined a world in which technology was more important than geography.

It wasn't until the mid–nineteenth century that people began to grasp that awesome possibility. When Samuel Morse tapped out the first telegraph message, on May 24, 1844, on a line strung between Washington and Baltimore, he spoke for the world: "What hath God wrought?" The rise of the machine—railroads, telegraph lines, soon an undersea cable—created something that hadn't yet become powerful in George Washington's day: nostalgia for the pastoral world. When Henry David Thoreau listened to the wind vibrating the telegraph line in the railroad cut near his home, he thought it sounded like an aeolian harp. He did not reject this new tool. But he wondered what it foretold of human destiny. He felt compelled to return to the woods, and the simple life. He wrote:

> Our inventions are wont to be pretty toys, which distract our attention from serious things. They are but improved means to an unimproved end, an end which it was already but too easy to arrive at; as railroads lead to Boston or New York. We are in great haste to construct a magnetic telegraph from Maine to Texas; but Maine and Texas, it may be, have nothing important to communicate.

So much had been accomplished since George Washington laid out his vision of a connected, unified, commercially prosperous nation. But the triumphs had come at a cost. People yearned for the lost gardens of the past.

14

The Border

IN PUTTING TOGETHER his grand plan for the Potomac, George Washington had plenty of his own financial interests in mind. But the element that seemed to concern him most, that most animated his 1784 treatise, was the river's potential to unite the country, to stave off disunion, to serve as a powerful binding agent between West and East.

Instead, it became a fracture line. A border between warring armies.

Washington would have found this a particularly painful irony. He always had a foreboding about the divisiveness of slavery, and the institution had been a subject of debate at every significant turn in the young nation's history, but in Washington's mind it had never been the most pressing threat to the Union. He seems to have viewed the mountains as a bigger problem. Slavery might gradually dissipate, he thought, but the erosion of mountains was too slow a process for a nation in a hurry. Men of vigor had to breach the Appalachian wall.

Slavery in the 18th century did not divide the nation as starkly as it did just a few decades later. In the early decades of the republic, slaves could be found in every state, even Massachusetts. Even the concept of "North" and "South" was a bit fuzzy. Some political leaders still talked of the "eastern" states, in reference to New England. Racism was hardly the sole province of the South; a great deal of early sentiment against slavery in the North was driven by a desire to keep the region free of blacks. Washington can be forgiven for underestimating the shearing effect of slavery, and focusing on the possibility of the western settlers going their own way. As in so many cases, he got the details wrong (a major detail, in this case) but the big picture right: Membership in his United States was voluntary. He knew that a central ideal of the Revolution—the principle that a people had a right to separate from their Mother Country—carried with it the threat of disunion.

Washington may have made a more fundamental miscalculation. He believed that only "interest" could bind people together, that human beings were economic entities, pragmatic thinkers, unlikely to be swayed by ideology and rhetoric. Perhaps life in an army camp had taught him that. His own officers had wanted to turn on the United States when Congress failed to pay them. He'd seen his men suffer through Valley Forge and countless other miseries while the distant politicians did little to support them. He rarely had the luxury of being an armchair idealist. But ultimately the ideals matter, the beliefs matter, and such evanescent concepts as "liberty" matter. It turned out that commerce, trade, the "cement of interest," the building of roads, the construction of canals and railroads, and so on, would not cure the nation's chronic disease.

The Revolutionary generation and the generations that came afterward refused to deal with the evil in their midst. They postponed the reckoning, letting the institution of slavery grow and fester. They consigned millions of men and women and children to a fate that defied the very words of the nation's founding document. You might say that they failed to make the most important kind of internal improvements, those of the spirit.

Harpers Ferry, Virginia, October 17, 1859

*T*HE TOPOGRAPHY of Harpers Ferry had always inspired visionary men. Thomas Jefferson read the landscape as a kind of geological dramatization of man's destiny, of his journey from barbarism to civilization, from tumult to serenity. In blasting away the mountain the combined waters of the Potomac and Shenandoah had shown us the way to smooth blue horizons. For George Washington, the scene triggered ideas of public utility: The fall of the water could be harnessed for power. He would put the federal armory there, and manufacture guns. Washington was not blind to the beauties of nature, but what always grabbed his attention was a piece of terrain that could be put to good use. With the C&O and the B&O and the wagon roads all converging, and with smoke from the chimneys and the mills and the armory, the scene had been transformed dramatically from the day when Jefferson stood on that rock and rhapsodized about the water gap in the Blue Ridge. It had become an industrial site.

John Brown saw it as the perfect setting for a guerrilla war. He was an accomplished man of stealth and violence, determined to excise the evil of slavery, unwilling to compromise. Brown had spent the past five years roaming the country, from Kansas to Massachusetts and finally to a farmhouse in Maryland, where in October 1859 he plotted his assault on the federal armory at Harpers Ferry. He had dined along the way with Thoreau and Emerson, and met with Frederick Douglass, failing to recruit him to a raid that Douglass viewed as suicide. Brown chose his target carefully: Harpers Ferry sat at a crossroads of the nation, with roads and rivers and rail lines skewing off in every direction. The armory would offer the raid both a symbolic significance and a real source of guns for arming slaves in what would surely be a widening insurrection. Brown knew how to strike at a target and flee to safety, and Harpers Ferry was his kind of landscape. There were so many hills and hollows, so many rivers and creeks, and deserted islands up and down the Potomac, even some deep, dry caves in the limestone bluffs. The trees had been cleared from the surrounding heights, and a spy could stand on the overlook across the Potomac and feel as though he were suspended in a hot-air balloon above the little manufacturing village.

Harpers Ferry sat in Virginia, a slave state, with the slave state of Maryland just across the Potomac, but the industrial economy made the town something of an island of the North. Slaves were greatly outnumbered here by free African Americans: The population included 1,212 whites, 1,251 free blacks, and only 88 slaves.

Scouting out the area in the weeks before the raid, one of Brown's men had visited a local farmer, Colonel Lewis W. Washington, great-grandnephew of President Washington. During the course of what Colonel Washington had assumed was an innocuous conversation, he'd shown the raider a ceremonial sword that he had inherited from his famous ancestor. This came to General Washington from Lafayette, and originally belonged to Frederick the Great, the colonel bragged. The raider made a note of it.

The night of the raid, Colonel Washington woke with a start at half past one in the morning, hearing voices. He opened his door and saw two men armed with revolvers. They told him he was their prisoner. "I should doubt your courage," the colonel said, "you have too many arms to take one man."

One of the raiders replied, "We have come here for the purpose of liberating all the slaves of the South."

They took the prisoner and General Washington's ceremonial sword to John Brown. Brown knew how to use a sword for more than mere ceremony, for three years earlier, in Kansas, during a period of open warfare between proslavery and free-state forces, he and his men had used broadswords to kill five men at Pottawatomie Creek.

The raiders crossed the Potomac from Maryland on a covered railroad bridge. There was no moon, hardly anyone on the streets, and they easily seized the armory and arsenal. The raiders rounded up hostages, including Colonel Washington, and put them in the engine house in the armory yard. But things started going badly within minutes. A commotion broke out at the railroad station, and one of the raiders shot and killed an African-American railroad porter, Heyward Shepherd. The raid triggered alarms throughout the village and the surrounding countryside, but instead of a spreading slave insurrection there was a mobilization of white farmers, who stormed across the Potomac bridges and attacked the raiders. One of Brown's men, Dangerfield Newby, took a bullet through the throat, and the villagers bludgeoned and mutilated his corpse, after which the ravenous village swine went to work on it. Town residents captured raider Will Thompson, took him down to the river, shot him, and spent the rest of the afternoon firing at the body, which took so much lead shot that it sank to the bottom. The corpse remained there for more than a day, "his ghastly face still exhibiting his fearful death agony," in the words of the *New York Herald*. William Leeman, another raider, tried to flee across the Potomac but made it only to an island in the river before the locals gunned him down. He served as target practice for many hours thereafter.

Brown, holed up in the fire-engine house, sent his son Watson and another man, Aaron Stevens, to negotiate with the furious mob under a white flag of truce. They were promptly gunned down. Watson Brown crawled back to cover and spent the following hours in excruciating pain. John Brown's other son, Oliver, took a bullet as well, and spent the night begging his father to put him out of his misery. His father refused. "If you must die, die like a man," he said.

By now the government had become aware that an insurrection was under way, and dispatched Colonel Robert E. Lee to make the counterattack. Lee had grown up on the Potomac, for he was the son of the ill-fated war hero, land speculator, and Washington eulogist Henry "Light-Horse Harry" Lee. Commanding a combined force of Maryland militia, Army troops from Fort Monroe, and Marines from the Washington Navy Yard, Colonel Lee arrived at Harpers Ferry by train that night, expecting to find 500 insurgents (as with the Whiskey Rebellion, rumors had a way of inflating numbers). Lee soon sent a message to Brown saying he had no possibility of escape. Brown refused to surrender.

Lee organized a squad of marines for a dawn assault on the fire-engine house. Lee's deputy, Jeb Stuart, advanced under a white flag and dictated surrender terms to Brown. Brown answered by thrusting a carbine through a crack in the door and demanding that he be allowed to cross the bridge back into Maryland before releasing his hostages. A voice in the back shouted, "Never mind us, fire!"

That was Colonel Washington.

Lee, about 40 feet away, recognized Washington's voice, and said out loud, "The old revolutionary blood does tell!"

Stuart waved his hat to signal that the negotiations were going nowhere and that the time had come to storm the building. The marines battered their way inside, many of them wielding swords themselves. Two marines were shot instantly. Their comrades quickly cut down two of Brown's men—ran them through with swords—and then the leader of the marines, Lieutenant Israel Green, did his best to dispatch Brown on the spot. Green's sword hit something hard—a belt buckle, possibly—and the sword bent. Green resorted to pounding Brown on the head with the hilt of his sword until Brown blacked out. Oliver Brown was already dead, and Watson Brown had only a matter of hours left. The hostages were frazzled but alive. Colonel Washington, like his relative, had a sense of propriety about his appearance and would not emerge from the building until someone brought him gloves to cover his dirty hands.

On December 2, 1859, Brown went to the gallows in Charles Town, on the lawn of the courthouse, not far from Happy Retreat, where George Washington had visited his brother in 1784. Brown had written a final statement, and handed it over a few minutes before his death: "I John Brown am now quite *certain* that the crimes of this *guilty, land: will* never be purged *away*; but with Blood."

*   *   *

GEORGE WASHINGTON had wished for slavery to vanish painlessly—by slow, sure, and imperceptible degrees. But abolition came only after more than 600,000 Americans killed one another, their bodies piled up in places that history buffs know simply as the Cornfield, the Sunken Road, Devil's Den, the Crater, the Hornet's Nest, Little Round Top, the Bloody Lane. In the fields near Antietam Creek, just a few miles from the Potomac, more Americans would die in a single day than in the War of 1812, the Mexican War, and the War of Independence combined.

Loyalty to the Union did not follow precisely the course of the Potomac. The people in northern and western Virginia, including those in Harpers Ferry and Berkeley Springs (Bath), had no interest in being allied to a rebellion led by slave-owners (western Virginia had only a 4 percent slave population), and soon formed the state of West Virginia. Southern Maryland, east of the river, had a fanatical devotion to the Confederate cause, which is why, in April 1865, after assassinating Lincoln at Ford's Theatre, John Wilkes Booth had no trouble escaping through the region and across the Potomac.

Even if the Potomac did not exactly describe the boundary of emotional loyalty to the United States, the river played a key psychological role in the war. Everyone on both sides was keenly aware that this was the formal dividing line between North and South. Lee, who took command of the Army of Northern Virginia, twice took his troops across the Potomac in highly calculated invasions of the North. He didn't need to conquer territory, but merely to sap the will of the Union to prosecute a war in which the status quo would equal a southern victory. So powerful was the symbol of the Potomac that some Confederate troops refused to cross it during the invasions of the North in 1862 and 1863. They said they had signed up to defend their country, not invade another.

"[T]he river was the principal theater of the war. It played the dominant strategic role. Potomac episodes of the war, important in themselves, epitomized the larger events in the national scene," Frederick Gutheim argued in *The Potomac*. Beyond Harpers Ferry, the effective line of battle, Gutheim noted, was the B&O Rail Road line.

The decision to place the permanent seat of government on the Potomac came back to haunt Lincoln and his commanders. President Washington, along with Jefferson and Madison, had put the federal town in a central location, a crossroads of America—so central that the capital was now, in 1861, stranded at the edge of the Union. The capital of the United States and one of the two capitals of the Confederate States of America faced each other across only 100 miles of Piedmont. Much of the war would be fought between those two points. Each side plotted the sacking of the other capital. The Confederates in

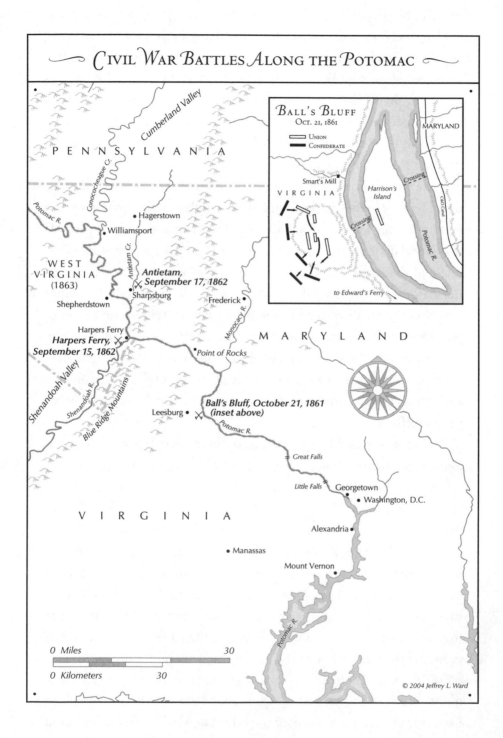

CIVIL WAR BATTLES ALONG THE POTOMAC

BALL'S BLUFF
OCT. 21, 1861

☐ UNION
▬ CONFEDERATE

MARYLAND

Smart's Mill

Harrison's
Island

VIRGINIA

Crossing

Crossing

C&O Canal

Potomac R.

to Edward's Ferry

Cumberland Valley

PENNSYLVANIA

Conococheague C.

Potomac R.

Hagerstown

Williamsport

WEST
VIRGINIA
(1863)

Antietam Cr.

Antietam,
September 17, 1862
Sharpsburg

Shepherdstown

Frederick

Monocacy R.

M A R Y L A N D

Harpers Ferry
Harpers Ferry,
September 15, 1862

Point of Rocks

Shenandoah Valley

Shenandoah R.

Blue Ridge Mountains

Leesburg

Ball's Bluff, October 21, 1861
(inset above)

Potomac R.

Great Falls

Little Falls Georgetown

Washington, D.C.

V I R G I N I A

Alexandria

Manassas

Mount Vernon

Potomac R.

0 Miles   30

0 Kilometers   30

© 2004 Jeffrey L. Ward

their first War Council, in July 1861, briefly considered a pincer move on Washington from north and south, which would culminate in the dictation of a peace treaty to Lincoln in the White House itself.

Lincoln and his commanders feared an attack; they worried that the rebels would simply march right across the Potomac on Chain Bridge. Early in the war the Union forces took positions in Arlington and se- cured the Potomac, but the rebels were never far away, and their most forward outpost, Munson's Hill, was within 10 miles of Washington, close enough to allow rebel troops to watch construction on the Capi- tol Dome. The two major supply lines for the capital, the B&O and the C&O, were fat targets for southern raiders. The Union army began ringing the capital with forts, including several on the devegetated bluffs above the Potomac.

Every day the leaders in Washington waited for news. The bulletin they most enjoyed was the one that said, "All quiet along the Po- tomac."

*   *   *

OF THE MANY BATTLES, skirmishes, and maneuvers along and near the Potomac, one event early in the war showed what can happen when military men misinterpret the landscape and forget the simplest rules for crossing a river.

As the leaves were turning in October 1861, the Union had not fully recovered from the shock of the First Battle of Bull Run (or Manassas, as it was called in the South). In July, 30,000 Union troops had taken the fight to the Confederate forces, fully expecting to smash the rebellion then and there. It was the first serious battle of the war, and Lincoln hoped it would be the last. Washington politicians and other leading citizens rode in carriages across the Long Bridge and over the roads of northern Virginia to see the great sport of modern warfare. Instead, they saw Union troops stampeding back to Washing- ton in panic, shouting, "Turn back! Turn back! We are whipped!" Fif- teen hundred federals had surrendered to the Rebels, and 481 had died. The Rebels had significant losses as well, but Bull Run gave the first strong evidence that this Civil War might not come to an expeditious end.

Now, three months later, 40,000 Confederate troops remained camped in northern Virginia near Centreville, only about 25 miles due west of the capital of the United States. More rebel forces occupied portions of the Shenandoah Valley. Major General George B. McClellan, who had taken command of the Union army from the doddering old war hero General Winfield Scott, and who had named his force the Army of the Potomac, dispatched Brigadier General Charles P. Stone and a division of 6,500 men to Poolesville, Maryland, with instructions to keep an eye on any rebels who might try to cross the river. McClellan hoped the rebels would pull back from Leesburg, Virginia, only 10 miles from Poolesville. He wired Stone, suggesting that "perhaps a slight demonstration on your part would have the effect to move them."

Stone sent two regiments across the Potomac at Edward's Ferry, and another regiment across at Harrison's Island. The soldiers would have to take boats, of course, since there wasn't a bridge for many miles, and the river can't be forded anywhere below Point of Rocks, where it emerges from the mountains.

Harrison's Island seemed like a decent stepping-stone from Maryland to Virginia. The island is 3 miles long and about 350 yards wide, and occupies a pronounced bend in the river between Leesburg and Poolesville. Looming over the island on the Virginia bank is a bluff, about 100 feet high. It was called Ball's Bluff, after a local farming family. The river channel between the island and the Virginia bank was narrow but deep, the current swift.

Stone's men could scrounge together only a flatboat that could carry 25 men and a skiff that could carry 10. In the darkness after midnight, October 21, some 400 men took turns using these boats to cross the river. With the advantage of surprise, they assumed they did not need to transport themselves swiftly. A few boats were enough. Still, Stone had sent a message to McClellan: "We are a little short of boats."

Colonel Edward D. Baker led the Union regiment as, struggling up a cowpath, it ascended the bluff. Baker continued to serve as a United States senator from Oregon and numbered President Lincoln among his closest friends. He could have accepted a commission as a major general but by law would have had to resign from the Senate (in news accounts, however, he would be usually referred to as General Baker). As historian Shelby Foote tells it, the dual status of soldier and senator allowed Baker to make swashbuckling full-uniform appearances in the well of the Senate, laying his sword on his desk and railing against any compromise with secession. "I want sudden, bold, forward, determined war," he declared.

He crossed the river, charged up the bluff, and saw with satisfaction a clearing at the top. Baker didn't know that the Confederate commander, General Nathan G. "Shanks" Evans (so nicknamed because of his skinny legs), had withdrawn most of his men from their position downriver near Edward's Ferry and ordered them to concentrate their firepower on Ball's Bluff. The woods were lousy with rebels.

Baker welcomed another colonel, Milton Cogswell of the 42nd New York Infantry, with a quotation from Walter Scott: "One blast upon your bugle horn/Is worth a thousand men." Cogswell couldn't believe what he saw. This was an obvious trap, self-created. Cogswell told the effervescent Colonel Baker that his forces would be destroyed easily by the enemy if the rebels were to occupy the wooded ground on the edge of the clearing.

Twenty minutes later that ceased to be a hypothetical. The rebels began sniping from behind trees and bushes, picking off the federals as easily as shooting tin cans on a fence. Baker and Cogswell worked the artillery pieces themselves as their men and officers fell around them. The rebels broke from the woods, charging, whooping. Men fought hand-to-hand. The rebels kept surging forward, taking prisoners. Hold your ground, Baker told his troops. Baker shouted, "Who are those men?" only to hear a rebel answer, "Confederate troops, you damned Yankee!" Baker had seconds to live.

"One huge red-haired ruffian drew a revolver," the *New York World* reported, "came close to Baker, and fired four balls at the general's head, every one of which took effect, and a glorious soul fled through their ghastly openings."

Cogswell—now in command, despite a bullet through his wrist—wanted to fight his way through the rebel lines to Edward's Ferry and cross back into Maryland there, but his men couldn't push through. The fog of war took its toll: A Confederate officer suddenly appeared in front of the New York regiment as if he belonged to the Union side and ordered the federals to charge the enemy. The Union soldiers rushed forward, only to be massacred.

Cogswell ordered a retreat to the bluff. Union soldiers spilled over the precipice, tumbling and sprawling and piling up at the base of the bluff, slipping on wet clay and blood. Many couldn't swim. Some struggled to cross the river in their heavy uniforms and boots. The rebels stood on top of the bluff and fired down at the panicked and screaming men. The surface of the Potomac spattered as though in a hailstorm.

Dozens of soldiers climbed onto the flatboat, but there were too many of them, and it foundered. Almost everyone on the boat, at least 20 men, drowned.

The bodies of Union soldiers floated down the river toward the Great Falls. Some tumbled through the cataract and down the lovely gorge. A few may have found a purchase in the vegetation along the riverbank, only to be flushed further downstream as rains drenched the region. One body eventually reached Chain Bridge, having negotiated the violent sluice of Little Falls; another washed up by the wharf at Sixth Street, where slaves had been bought and sold for years. Citizens could see a body lying on driftwood near the Long Bridge. One private's body made it almost to Mount Vernon.

The battle left 49 Union soldiers dead, 158 wounded, and 714 captured or missing. The Confederate casualties included 33 dead and 115 wounded, and none captured. It was a smashing rebel victory, emphasized all the more horribly by its detritus, the macabre spew of warfare in the river itself.

Just five days after the battle, the *Morning Courier & New-York*

Enquirer demanded to know who had ordered the crossing of the Potomac: "Who is responsible for this appalling blunder? . . . Who is responsible for the fact that in view of the necessity of crossing, and the possibility of having hastily to re-cross the river, no pontoon train or suitable provision of boats has been provided anywhere on the upper Potomac?"

River crossings! The bane of the young republic's existence. For Washington and Jefferson it had been a maddening inconvenience. For decades the leaders of the nation had struggled to figure out how to build bridges and roads and a decent transportation network. The lack of fluidity in movement, for humans and their cargo, had been a constant frustration. Now, for the Union, it had become a tragedy.

After the disaster sank in, Congress appointed a Joint Committee on the Conduct of the War. The panel kept generals looking over their shoulders for the next four years. General Stone met his own personal catastrophe, for suspicions surfaced within the committee that he had conspired with the enemy to lead the federals into a trap. It was a preposterous and paranoid allegation, but this was a Star Chamber, unencumbered by such awkward notions as due process. In February 1862, McClellan ordered Stone arrested. The general, transported to Fort Lafayette in New York Harbor, languished in a cell for 189 days. The military never charged him with treason or any other crime. By the time he walked out, ruined as an officer, half of the soldiers under his command had become casualties of the war.

The Union defeat at Bull Run had been a warning shot across the bow; now Ball's Bluff confirmed the worst fears of the Unionists. The war would be long and bloody. The American experiment had not yet failed, but it was in grave peril. There was no talk now of a Great National Project, or the Progress of Man, or even of the inexorable, wondrous, westward march of empire. There was no one who could speak now of Americans as actors in a most conspicuous theater, *peculiarly designated by Providence for the display of human greatness and felicity.* Gone was any thought that you could bring people together, and cement their union, with some improvements to a river.

15

The River Today

GEORGE WASHINGTON'S plan for a Potomac Route to the West managed to survive deep into the second half of the nineteenth century, despite the hazards of war, floodwater, technological change, and financial calamity. As late as the 1870s, C&O officials talked of resurrecting the plan to extend the canal across the mountains. It was hard to let go of the dream. For all the talk of railroads obviating canals, the C&O still had plenty of business, indeed more than ever, thanks to the appetite for all that bituminous coal spilling from the mountains of the Upper Potomac. A decade after the Civil War, no fewer than 500 canal barges floated up and down the canal at any given moment. Maybe canals could make a comeback.

As always, the demon river dashed those thoughts. The cutting of the Eastern Forest reached its peak in the later years of the nineteenth century, and floods were more devastating than ever. In 1889 the storm that caused the disastrous Johnstown Flood in central Pennsylvania also drove the Potomac far over its banks, and this time the floodwaters put the C&O company out of business. The canal was repaired and allowed to linger a few decades longer only because the B&O, which had obtained financial control of it, wanted to keep it going to prevent a competitor from snapping up the right-of-way. A few canal boats still plied the route until the flood of 1924, when finally there were no dreamers to repair the Great National Project. Gutheim writes in *The Potomac*, "The fate of the canal also marked the tendency of the Potomac to recede from its position as one of the great American rivers, important in the life of the nation, and to become just another regional artery."

Trees and vines and weeds reclaimed the old ditch. Driftwood from high water plugged the locks. The abandoned lockhouses gradually filled with dirt, mold, and cobwebs. Leaf litter and eroded soil filled the canal basins, and where boats once floated, there were now wildflowers—Virginia bluebells and Dutchman's breeches. A century after John Quincy Adams struck that root as he inaugurated the C&O, the canal had become a ruin.

After the devastating floods in 1936 and 1937, the B&O wanted to get rid of the canal. The railroad found a buyer: what George Washington used to call the General Government. It was suddenly a different sort of entity, juiced by the New Deal, an active, dynamic agent of social change, pretty much the opposite of Jefferson's boutique operation. Franklin Delano Roosevelt was doing what the Founding Generation never could: moving the de facto capital of the country to Washington. The capital had always thrived in troubled times, particularly wars, when the consolidation of authority became attractive. The Depression brought the city a population boom not seen since the Civil War. The city's motto could easily be Trouble Is Our Business.

Thus began the resurrection of the canal and the river it parallels. Several hundred young African Americans in the Civilian Conservation Corps restored the lower 22 miles of the canal. The Army Corps of Engineers meanwhile approached the situation in a way that would have made George Washington proud. It was always eager to bring nature to heel, and having a talent for turning rivers into industrial corridors (the Corps, when faced with the Chicago River, had managed to *reverse* its flow altogether), developed a new plan for the Potomac: Dam it. Dam the whole thing, from tidewater to the far upper reaches of the North Branch. That would yield hydroelectric energy and end the threat of floods.

A 105-foot-high dam at Little Falls would create an 8-mile lake going back to the base of Great Falls. A 119-foot-high dam just above Great Falls would create slackwater all the way back to Harpers Ferry; motorists could drive right across the river at the falls. Places like Harrison's Island and Mason's Island would cease to exist. The dam at Harpers Ferry would flood the lower town, where John Brown had made his stand. Under the Army Corps plan, fourteen dams would turn the Potomac into a necklace of lakes.

But the National Park Service took over administration of the canal, and had its own peculiar ideas for what to do with it. It set out to revive George Washington's dream of a highway to the west, but this highway wouldn't be a river, and it wouldn't be a canal. It would *literally* be a highway. No more metaphors. The Park announced plans to build a "parkway" on top of, or paralleling, the canal, the full distance from Washington to Cumberland.

Nature required human access. The Park Service was in the business of serving people, of getting them to the parks and monuments. A strip of asphalt along the river, and on both banks in some places, seemed the right approach, especially if combined with picnic areas, parks, marinas, boat ramps, and other recreational facilities. In 1946 a lawyer for the Park Service said there was "no legal objection, in my opinion, to filling the canal with dirt . . . as a step toward its conversion into a parkway."

What happened next is local lore. Though there weren't "environmentalists" in the 1950s, there were "conservationists." One of them was William O. Douglas, the Supreme Court justice, who lived in the District and took frequent walks on the towpath. When the *Washington Post* editorial board endorsed the parkway plan, saying it "would enable more people to enjoy beauties now seen by very few," Douglas responded with a letter inviting the *Post* editors to hike along the towpath for the length of the canal. They did just that, amid much publicity, and partially revised their stance. In the end, only a small portion of the planned road (now called the Clara Barton Parkway) materialized, and it spared the canal.

In effect, Douglas and others had discovered an entirely new use for the river: It would be an antidote to the industrialized society. It would be a sedative for a hyperactive, manic culture. Rather than providing the cement of interest, it would provide relief from the world of cement.

In his letter to the *Post*, Douglas wrote, "It is a refuge, a place of retreat, a long stretch of quiet and peace at the Capitol's back door . . . a wilderness area where man can be alone with his thoughts, a sanctuary where he can commune with God and with nature, a place not yet marred by the roar of wheels and sound of horns."

And so the river became, quite specifically, and therapeutically, the thing that was *not* the city.

In 1958, Congressman DeWitt S. Hyde of Maryland introduced a bill to create the Chesapeake & Ohio Canal National Historical Park— what he called "a poor man's national park." He wrote, "This park will run through probably one of the most beautiful, least known, and least developed river valleys in the East." Note that, by the late 1950s, the attractions of the Potomac included the fact that no one knew anything about it. (Didn't George Washington once have some kind of river project around here?) Hyde's bill, and others in the late '50s, got bogged down in Congress, but in January 1961, a few days before he left the White House, President Eisenhower named the canal lands from Seneca to Cumberland a National Monument. A more ambitious idea came along in 1965: Make the entire Potomac, Washington to Cumberland, a national park. President Lyndon Johnson instructed Interior Secretary Stewart Udall to find a way to make the river a model of conservation. Udall decided that the river should become the "Potomac National River," with federal parkland along both sides of the river.

But political geography posed a problem, just as it had when the general tried to figure out how to make a route to the Ohio without going through Pennsylvania. The Potomac was still a fracture line, flowing between the generally liberal, slow-growth state of Maryland and the more conservative, pro-business states of West Virginia and Virginia. The latter two states felt that the Potomac National River was just a federal land grab. Even Justice Douglas thought Udall had fallen victim to delusions of grandeur. The conservationists, thinking strategically, rallied behind a slightly more modest proposal by Rep. Gilbert Gude and Sen. Charles Mathias to turn the C&O Canal into a national historical park. Congress finally passed the park bill in 1970. Udall's Potomac National River had been split lengthwise.

Today the Chesapeake & Ohio Canal National Historical Park stretches 184.5 miles, from Georgetown to Cumberland, and at every significant entrance to the park, at every old lock, boat ramp, and picnic ground, there's a chocolate-brown sign that gives the name of the park and the name of the man to whom it is dedicated. You could argue that it should be dedicated to the man who did more than anyone to make the Potomac a westward-leading highway, who saw the possibilities of the Potomac in the 1750s, who began pushing for improvements in the river in 1769, who supervised the first canal at Great Falls, and whose vision inspired the builders of the C&O a full generation after his death. But Congress didn't see it that way. The historical park is dedicated to Justice Douglas.

The message is that the canal's construction is so remote from us in time that we celebrate not its creation, but our success in refraining from destroying its remnants. One of the great national projects of the twenty-first century is, in fact, Preservation. It's a daunting challenge, trying to save the things we consider authentic from the ravages of a synthetic culture. George Washington could not have imagined a day when people would feel that there weren't enough trees, that there wasn't enough empty space, that there was too much infrastructure and not enough wilderness.

*   *   *

THE POTOMAC failed to become what George Washington wanted it to be, and instead became something much better. Instead of a heavily industrialized, reengineered, dammed, channelized, straightened, and filthy river, the Potomac today is a pretty decent model for the stewardship of natural and historical resources. Gone are the days when the park police advised boaters who fell into the river to get a tetanus shot.

The failure of Washington's plan was the best thing that ever happened to the river. The Potomac has survived, so far, the attempts to make it *useful* in the traditional sense. It has overcome the schemes of Founding Fathers, canal-builders, railroad magnates, coal-mining conglomerates, power companies, sewage treatment authorities, highway planners, and the Army Corps of Engineers. The best use of the river, it turns out, is to let it be a river.

Little Falls has become something of a headquarters for the U.S. Olympic kayaking team, which has created a slalom run in a portion of the old skirting canal built by Ballendine in the 1770s and improved by the Patowmack Company. It's hard to find anyone who knows that piece of historical trivia. People understand that there's history all around them, but the details are fuzzy.

One historical quirk of the Potomac intruded into a recent legal battle that went all the way to the Supreme Court. The Potomac is the main source of drinking water for the Washington metropolitan area. Virginia wanted to extend its intake pipe to the middle of the river to get cleaner water, but Maryland objected, citing the seventeenth-century charter giving it jurisdiction over the Potomac. Virginia countered by invoking the Mount Vernon Compact of 1785. Didn't Washington and Madison and their cohort work out a deal for precisely this sort of dispute? And didn't that lead to the Annapolis Convention and then the Constitutional Convention? Lawyers were diving deep into the historical archives to make their point. Maryland contended that the Compact referred to the "shore" of the Potomac, and thus did not refer to the entire 395 miles of river from the headspring of the North Branch to the mouth on the Chesapeake, but rather only to that section of the river below the falls, where it is a wide, tidal river. The Supreme Court eventually ruled in favor of Virginia.

Desirable though its water may be, the river is not exactly pristine.

There are moments when the water can suddenly appear sudsy, as though gushing from a laundromat. When you walk along the banks, you will almost inevitably come across a colony of debris, an environmental niche of trash and flotsam, starring Styrofoam cups, unsinkable plastic soda bottles, and the obligatory soggy tennis ball, a serve gone catastrophically awry. Millionaires build castles on the bluff. One dot-com tycoon, unburdened by shame, has aimed five backyard floodlights on the cataract at Little Falls, making the river look like a crime scene.

The Potomac Conservancy, one of many nonprofit groups that try to protect the river, calls the gorge from Great Falls to Georgetown the wildest urban river in the world, and one of the most endangered scenic landscapes in America. The Potomac is still silted up from erosion, and some stretches of the Upper Potomac are still poisoned with acid tailings from coal mines. The section below the capital becomes a dumping station for raw urban waste whenever a heavy rainfall overwhelms the storm sewers. The central section of the capital, in particular the part laid out by L'Enfant, has combined sanitary and storm sewers.

The gorge is overrun with invasive species, like kudzu, porcelainberry, and English ivy. On Theodore Roosevelt Island, a forested park in the middle of the Potomac in Washington, D.C., a sign brags, "The Forest Returns," and says, "Although most of the island was cleared for farming in the 1800s, the forest is now much as it was nearly 400 years ago when Captain John Smith saw it." Without intervention this sign would literally be smothered by invasive plants and vines within a single season.

The sturgeon have largely disappeared, and the shad have declined. White-tailed deer run rampant, a weed species. By no means is this an unchanged landscape. The very walls of the gorge have been hacked, blasted, and sliced for the stones of monumental buildings.

And yet it is still a remarkably tranquil, natural environment. On the Potomac Heritage Trail, which runs along the Virginia bluff for 10 miles upstream from Georgetown, you can easily find solitude in the middle of the metropolis. On an average day you'll see a fisherman, a dog-walker, and a few deer. Geographically in the heart of metropolitan Washington, you're surrounded by heroic oaks, maples, beeches, and tulip poplars, and if you're so inclined, you might venture out upon the trunk of a sycamore that leans across the river like a diving board. There are a lot of geese, hissing comically to protect their goslings. Great blue herons glide low over the water, fishing. The beavers are back, gnawing up a storm. If it weren't for the deafening white noise of Beltway traffic, the jets flying toward Reagan National, and your cell phone trilling, you'd think you were Daniel Boone in the howling wilderness.

*   *   *

THE C&O TOWPATH is like a country road through the forest. The river is an ever-changing presence, sometimes right next to the canal, sometimes hidden behind a wooded flood plain. The canal in places comes directly onto the riverbank, propped up by stone walls. In several places the bluff collects itself as a promontory of dark rock and lunges toward the river, kinking the canal. The palisade is pocked by quarries. Near Seneca, where Washington supervised the yanking of rocks from the river, the skeleton of a stonecutting mill still stands in the woods, a secret fortress for intrepid kids.

As you get further from the city, the towpath starts to feel utterly isolated. The city dweller thinks: *Where are the concessions?* But then there's another sound: airplanes. You can find yourself in what seems to be a wilderness, but you're still in the flight path for Dulles International Airport. This is a manufactured wilderness, a wilderness designed by landscape architects, park service administrators, county zoning boards.

The National Park Service, with an efficiency bordering on ruthlessness, has torn down more than 2,000 houses, cabins, trailers, and other "improvements" in the river valley. Doug Faris, the C&O Canal superintendent, said the park's goal was to "restore the cultural landscape to a period pre-1924." Anything too modern, that doesn't look like a canal-era structure, has to come down. What is left is not the pre-1924 world, of course, but a distinctly twenty-first-century place, carefully planned, stripped clean of cultural debris, and reserved for politically sanctioned, low-impact activities by visitors on parole from their indoor life. The river is devoid of the hustle and bustle that marked its heyday as a commercial artery. The mills are gone, and the stores, and the taverns and brothels, and even the water is gone for most of the canal's length. When you explore the river now, you see foundations peeking from under the vegetation, and mysterious brick walls, and chimneys strangled by vines.

The maverick historian William Cronon has argued that "wilderness" is a human construct, a romantic, idealized place with no trace of human beings. The first Europeans to colonize America had no love for the wilderness. They considered it hideous, a moral affront, something that needed to be conquered, opened up, farmed. "The dream of an unworked natural landscape," Cronon has written, "is very much the fantasy of people who have never themselves had to work the land to make a living . . . urban folk for whom food comes from a supermarket or a restaurant instead of a field, and for whom the wooden houses in which they live and work apparently have no meaningful connection to the forests in which trees grow and die."

The Potomac fits the Cronon model. The "wild" stretches of the river seem almost like an exhibit in a museum.

*　　　*　　　*

THE AMERICAN LEGION MEMORIAL BRIDGE is a featureless, utilitarian slab of steel and concrete that carries the Capital Beltway across the Potomac River a few miles south of Great Falls. It is best known for its traffic jams. You could say the bridge is ugly, but that would imply that you paid any attention to it, that you observed the bridge as a single, designed piece of architecture, rather than as a stretch of pavement through a green depression in the Earth. The bridge is not really a bridge at all, but rather a road with some air under it.

This great highway, the Beltway, a 66-mile loop, is at once a commuter artery, a suburban Main Street, and an interstate highway, and so the vehicles roaring over the bridge are of every dimension and function imaginable, from puny hatchbacks to luxury sedans to bulked-up sport utes to fearsome, groaning eighteen-wheelers carrying who knows what kind of lethal hazmat cargo. The passage over the river would be considered scenic if taking your eye off the road did not invite an instant, public, spectacular death. And you really can't see much anyway. Only distant parts of the gorge are visible, because Jersey walls, those waist-high concrete barriers, attenuate the line of sight. There could be a three-masted sailing ship down below, or a modern hydroelectric plant, or a small liberal arts college, and you'd have no way to know it.

There are modest signs, eastbound and westbound, saying "Potomac River," but that is the entirety of the homage to this geological feature. Just keep your eyes on the road, buster.

The C&O runs perpendicular to, and underneath, the Beltway, and in fact Lock 13 is directly beneath the moaning concrete span, still watered, still solid-looking, with the massive stone blocks and the heavy wooden gate, the whole thing impossibly quaint, like a Victorian house preserved under the eave of a New York skyscraper. The sun never shines down there and hardly anything grows other than fungus.

Washington is now a megametropolis of 6 million people, a thoroughly modern, wired, tense, anxious, Information Age urban-suburban-exurban complex with a diminishing memory of its history and geographic significance. George Washington would be stunned (if his brain didn't simply explode). Perhaps he would be proud of what the country has become, amazed at the technological and cultural changes, perhaps heartened by the realization that he'd been utterly wrong about the possibility of a multiracial society. He'd surely be astonished and pleased that his federal town, where hardly anyone bought lots at auction, has turned into a world-class capital city. He might find it strange that so many people live their lives indoors, sedentary and stressed. Maybe he'd quickly take a limo to Middleburg, out near the Blue Ridge, where his fellow horse people still put on their jodhpurs and chase foxes through the woods and practice such maxims as "Spit not in the Fire," and "Kill no vermin as Fleas, lice, ticks &c in the Sight of others."

The metropolis so miniaturizes the old river that the city can no longer be described as "on the Potomac." Washington is on the southern section of the Boston-to-Richmond urban corridor.

Nearly a million people live in Fairfax County, in northern Virginia; nearly 2 million more live in Montgomery and Prince George's counties, in Maryland. Many of them, defiant of geography, work or shop on the opposite side of the river from their residence, and therefore must daily crawl over the Legion Bridge, or one of a handful of bridges farther south. For 44 miles, from Little Falls to Point of Rocks, the Legion Bridge is the only span across the Potomac. The problem that General Stone faced at Ball's Bluff—no easy way across the river—has never been rectified. The situation is such an anomaly that White's Ferry still carries cars across the river near Ball's Bluff.

A few years ago local business leaders and their political allies asked themselves, *Dare we build a road?*

They advocated the construction of a new highway across the Potomac, one that would link the high-tech areas of Montgomery County, Maryland, and northern Virginia. The Techway, it would be called. To the business leaders it made perfect sense. *The Washington Post* strongly endorsed the plan. Even Maryland officials, still far more reluctant to embrace development than their Virginia counterparts, went along with a $2 million study of the feasibility of building the Techway. But the opponents mobilized, and not just the usual band of environmentalists who didn't want to see the river spanned by a new bridge. The loudest yelps of protest came from the wealthy residents along the river. Back in 1802, as the Patowmack Company canal was about to open at Great Falls, a traveler named Manasseh Cutler had commented on the degenerate nature of the fields and woods in this part of the river, the general impoverishment of the people, their lazinesss, their idleness. Today this is a land of mansions. These people had seen maps of possible routes for the Techway, and no one wanted a highway through their little piece of paradise.

And so the government, for the time being, did not dare to build a road.

*   *   *

THE EARLY VISION of the river was that it was a tool, a means for making connections. It would increase fluidity, the fluidity of people, products, information, in a country in which none of those things moved very quickly. As it turns out, we've become a hyperfluid society. Technology has obliterated most natural obstacles. It has liberated us from our hometowns, from ancestral turf, from conventions and traditions. We are free and unencumbered, but we can also feel a little lost. We live in unfamiliar environments. We are cut off from family history. Our parents and grandparents are in distant cities. We don't know the local lore or the names of the plants and trees around us. Our new neighbors are, like us, from somewhere else. Many of us don't really know where we are.

In Washington, D.C., the river is increasingly popular, and yet it is easy to find people who know absolutely nothing about it, not even the most basic geographic data. They ask, "Where does it begin?" "How long is it?" "What direction does it flow?"

"You *swim* in it?!"

George Washington's canal at Great Falls is just a depression through a grassy picnic area, overlooked by people throwing Frisbees and munching hot dogs. Until Wilbur Garrett wrote a story in the *National Geographic* in 1987 championing the old canal, it was overgrown and untidy. The Park Service has since cleaned it up, but it's still rather lost amid the landscape. When it reaches the woods, the ditch deepens, becoming more clearly the ruin of a canal, with crumbling stones lining the edge; as it nears the river once again, it passes through the remnants of several locks, stairstepping down through the solid rock that flanks the Potomac gorge. It's an impressive piece of engineering even after two centuries. Nearby are the ruins of Henry Lee's town, Matildaville. It's certainly true, as the editors of the Madison papers note, that Matildaville "has disappeared from the map," but the place is still there, back in the bushes, a small collection of foundations and chimneys and crumbling stone walls. A ghost town. You have to close your eyes and shut out the songbirds and the swish of overhead branches to hear the noise of the boatmen, the lockkeepers, the wagoners, the drunks, the hustlers, the people looking for their main chance.

The dreamers.

*   *   *

GEORGE WASHINGTON'S greatest gamble involved something larger than the Potomac scheme. He believed that American independence, won with the sword, if aided by a sound national government, could give rise to an empire of stunning power and endurance.

The United States today is, in many ways, the country that Washington envisioned, only more so, an exaggeration of his Union, not merely an actor in a most conspicuous theater, but a dominating force on the planet. History doesn't turn on one man's life, but if it did, then Washington might well be considered the man who made America as we know it.

He wanted to find some way to make a transportation link between the tidewater Potomac and the upper Ohio River watershed. Today the journey from Washington to Pittsburgh takes a tad over four hours. You can move mountains with a car—just press on the gas pedal and they'll slowly come into view. By car you obliterate the details of your surroundings. You miss everything smaller than a barn. The secret to pleasurable travel these days is to find a way to go *slower*.

Of the places Washington visited in his western journey of 1784, some have changed little (there are villages with rigid zoning codes that preserve their eighteenth-century architecture—never mind the BMW parked out front), and some have undergone a drastic transformation (it's hard to imagine that there's a chain store in America without an outlet on the Leesburg Pike). And some have become hybrid versions of what they had been. On the eastern side of the Blue Ridge some of the remaining farms exist as a kind of performance art.

They open their doors to urbanites, who pay 10 dollars a head for the experience of wandering among pigs and turkeys and goats. Cornfield mazes are popular. The farmer mows a path through the cornfield and the city people pay money to get lost among the stalks. In urbanizing areas the concept of corn—corn as a symbol of earthiness and cultural authenticity—is now more valuable than corn as a foodstuff. "Corn" is more valuable than corn.

Happy Retreat, where George Washington stayed the night of September 3, 1784, still stands, a relic of colonial grandeur in a county bursting with freshly planted subdivisions. From inside, the view of the lawn, through a window, is distorted by waves in the antique glass. In these old houses one is always struck by the smallness of even the stately rooms. A typical suburban ranch house has a larger dining room or entry hall. The stairs where Washington retired to his bedroom are extremely narrow by modern standards. A September night in the valley would have been hot and muggy. One thinks of candlelight, a smokiness to everything, dust, the smell of mud and manure. In Charles Town today the hot action is at the racetrack. On any night of the year the place is crammed with tourists feeding coins to the slot machines. Washington liked to gamble a bit, but one guesses that his accountant's mind would see the slots as a low-percentage venture. He would think it better to own the machines, to be master of the racetrack, which is, after all, a kind of plantation of gambling.

On September 4, 1784, George Washington crossed Opequon Creek on his way to the West, and if you look at old maps and compare them with the general's diary you might well conclude that he splashed across at Burn's Ford, at the eastern edge of Captain James Strode's property. Today it's still a rural place, with isolated homes and farms and a thick buffer of trees along the creek. There's nothing at the ford now but a modest bridge. One day not long ago two teenagers were using it for skateboarding. A stranger walked up and volunteered that George Washington had very likely traveled over the creek at this very spot.

"Huh," said one of the skateboarders. "I took a leak here once."

When you're fifteen, George Washington is from the Age of Trilo-
bites.

At least some of the general's journey on that distant September 4
was on what was then called the Warm Springs Road, and is now
called Highway 9. It's a death trap of a rural highway, a roller coaster.
The locals want it four-laned. Progress smooths out the rough edges
of a landscape, straightens the roads, eliminates eccentricities.

Many towns on the river have survived by becoming museum ex-
hibits, like Harpers Ferry. The town has only a few hundred residents
(more live farther up the hill, in Bolivar), and is as quaint as a movie
set, which it sometimes becomes when a director needs a Civil War lo-
cale. Up the river, Shepherdstown thrives thanks to a college, Civil
War buffs, and affluent visitors in search of an "authentic" small town
that's not so authentic as to forbid gourmet restaurants. A monument
to James Rumsey soars from a bluff above the Potomac, remembering
his steamboat triumph; in a graveyard on the other side of town, more
than 100 Confederate soldiers, many unnamed, lie "in obedience to
the commands of our sovereign states," as a sign puts it.

Many towns and villages along the river valley are not so polished
as Shepherdstown, and one senses that quaintness is in a protracted
battle against decrepitude. They're as sad as faded postcards. They
need some coats of paint, some people downtown, some laughter on
the sidewalk. They're on the Potomac Route to the West, but what's
that got to do with the twenty-first century? You go away from these
towns with mental images in black-and-white.

Bath, now Berkeley Springs, has survived beautifully, and there's
still a creek running through the center of town, ready for someone like
James Rumsey to come along and experiment with a magical boat. For
a mountain village, healing water is a resource that has proved more
durable than coal, iron, lime, copper, or timber. Bath has that mystical
water percolating through the limestone. The town now features
Roman bathhouses, a steaming outdoor pool, and private spas and sa-
lons. Almost lost in the shuffle is a curious little hole in the ground with
some water in the bottom, identified as "Washington's Bathtub."

Washington's worst-road-trod-by-man-or-beast lingers in the form of the Old Town Road, a winding, dipping, abruptly veering graded path that occasionally ascends a height and offers a grand view of the Potomac, the canal, and the B&O railroad. The 3,118-foot Paw Paw Tunnel is still intact, more than a century and a half after the canal workers laid the final brick, and it makes for a dark, creepy towpath hike. There are surprises up the river, for in addition to fishing shacks and trailer homes and some elegant boarded-up Victorians that haven't had an occupant for decades, there are fine mansions perched on bluffs, and expensive resorts that would be happy to lure George Washington out of the rain. The powerful senator from West Virginia has brought plush federal facilities to the oddest places ("They just built another Taj Mahal there," a local says of an agricultural research station near Shepherdstown). Some of the newly paved roads through the backcountry are as smooth as a bowling lane.

Going west on Interstate 68, about two and a half hours from the Beltway, you pass through a notch in a mountain and suddenly find yourself in Cumberland, once the Queen City of the Alleghenies, now a dowager. The first impression is of steeples. A booster recently had the notion to light all the steeples at night, to enhance city pride, but this does not seem to be enforced of late. The second impression is of roads, bridges, railroad tracks, and rivers. Cumberland is the nexus of every form of transportation employed in the United States prior to the twentieth century. Will's Creek is now lined with concrete, artificially enclosed as a means of flood control. The Potomac spills over a short dam underneath a steel truss bridge.

The third impression is of abandonment. Many of the roughly 21,000 people who remain wouldn't mind leaving either, in all likelihood. Here's a woman working at McDonald's, talking about what she'd do if she won the lottery: "The very first thing I'd do is get out of here. Find a place *way* out. You know over the state line, where those nice new houses are?"

Cumberland had such promise! It had the providential geography. The canal came here, and the railroad, and here was born the Cumberland Road. And yet somewhere along the way, Cumberland became isolated again. On a Sunday you could fire a cannonball down the center of Baltimore Street, the main drag through downtown, and imperil not a single pedestrian. Cumberland is an industrial city with no industry. Since World War II virtually every major employer has packed up and fled. The breweries (Old German, Queen City, etc.) are gone. Celanese, a textile company based in England, had employed 13,000 people on the banks of the Potomac just south of town, but it closed in 1983. Soon after that, Pittsburgh Plate Glass shut its doors. Kelly-Springfield, a tire manufacturer, was the last to close shop, in 1987. The Celanese site now houses two prisons. Prisons and hospitals are just about the only businesses still doing well.

In Cumberland the economy is about what you'd expect in a place built around nineteenth-century industries (it's always a bad sign when one of your major claims to economic significance is a canal). The B&O line and other railroad assets have been consolidated under a single corporation with the unromantic name CSX. CSX is based in Jacksonville, Florida. Even the switches are controlled there. When a train accident occurred in Cumberland a few years ago, it was because of a switching error in Jacksonville.

As technology changed, Cumberland increasingly became a city that wasn't anywhere in particular. Who cares if it's on the Potomac? The Potomac is irrelevant. The important geographical feature in this part of the world is Interstate 70. The interstate links Baltimore with Pittsburgh. At Hancock, Maryland, about 40 miles east of Cumberland, it jukes north into Pennsylvania, and bypasses western Maryland entirely. Not until the early 1990s did a full-blown interstate highway reach Cumberland, but by then the city had already been isolated for decades. Civic leaders look with envy on Hagerstown, an hour to the east, which squats at the junction of I-70 and I-81, and which is still in the economic orbit of metropolitan Washington.

Cumberland is a victim of the hyperfluid society. Everything moves faster and easier now: information, capital, jobs, people. A young person graduating from high school in Cumberland is not going to stay, in most cases. There are better options, better places to find work, places with more young people, more movies and bars and clubs and coffee shops, more stores, more action. Some places win in that competition, and some of them lose.

Cumberland might be ammunition for those who dispute the notion of Progress, who see history as a zero-sum game, a process with as many failures as triumphs, with one person's gain balanced by another's loss. But that's a hard ledger to balance, and is probably too grim a view of history, for even losers have a way of adapting, bouncing back, coming up with a new scheme to improve the world. Perhaps the dreams of civic leaders in Cumberland will come true, and people will rediscover this mountain town, will feel compelled to look for the old path of Nemacolin, the hacked road of young George Washington and the doomed Braddock. Perhaps they'll wander around the site of the old fort, or down by the junction of Will's Creek and the Potomac, where the C&O canal takes off for tidewater, and where an old steam locomotive with vintage rail cars offers to haul tourists through the rocky countryside on its way to the top of the Allegheny Plateau.

A bike trail from Pittsburgh to Washington and passing right through Cumberland is nearly complete, taking advantage of the canal towpath and, in higher terrain, abandoned railroad tracks and the heroic tunnels through the mountains. People will be able to cycle from Mount Vernon to the Forks of the Ohio, using George Washington's commercial corridor as a nifty recreational opportunity, a tool for athletic achievement and the burning of unwanted body fat.

The Potomac Bike Route to the West!

*　　　*　　　*

THERE'S A STEAKHOUSE on top of Cacapon Mountain where George Washington in 1784 looked out over the Potomac and the receding Appalachian ridges. The view from the roadside overlook is still sublime. The landscape retains the imprint of human beings, including a railroad, a canal, and some hayfields and pastures, but the first impression is one of trees, of endless woods filled with game and songbirds. The Great Eastern Forest has been slowly reconstituting itself since the Second World War. Farmers have abandoned unprofitable fields, and the mining and lumber and paper mill jobs have long disappeared. The forest is surely not the same as the one that George Washington knew, for gone is the American chestnut, rare is the white pine, too abundant is the red maple, and the sycamores leaning over the Potomac are not the giants of the eighteenth century. No wolves anywhere, no cougars, certainly no elk or buffalo, but the bears are coming back, and you might find a dark and gloomy wood that would be worthy of being called the Shades of Death.

There is something about a panoramic view of mountains and trees and rivers that connects us to anyone who has stood in such a place before. Broad views inspire big ideas, it's a universal reaction. The expansive vista makes it obvious that the world is grander than any one human life, that forces are at play that are difficult to discern, that there are things going on that we may never fully understand. We sense, as Thomas Jefferson did at the water gap at Harpers Ferry, that the world was created in time, that it is a dynamically changing and tumultuous place, that there are messages written in the lay of the land. George Washington looked at the land as a challenge, sensing that the American experiment in self-government would not be accomplished without the aid of navigable rivers and clear paths through the forest. He knew he had work to do, that someone had to put his shoulder to the task of improving the natural world. It was his duty.

Washington and those who carried on his vision were wildly successful in creating a connected society, and today all the links and hyperlinks are in place. People, products, and data move freely across a continent that no longer seems to have barriers. You can get there from here. Anything goes anywhere. And when people go off into the mountains these days, and look for a place with a lovely view, they often have no goal in mind other than *getting away from it all*.

The mountains endure, even if they no longer seem so lofty. They can be eroded by wind and water and the occasional stick of dynamite, and there are places where their forests have given way to houses and roads, and at Sideling Hill, Interstate 68 slices through the mountain in a 300-foot vertical notch that reveals the convoluted innards of the thrust-and-fold system—but for the most part the mountains are inde-structible even in the age of the bulldozer and the backhoe. The mountains exist on a time scale different from ours. They were here before the coming of human beings, and they will be here when we're gone.

The river below is a memory bank, of geological events, of the evolution of plants and animals, of the coming of men and their ingenious methods for improving their environment. The river belongs to the living and the dead. The Potomac corridor of George Washington is a land of many ghosts—the spirits of the hunters and fishermen of tribes we label archaic; of the Spanish explorers, the English colonists, the indentured servants, and the kidnapped Africans; of Washington and Jefferson and Madison, with their dreams of an empire of liberty; of Gist, Croghan, Cresap, Boone, who, like the Indians, did not get lost in the woods; of all the forgotten characters of the American drama who were every bit as real and alive as the ones who get the ink; of Crawford the surveyor, begging for death; of the Scotch-Irish farmers of western Pennsylvania who found themselves evicted by the most powerful man in America; of the canal builders, the Irish combatants, John Brown, and those federals washing away in the gloaming of a disastrous autumn day.

And yet even as all this history saturates the landscape, it has an astonishing ability to remain invisible. One day a painter set up his easel at the mouth of the Monocacy, a place mentioned once as the possible capital of the United States. The man was painting the scene, capturing the confluence of the river and the curious works of human engineering. The canal in this area is dry, just a low area covered in grass. The stones of the C&O aqueduct are crumbling. The painter said he loved the light here. Everything was green and peaceful and natural—except, of course, this strange old canal.

He looked genuinely puzzled for a moment, and asked:

"Were there ever any boats on this thing?"

NOTES

Unless otherwise noted, quotes from the correspondence and diaries of Washington are based on the transcriptions published by *The Papers of George Washington*, edited by W. W. Abbot, Dorothy Twohig, et al. (Charlottesville: University Press of Virginia), referred to here as *Papers* and *Diaries*, respectively. I've given GW free rein in his spelling and punctuation.

Quotations from Jefferson, unless otherwise noted, are based on *The Papers of Thomas Jefferson*, edited by Julian P. Boyd et al. (Princeton, NJ: Princeton University Press). I refer to them as *Jefferson Papers*.

This story of George Washington, his era, and the river he loved has been shaped by a number of scholars whose insights percolate throughout my text. Frederick Gutheim's *The Potomac* (New York: Rinehart & Co., 1949), published as part of the Rivers of America series, remains unsurpassed as a history of the river, combining a breadth of information with an enviable lyricism. I relied on many biographies of Washington, including those of James Thomas Flexner, Douglas Southall Freeman, John Ferling, Paul Longmore, and Richard Norton Smith. Flexner's third volume offers a provocative (if perhaps slightly speculative) portrait of a melancholic postwar Washington, waiting to die, and it got me thinking about what a person would do with himself after he'd just won independence for his country. D. W. Meinig's *The Shaping of America: A Geographical Perspective on 500 Years of History* (New Haven, CT: Yale University Press, 1986) offered a primer in the fragmented nature of the early republic. Alan Taylor's *American Colonies* (New York: Viking, 2001) tutored me in the early history of the continent.

Other secondary sources that I've relied on for general background, hard facts, wisdom, and inspiration include Bernard Bailyn, *Voyagers to the West: A Passage in the Peopling of America on the Eve of the Revolution* (New York: Vintage, 1988); Ira Berlin, *Many Thousands Gone: The First Two Centuries of Slavery in North America* (Cambridge, MA: Harvard University Press, 1988); Daniel Boorstin, *The Americans: The National Experience* (New York: Vintage, 1965); James MacGregor Burns, *The Vineyard of Liberty* (New York: Knopf, 1982);

Joseph Ellis, *American Sphinx: The Character of Thomas Jefferson* (New York: Knopf, 1997), and, by the same author, *Founding Brothers: The Revolutionary Generation* (New York: Knopf, 2000); John Ferling, *A Leap in the Dark: The Struggle to Create the American Republic* (New York: Oxford University Press, 2003); Don Higginbotham, ed., *George Washington Reconsidered* (Charlottesville: University Press of Virginia, 2001); Warren R. Hofstra, ed., *George Washington and the Virginia Backcountry* (Madison, WI: Madison House, 1998); Margaret Leech, *Reveille in Washington, 1860–1865* (New York: Harper & Brothers, 1941); David McCullough, *John Adams* (New York: Simon & Schuster, 2001); Charles Royster, *The Fabulous History of the Dismal Swamp Company* (New York: Knopf, 1999); Gore Vidal, *Burr* (New York: Random House, 1973); Roger Wilkins, *Jefferson's Pillow: The Founding Fathers and the Dilemma of Black Patriotism* (Boston: Beacon Press, 2001); and Garry Wills, *Cincinnatus: George Washington and the Enlightenment* (Garden City, NY: Doubleday, 1984).

Washington's river scheme, its role in American history, and the state of the Potomac today are the subject of an excellent article by Wilbur E. Garrett, "George Washington's Patowmack Canal," *National Geographic,* vol. 171, no. 6 (June 1987). Particularly helpful was the accompanying map showing George Washington's many backwoods travels.

A final suggestion for those wishing to follow up this story: Despite the powers of the Internet, which make it possible to find, for example, the full text of a Washington quote simply by searching for a phrase, there is nothing quite like browsing the shelves of a good library, where many fine books, too geriatric or obscure to be transferred to the digital realm, languish unread, in serious danger of being consigned to the category of lost information.

Chapter 1: The Surveyor

1 *such a flourish of Enlightenment virtue:* Garry Wills, in *Cincinnatus: George Washington and the Enlightenment* (Garden City, NY: Doubleday, 1984), explains the classical significance of Washington's retirement and his ability to gain power by surrendering it.

1 *"I am become":* GW to Lafayette, 1 February 1784, *Papers,* Confederation Series, vol. 1, pp. 87–89.

2 *(from 1 Kings 4:25):* See also 2 Kings 18:31 and Micah 4:4.

3 *"Having now finished":* "Address to Congress on Resigning His Commission," 23 December 1783, in John C. Fitzpatrick, ed., *The Writings of George Washington,* vol. 27 (Washington, DC: U.S. Government Printing Office, 1938), p. 285.

3 *"that Country from whence":* See Peter R. Henriques, "The Final Struggle Between George Washington and the Grim King," in Don Higginbotham,

ed., *George Washington Reconsidered* (Charlottesville: University Press of Virginia, 2001), p. 262. He cites GW to Alexander Hamilton, 17 December 1797, and GW to Richard Washington, 20 October 1761.

3   *(Pine later "corrected" the portrait):* William M. S. Rasmussen and Robert S. Tilton, *George Washington: The Man Behind the Myths* (Charlottesville: University Press of Virginia, 1999), pp. 152–53.

3   *"there is not a king in Europe":* Dorothy Twohig, "The Making of George Washington," in Warren R. Hofstra, ed., *George Washington and the Virginia Backcountry* (Madison, WI: Madison House, 1998), p. 3.

4   *He could bend a horseshoe:* W. E. Woodward, *George Washington: The Image and the Man* (New York: Boni & Liveright, 1926), p. 390.

4   *The piazza was a Washington innovation:* See Robert F. Dalzell, Jr., and Lee Baldwin Dalzell, "Interpreting George Washington's Mount Vernon," in Higginbotham, ed., *George Washington Reconsidered*, p. 105. The essay discusses Washington's decision in the later years of his life to make the setting of Mount Vernon less linear and formal and stark, replacing straight lines with curves, adding trees in a random nature, transforming the imperial setting of the mansion into something humbler. The authors also make the point that in dividing his estate in his will into small parcels, distributing the proceeds of the sale of his western lands to so many individuals, and freeing his slaves, he effectively dismantled the estate he'd spent his life assembling.

5   *"No estate in United America is more pleasantly":* GW to Arthur Young, 12 December 1793, Fitzpatrick, ed., *Writings*, vol. 33 (Washington, DC: U.S. Government Printing Office, 1931), pp. 175–76.

5   *A mansion on a river was essential:* See Howard Mumford Jones and his lively, quirky *O Strange New World* (New York: Viking, 1964), particularly a nice passage on p. 245: "What emerged more immediately, to continue well past the American Revolution, was an ideal curious among men we are taught to regard as activists—an ideal of retreat, the model of which was Horace's Sabine Farm. That poet's little house and little fields, the garden that yielded its adequate wine, the fountain of Bandusia, the flocks and herds, the site that was never too hot or too cold, a hospitable place for friends and not without the hope of female companionship—here was a model for the American gentleman amid 'rural scenes,' whether on the Potomac, the Schuylkill, or Narragansett Bay, or in the foothills of the Appalachians."

5   *"I am not only retired":* GW to Lafayette, 1 February 1784, *Papers*, Confederation Series, vol. 1, pp. 87–89.

6   *Other than a brief trip to Philadelphia:* Washington attended a meeting of

the Society of the Cincinnati, an organization of retired military men that, according to Jefferson, came dangerously close to being a new American aristocracy. Washington, at Jefferson's behest, insisted that the organization end its provision that membership would be passed along through primogeniture.

6 *"I have come to a resolution":* GW to James Craik, 10 July 1784, *Papers, Confederation Series,* vol. 1, pp. 492–93.

6 *He owned 4,691 acres:* My numbers come from the ever reliable Philander Chase, "A Stake in the West: George Washington as Backcountry Surveyor and Landholder," in Hofstra, ed., *George Washington and the Virginia Backcountry.*

7 *"abounding plentiously in Fish":* GW to John Witherspoon, 10 March 1784, *Papers, Confederation Series,* vol. 1, pp. 197–203.

7 *". . . one object of my journey":* 3 September 1784, *Diaries,* vol. 4, p. 4.

9 *Douglas Southall Freeman allots the journey:* Douglas Southall Freeman, *George Washington: A Biography:* vol. 6: *Patriot and President* (New York, Charles Scribner's Sons, 1954), pp. 14–22.

9 *John Marshall, possibly the most ponderous:* Here is the full sentence: "In the autumn of 1784, General Washington made a tour as far west as Pittsburgh; after returning from which, his first moments of leisure were devoted to the task of engaging his countrymen in a work which appeared to him to merit still more attention from its political, than from its commercial influence on the union." John Marshall, *The Life of George Washington:* vol. 4: *Fredericksburg: The Citizen's Guild of Washington's Boyhood Home,* 1926, p. 123.

9 *David Ramsay is even more efficient:* David Ramsay, *The Life of George Washington* (London: Luke Hanfard & Sons, 1807), p. 269.

9 *(that is what even his wife called him):* Joseph E. Fields, ed., *Worthy Partner: The Papers of Martha Washington* (Westport, CT: Greenwood Press, 1994), pp. 194–95.

11 *("The United States of America have terminated"):* Journals of Congress, 9 December 1784, in *Journals of the Continental Congress 1774–1789,* vol. 27, 1784 (Washington, DC: U.S. Government Printing Office, 1928), p. 676. The final version of the Declaration of Independence referred to "the thirteen united States of America" and said that "as Free and Independent States, they have full Power to levy War, conclude Peace, contract Alliances, establish Commerce, and to do all other Acts and Things which independent States may of right do." The Articles of Confederation explicitly stated that "each state retains its sovereignty, freedom and independence." The Treaty of Paris listed each of the former British colonies by name and

declared them to be "free, sovereign and independent states." At the Constitutional Convention of 1787 there would be no mention of a singular nation or "national" government.

11   *In remote communities:* Richard Norton Smith, *Patriarch: George Washington and the New American Nation* (Boston: Houghton Mifflin, 1993), p. 109. Smith drops in this nice detail (oxen as currency—what happens when you need to make change?) in a discussion of the speculative fever sweeping the country after the opening of Alexander Hamilton's Bank of the United States in 1791.

11   *When the general kept his books:* John Bach McMaster, *A History of the People of the United States, from the Revolution to the Civil War,* vol. 1 (New York: D. Appleton, 1893), p. 23. McMaster provides the data here about currency, such as the number of grains of silver in a pound in different states.

12   *A map of the nation revealed a patchwork:* The invaluable source for any discussion of the geography of early America is D. W. Meinig, *The Shaping of America: A Geographical Perspective on 500 Years of History,* vol. 1 (New Haven, CT: Yale University Press, 1986).

13   *The Citizens of America:* GW Circular to the States, 8 June 1783, in Fitzpatrick, ed., *Writings,* vol. 26, pp. 483–96.

13   *"the one big thing he knew":* Joseph Ellis, *Founding Brothers: The Revolutionary Generation* (New York: Knopf, 2000), p. 134. Ellis is using Isaiah Berlin's notion of the hedgehog and the fox, where the hedgehog knows one big thing and the fox knows many little things. Washington, Ellis writes, "was an archetypal hedgehog." I'd suggest that, although Washington knew that America's future lay in the West, and could strike an optimistic note about that future in his public addresses, in his private comments he showed an unusual degree of anxiety about the situation on the ground. He worried that the West was spinning out of control, that it needed the imposition of order from the leaders of the East, and some kind of binding agent that would create the "cement of interest." That this agent would be the Potomac is Washington's obsessively held belief—what I call his "grand idea."

14   *"progressive refinement of Manners":* GW Circular to the States, 8 June 1783, in Fitzpatrick, ed., *Writings,* vol. 26, pp. 483–96.

14   *"like a young heir":* GW to Benjamin Harrison, 18 January 1784, *Papers,* Confederation Series, vol. 1, pp. 56–57.

14   *the fourth-largest country in the world by size:* Meinig, *Shaping of America,* vol. 2, p. 4.

15   *"a most happy asylum":* GW Farewell Orders to the Armies of the United

States, 2 November 1783, in Fitzpatrick, ed., *Writings of George Washington*, vol. 27, pp. 222–27.

16 *He should have died:* Washington's narrative of these adventures can be found in Fitzpatrick, ed., *Writings of George Washington,* vol. 1, pp. 22–30. My account also draws on Douglas Southall Freeman, *George Washington: A Biography, vol. 1* (New York: Scribner, 1954), pp. 320–23.

17 *("The Cold was so extremely severe"):* 23 December 1753, Fitzpatrick, ed., *Writings,* vol. 1, p. 30.

17 *("He was incapable of fear"):* TJ to Walter Jones, 2 January 1814, in Andrew A. Lipscomb, ed., *The Writings of Thomas Jefferson,* Library ed. (Washington, DC: Thomas Jefferson Memorial Association, 1903), vol. 14, pp. 46–52.

17 *"to reconnoitre the Country":* GW to Robert Dinwiddie, 29 May 1784, *Papers,* Colonial Series, vol. 1, pp. 107–15.

18 *scooped out the contents of Jumonville's skull:* Fred Anderson, *Crucible of War: The Seven Years' War and the Fate of Empire in British North America 1754–1766* (New York, Knopf, 2000), p. 6.

18 *In a Pennsylvania field called Great Meadows:* See "Account by George Washington and James Mackay of the Capitulation of Fort Necessity," 19 July 1754, *Papers,* Colonial Series, vol. 1, pp. 159–72.

18 *"I heard the bullets whistle":* GW to John Augustine Washington, 31 May 1754, *Papers,* Colonial Series, vol. 1, pp. 118–19. This example of youthful bravado incited a famous retort from George II: "He would not say so, if he had been used to hear many" (ibid., p. 119fn). But a less-noted part of the letter is Washington's observation that he could easily have died: "I fortunately escaped without a wound, tho' the right Wing where I stood was exposed to & received all the Enemy's Fire and was the part where the man was killed & the rest wounded." He had begun to sense that bullets couldn't hit him.

19 *burned at the stake:* See James Smith, *An Account of the Remarkable Occurences in the Life and Travels of Col. James Smith During His Captivity with the Indians* (Cincinnati, OH: Robert Clarke Co., 1907), p. 12.

20 *"It's a fine fox chase, my boys!":* See James Thomas Flexner, *Washington: The Indispensable Man* (Boston: Little, Brown, 1974; first published 1969), p. 97. Flexner based this on the account of George Washington Parke Custis, and so it is firmly in the category of oral tradition rather than documented fact.

20 *"my frequent long Journeys":* Joseph E. Fields, ed., *Worthy Partner: The Papers of Martha Washington* (Westport, CT: Greenwood Press, 1994), p. 193.

21   *"It may be compared to a well resorted tavern"*: GW to Mary Washington, 15 February 1787, *Papers,* Confederation Series, vol. 5, pp. 33–36. There's a terrific summary of the rise and fall of the Washington cult in James Morton Smith's introduction to his work *George Washington: A Profile* (New York: Hill & Wang, 1969).

21   *"the expensive mansion"*: GW to George Augustine Washington, 25 October 1786, Fitzpatrick, ed., *Writings of George Washington,* vol. 29, p. 28.

21   *"Her cry excited in me a disposition to smile"*: Quoted in James Thomas Flexner, *George Washington and the New Nation, 1783–1793* (Boston: Little, Brown, 1969), p. 25.

22   *"Spit not in the Fire"*: Dorothy Twohig, "The Making of George Washington," in Hofstra, *George Washington,* pp. 9–10.

22   *"They are the archives of someone"*: W. W. Abbot, "An Uncommon Awareness of Self," in Higginbotham, ed., *George Washington Reconsidered,* p. 279.

22   *"He was obsessed with having things in fashion"*: Gordon Wood, "The Greatness of George Washington," in Higginbotham, ed., *George Washington Reconsidered,* p. 315. Wood's essay is a wonderful primer on Washington's personality, and it has significantly influenced my own description of the man and his career. He points out that Washington, though not an intellectual, was a man of affairs, running his plantation far better than Jefferson ran Monticello. Wood notes that, as president, Washington's letters instructing his manager how to run the plantation were longer than his letters about running the federal government. Wood has a good explanation for Washington's seemingly unknowable nature: "He belonged to the pre-democratic and pre-egalitarian world of the 18th century, to a world very different from the world that would follow. No wonder then that he seems to us so remote and so distant. He really is. He belonged to a world we have lost and we were losing even as Washington lived" (p. 312). Washington's concern with his reputation may seem obsessive to modern eyes, Wood writes, but he lived in a time when a man's reputation was considered the same thing as his honor.

An interesting discussion of Washington's ambitions is in Paul K. Longmore, *The Invention of George Washington* (Charlottesville: University Press of Virginia, 1999). Longmore writes, "To hold securely one's own sense of honor, one's self-assessment must concur with the community's assessment. Personal identity was, then, inseparable from public reputation" (p. 2).

22   *"I do not recollect that in the course of my life"*: GW to William Triplet, 25 September 1786, Fitzpatrick, ed., *Writings,* vol. 29, p. 18.

23 *"a persistent mediocrity"*: Woodward, *George Washington: The Image and the Man*, p. 9.

23 *"He speaks of the American War"*: Wood, in Higginbotham, ed., *George Washington Reconsidered*, citing J. P. Brissot de Warville, *New Travels in the United States of America, 1788*, edited by Durand Echeverria (Cambridge, MA: Belknap Press of Harvard University, 1964), p. 199.

23 *"He is slow of perception"*: Gijsbert Karel van Hogendorp, a 22-year-old Dutchman, quoted in Freeman, *George Washington: A Biography*, vol. 6, p. 34. Freeman concludes that van Hogendorp, as a stranger, should not have expected Washington, already besieged by guests, to be anything other than reticent.

24 *"Sum of money due to me"*: GW to John Stephenson, 13 February 1784, *Papers*, Confederation Series, vol. 1, pp. 118–19. Stephenson's half-brother William Crawford had surveyed many western tracts for GW, including the Millers Run land that would present the general with so many troubles in the years after the war. Washington's all-business tone reflects his deep anxiety, in February 1784, that he has lost control of his western properties and lacks even the proper paperwork to prove his title. See also GW to Thomas Lewis, 1 February 1784, *Papers*, Confederation Series, vol. 1, pp. 95–100, and GW to John Harvie, 10 February 1784, ibid., pp. 107–9.

24 *"How profitable our partnership has been"*: GW to Gilbert Simpson, 13 February 1784, ibid., pp. 117–18.

24 *"There was a great space"*: GW to Fielding Lewis, Jr., 27 February 1784, ibid., pp. 161–62.

25 *"recover my business"*: GW to Thomas Lewis, 1 February 1784, ibid., pp. 95–97.

25 *Where could he find paperwork*: See GW to John Harvie, 10 February 1784, ibid., pp. 107–9.

25 *"ignorantly, or under a mistaken belief"*: GW to John Lewis, 14 February 1784, ibid., pp. 123–24.

26 *Washington had seen more of America*: For a description of Washington as a rambling woodsman, see J. Frederick Fausz, "Engaged in Enterprises Pregnant with Terror!: George Washington's Formative Years among the Indians," in Hofstra, ed., *George Washington and the Virginia Backcountry*.

27 *"I shall not rest contented"*: GW to Chevalier de Chastellux, 12 October 1783, Fitzpatrick, ed., *Writings of George Washington*, vol. 27, pp. 188–90.

27 *"I have it in contemplation"*: GW to Lafayette, 12 October 1783, ibid., pp. 185–88.

28 *"dealt her favors to us with so profuse a hand"*: GW to Chevalier de Chastellux, 12 October 1783, ibid., p. 190.

Chapter 2: The Race to the West

30 *"Really there ought not to be a state":* Quoted in David McCullough, *John Adams* (New York: Simon & Schuster, 2001), p. 149.

30 *The Potomac's rivals among American rivers:* Jon Kukla's *A Wilderness So Immense* (New York: Knopf, 2003) has an excellent description of the competition among American rivers for the western trade. See pp. 95–102.

32 *Jefferson had made his greatest contribution:* Any sketch of Jefferson is necessarily subjective, since there are so many potential Jeffersons to choose from. A book I found immensely helpful was Peter S. Onuf, ed., *Jeffersonian Legacies* (Charlottesville: University of Virginia Press, 1993), a collection of papers presented at a conference at the University of Virginia in 1993 (I covered it for *The Washington Post*). I also found Joseph J. Ellis, *American Sphinx: The Character of Thomas Jefferson* (New York: Knopf, 1997), delightful and persuasive. I tried to sample the Jeffersoniana, from Dumas Malone to Merrill Peterson to Richard K. Matthews to Conor Cruise O'Brien (who seems to think that Western Civilization will collapse if it doesn't officially denounce Jefferson and tear down his memorial at the Tidal Basin in Washington), but the writer who is most captivating is, predictably, Jefferson himself. I kept *The Portable Thomas Jefferson*, edited by Merrill D. Peterson (New York: Viking, 1975), handy at all times.

34 *"[T]he Ohio, and it's branches":* TJ to James Madison, 20 February 1784, Jefferson *Papers*, vol. 6, p. 548.

34 *"What an example this is!":* Ibid.

34 *"His mind was great and powerful":* TJ to Walter Jones, 2 January 1814, in *The Writings of Thomas Jefferson*, Andrew Lipscomb, ed. (Washington, DC: Thomas Jefferson Memorial Association, 1903), vol. 14, pp. 46–52.

35 *"All the world is becoming commercial":* TJ to GW, 15 March 1784, Jefferson *Papers*, vol. 7, p. 26. Jefferson and Washington talked of many things other than Potomac navigation, of course. In this spring of 1784, for example, Washington requested an assessment by Jefferson of the merits of the Society of the Cincinnati, of which Washington was the leading light, and which restricted membership to military officers and their eldest male offspring. (See GW to TJ, 8 April 1784, Jefferson *Papers*, vol. 7, p. 88.) Jefferson smelled the creation of an American aristocracy. He told Washington that the new government was founded on "the natural equality of man," and this meant the denial of any preeminence by birth alone. The Revolution hadn't ended with the despotism of the military commander because that commander exhibited moderation and virtue, but—and Jefferson continued to speak of Washington in the third person—"he is not immortal, and his successor or some one of his successors at the head of this institu-

tion may adopt a more mistaken road to glory." Jefferson warned Washington that leadership of such a group might damage his reputation and standing in history. That did the trick. Washington immediately insisted that the Society of the Cincinnati in its constitution strike out anything remotely involving heredity, politics, or anything else that might inflame observers. See TJ to GW, 16 April 1784, in Jefferson *Papers*, vol. 7, pp. 105–10.

36 *The United States Geological Survey reports the following variations:* Jon Campbell, U.S. Geological Survey, personal communication.

36 *"I am not so disinterested":* GW to TJ, 29 March 1784, Jefferson *Papers*, vol. 7, pp. 49–52.

37 *"I know the Yorkers":* Ibid.

37 *Between 1749 and 1753:* For more on Washington and his early western interests, see Philander Chase, "A Stake in the West: George Washington as Backcountry Surveyor and Landholder," in Warren R. Hofstra, *George Washington and the Virginia Backcountry* (Madison, WI: Madison House, 1998).

38 *"there is no other obstacle":* GW to Charles Carter, August 1754, *Papers*, Colonial Series, vol. 1, pp. 196–98. See also the entry for July–August 1754, "Notes on the Navigation of the Potomac River Above the Great Falls," ibid., pp. 179–80.

38 *"the luckless Fate of poor Virginia":* GW to John Robinson, 1 September 1758, *Papers*, Colonial Series, vol. 5, pp. 432–33. See also W. W. Abbot, "George Washington, the West, and the Union," in Don Higginbotham, ed., *George Washington Reconsidered* (Charlottesville: University Press of Virginia, 2001). Abbot says GW hinted that he should be sent to London to reveal to George II the idiocy of General Forbes.

39 *In 1770 Washington urged Thomas Johnson:* GW to Thomas Johnson, 20 July 1770, *Papers*, Colonial Series, vol. 8, pp. 357–60. Washington was not the first Potomac promoter. In 1769 a man named John Semple took a broad view of the significance of Potomac improvements. With a little effort, costing no more than 5,000 pounds sterling, Semple wrote, "The best Channel Is opened for inland trade that can be possibly had in British America, The land Carriage between the bay of Chesapeak and the mouth of the Mississippi, The Ilenois, three hundred Miles up the Missuri and to the different lakes, by very small Portages is reduced to Seventy Miles. . . ." See John Semple's Proposal for Potomac Navigation, *Papers*, Colonial Series, vol. 8, pp. 284–90.

In 1774, shortly before Christmas, Washington attended a meeting in Alexandria headed by John Ballendine. Ballendine intended to open the Potomac to navigation above Little Falls and persuaded Washington and other prominent citizens to put up money for the construction of skirting canals. Work began on a canal around Little Falls—built, apparently, by slaves hired for the purpose. An ad in the *Virginia Gazette* of 14 January 1775 said Washington et al. had approved the hiring of fifty slaves. See Corra Bacon-Foster, *Early Chapters in the Development of the Patomac Route to the West* (New York: Burt Franklin, 1971; originally published 1912), p. 28.

41 *("I have taken my final leave of everything"):* TJ to Edmond Randolph, 16 September 1781, Jefferson *Papers*, vol. 6, p. 118. Jefferson made a similar statement in 1794, when he retired as Secretary of State, saying he wanted "to be liberated from the hated occupations of politics, and to remain in the bosom of my family, my farm, and my books." Quoted in Ellis, *American Sphinx*, p. 119.

41 *Jefferson proposed:* See Jefferson *Papers*, vol. 6, "Plan for Government of the Western Territory" and the Editorial Note, pp. 581–606.

42 *reference points in the blank spaces of the map:* I'm indebted for this insight to D. Graham Burnett, who calls the sources of rivers "points whose existence could be deduced, even if unknown, providing goals within a terra incognita." See p. 180 of his book *Masters of All They Surveyed: Exploration, Geography, and a British El Dorado"* (Chicago: University of Chicago Press, 2000).

42 *Jefferson used* Notes *to refute the notion:* See the discussion in Donald Jackson, *Thomas Jefferson and the Stony Mountains: Exploring the West from Monticello* (Norman: University of Oklahoma Press, 1993), pp. 26–27.

43 *The passage of the Patowmac:* From *Notes on the State of Virginia*, in Peterson, ed., *Portable Thomas Jefferson*, pp. 48–49. There was a minor controversy late in Jefferson's life about whether his description was original or had been lifted from a French engineer. See *Writings of Thomas Jefferson*, Lipscomb, ed., vol. 12, p. 280. In a 14 May 1809 letter to Horatio G. Spafford, Jefferson explained the mix-up: "Mr. Volney was mistaken in saying I told him I had received the description from a French engineer. By an error of memory he has misapplied to this scene what I mentioned to him as to the Natural Bridge. I told him I received a *drawing* of that from a French engineer sent there by the Marquis de Chastellux, and who has published that drawing in his travels. I could not tell him I had the description of the passage of the Potomac from a French engineer, because I never heard any Frenchman say a word about it, much less did I ever receive a description of it from any mortal whatever."

44 *never mentioned Oregon:* Jackson, *Thomas Jefferson and the Stony Mountains*, p. 82.

44 *"view the world at different scales":* John Logan Allen, "Imagining the West: The View from Monticello," in James P. Ronda, ed., *Thomas Jefferson and the Changing West* (St. Louis: Missouri Historical Society Press, 1997), p. 5.

44 *"An ash standing on the upper side":* These quotes are from a survey map made by Washington on his 1770 trip down the Ohio. The map is in the Maps Division of the Library of Congress, and can be viewed online via the American Memory link at www.loc.gov.

45 *"Those who labor in the earth":* Thomas Jefferson, *Notes on the State of Virginia,* in *The Writings of Thomas Jefferson,* Lipscomb, ed., vol. 2, p. 229. Joseph Ellis, in *American Sphinx,* makes the point that, for Jefferson, the West offered the hope of an endless renewal of the revolutionary spirit; the frontier would have a cleansing effect, scrubbing out the inevitable corruptions of the imperfect experiment in self-government. "For Jefferson more than any other major figure in the revolutionary generation, the West was America's future. Securing a huge swatch of it for posterity meant prolonging for several generations the systemic release of national energy that accompanied the explosive movement of settlements across the unsettled spaces" (p. 212).

46 *Jefferson's first memory:* Roger Wilkins, *Jefferson's Pillow: The Founding Fathers and the Dilemma of Black Patriotism* (Boston: Beacon Press, 2001).

Chapter 3: Up the River

47 *two kegs of West Indian rum:* See the entry for 22 September 1784, *Diaries,* vol. 4, p. 32.

48 *Craik was something special and rare:* See Frank Grizzard, *George Washington: A Biographical Companion* (Santa Barbara: ABC-CLIO, 2002), pp. 59–61.

48 *"the best horseman of his age":* TJ to Walter Jones, 2 January 1814, in Lipscomb, ed., *The Writings of Thomas Jefferson,* pp. 46–52.

49 *"[W]hen the country was cover'd with Woods":* Quoted in Leland Baldwin, *Pittsburgh: The Story of a City* (Pittsburgh: University of Pittsburgh Press, 1937), p. 2.

50 *"Nothing is to be seen here":* Isaac Weld, Jr., *Travels Through the States of North America, and the Provinces of Upper and Lower Canada,* 4th ed., vol. 1 (London: John Stockdale, 1807), pp. 138–39.

51 *"purgeth superfluous fleame and other grosse humours":* Thomas Harriot, "A Briefe and True Report of the New Found Land of Virginia," in *The Heath Anthology of American Literature,* 4th ed. (Boston: Houghton Mif-

flin, 2002), pp. 226–33. I used this anthology as a reference for much classic American writing.

51 *The first European to see the Potomac proper:* This summary comes from *Washington: City and Capital*, Federal Writers' Project (Washington, DC: U.S. Government Printing Office, 1937), p. 35. I have also relied on the lecture notes of the late Philip W. Ogilvie, which he titled "An Eco-History of the Potomac Basin" (Philip W. Ogilvie, 2000). For more on early inhabitants of the Potomac Valley, see Stephen R. Potter, *Commoners, Tribute, and Chiefs: The Development of Algonquian Culture in the Potomac Valley* (Charlottesville, VA: University Press of Virginia, 1993).

51 *"abundance of fish lying so thicke":* Capt. John Smith, quoted in Frederick Guthcim, *The Potomac* (Baltimore: Johns Hopkins University Press, 1986), p. 24.

51 *"mirey, inconvenient and troublesome":* Diaries, vol. 4, p. 3n.

53 *"most beautiful Groves": The Writings of George Washington*, vol. 1, edited by John C. Fitzpatrick (Washington, DC: U.S. Government Printing Office, 1931), p. 6.

53 *we got our supper and was lighted into a Room:* Ibid. p. 7.

54 *They clear a Large Circle:* Ibid., p. 9.

54 *"Ah! woe's me, that I should Love and conceal":* Circa 1749–1750, ibid.

54 *"look to Frederick":* GW to John Posey, 24 June 1767, *Papers*, Colonial Series, vol. 8, pp. 1–4.

55 *"It cannot be laid to my charge":* GW to Charles Simms, 22 September 1786, Fitzpatrick, ed., *Writings of George Washington*, vol. 29, pp. 8–9.

55 *"The Revolution which the Virginia aristocracy":* Daniel Boorstin, *The Americans: The Colonial Experience* (New York: Vintage Books, 1964), p. 143.

56 *"the new Country":* John Augustine Washington to GW, 24 July 1784, *Papers*, Confederation Series, vol. 2, pp. 8–9.

56 *"[T]he golden opportunity I conceive":* GW to John Augustine Washington, 29 July 1784. Phil Chase brought my attention to this letter, which has only recently surfaced and is not yet published.

57 *"I held much conversation with him":* 4 September 1784, *Diaries*, vol. 4, p. 6.

58 *"Went out a Hunting":* Ibid., vol. 2, p. 284n.

59 *As the historian Archer Hulbert noted:* Archer Hulbert, *Washington and the West* (New York: Century Company, 1905). Hulbert writes, "Great as the mass of Washington's literary remains seems to be, consisting of so many letters, journals, diaries, and memoranda, it is rare that one can find a single instance where the man breaks through the crust of stolid indiffer-

ence of everything that is suggested by the words sentiment and romance and speaks in a reminiscent strain" (pp. 134–35).

61   *by one historical estimate:* Frank Monaghan and Marvin Lowenthal, *This Was New York: The Nation's Capital in 1789* (Garden City, NY: Doubleday, Doran & Co., 1943), p. 4.

62   *he appears in a portrait by Benjamin West:* See frontispiece, Ella May Turner, *James Rumsey: Pioneer in Steam Navigation* (Scottdale, PA: Mennonite Publishing House, 1930).

63   *". . . the principles of this were not only shewn":* 6 September 1784, *Diaries,* vol. 4, p. 9.

63   *"been an eye witness":* Certificate for James Rumsey, 7 September 1784, *Papers,* Confederation Series, vol. 2, p. 69.

63   *"justly represent a greater object":* GW to Hugh Williamson, 15 March 1785, *Papers,* Confederation Series, vol. 2, pp. 439–40.

63   *"Convicts almost Every person":* James Rumsey to GW, 19 October 1784, ibid., p. 101.

64   *"to almost every Mans door":* GW to James Madison, 30 November 1785, *Papers,* Confederation Series, vol. 3, pp. 419–21.

Chapter 4: Ridge and Valley

66   *Two streams flowing in opposite directions:* This process is well described in John McPhee, *Annals of the Former World* (New York: Farrar, Straus & Giroux, 1998), pp. 239–42.

66   *"Apalacheon Mountains":* 1 September 1784, *Diaries,* vol. 4, p. 1.

67   *Only the hardest layers of rock survived:* See also Chet Raymo and Maureen E. Raymo, *Written in Stone: A Geological History of the Northeastern U.S.* (Las Vegas: Nevada Mineral & Book Company, 1989). "Coarse-textured sediments near the base of the mountains degraded into clays and lime to the west. Compression and deformation of these sediments during later mountain-building episodes created the anticlines (uparching folds) and synclines (downarching folds) of the Ridge and Valley Province. Erosion left the more resistant strata, chiefly the conglomerates and the sandstones, standing as ridges while the less resistant strata, the limestones, the dolostones, and the claystones, form the valley floors. Intense pressure and deformation also converted the buried plant remains of the deltaic deposits into the high-grade coal of northeastern Pennsylvania's famed anthracite fields" (p. 41). The plateaus feature "flat-lying, sedimentary Paleozoic strata," and the isolated outliers and promontories of Kentucky and Ohio, called knobs, are formed of more resistant Mississippian and Pennsylvanian aged rocks. Some of these strata also contain bi-

tuminous coal. The Raymos suggest that the Piedmont and New England represent accreted terrane, like volcanic islands or fragments of continents.

67 *"To look from the hills into the lower Lands":* Quoted in Leland D. Baldwin, *Pittsburgh: The Story of a City, 1750–1865* (Pittsburgh, PA: University of Pittsburgh Press, c. 1937), p. 4.

67 *commensurate with his capacity for wonder:* This phrase comes very near the end of F. Scott Fitzgerald's *The Great Gatsby:* ". . . for a transitory enchanted moment man must have held his breath in the presence of this continent, compelled into an aesthetic contemplation he neither understood nor desired, face to face for the last time in history with something commensurate to his capacity for wonder."

67 *From a bluff a traveler looking down:* Particularly helpful in this description of the primeval forest was Gordon G. Whitney, *From Coastal Wilderness to Fruited Plain: A History of Environmental Change in Temperate North America, 1500 to the Present* (New York: Cambridge University Press, 1994).

68 *(Washington once found a sycamore): Diaries,* vol. 2, p. 309.

68 *"this earth has been created in time":* "Notes on the State of Virginia," in Merrill Peterson, ed., *The Portable Thomas Jefferson* (New York: Viking, 1975), p. 48.

69 *"which I find exceedingly rich": Diaries,* vol. 4, p. 14.

69 *"the Worst Road that ever was trod":* Ibid., vol. 1, p. 12.

69 *Shawnees . . . had relocated to the Ohio Valley:* The precise details of why the Shawnees abandoned the village are unknown, but they and other native peoples had long before been decimated by European diseases. It would be hard to imagine a more lucid explanation of the effects of disease on Native Americans than that in Jared Diamond's *Guns, Germs, and Steel: The Fates of Human Societies* (New York: W. W. Norton, 1999). See pages 210–12 for a summary of the high mortality rates of epidemic diseases among a native population with no immunity. Diamond makes the important observation that the very first contacts between Europeans and Indians led to staggering pandemics. When Hernando De Soto traveled through the area that became the southeastern United States, he found villages already abandoned. "The Spaniards' microbes spread to the interior in advance of the Spaniards themselves," Diamond writes. One reason the whites perceived the continental interior as essentially empty is that European diseases had wiped out a thriving civilization. The estimates of the number of native people in North America north of Mexico used to be in the vicinity of 1 million, but Diamond cites a more recent estimate of 20 million.

70   *Cresap was the prototypical frontiersman:* My account of Cresap is based largely on Kenneth Bailey, *Thomas Cresap: Maryland Frontiersman* (Boston: Christopher Publishing House, 1944), and on the sketch in Corra Bacon-Foster, *Early Chapters in the Development of the Patomac Route to the West* (New York: Burt Franklin, 1971; originally published 1912), p. 3n.

71   *Nemacolin's Trail thus begat Washington's Road:* See Archer B. Hulbert, *Washington's Road (Nemacolin's Path): The First Chapter of the Old French War* (New York: AMS Press, 1971, originally published 1902).

72   *"one Servant only":* 10 September 1784, *Diaries,* vol. 4, p. 16.

72   *It is unlikely the man was Billy Lee:* On 28 July 1784, Washington wrote to Clement Biddle asking him to arrange for Lee's wife to travel to Mount Vernon to join her husband. Washington didn't care for Mrs. Lee but tolerated her out of gratitude for the loyalty of his servant. There is no evidence that she made the journey. See Fritz Hirschfeld, *George Washington and Slavery: A Documentary Portrayal* (Columbia: University of Missouri Press, 1997), p. 106.

72   *"Crossing the Mountains":* 12 September 1784 *Diaries,* vol. 4, pp. 18–19.

73   *"behind the successive ridges":* "Notes on the State of Virginia," in Peterson, ed., *Portable Thomas Jefferson,* p. 49.

73   *("Ideas of immensity swelled and exalted"):* Thaddeus Mason Harris, "The Journal of a Tour into the Territory Northwest of the Alleghany Mountains," in Reuben Gold Thwaites, ed., *Early Western Travels, 1748–1846,* vol. 3 (Cleveland, OH: The Arthur H. Clark Co., 1904), p. 366. The full quote: "From this summit a sweep of hundreds of miles is visible, except where remote intervening mountains break the line of the horizon, which in other parts is lost in the interminable azure wherewith the heaven and the earth are blended. Ideas of immensity swelled and exalted our minds as we contemplated a prospect partaking of so much of infinitude; and we felt some wonderful relations to an universe without boundary or end."

73   *"The Road from the Old Town to Fort Cumberland":* 10 September 1784, *Diaries,* vol. 4, p. 17.

74   *what an economist might call their "action radius":* The phrase is from Arnulf Grubler, *The Rise and Fall of Infrastructures: Dynamics of Evolution and Technological Change in Transport* (Heidelberg: Physica-Verlag, 1990), p. 1.

75   *Historian Eric Hinderaker reports:* Eric Hinderaker, *Elusive Empires: Constructing Colonialism in the Ohio Valley, 1673–1800* (New York: Cambridge University Press), p. 68.

75   *"There, remote from the power of example":* J. Hector St. John de Crève-

coeur, *Letters from an American Farmer* (Franklin Center, PA: Franklin Library, 1982), pp. 55–57.

75 *"I found the people belong'd":* Margaret Van Horn Dwight, *A Journey to Ohio in 1810, As Recorded in the Journal of Margaret Van Horn Dwight,* Max Farrand, ed. (New Haven, CT: Yale University Press, 1920), pp. 59–60.

76 *"Found a dead Man":* Conrad Weiser, "Conrad Weiser's Journal of a Tour to the Ohio, August 11–October 2, 1748," in Thwaites, *Early Western Travels,* vol. 1, p. 23.

76 *"his eyes were filled with madness":* Crèvecoeur, *Letters from an American Farmer,* p. 188.

76 *Alcohol is a recurrent element:* François André Michaux, "Travels to the West of the Alleghany Mountains," in Thwaites, *Early Western Travels,* vol. 3, p. 144. See also "Alexander McClean's Journal of the 1786 Survey of the Western Boundary of Pennsylvania: Volume 2," edited by James L. Murphy, in *Western Pennsylvania Historical Magazine,* vol. 63, no. 4 (October 1980), pp. 342–43. McClean writes, "The Captain having sent them a Small Cag of Whisky, their thirsty Souls were soon overwhelmed & their reason sunk into Oblivion. At length the martial spirit burst into a Flame & they got to fighting & playing the Devil in all Quarters. . . . after they had exhausted Nature by Wallowing in their filth until 9 oClock at Night, they went to Bed & a sullen Silence remained in Camp till morning. . . . As soon as the Brutes had opened their eyes, they were prepared for the other round and began afresh to beating each other in the most barbarous manner."

76 *Whiskey cost 3 cents a glass:* For this portrait of backcountry life, including the etymology of "stogies," I've relied on William Chauncy Langdon, *Everyday Things in American Life: 1776–1876* (New York: Charles Scribner's Sons, 1937).

76 *There was no need of a scramble:* George Bancroft, *History of the United States from the Discovery of the American Continent,* 15th ed., vol. 1, (Boston: Little, Brown, 1857), pp. 234–35.

77 *. . . the stern depths of immemorial forests:* Francis Parkman, *France and England in North America,* vol. 1 (New York: Viking, 1983), pp. 1, 322. I am indebted to Gordon G. Whitney for this citation.

77 *"I always found the roads":* Constantin Volney, *A View of the Soil and Climate of the United States of America* (New York: Hafner Publishing Company, 1968), pp. 6–7.

78 *He did not know at what tread:* Joseph Doddridge, *Notes on the Settlement and Indian Wars of the Western Parts of Virginia and Pennsylvania, from 1763 to 1783* (Albany, NY: Joel Munsell, 1876), pp. 64–65.

78 *There were thousands of girdled trees:* Gordon G. Whitney, *From Coastal Wilderness*, pp. 132–33.

78 *The scene could become rather hellish:* See D. Griffiths, Jr., *Two Years' Residence in the New Settlements of Ohio, North America: With Directions to Emigrants* (London: Westley & Davis, 1835), p. 42.

78 *"Each lifeless Trunk":* Sarah Kemble Knight, "The Journal of Madam Knight," in *Colonial American Travel Narratives,* Wendy Martin, ed., (New York: Penguin, 1994), p. 55.

79 *The French went farther than anyone else:* For more on French exploration of the continent, see Alan Taylor, *American Colonies* (New York: Viking, 2001).

80 *"which appears to have been but little improved":* 12 September 1784, *Diaries*, vol. 4, p. 18.

81 *"will gladly send you off":* Alexis de Tocqueville, *Journey to America* (Garden City, NY: Doubleday, 1971), p. 335.

Chapter 5: Squatters

83 *The modest wooden wheel:* Description from photo in Solon J. Buck and Elizabeth Hawthorn Buck, *The Planting of Civilization in Western Pennsylvania* (Pittsburgh: University of Pittsburgh Press, 1939).

84 *I do not find the Land:* 14 September 1784, *Diaries*, vol. 4, pp. 20–21.

84 *"stream is rather too slight":* 15 October 1770, ibid., vol. 2, p. 290.

84 *"extreame stupidity":* GW to Lund Washington, 20 August 1775, *Papers*, Revolutionary War Series, vol. 1, p. 335.

84 *I have been here Twelve Years:* Gilbert Simpson to GW, 27 April 1794, *Papers*, Confederation Series, vol. 1, p. 315.

85 *Thomas Bigger, had narrowly escaped:* See Address of Judge Thomas M. Bigger, of Columbus, Ohio, on genealogy in Washington County, Pennsylvania, Web site: http://www.chartiers.com/pages-new/articles/bigger.html.

85 *"look me out a tract of about fifteen hundred":* GW to William Crawford, 17 September 1767, *Papers*, Colonial Series, vol. 8, p. 27.

86 *The energetic researchers at* The Papers: For an extensive editor's note on the Millers Run controversy, see Thomas Smith to GW, 9 February 1785, *Papers*, Confederation Series, vol. 2, pp. 338–58. See also GW to Charles Simms, 22 September 1786, *Papers*, Confederation Series, vol. 4, pp. 254–59. Adding to the confusion was the fact that this part of Pennsylvania had been, until the late 1770s, part of Virginia. The State of Pennsylvania went no farther west than the dividing ridge between the eastern and western waters. Thus a 1771 survey of the Millers Run land by Crawford, conducted on Washington's behalf, had to be filed first with the county

surveyor of Augusta County, Virginia, stationed far to the south, and from there sent to the colonial capital in Williamsburg, so far away as to be practically in the Caribbean. Crawford waited several years before sending the document to the county surveyor, apparently waiting for the Virginia Council to pass a law allowing the holders of military patents to retain their western properties despite a general ban on settlement west of the mountains (a concession at the time to the Indians).

88 *"The only entrance to it"*: John Bach McMaster, *A History of the People of the United States, from the Revolution to the Civil War*, vol. 1 (New York: D. Appleton, 1893), p. 99.

88 *They were being pushed*: Roger Kennedy, personal communication. Kennedy's book, *Mr. Jefferson's Lost Cause: Land, Farmers, Slavery, and the Louisiana Purchase* (New York: Oxford University Press, 2003), fleshes out this idea.

88 *"we killed in the journey 13 buffaloes"*: "Journal of Doctor Thomas Walker," in J. Stoddard Johnson, *First Explorations of Kentucky* (Louisville, KY: John P. Morton & Company, 1898), p. 75.

89 *(the rarity of stone or brick)*: Buck and Buck, *The Planting of Civilization*, pp. 318–24.

89 *"[It] is inhabited almost entirely by Scots and Irish"*: Quoted in Richard C. Wade, *The Urban Frontier: The Rise of Western Cities, 1790–1830* (Urbana: University of Illinois Press, 1996), p. 10.

89 *"The haze which covered the New World"*: Daniel Boorstin, *The Americans: The Colonial Experience* (New York: Vintage Books, 1958), p. 159.

89 *a kind of men who cannot settle upon the soil*: François André Michaux, "Travels to the West of the Alleghany Mountains," in Reuben Gold Thwaites, *Early Western Travels, 1748–1846*, vol. 3 (Cleveland, OH: Arthur H. Clark Co., 1904), vol. 3, p. 192.

90 *a "company of hellhounds"*: See "A Narrative at the Captivity and Restauration of Mrs. Mary Rawlandson," in *The Heath Anthology of American Literature*, 4th ed. (Houghton Mifflin, 2002), pp. 428–56.

90 *"deep into the American psyche"*: Bernard Bailyn, *The Peopling of British North America: An Introduction* (New York: Vintage Books, 1988), p. 116.

90 *the Cumberland Gap*: The Cumberland Gap is nowhere near, and should not be confused with, the Cumberland Road, which terminates at Cumberland, Maryland, the jumping-off point for Washington's trips to the West. The Cumberland Gap was originally dubbed Cave Gap by Thomas Walker, who in 1750 had followed a heavily trod Indian trail from the Shenandoah Valley into the western Appalachians.

90 *"Many dark and sleepless nights"*: John Filson, *The Discovery, Settlement,*

and the Present State of Kentucke (Fairfield, WA: Ye Galleon Press, 2001), pp. 80–81.

91   *"The whole society was"*: William Winans, quoted in Thomas P. Slaughter, *The Whiskey Rebellion* (New York: Oxford University Press, 1986), p. 64.

91   *The historian Leland Baldwin:* Leland D. Baldwin, *Pittsburgh: The Story of a City* (Pittsburgh, PA: University of Pittsburgh Press, 1937), p. 136.

91   *The "rage for speculating":* GW to Jacob Read, 3 November 1784, *Papers,* Confederation Series, vol. 2, p. 119.

92   *"The immediate needs of western settlers":* Slaughter, *Whiskey Rebellion,* pp. 87–88.

92   *"he lied, broke the law, and betrayed public trusts":* Ibid., p. 248n.

92   *"possibly be evaded":* See Bernhard Knollenberg, *Washington and the Revolution: A Reappraisal* (The Macmillan Company, 1941), p. 153. Knollenberg added that he did not mean to imply Washington was wicked, only that he "was not the paragon of humaneness, magnanimity, and honesty that Sparks and his followers have portrayed him to be" (p. 155).

93   *"the grazing multitude":* Quoted in Gordon Wood, "The Greatness of George Washington," in Don Higginbotham, ed., *George Washington Reconsidered* (Charlottesville: University Press of Virginia, 2001), p. 27.

93   *"I really think they seem to be":* Diaries, vol. 1, p. 18.

93   *"blow out my brains":* quoted in Warren R. Hofstra, *George Washington and the Virginia Backcountry* (Lanham, MD: Rowman & Littlefield, 1998), p. 89.

93   *("His heart was not warm in its affections"):* TJ to Walter Jones, 2 January 1814, in Saul Padover, ed., *The Complete Jefferson* (New York: Tudor, 1943), p. 925.

94   *"If the powers of the country":* Quoted in W. E. Woodward, *George Washington: The Image and the Man* (New York: Boni & Liveright, 1926), p. 120.

94   *"lawless tyrannical rabble":* Quoted in *Heath Anthology of American Literature,* p. 1008.

94   *(Abigail Adams likewise declared):* Abigail Adams to John Adams, 31 March 1776. See http://www.thelizlibrary.org/suffrage/abigail.htm.

94   *"the people are turbulent and changing":* Quoted in Arthur M. Schlesinger, Jr., *The Age of Jackson* (Boston: Little, Brown, 1945), p. 10.

94   *"The evils we experience":* Quoted in Walter Isaacson, *Benjamin Franklin: An American Life* (New York: Simon & Schuster, 2003), p. 447.

94   *"men of enterprising, violent":* Thomas Scott, congressman from western Pennsylvania, speaking on 13 July 1790. See *Annals of Congress,* 1st Congress, compiled by Joseph Gales (Washington: Gales & Seaton, 1834), Library of Congress Web site.

94 *"As explorers, adventurers, fighters"*: Henry Adams, *History of the United States During the Administration of Thomas Jefferson* (New York: Albert and Charles Boni, 1930, p. 137.

95 *"came here to set forth their pretensions"*: 14 September 1784, *Diaries*, vol. 4, p. 21.

97 *Ending a business partnership*: See the editor's note for 17 September 1784, *Diaries*, vol. 4, p. 25.

97 *"Being Sunday, and the People"*: 19 September 1784, *Diaries*, vol. 4, p. 26.

99 *"Gentlemen, I will have this land"*: Boyd Crumrine, ed., *History of Washington County, Pennsylvania* (Philadelphia: L.H. Everts, 1882), pp. 858–59.

99 *"Gentlemen, you will permit me"*: See James Thomas Flexner, *George Washington in the American Revolution (1775–1783)* (Boston: Little, Brown and Company, 1967), p. 507.

Chapter 6: A Darker Wood

102 *"Indeed, comparatively speaking"*: For this document and a thorough discussion of the Millers Run case, see Editorial Note, Thomas Smith to GW, 9 February 1785, *Papers*, Confederation Series, vol. 2, pp. 338–58. The "comparatively speaking" line is in the first of his answers to the anticipated pleas of the squatters.

102 *"would certainly result in the establishment"*: Archer B. Hulbert, *Washington and the West* (New York: Century Co., 1905), p. 155. Hulbert's book is unusual in that he prints the entire diary and then comes in with his own narrative version of the same events, peppered with insights.

103 *"The Accts. given by those"*: 12 September 1784, *Diaries*, vol. 4, p. 19. It's important to note that even before his difficult meeting with Gilbert Simpson or with the Seceders at Millers Run, GW decides that he probably won't go all the way down the Ohio River to his westernmost properties. He finalizes that decision only after he starts dealing with the western settlers.

103 *"better to return, than to make a bad matter worse"*: GW to Henry Knox, 5 December 1784, *Papers*, Confederation Series, vol. 2, pp. 170–72.

103 *"The Indians by what means I can't say"*: Thomas Freeman to GW, 9 June 1785, *Papers*, Confederation Series, vol. 3, pp. 43–45.

104 *The militiamen rounded up the Moravians*: My account is based largely on Boyd Crumrine, *History of Washington County, Pennsylvania* (Philadelphia: L.H. Everts, 1882), pp. 115–26.

105 *"particularly affected"*: GW to William Irvine, 10 July 1782, John C. Fitzpatrick, ed., *The Writings of George Washington* (Washington, DC: U.S. Government Printing Office, 1931), vol. 24, p. 417.

105 *"no other than the extremest"*: GW to William Irvine, 6 August 1782, ibid., p. 474.

105 *treated his Indian allies as though they were his slaves: The Papers of Benjamin Franklin,* edited by Leonard W. Labaree (New Haven: Yale University Press, 1962). vol. 5, p. 66n.

106 *"Several of our young People":* Benjamin Franklin, "Remarks Concerning the Savages of North America," in *Heath Anthology of American Literature,* pp. 798–99.

107 *They had their own chaotic history in the region:* See Richard White, *The Middle Ground: Indians, Empires, and Republics in the Great Lakes Region, 1650–1815* (New York: Cambridge University Press, 1991); Michael N. McConnell, *A Country Between: The Upper Ohio Valley and Its Peoples, 1724–1774* (Lincoln: University of Nebraska Press, c1992); and Eric Hinderaker, *Elusive Empires: Constructing Colonialism in the Ohio Valley, 1673–1800* (New York: Cambridge University Press, 1997).

108 *Indians started wearing cloth instead of skins:* See Hinderaker, *Elusive Empires,* pp. 69–70. He writes, "in place of their distinctive material cultures, a single, pan-indian culture had emerged that was defined primarily by European artifacts."

109 *"By the 1770s, chaos reigned in the Ohio Valley":* Ibid., p. 175.

110 *"Generosity, Clemency and Mercy":* See report of Committee on State of Indian Affairs in the Southern Department, 27 May 1784, *Journals of the Continental Congress 1774–1789,* vol. 27 (Washington, DC: U.S. Government Printing Office, 1928), p. 455.

110 *"but as we prefer Peace":* GW to James Duane, 7 September 1783, in Fitzpatrick, ed., *Writings,* vol. 27, p. 134.

111 *Thomas Smith, a Scotsman:* Burton Alva Konkle, *The Life and Times of Thomas Smith, 1745–1809* (Philadelphia: Campion & Company, 1904), pp. 171–72.

112 *At Beason Town I met with Captn. Hardin:* 22 September 1784, *Diaries,* vol. 4, p. 32.

113 *"[T]he Cheat River had been passed":* 23 September 1784, ibid., p. 38.

113 *The colour of the two Waters:* 24 September 1784, ibid.

114 *"You are right, sir":* Henry Adams, *The Life of Albert Gallatin* (Philadelphia: J. B. Lippincott, 1879), pp. 56–57. The account cites John Russell Bartlett's "Reminiscences of Mr. Gallatin."

114 *"That from the fork of Monongahela & Cheat":* 24 September 1784, *Diaries,* vol. 4, p. 39.

114 *"very blind":* 25 September 1784, ibid, p. 43.

115 *"choak the river":* Ibid.

115 *"which owes it origen to Buffaloes:"* Ibid., p. 44.

116   *"might be eased, & a much better way"*: Ibid.

116   *"At the entrance of the above glades"*: Ibid. (There's a nice passage in Douglas Southall Freeman, *George Washington: A Biography*: vol. 6, *Patriot and President*, p. 21: "Whenever the rain ceased momentarily to pour on the resounding carpet of golden leaves and pine needles around Washington's bivouac, silence was as intense as it had been almost thirty years previously. The wilderness seemed as bare of habitation; but in the darkness of '84 as in the black night of '55, the woods were peopled with promise and with the echoing shouts of men—not of wounded, retreating redcoats, but of oncoming settlers in hunting shirts.")

116   *"It may not be amiss to observe," he wrote*: 25 September 1784, *Diaries*, vol. 4, p. 44.

116   *"Having found our Horses readily"*: 26 September 1784, ibid., p. 45.

117   *"would admit an exceeding good Waggon road"*: Ibid.

117   *"[T]hese difficulties, in the eyes of a proper examiner"*: Ibid., p. 46.

117   *as Washington put it, "infamous"*: Ibid., p. 47.

118   *"[T]heir accts. are to be received"*: Ibid.

118   *"Remained at Colo. Hite's"*: 28 September 1784, ibid., p. 51.

120   *"pitiful house." But then he was hospitably entertained*: 2 October 1784, ibid., p. 56.

120   *"The more then the Navigation of Potomack"*: 4 October 1784, ibid., p. 58.

Chapter 7: Skirting the Falls

121   *This would be the ultimate synthesis*: 4 October 1784, *Diaries*, vol. 4, pp. 57–71. Washington also wrote a long letter to Gov. Benjamin Harrison of Virginia, laying out his plan and warning that the western settlers could easily be lured into the orbit of Spain or Britain. His language in many cases is identical or similar to the diary entry. See 10 October 1784, *Papers*, Confederation Series, vol. 2, pp. 86–99.

124   *They were from somewhere else*: See GW to Richard Henry Lee, 22 August 1785, *Papers*, Confederation Series, vol. 3, pp. 195–97.

125   *he sent a more polished version*: GW to Benjamin Harrison, 10 October 1784, *Papers*, Confederation Series, vol. 2, pp. 89–96.

125   *"as unconnected with us, indeed more so"*: GW to Jacob Read, 3 November 1784, ibid., pp. 118–22.

125   *"become a distinct people from us"*: GW to Henry Knox, 5 December 1784, ibid., pp. 170–72.

125   *"what we might be"*: Ibid.

125   *"[T]he motives which predominate most"*: GW to James Madison, 3 December 1784, ibid., pp. 165–67.

126 *"[A]ll I would be understood to mean"*: GW to George Plater, 25 October 1784, ibid., pp. 106–9.

126 *"a half starved, limping Government"*: GW to Benjamin Harrison, 18 January 1784, ibid., vol. 1, pp. 56–57.

126 *"shut my hand against every pecuniary recompense"*: GW to Maryland House of Delegates, quoted in *Maryland Gazette*, 16 February 1786.

126 *"ostentatious display of disinterestedness"*: GW to TJ, 25 February 1785, ibid., pp. 379–82.

127 *"The opening of the navigation of Patowmack"*: *Maryland Gazette*, 2 December 1784.

127 *I often asked myself*: GW to Lafayette, 8 December 1784, *Papers*, Confederation Series, vol. 2, pp. 175–76.

128 *"It is now near 12 at night"*: GW to James Madison, 28 December 1784, ibid., pp. 231–33.

128 *"He modestly waived all allusions"*: Quoted in Douglass Southall Freeman, *George Washington: A Biography;* vol. 6, *Patriot and President* (New York, Charles Scribner's Sons, 1954), p. 37.

129 *"The General sent the bottle about pretty freely"*: *Quebec to Carolina in 1785–1786: Being the Travel Diary and Observations of Robert Hunter, Jr., a Young Merchant of London,* edited by Louis B. Wright and Marion Tinling (San Marino, CA: Huntington Library, 1943), p. 193.

129 *"The earnestness with which he espouses"*: James Madison to TJ, 9 January 1785, *Jefferson Papers*, vol. 7, pp. 588–98.

130 *The New Bremen glassworks*: Frederick Gutheim, *The Potomac* (Baltimore, MD: Johns Hopkins University Press, 1986; first published 1949), pp. 204–10.

130 *"[M]en who can afford"*: GW to Lafayette, 15 February 1785, *Papers*, Confederation Series, vol. 2, pp. 363–66.

130 *"To describe the usefulness of water transportation"*: GW to George Plater, 25 October 1784, ibid., pp. 106–9.

130 *"[N]othing is more practicable"*: Stephen Sayre to GW, 15 October 1784, ibid., p. 99.

130 *they would pay "liberal wages"*: Corra Bacon-Foster, *Early Chapters in the Development of the Patomac Route to the West* (New York: Burt Franklin, 1971; originally published 1912), p. 62.

132 *"The principle difficulties lye in rocks"*: 3 August 1785, *Diaries*, vol. 4, pp. 171–73.

132 *"The President and Directors have no doubt"*: GW to James Rumsey, 8 August 1785, *Papers*, Confederation Series, vol. 3, pp. 174–75.

133 *"In a word nature"*: 11 August 1785, *Diaries*, vol. 4, p. 181.

134 *"are irregular and disorderly"*: GW to Thomas Johnson and Thomas Sim Lee, 10 September 1785, *Papers*, Confederation Series, vol. 3, pp. 243–44 and 244n.

134 *"will be more valuable than that of common white Hirelings"*: Thomas Johnson to GW, 21 September 1785, ibid., pp. 269–71.

134 *Premature ignition had grisly results:* James D. Dilts, *The Great Road: The Building of the Baltimore and Ohio, The Nation's First Railroad, 1828–1853* (Stanford, CA: Stanford University Press, 1993), p. 257.

134 *"both his hands most horridly maimed"*: Quoted in Peter Way, *Common Labor: Workers and the Digging of North American Canals, 1780–1860* (Baltimore, MD: John Hopkins University Press, 1997), p. 33.

134 *"His situation is scarcely to be described"*: Way, *Common Labor*, p. 33.

135 *"To me it seemed, as if we had advanced"*: 22 September 1785, *Diaries*, vol. 4, p. 196.

136 *"We have been much Imposed upon"*: Dilts, *Great Road*, p. 17.

136 *"She goes, by God, she goes!"*: Ella May Turner, *James Rumsey: Pioneer in Steam Navigation* (Scottdale, PA.: Mennonite Publishing House, 1930), pp. 88–89.

137 *"Overplied with energies of thinking"*: Ibid., p. 200.

Chapter 8: Trial and Tribulation

139 *Clear & warm:* 8 July 1786, *Diaries*, vol. 5, p. 5.

140 *Rid to the Plantations:* 17 July 1786, ibid., p. 11.

140 *Examined the low:* 24 July 1786, ibid., p. 14.

140 *Quite calm and exceedingly Sultry:* 23 August 1786, ibid., p. 29.

140 *"no dray moves more readily"*: GW to Francis Hopkinson, 16 May 1785, *Papers*, Confederation Series, vol. 2, p. 562.

140 *A rumor reached his ear:* GW to Thomas Johnson, 31 August 1788, John C. Fitzpatrick, ed., *The Writings of George Washington*, vol. 30 (Washington, DC: U.S. Government Printing Office, 1931), pp. 70–79.

140 *"The arts of peace"*: GW to La Luzerne, 1 August 1786, *Papers*, Confederation Series, vol. 4, p. 186.

141 *"it being among my first wishes"*: GW to John Francis Mercer, 9 September 1786, ibid., pp. 243–44.

141 *"a certain species of property"*: GW to Tobias Lear, 6 May 1794, *Writings*, Fitzpatrick, ed., vol. 33, p. 358.

142 *"at their work as soon as it is light"*: GW to John Fairfax, 1 January 1789, *Papers*, Presidential Series, vol. 1, pp. 216–25.

142 *"the ingratitude of the girl"*: GW to Alexander Hamilton, 1 September 1796, Fitzpatrick, ed., *Writings*, vol. 35, pp. 201–02.

143 *"Neither lust . . . nor sadism"*: James Thomas Flexner, *Washington: The Indispensable* Man (New York: New American Library, 1984; first published 1974), p. 391.

143 *[I]t is foremost in my thoughts*: GW to Anthony Whitting, 14 October 1792, *Papers*, Presidential Series, vol. 11, pp. 222–31.

144 *Were it not then, that I am principled*: GW to Alexander Spotswood, 23 November 1794, Fitzpatrick, ed., *Writings*, vol. 34, pp. 46–48.

144 *"I think nothing more is necessary"*: GW to Thomas Smith, 14 July 1785, *Papers*, Confederation Series, vol. 3, pp. 121–25.

145 *"you will sue them respectively for Trespasses"*: GW to Thomas Smith, 10 September 1785, ibid., pp. 245–46.

145 *"may produce a bad effect"*: Thomas Smith to GW, 17 November 1785, ibid., pp. 365–69.

145 *"I never should have thought"*: Ibid., 7 December 1785, pp. 438–39.

146 *he wrote down the squatters' "Pleas"*: See Editorial Note, Thomas Smith to GW, 9 February 1785, ibid., vol. 2, pp. 338–58.

147 *He'd never been more agitated*: Thomas Smith to GW, 7 November 1786, *Papers*, Confederation Series, vol. 4, pp. 339–43.

147 *"take the Bull by the Horns"*: Ibid.

149 *"You have now* thirteen *plantations"*: Ibid.

149 *Washington turned to John Cannon*: GW to John Cannon, 28 November 1786, ibid., pp. 405–6.

150 *Glenn gave his new estate a forlorn name*: See the Mount Pleasant Township Warrantee Map, published 1945, based on original plats. I examined the copy in the Heinz History Center, Pittsburgh.

150 *Even so, it would not be a lump sum*: Frank Grizzard, *Washington: A Biographical Companion* (Santa Barbara: ABC-CLIO, 2002), pp. 219–21.

150 *"He could not be considered"*: Editorial Note, Thomas Smith to GW, 9 February 1785, *Papers*, Confederation Series, vol. 2, p. 356n.

151 *earn the general more than 600 dollars*: Paul Leicester Ford, *George Washington* (Philadelphia: J. B. Lippincott, 1924), p. 125.

151 *The Ice on the river*: 22 January 1788, *Diaries*, vol. 5, p. 268.

151 *The River, which had opened*: 5 February 1788, ibid., p. 273.

151 *There remains now no doubt*: GW to TJ, 31 August 1788, Fitzpatrick, ed., *Writings*, vol. 30, pp. 79–84.

153 *"We are either a United people, or we are not"*: GW to James Madison, 30 November 1785, *Papers*, Confederation Series, vol. 3, pp. 419–21.

153 *Historian John Ferling*: John Ferling, *A Leap in the Dark: The Struggle to Create the American Republic* (New York: Oxford University Press, 2003), p. 277.

154 *"[F]or Gods sake tell me, what is the cause":* GW to David Humphreys, 22 October 1786, *Papers,* Confederation Series, vol. 4, pp. 296–97.

154 *"The want of energy in the foederal government":* GW to Thomas Johnson, 12 November 1786, ibid., pp. 359–60.

155 *"How does the grass Seeds":* GW to George Augustine Washington, 27 May 1787, *Papers,* Confederation Series, vol. 5, pp. 196–99.

155 *"as little room for partiality and prejudice to operate":* GW to TJ, 30 May 1787, ibid., pp. 203–8.

Chapter 9: A Capital Idea

158 *"But how can I know what is best":* GW to Jonathan Trumbull, 4 December 1788, *Papers,* Presidential Series, vol. 1, pp. 158–59.

158 *"be chargeable with levity and inconsistency":* GW to Henry Lee, 22 September 1788, *Papers,* Confederation Series, vol. 6, pp. 528–31.

158 *"[M]y movements to the chair of Government":* GW to Henry Knox, 1 April 1789, *Papers,* Presidential Series, vol. 2, p. 2.

159 *"[N]obody who has tried both public and private life":* TJ to GW, 10 May 1789, ibid., pp. 258–60.

160 *"I enclose you such a rough sketch":* GW to TJ, 13 February 1789, ibid., vol. 1, pp. 299–304.

160 *Washington had previously written Secretary of War Henry Knox:* See Douglas Southall Freeman, *George Washington: A Biography:* vol. 6: *Patriot and President,* pp. 157–58. Freeman points out that Knox mentioned the election returns in a casual way, without even a transitional sentence.

160 *Knox wrote to inform the general:* Henry Knox to GW, 16 February 1789, *Papers,* Presidential Series, vol. 1, p. 316.

161 *"Sir, I have been long accustomed to entertain":* Address to Charles Thomson, 14 April 1789, ibid., vol. 2, p. 56.

161 *"I think it was much too late for him":* Joseph E. Fields, ed., *Worthy Partner: The Papers of Martha Washington* (Westport, CT: Greenwood Press, 1994), p. 213.

162 *"I feel great difficulty how to act":* Kenneth R. Bowling and Helen E. Veit, eds., *The Diary of William Maclay and Other Notes on Senate Debates* (Baltimore, MD: Johns Hopkins University Press, 1988), p. 6.

162 *"This great man was agitated and embarrassed":* Ibid.

163 *Men, wrote Hamilton, "are ambitious":* in *The Federalist* No. 6, Benjamin Fletcher Wright, ed. (Cambridge: Harvard University Press, 1961), pp. 108–13.

164 *"Is it not time to awake":* Ibid.

164 *"practise with success the vicious arts":* Federalist No. 10, pp. 129–36.

165   *Was there a hamlet in all America:* The outstanding source for informa-
      tion on the founding of Washington, D.C., is Kenneth Bowling, *The Cre-
      ation of Washington, D.C.: The Idea and Location of the American Capital*
      (Fairfax, VA: George Mason University Press, 1991). Joseph J. Ellis, in
      Founding Brothers: The Revolutionary Generation (New York: Knopf,
      2000), captures the drama of the debate over Residency and Assumption
      and the role of the Potomac in the grand compromise. A tip from Jon Kukla
      led me to the excellent primary documents for this section, the *Letters
      from Delegates* of the Continental Congress.

166   *"remoteness from the influence":* "Notes on Congress' Place of Resi-
      dence" [*ca.* 14 October 1783], *Madison Papers*, vol. 7, pp. 378–82.

167   *"grand Virginia illusion":* Ellis, *Founding Brothers*, p. 71.

167   *As historian Kenneth Bowling has explained:* Bowling, *The Creation of
      Washington, D.C.*, p. 53.

168   *"in the fifth generation":* Charles Royster, *Light-Horse Harry Lee and the
      Legacy of the American Revolution* (New York: Knopf, 1981), p. 71.

168   *"The advantages infinitely exceed":* Henry Lee to James Madison, 29 Oc-
      tober 1788, *Madison Papers*, vol. 11, pp. 321–22.

169   *("may be too sanguinely dilated"):* GW to James Madison, 17 November
      1788, *Madison Papers*, vol. 11, pp. 349–51.

170   *There is such an intimate connection:* GW to David Stuart, 8 April 1792,
      Papers, Presidential Series, vol. 10, pp. 229–30.

171   *John Ferling, reads this as a confession:* John E. Ferling, *The First of Men: A
      Life of George Washington* (Knoxville: University of Tennessee Press,
      c1988), p. 398. Ferling concludes, "Few public figures in American history
      could match Washington's record of virtuous and selfless service, but even
      he stumbled when the vast potential of the frontier West was at stake. This
      was the man who had exhorted Forbes and Bouquet to cut a wilderness
      road through a route that would be of benefit to him, the man whose atten-
      tive amassing of the best bounty lands available to the Virginia Regiment
      bore the stench of scandal."

171   *Madison, using the kind of statistics:* Debates in the House of Representa-
      tives, Second Session: April—August 1790, Helen E. Veit et al., eds. (Balti-
      more: Johns Hopkins University Press, 1994), p. 1648.

171   *"an astonishing mass of people":* James Madison, 4 September 1789, in *De-
      bates in the House of Representatives, First Session: June–September 1789*,
      Charlene Bangs Bickford et al., eds. (Baltimore: Johns Hopkins University
      Press, 1992, p. 1438. See also C. M. Harris, "Washington's Gamble, L'Enfant's
      Dream: Politics, Design, and the Founding of the National Capital," *William
      and Mary Quarterly*, 3rd Series, vol. 56, no. 3, July 1999, pp. 527–64. "Sig-
      nificantly, Washington's market-oriented new-town strategy required a

grand vision and great risk taking to be at all practical. An expansive city, even if only in outline, was necessary to guarantee an ample supply of saleable land to fund the construction of public buildings. . . . George Washington's grand scheme was in fact to be funded by the familiar mechanism of the land bubble, and, like all promotions dependent upon the rapid rise of asset prices, the physical creation of the Federal City required highly visible activity, measurable progress, and, certainly, a bit of magic" (pp. 536–37).

171 *the northerners adopted "Conococheague"*: Elbridge Gerry, on 6 July 1790, spoke for many: "Enquiries will be made, where in the name of common sense is Connogocheque, and I do not believe that one person in a thousand in the United States knows that there is such a place on earth. . . . [F]or the grave council of the United States, to pass a bill that the seat of government should be removed to that place, is a measure too ridiculous to be credited." See Jefferson *Papers*, vol. 27, Editorial Note, pp. 453–54.

172 *"Hamilton was in despair"*: "The Anas," in *The Writings of Thomas Jefferson*, Library Edition, Andrew A. Lipscomb, ed. (Washington, DC: The Thomas Jefferson Memorial Association, 1903), vol. 1, pp. 274–75. The only account of the dinner is from Jefferson, and initially, in a memorandum written no earlier than 1791, he gave a stripped-down version of events, saying, "It ended in Mr. Madison's acquiescence in a proposition that the question (assumption) should be again brought before the house by way of amendment from the Senate, that tho' he would not vote for it, nor entirely withdraw his opposition, yet he should not be strenuous, but leave it to it's fate." Jefferson *Papers*, vol. 17, pp. 206–7.

172 *"the savory viands and mellow Madeira"*: Federal Writers' Project, *Washington: City and Capital* (Washington, DC: U.S. Government Printing Office, 1937), p. 42.

172 *"I was duped"*: TJ to GW, 9 September 1792, *Papers*, Presidential Series, vol. 11, pp. 96–105.

172 *"Hamilton was not only a monarchist"*: "The Anas," in Lipscomb, ed., *The Writings of Thomas Jefferson*, p. 278.

173 *"a populous city better than building a palace"*: See *Annals of Congress*, vol. 2, Joseph Gales, comp. (Washington: Gales & Seaton, 1834), p. 1719.

173 *"I can conceive none"*: Ibid., p. 1723.

174 *"subject to the President's direction"*: TJ to GW, 29 August 1790, *Papers*, Presidential Series, vol. 6, pp. 368–69.

175 *"In Paris it is forbidden"*: Ibid.

175 *". . . upon unpacking the china ornaments"*: GW to Tobias Lear, 17 September 1790, ibid., pp. 465–67.

176 *spent the time well, meandering around*: Thomas Lee Shippen to William Shippen, 15 September 1790, Jefferson *Papers*, vol. 17, p. 464–65.

176 *The federal district's boundary:* Ibid.; see also Dumas Malone, *Jefferson and His Time;* vol. 2: *Jefferson and the Rights of Man* (Boston: Little, Brown, 1948–1981), p. 319; and TJ to GW, 14 September 1790, *Papers,* Presidential Series, vol. 6, pp. 434–36.

176 *"1. . . . it's being at the junction":* TJ to GW, 17 September 1790, *Papers,* Presidential Series, vol. 6, p. 463.

177 *George Thompson received a grant of 1,000 acres:* Federal Writers' Project, *Washington: City and Capital,* p. 38.

179 *Kenneth Bowling is a leader:* Personal communication.

179 *"You ride through some delightful corn":* Louis B. Wright and Marlon Tinling, eds., *Quebec to Carolina in 1785–1786: Being the Travel Diary and Observations of Robert Hunter, Jr., a Young Merchant of London* (San Marino, CA: Huntington Library, 1943), p. 188.

179 *surveying trip up the river:* See 13 October 1790, *Papers,* Presidential Series, vol. 6, p. 557n.

Chapter 10: The Final Measurement

186 *"I was in imminent danger":* 24 March 1791, *Diaries,* vol. 6, pp. 100–101. The remaining quotes from Washington's southern tour are in this volume; see pp. 99–163.

186 *Colonel Allen and his family:* 20 April 1971, ibid., p. 115. See the account in Richard Norton Smith, *Patriarch: George Washington and the New American Nation* (Boston: Houghton Mifflin, 1993), p. 94.

188 *"I am a friend to all, and hurt none":* 1 February 1793, Jefferson *Papers,* vol. 25, p. 112–18.

189 *He felt himself a "slave" to the public:* GW to Henry Lee, 21 July 1793, John C. Fitzpatrick, ed., *The Writings of George Washington,* vol. 33 (Washington, DC: U.S. Government Printing Office, 1931), pp. 22–24.

189 *"the most vulnerable part of me":* Ibid.

189 *"feels those things more":* TJ to James Madison, Jefferson *Papers,* vol. 26, pp. 239–42.

190 *"The Presidt. was much inflamed":* "Notes on Cabinet Meeting on Edmond Charles Genet," Jefferson *Papers,* vol. 26, pp. 601–3.

191 *Build a new rail fence along that property line:* For the various instructions in this paragraph, see GW to William Pearce, 26 January 1794 and 9 February 1794, Fitzpatrick, ed., *Writings,* vol. 33, pp. 252–56, 263–67; GW to Overseers, 14 July 1793, ibid., pp. 5–12; GW to William Pearce, 13 July 1794, ibid., pp. 424–30; GW to Hyland Crow, 4 August 1793, ibid., pp. 36–37; GW to William Pearce, 17 August 1794, ibid., p. 470.

192 *("the roguest people about the house"):* GW to Howell Lewis, 18 August 1793, ibid., pp. 49–54.

192 *"the importance of giving attention"*: Ibid.

193 *Historian Dennis Pogue has contended*: Dennis Pogue, "George Washington and the Politics of Slavery," in manuscript. Pogue says of the cost of freeing the Custis slaves, "At an estimated average value of 40 pounds sterling per slave, this would have amounted to a payment of more than 6000 pounds. By way of comparison, the total profit that Washington received from all of his plantation operations for the year 1797 was valued at little more than 900 pounds sterling." See also GW to Tobias Lear, 6 May 1794, Fitzpatrick, ed., *Writings*, vol. 33, pp. 353–60.

194 *"They entertain suspicions that it is not the wish"*: Edmund Randolph to GW, 15 July 1794, uncollected papers, no. 52164. (These are the papers of Washington at the University of Virginia, not yet published in bound editions.)

194 *the westerners distilled ten times as much whiskey*: Hugh Henry Brackenridge, *Incidents of the Insurrection*, edited by Daniel Marder (New Haven, CT: College & University Press, 1972), p. 47. See also Hugh Cleland, *George Washington in the Ohio Valley* (Pittsburgh, PA: University of Pittsburgh Press, 1955), p. 337: "The distillery, therefore, took the place of transportation."

195 *"The whole country was [an] inflammable mass"*: Brackenridge, *Incidents of the Insurrection*, p. 93.

196 *"there was an end to our Constitution & laws"*: 2 August 1794, *Papers of Alexander Hamilton*, Harold C. Syrett, ed. (New York: Columbia University Press, 1972), vol. 17, pp. 9–13.

196 *Hamilton urged him to go full bore*: Alexander Hamilton to GW, 2 August 1794, ibid., p. 18.

197 *"sink into the profoundest retirement"*: GW to Henry Lee, 26 August 1794, Fitzpatrick, ed., *Writings of George Washington*, vol. 33, p. 476.

197 *He jotted off a note with that observation*: GW to William Pearce, 1 October 1794, uncollected papers, no. 58353.

197 *("Resolved unanimously")*: Washington County, Pennsylvania, Citizens to GW, 2 October 1794, uncollected papers, no. 8340.

198 *"The sword of justice"*: Carlisle, Pennsylvania, Citizens to GW, 6 October 1794, uncollected papers, no. 52218.

198 *"Let us hope that the delusion can not be lasting"*: GW to Carlisle, Pennsylvania, Citizens, 6 October, 1794, uncollected papers, no. 32539.

199 *"the extreme badness of the Road"*: 15 October 1794, *Diaries*, vol. 6, pp. 191–92.

199 *"[T]hough Submission is professed"*: 17 and 18 October 1794, ibid., p. 193.

199 *"opened by Troops under my command"*: 19 October 1794, *Diaries*, vol. 6, p. 194.

199 *As it happened, none of the Seceders:* Elizabeth J. Wall, ed., *Men of the Whiskey Insurrection in Southwestern Pennsylvania* (Pittsburgh, PA: E. J. Wall, 1988), p. 42.

200 *He feared the federal dragoons:* Brackenridge, *Incidents of the Insurrection*, pp. 193–201.

200 *penned up in a wet stable and thrown raw meat:* Ibid., p. 202.

200 *"so patient of the kicks and scoffs":* TJ to James Madison, 28 December 1794, Jefferson *Papers*, vol. 28, p. 229.

201 *"The motion of my blood":* TJ to James Madison, 9 June 1793, Ibid., vol. 26, pp. 239–42.

201 *"The Albany Pea":* GW to TJ, 4 October 1795, Fitzpatrick, ed., *Writings*, vol. 34, pp. 324–25.

202 *"His memory was already sensibly impaired":* "The Anas," in *The Writings of Thomas Jefferson*, Library Edition, Andrew A. Lipscomb, ed. (Washington, DC: The Thomas Jefferson Memorial Association, 1903), vol. 1, p. 282.

202 *"more than usually grave, cool, and reserved":* Quoted in Henry Adams, *The Life of Albert Gallatin* (Philadelphia, PA: J. B. Lippincott, 1879), p. 182.

202 *"It would give you a fever":* TJ to Philip Mazzei, 24 April 1796, in Jefferson *Papers*, vol. 29, pp. 73–83.

203 *"I put away this disgusting dish":* TJ to GW, 19 June 1796, ibid., pp. 127–29.

203 *"As you have mentioned the subject yourself":* GW to TJ, 6 July 1796, Fitzpatrick, ed., *Writings*, vol. 35, pp. 118–22.

204 *"every citizen would take pride":* Farewell Address [First Draft], 15 May 1796, ibid., pp. 51–61.

205 *"for all his talk of longing to sit undisturbed":* W. W. Abbot, "George Washington in Retirement," the Lowell Lecture Series, the Museum of Our National Heritage, 5 December 1999, pp. 14–17.

206 *Should the flap be embroidered?:* Ibid.

206 *"Much is it to be regretted":* GW to John Fitzgerald, 27 July 1799, *Papers*, Retirement Series, vol. 4, pp. 211–12.

206 *"To dilate on the benefits":* GW to William Berkeley, 11 August 1799, Fitzpatrick, ed., *Writings*, p. 330.

207 *"dissipation and extravagence" so common in colleges:* George Washington's Last Will and Testament, 9 July 1799, *Papers*, Retirement Series, vol. 4, pp. 477–92.

208 *These swords are accompanied:* Ibid.

209 *a "settled cold Rain":* 12 December 1799, *Diaries*, vol. 6, p. 378.

209 *"You know I never take any thing for a cold":* Tobias Lear's Narrative Accounts of the Death of George Washington, *Papers*, Retirement Series, vol. 4, pp. 542–55. See the diary account, p. 548.

209 *"Morning Snowing"*: 13 December 1799, Diaries, vol. 6, pp. 378–79.

209 *In his body, a microbial storm raged:* "During the rest of the day—nearly twenty hours—George Washington slowly and painfully choked to death," writes Peter R. Henriques, who identifies Washington's ailment as possibly *Hemophilus influenza* Type B, triggering acute epiglottitis. See Peter R. Henriques, "The Final Struggle Between George Washington and the Grim King," in Don Higginbotham, ed., *George Washington Reconsidered* (Charlottesville: University Press of Virginia, 2001), p. 254.

Chapter 11: The Second American Revolution

214 *Fortunately, the Patowmack Company:* The best account of the company is still Corra Bacon-Foster, *Early Chapters in the Development of the Patomac Route to the West* (New York: Burt Franklin, 1971; originally published 1912).

215 *The revenues of the Patowmack Company:* Ibid., p. 185.

216 *"The waters fret and boil"*: Constantin Volney, *A View of the Soil and Climate of the United States of America* (Philadelphia: J. Conrad & Co. 1804), p. 63.

217 *"the pompous appellation of 'Tyber'"*: Henry Adams, *The Life of Albert Gallatin* (New York: Peter Smith, 1943), p. 252–53.

218 *"graced by not a single vessel"*: Ibid.

218 *"lodge, like cattle, in the fields"*: TJ to Alexander White, 10 September 1797, Andrew A. Lipscomb, ed., *The Writings of Thomas Jefferson,* vol. 9 (Washington, DC: Thomas Jefferson Memorial Association, 1903), p. 426.

218 *the perfect republican capital:* Joseph Ellis, *American Sphinx: The Character of Thomas Jefferson* (New York: Knopf, 1997), p. 171.

218 *"The nation's capital, in being removed"*: Stanley Elkins and Eric McKitrick, *The Age of Federalism* (New York: Oxford University Press, 1993), p. 174.

219 *"they live like fishes, by eating each other"*: Federal Writers' Project, American Guide Series, *Washington: City and Capital* (Washington, DC: U.S. Government Printing Office, 1937), p. 47.

219 *"holding down and breaking bows of trees"*: Thomas Froncek, ed., *The City of Washington: An Illustrated History* (New York: Wings Books, 1992), p. 81.

219 *"To be under the necessity"*: Isaac Weld, Jr., *Travels Through the States of North America, and the Provinces of Upper and Lower Canada, During the Years 1795, 1796, and 1797,* 4th ed., vol. 1 (London: John Stockdale 1807), p. 86.

219 *"After some time, a coach passed"*: William Cabell Bruce, *John Randolph of Roanoke,* vol. 1 (New York: Octagon Books, 1970), p. 562.

219 *"How I wish that I possessed"*: Margaret Bayard Smith (Mrs. Samuel Harrison Smith), *The First Forty Years of Washington Society*, edited by Gaillard Hunt (New York: Charles Scribner's Sons, 1906), pp. 10–11.

221 *"We have no villages in America"*: Quoted in Jack Larkin, *The Reshaping of Everyday Life, 1790–1840* (New York: Harper & Row, 1988), pp. 6–7.

222 *More than seventy turnpike companies*: See Carter Goodrich, *Government Promotion of Canals and Railroads, 1800–1890* (New York: Columbia University Press, 1960), pp. 21–22.

222 *the astonishing array of merchandise*: See Jon Kukla, *A Wilderness So Immense: The Louisiana Purchase and the Destiny of America* (New York: Knopf, 2003), pp. 210–11.

222 *the journey took four months*: James MacGregor Burns, *The Vineyard of Liberty* (New York: Knopf, 1982), p. 277.

222 *The news of George Washington's death*: Allan R. Pred, *Urban Growth and the Circulation of Information: The United States System of Cities, 1790–1840* (Cambridge, MA: Harvard University Press, 1973), p. 14.

222 *"Even after two centuries of struggle"*: Henry Adams, *History of the United States of America During the First Administration of Thomas Jefferson*, vol. 1 (New York: Charles Scribner's Sons, 1921), p. 1.

223 *"sink Federalism into an abyss"*: Samuel Eliot Morison et al., *The Growth of the American Republic*, 7th ed. (New York: Oxford University Press, 1980), p. 332.

223 *"Our country is too large"*: TJ to Gideon Granger, 13 August 1800, quoted in *The Annals of America; vol. 4: 1797–1820: Domestic Expansion and Foreign Entanglements* (Chicago: Encyclopaedia Britannica, 1976), pp. 140–41.

225 *"Jefferson could not maintain his extravagant life style"*: Paul Finkelman, "Jefferson and Slavery," in Peter S. Onuf, ed., *Jeffersonian Legacies* (Charlottesville: University Press of Virginia, 1993), p. 183. For a cogent analysis of Jefferson's desire to have the fruits of power without the nasty consequences of its exercise, see Robert W. Tucker and David C. Hendrickson, *Empire of Liberty: The Statecraft of Thomas Jefferson* (New York: Oxford University Press, 1990), p. 18.

225 *the election fiasco of 1800*: See the excellent account in Burns, *Vineyard of Liberty*, pp. 151–55. Also see John Ferling, *A Leap in the Dark: The Struggle to Create the American Republic* (New York: Oxford University Press, 2003), pp. 477–88.

225 *"separated by nature and a wide ocean"*: Merrill D. Peterson, ed., *The Portable Thomas Jefferson* (New York: Viking Press, 1975), p. 292.

226 *"Among these mountains, those that lie"*: Jonathan Carver, *Three Years' Travels Thoughout [sic] the Interior Parts of North America* (Walpole, NH: Isaiah Thomas & Co., 1813), p. 77.

227   *If someone were to go up the Missouri:* See John Logan Allen, *Passage Through the Garden: Lewis and Clark and the Image of the American Northwest* (New York: Dover, 1991), pp. 6–7. An excellent source on Jefferson and the West is Donald Dean Jackson, *Thomas Jefferson & the Stony Mountains: Exploring the West from Monticello* (Urbana: University of Illinois Press, 1981).

227   *(a land carriage of 340 miles):* Henry Nash Smith, *Virgin Land: The American West as Symbol and Myth* (Cambridge, MA: Harvard University Press, 1950), p. 17.

227   *"the most direct & practicable water communication":* TJ to Meriwether Lewis, 20 June 1803, *The Annals of America,* vol. 4, pp. 160–64.

227   *"as characterized by the thermometer":* Ibid.

228   *"extreemly dusty" roads:* Quoted in Stephen E. Ambrose, *Undaunted Courage: Meriwether Lewis, Thomas Jefferson, and the Opening of the American West* (New York: Simon & Schuster, 1996), p. 103.

229   *"the greatest consternation":* Lewis started his journal of the expedition in Pittsburgh, and describes this near-disaster. See Gary E. Moulton, ed., *The Journals of the Lewis & Clark Expedition,* vol. 2 (Lincoln: University of Nebraska Press, 1983), p. 65.

229   *"The Mississippi is . . . the Hudson":* James Madison to Charles Pinckney, 27 November 1802, *The Papers of James Madison,* Secretary of State Series, vol. 4: 8 October 1802–15 May 1803 (Charlottesville: University Press of Virginia, 1998), pp. 146–48.

Chapter 12: The Progress of Man

231   *One man kept alive the dream:* A "National Road," Gallatin said, would help the Union by "cementing the bonds" between rival states. See John Lauritz Larson, *Internal Improvement: National Public Works and the Promise of Popular Government in the Early United States* (Chapel Hill: University of North Carolina Press, 2001), p. 54. Jefferson had cement on his mind as well, for he later said that he wanted to increase the communication among the states so that "the lines of separation will disappear, their interests will be identified, and her union cemented by new and indissoluble ties." See Henry Adams, *The Life of Albert Gallatin* (New York: Peter Smith, 1943), p. 350. Gallatin didn't say where the road should be built. Congress recognized three options: an all-Pennsylvania route, a Potomac route that followed more or less the path of Braddock's Road, and an all-Virginia route via the James and New/Kanawha rivers. The Pennsylvania route lost luster for the simple reason that the intrepid folks of that state were already building it with their own money, and didn't really need the federal largess. The Virginia route suffered from remoteness.

232   *If Congress could establish banks:* John Lauritz Larson, "Jefferson's Union
       and Internal Improvements," in Peter S. Onuf, ed., *Jeffersonian Legacies*
       (Charlottesville: University Press of Virginia, 1993), p. 363. Larson writes
       that the legacy of Jefferson's career as a democratic revolutionary was "a
       kind of radical political temper that instinctively favored libertarian rheto-
       ric and resented the exercise of power even in behalf of the interests of ma-
       jorities" (p. 364).

232   *"four necks of land": Report of the Secretary of the Treasury [Albert Gal-
       latin] on the Subject of Roads and Canals* [1808] (New York: Augustus M.
       Kelley, 1968), p. 9. Gallatin detailed his vision of an inland waterway: "[A]
       sea vessel, entering the first canal in the harbor of Boston, would through
       the bay of Rhode Island, Long Island sound, and the harbor of New York,
       reach Brunswick on the Rariton; thence pass through the second canal to
       Trenton on the Delaware, down that river to Christiana, or New Castle, and
       through the third canal to Elk river, and the Chesapeake; whence sailing
       down that bay, and up Elizabeth river, it would, through the fourth canal,
       enter the Albemarle sound, and by Pamptico, Core and Bogue sounds,
       reach Beaufort and Swansborough, in North Carolina. From the last men-
       tioned place, the inland navigation, through Stumpy and Toomer's sounds,
       is continued with a diminished draft of water, and by cutting two low and
       narrow necks, not exceeding three miles together, to Cape Fear river; and
       thence, by an open but short and direct run along the coast, is reached that
       chain of islands between which and the main, the inland navigation is
       continued to St. Mary's, along the coast of South Carolina and Georgia"
       (pp. 9–10).

233   *an intracoastal waterway:* Robert Fulton, the steam pioneer, declared that
       when the nation was bound together by canals, it would be no more possi-
       ble to split the United States than it would be for England to divide into
       seven kingdoms. Joshua Forman, an assemblyman in New York, was elated
       at the prospect of 3 million dollars in federal money going to a canal be-
       tween the Hudson and Lake Erie. He traveled to Washington and obtained
       an audience with President Jefferson. The session went badly for the New
       Yorker, however. Jefferson, though he had been estranged from George
       Washington in the great man's final years, still adhered to the Potomac
       plan that he and the general had discussed in the 1780s. Forman recalled
       what Jefferson told him: "Why, sir, here is a canal for a few miles, projected
       by George Washington, which if completed would render this a fine com-
       mercial city, which has languished for many years because the small sum
       of 200,000 dollars necessary to complete it, cannot be obtained from the
       general government, the state government, or from individuals—and you
       talk of making a canal 350 miles through the wilderness—it is little short

of madness to think of it at this day." Quoted in James MacGregor Burns, *The Vineyard of Liberty* (New York: Knopf, 1982), p. 306.

234 *The Americans had a republican defense:* See Garry Wills, *James Madison* (New York: Times Books, 2002). See also J. Mackay Hitsman, *The Incredible War of 1812: A Military History* (Toronto: University of Toronto Press, 1965).

234 *"[W]hat the devil will they do here":* Irving Brant, *The Fourth President: A Life of James Madison* (Indianapolis: Bobbs-Merrill, 1970), p. 568. His account of the burning of Washington informs much of my narrative.

234 *Among the invaders were African-Americans:* James Oliver Horton and Lois E. Horton, *Hard Road to Freedom: The Story of African America* (New Brunswick, NJ: Rutgers University Press, 2001), p. 99.

236 *"an alliance by constraint": Annals of America,* vol. 4, 1797–1820, p. 371.

237 *"The United States form, for many":* D. W. Meinig, *The Shaping of America,* vol. 2 (New Haven, CT: Yale University Press, 1986), p. 399. For more on rising nationalism, see Kendric Charles Babcock, *The Rise of American Nationality,* 1811–1819 (New York: Greenwood Press, 1969, originally published 1906).

238 *The first Potomac bridge had gone up in 1797:* For a history of bridges on the Potomac, see Donald Beekman Myer, *Bridges and the City of Washington* (Washington, DC: U.S. Commission of Fine Arts, U.S. Government Printing Office, 1974).

238 *The country was better at creating East-West connections:* See Albert Fishlow, *American Railroads and the Transformation of the Antebellum Economy* (Cambridge, MA: Harvard University Press, 1965).

239 *("sawyers" if they bobbed):* Seymour Dunbar, *A History of Travel in America,* vol. 1 (New York: Greenwood Press, 1968), pp. 296–300. See also Ralph H. Brown, *Historical Geography of the United States* (New York: Harcourt, Brace, 1948). He reports that in 1811 the *New Orleans* became the first Ohio River steamboat, but lacked the power for upriver journeys (p. 261). The *Aetna,* however, managed to travel against the current in 1815, carrying 200 tons of freight and a few passengers. Leaving New Orleans, it reached Louisville in sixty days.

239 *The road had a remarkable feature:* At its highest point the road would be 2,325 feet above sea level. The total land portage between the navigable Potomac and the navigable Monongahela would be 66.5 miles. See Thomas Searight, *The Old Pike* (Uniontown, PA: self-published, 1894), p. 32.

241 *By 1817 the company had managed:* Corra Bacon-Foster, *Early Chapters in the Development of the Patomac Route to the West* (New York: Burt Franklin, 1971; originally published 1912), p. 123.

242 *". . . its dangerous character, arising from the wildness":* U.S. House of

Representatives, "Chesapeake and Ohio Canal," 20th Congress, 1st Session, Committee on Roads and Canals, Report No. 47, pp. 47–48. (This is an "extract from the report of the Virginia and Maryland Commissioners, printed by order of the Senate of the United States, January 27, 1823.")

243 *"dregs and froth":* Charles Fenton Mercer, *Weakness and Inefficiency of the Government of the United States of North America* (London: Houlston & Wright, 1863; originally self-published 1845), p. 52. For the biography of Mercer, see Douglas R. Egerton, *Charles Fenton Mercer and the Trial of National Conservatism* (Jackson: University Press of Mississippi, 1989).

243 *an ailing Mercer appeared in the Capitol:* See "Speech of Mr. C. F. Mercer on the Subject of the Chesapeake and Ohio Canal, Delivered in the Convention of Delegates, Held at the City of Washington, November 7, 1823 (Washington, DC: Gales & Seaton, 1823).

243 *Here were men with names long known:* U.S. House of Representatives, "Chesapeake and Ohio Canal," pp. 6–10.

244 *"For its prime mover":* "Speech of Mr. C. F. Mercer," pp. 3–4.

244 *"It has even been whispered":* Ibid., pp. 9–10.

245 *"I regret that I am now to die":* TJ to John Holmes, 22 April 1820, Merrill D. Peterson, ed., *The Portable Thomas Jefferson* (New York: Viking, 1975), pp. 568–69.

246 *"Let a philosophic observer":* TJ to William Ludlow, 6 September 1824, ibid., p. 583.

247 *"The United States lies like a huge page":* Frederick Jackson Turner, *The Frontier in American History* (New York: Henry Holt, 1920), pp. 1–3. Turner writes, "American social development has been continually beginning over again on the frontier. This perennial rebirth, this fluidity of American life, this expansion westward with its new opportunities, its continuous touch with the simplicity of primitive society, furnish the forces dominating American character." He continues: "The frontier is the line of most rapid and effective Americanization. The wilderness masters the colonist. It finds him a European in dress, industries, tools, modes of travel, and thought. It takes him from the railroad car and puts him in the birch canoe. It strips off the garments of civilization and arrays him in the hunting shirt and the moccasin. It puts him in the log cabin of the Cherokee and Iroquois and runs an Indian palisade around him. Before long he has gone to planting Indian corn and plowing with a sharp stick; he shouts the war cry and takes the scalp in orthodox Indian fashion" (p. 4). Edward Countryman has written, "Turner was right in one important sense: on 'the frontier' people became what they had not been before. We have turned away from him in part because Turner was so very wrong in asserting that

westward-moving, English-speaking whites were the only people involved." See Edward Countryman, "Why the West is Lost: Comments and Response," *William and Mary Quarterly*, 3rd series, vol. 51, no. 4 (October, 1994), p. 723.

248 *But the creditors took what they could:* Lucia Stanton, "Those Who Labor for My Happiness: Thomas Jefferson and His Slaves," in Peter S. Onuf, ed., *Jeffersonian Legacies* (Charlottesville: University Press of Virginia, 1993), p. 147. See also the discussion of Jefferson's racial attitudes in Winthrop D. Jordan, *White Over Black: American Attitudes Toward the Negro, 1550–1812* (Chapel Hill: University of North Carolina Press, 1968).

Chapter 13: A Heroic Age

250 *The sun came out from behind a cloud:* This account, including the quotes from Mercer and Adams, is largely based on the detailed story in the *Daily National Intelligencer* (Washington), vol. 16, July 7, 1828. See also *Memoirs of John Quincy Adams*, edited by Charles Francis Adams, vol. 8 (Freeport, NY: Books for Libraries Press, 1969), especially pp. 49–50, where he discusses being nervous: "As has happened to me whenever I have had a part to perform in the presence of multitudes, I got through awkwardly, but without gross and palpable failure. The incident that chiefly relieved me was the obstacle of the stump, which met and resisted the space, and my casting off my coat to overcome the resistance. It struck the eye and fancy of the spectators more than all the flowers of rhetoric in my speech, and diverted their attention from the stammering and hesitation of a deficient memory."

252 *And the rival had chosen this very same day:* My account relies on the dispatch from the *Baltimore Gazette*, 8 July 1828, in the *Daily National Intelligencer* (Washington); on Edward Hungerford, *The Story of the Baltimore & Ohio Railroad, 1827–1927* (New York: G. P. Putnam's Sons, 1928), and James D. Dilts, *The Great Road: The Building of the Baltimore and Ohio, the Nation's First Railroad, 1828–1853* (Stanford, CA: Stanford University Press, 1993). An estimate of 70,000 people in attendance can be found in Herbert H. Harwood, Jr., *Impossible Challenge II: Baltimore to Washington and Harpers Ferry from 1828 to 1994* (Baltimore, MD: Barnard, Roberts, 1994), p. 9.

252 *"So perfect was the symmetry of her form":* *Baltimore Gazette*, reprinted in *Daily National Intelligencer* (Washington), 8 July 1828.

253 *"make the East and the West":* Ibid.

254 *The longest railroad in the world:* Harwood, *Impossible Challenge II*, pp. 9–10.

257 *"a horrid hole"*: Benjamin H. Latrobe, Jr., after a visit in 1833, quoted in Dilts, *Great Road*, p. 187.

258 *"[C]anallers were miners and sappers"*: Peter Way, *Common Labor: Workers and the Digging of North American Canals, 1780–1860* (Baltimore, MD: Johns Hopkins University Press, 1997), p. 4.

258 *"It was at least necessary"*: *The Frederick Douglass Papers*, Series 2: *Autobiographical Writings*, vol. 1: *Narrative*, John W. Blassingame et al., eds. (New Haven: Yale University Press, 1999), p. 33.

258 *"all equal one to the other, all belonging to the same family"*: Alexis de Tocqueville, *Democracy in America*, Phillips Bradley, ed. (New York: Knopf, 1951), p. 434.

259 *"only a few nights"*: Fanny Trollope, *Domestic Manners of the Americans* (New York: Penguin Books, 1997: first published 1832), p. 148.

259 *"as a valuable horse is watched and physicked"*: Ibid., p. 225.

259 *Working conditions were even worse:* An excellent source is Katherine A. Harvey, *The Best-Dressed Miners: Life and Labor in the Maryland Coal Region, 1835–1910* (Ithaca, NY: Cornell University Press, 1969).

259 *the Corkmen and Longfords squared off:* Niles Weekly Register, 25 January 1834.

260 *they went berserk, bludgeoned several Germans:* Dilts, *Great Road*, p. 266.

260 *("The Canal sometimes passes along the rocky cliffs"):* Daily National Intelligencer (Washington), July 9, 1839.

261 *canal boats clotted, blocking the final short passage:* Walter Sanderlin, *The Great National Project: A History of the Chesapeake and Ohio Canal* (New York: Arno Press, 1976), pp. 191–92. I should note that the railroad had its own problems, its own financial low points, labor disputes, and shenanigans with scrip. But railroad mania took hold in America in the 1830s in the same way that canals had boomed a decade earlier. President Jackson in 1833 became the first president to travel by rail. In 1830 the United States had roughly 1,200 miles of canal, and only about 73 miles of rail, including the spur lines from coal mines. By 1840 there were 3,326 miles of canal and 3,328 miles of rail—a dead heat. And by 1850, there would be no doubt about the winner of the contest. There were still less than 4,000 miles of canal, but nearly 9,000 miles of rail, a number that would more than triple by the start of the Civil War. See also George Rogers Taylor, *The Transportation Revolution: 1815–1860* (New York: Rinehart, 1951), an excellent overview. For a discussion of the railroad boom's effect on business practices in America, see Alfred Dupont Chandler, Jr., *The Visible Hand: The Managerial Revolution in American Business* (Cambridge, MA: Harvard University Press, 1977).

261 ("Cumberland," predicted Horace Greeley): Dilts, Great Road, p. 279.

262 a Potomac flood crested six feet higher: Sanderlin, Great National Project, p. 207.

262 "Spacious avenues that begin in nothing": From American Notes, 1842, excerpted in Christopher Ricks and William L. Vance, eds., The Faber Book of America (London: Faber & Faber, 1992), p. 123.

263 "All is as shabby as possible": Grace King, Mount Vernon on the Potomac: History of the Mount Vernon Ladies' Association of the Union (New York: Macmillan, 1929), p. 10.

263 "Ladies of the South!": Ibid., p. 20.

264 "Washington's dream": John Lauritz Larson, Internal Improvement: National Public Works and the Promise of Popular Government In the Early United States (Chapel Hill: University of North Carolina Press, 2001), p. 21.

265 "What hath God wrought?": See Allan R. Pred, Urban Growth and the Circulation of Information: The United States System of Cities, 1790–1840 (Cambridge, MA: Harvard University Press, 1973). "Prior to that date," writes Allan Pred, "the long-distance movement of news and information was synonymous with human spatial interaction," (p. 12). Within three years, as entrepreneurs realized the potential of the technology, an almost continuous line ran from Boston to Washington (with a gap at the Hudson River). In 1858, communications reached another milestone with the laying of the first transatlantic cable.

266 "Our inventions are wont to be pretty toys": Henry David Thoreau, Walden, ed. by J. Lyndon Shanley (Princeton, NJ: Princeton University Press, 1971), p. 52. Leo Marx, in The Machine in the Garden: Technology and the Pastoral Ideal in America (New York: Oxford University Press, 2000: originally published 1964), shows that American literature reverberates with a common image, the sudden interruption of a pastoral reverie by the appearance of a machine, a factory, a steamboat. The machine is the great disrupter of the tranquil life. This was what Jefferson had feared. Was he not prophetic in his warnings against manufacturing and urban decay? Marx says that Jefferson was not espousing an agrarian ideal so much as a pastoral one, for he sees agriculture not so much as a superior economic system but as one that enforces superior values (p. 127).

Chapter 14: The Border

270 "We have come here for the purpose of liberating": Edward Stone, Incident at Harper's Ferry (Englewood Cliffs, NJ: Prentice-Hall, 1956), pp. 74–75.

270   *The raiders crossed the Potomac:* My account is based on Stephen B. Oates, *To Purge This Land with Blood: A Biography of John Brown* (Amherst: University of Massachusetts Press, 1984), pp. 290–306.

271   *"his ghastly face":* Edward Renehan, *The Secret Six: The True Tale of the Men Who Conspired with John Brown* (New York: Crown, 1995), p. 202.

271   *expecting to find 500 insurgents:* See the account in Douglas Freeman, *R. E. Lee: A Biography*, vol. 1 (New York: Charles Scribner's Sons, 1934), pp. 394–404.

272   *"The old revolutionary blood does tell!":* Ibid.

272   *"I John Brown am now quite certain":* Quoted in Oates, *To Purge This Land*, p. 351.

273   *So powerful was the symbol of the Potomac:* James M. McPherson, *Crossroads of Freedom: Antietam* (New York: Oxford University Press, 2002), p. 100.

273   *"[T]he river was the principal theater":* Frederick Gutheim, *The Potomac* (Baltimore, MD: Johns Hopkins University Press, 1986; first published 1949), p. 296.

275   *"All quiet along the Potomac":* For the definitive account of the nation's capital during the Civil War, see Margaret Leech, *Reveille in Washington, 1860–1865* (Garden City, NY: Garden City Pub. Co., 1945). See also *Official Records of the Union and Confederate Navies in the War of the Rebellion*, Series 1, vol. 4 (Washington, DC: U.S. Government Printing Office, 1896).

275   *one event early in the war:* In addition to sources mentioned below, my account of the battle of Ball's Bluff is based on *War of the Rebellion: Official Records*, vols. 5 and 51; Ted Ballard, *Battle of Ball's Bluff* (Washington, DC: Center of Military History, U.S. Army, 2001); and Robert Underwood Johnson and Clarence Clough Buel, eds., *Battles and Leaders of the Civil War*, vol. 2 (New York: Thomas Yoseloff, 1956).

275   *"Turn back! Turn back!":* Shelby Foote, *The Civil War: A Narrative*, vol. 1: *Fort Sumter to Perryville* (New York: Random House, 1958), p. 82.

277   *As historian Shelby Foote tells it:* Ibid., p. 105.

277   *"One blast upon your bugle horn":* Ibid., p. 106.

277   *"Who are those men?":* New York World, 29 October 1861. This is by far the most detailed of the contemporaneous newspaper accounts of the battle.

278   *One body eventually reached Chain Bridge:* Leech, *Reveille in Washington*, p. 116.

279   *"Who is responsible for this appalling blunder?":* Morning Courier & New York Enquirer, 26 October 1861.

Chapter 15: The River Today

282   *"The fate of the canal"*: Frederick Gutheim, *The Potomac* (Baltimore, MD: Johns Hopkins University Press, 1986), p. 264.

283   *Under the Army Corps plan:* The premier resource on the fate of the canal is Barry Mackintosh, *C&O Canal: The Making of a Park* (Washington, DC: Department of the Interior, 1991). For more on recent developments along the river, see my story "America's River," in *The Washington Post*, 5 May 2002, p. W12.

283   *"no legal objection, in my opinion, to filling the canal"*: Mackintosh, *C&O Canal*, pp. 54–55.

283   *"would enable more people to enjoy beauties"*: The Washington Post, 19 January 1954.

284   *"It is a refuge, a place of retreat"*: Ibid.

284   *Congressman DeWitt S. Hyde of Maryland:* Hearings before the Subcommittee on Public Lands of the Committee on Interior and Insular Affairs, House of Representatives, 86th Congress, 2nd Session, on S. 77 and H.R. 1145, p. 5, in U.S. Committee on Interior and Insular Affairs, House Hearings, 85th Congress, 1st Session, pp. 22–29.

284   *Udall decided that the river: The Potomac: A Report on Its Imperiled Future and a Guide for Its Orderly Development*, prepared by the Potomac Planning Task Force (Washington, DC: U.S. Government Printing Office, 1967), introduction by Stewart Udall, p. 6.

286   *a slalom run in a portion of the old skirting canal:* See Dan Guzy, "The Potomac Company's Canal and Locks at Little Falls," *Maryland Historical Magazine*, vol. 96, No. 4 (Winter 2001), pp. 421–37. Anyone wishing to explore the C&O Canal or the Potomac River can find excellent maps published by the National Park Service and the Interstate Commission on the Potomac River Basin. Among the many guidebooks to the canal, I found particularly useful Thomas F. Swiftwater Hahn, *Towpath Guide to the Chesapeake & Ohio Canal* (Harpers Ferry, WV: Harpers Ferry Historical Association, 1997). For the flora and fauna of the Potomac River valley, see Jack Wennerstrom, *Leaning Sycamores: Natural Worlds of the Upper Potomac* (Baltimore: Johns Hopkins University Press, 1996).

286   *One historical quirk of the Potomac intruded:* See "High Court Rules for Va. over Md. in Water Dispute," Charles Lane and Maria Glod, *The Washington Post*, 10 December 2003, p. A1.

289   *"The dream of an unworked natural landscape"*: William Cronen, ed., *Uncommon Ground: Toward Reinventing Nature* (New York: W. W. Norton, 1995), p. 80.

291   *The loudest yelps of protest:* See Michael D. Shear and Katherine Shaver, "Wolf Pulls Plug on 'Techway' over Potomac," *Washington Post,* 25 May 2001, p. A1. Rep. Frank Wolf of Virginia had inserted into a highway bill the funding for a $2 million study of possible "Techway" routes, but he succeeded in killing the study after protests from residents. There have been repeated efforts to revive the Techway plan. See Katherine Shaver, "Va. to Explore Need to Build Another Bridge," 16 July 2003, *Washington Post,* p. B1.

297   *along the way, Cumberland became isolated again:* Harry I. Stegmaier, Jr., et al., *Allegany County: A History* (Parsons, WV: McClain Printing Co., 1976), pp. 373–96.

ACKNOWLEDGMENTS

The labor that has gone into the publication of the papers of Washington, Jefferson, Madison, et al. has led to what has been called the democratization of history. This newspaper reporter has taken great advantage of that. This book is built on the work of others, whom I hope I have cited adequately in the Notes, and who, in many cases, gave me direct, personal help and encouragement.

In particular, the editors of *The Papers of George Washington*, at the University of Virginia, graciously welcomed an outsider who wandered up one day to pluck the ripest fruit of their historical vineyard.

Phil Chase, editor-in-chief of *The Papers of George Washington*, and his colleague Frank Grizzard gave detailed advice and corrected many an error. James Guba, the copy editor of the *Papers*, smartly annotated many chapters. Most importantly, they all bolstered my confidence at key moments when I might otherwise have been overwhelmed by the difficulty of the project. (For years I've been writing what might be called explanatory journalism, with a focus on the sciences, but I found that history is more complex and interpretive than physics, chemistry, biology, etc. I'm reminded of a comment by an astronomer, who said a frog is more complicated than a star. Well, a Founding Father is more complicated than a frog.)

In the fall of 2002, while I was on campus teaching a writing class, Will Howarth, professor of English at Princeton University, let me sit in on his undergraduate seminar on early American literature. He did something I've never seen a professor do: He insisted that the class be held in the rare books section of Firestone Library, and we were able to scrutinize and handle the original, priceless texts and artifacts from the seventeenth and eighteenth centuries, from Mary Rowlandson's captivity narrative to the captain's log of a slave ship to (going back even further) a pre-Columbian Aztec map. It was a brilliant way to make the past come alive, to make it tangible, and the course helped me see the extent to which the United States in the days of George Washington was already an old society. Professor Howarth and his wife, the author Anne Matthews, gave me detailed counsel on a number of chapters and offered great tips on finding new material.

I am indebted to a number of scholars who read some or all of the manuscript: W. W. Abbot, Kenneth Bowling, Karen Gray, Eric Hinderaker, Warren Hofstra, John Lauritz Larson, Jeff Looney, Doug MacGregor, and Dennis Pogue. Jennifer Albinson and Kristina Sherry were invaluable researchers in the home stretch. Peirce Lewis and Eugene Scheele gave advice on the maps. Tom Mann of the Library of Congress Main Reading Room guided me to treasures in that wonderful institution.

I benefited from the support and wisdom of many friends, colleagues, historians, and Potomac partisans, including: Michael Baker, Frank Baxter, Harry Belin, Don Briggs, Chris Buckley, Betty Burchell, Jon Campbell, Steve Coll, Murphy Donovan, Len Downie, Glenn Eugster, Marc Fisher, Stephanie Flack, Kyle Gibson, Bruce Glendening, Gilbert Gude, Mary Hadar, Deborah Heard, Tony Horwitz, Walter Isaacson, David Johnson, Bill Justice, Michael Lewis, Carl Linden, Matt Logan, Andy Masich, John McPhee, David Michaelis, Emily Notestein, Jim Notestein, Phil Ogilvie, Peter Onuf, John Parsons, Mark Patterson, Stephen Potter, William Powers, Steve Reiss, Paul Richard, Delia Rios, Gene Robinson, Paul Rosa, Jack Shafer, Martha Sherrill, James Spears, Dorothy Twohig, Jack Wennerstrom, Roger Wilkins, and Angus Yates.

I would never do anything so rash as attempt to publish a book without first exploiting the collective genius of my *Washington Post* colleagues and great friends Gene Weingarten, Pat Myers, David Von Drehle, and Tom Shroder. They have been rescuing me from disaster for decades—and must be tired of getting messages from me saying, "Can U read sumpin?"—and I need to make a mental note to thank them in person at some point.

I am lucky to have the best editor in the business, Alice Mayhew, who saw the shape of the book before I did, and who reined in my impulse to turn it into the history of the entire universe. I owe special thanks to Roger Labrie for his editing prowess and his patience. My agent, Michael Congdon, has been a steady advocate and editorial guide for many years.

Most of all, I thank Mary Stapp, who read the manuscript at every phase, supported me every paragraph of the way, and kept our daughters in line while I was lost in the eighteenth century.